SECOND EDITION

T·H·E

HOME BREWER'S

COMPANION

D0734931

SECOND EDITION

T·H·E

HOME BREWER'S

COMPANION

THE COMPLETE JOY OF
HOMEBREWING
MASTER'S EDITION

CHARLIE PAPAZIAN

WM

WILLIAM MORROW

An Imprint of HarperCollins*Publishers*

HarperCollins books may be purchased for educational, business, or sales promotional use. For information please e-mail the Special Markets Department at SPsales@harpercollins.com.

Library of Congress Cataloging-in-Publication Data has been applied for.

An Avon Books edition was published in 1994.

First Quill/HarperResource edition published 2002.

ISBN 978-0-06-221577-2

14 15 16 17 18 RRD 10 9 8 7 6 5 4 3 2 1

The Homebrewer's Companion, Second Edition is dedicated to homebrewers throughout the world. They have inspired an international renaissance in brewing and a respect for beer tradition and innovation.

I especially thank the following people who helped make the original edition of this book possible: Chris Miller, my original editor of over ten years at Avon Books, for her support and enthusiasm for my work. Michael Jackson as a friend and for his unparalleled dedication, furthering international awareness of beer and brewing. During his life, Michael afforded me continued insight and assistance. Tracy Loysen as a friend who had helped extract creativity, clarity, and insight with my original work with this book. Michael Saunders and Gina Truex for being there as great friends, during my abeyance while writing the first edition of this book.

I owe a continuing debt of gratitude to my friends and colleagues who have worked and volunteered with the Brewers Association and the American Homebrewers Association. Their knowledge, generosity, and passion for quality have inspired me throughout my life. And my parents, Aram and Lucy, who've had the patience to let me stumble into and enjoy the paths I've followed.

CONTENTS

to stop • **Some Practical Considerations** • Measuring the runoff • How fast the runoff? • Stuck runoff • How much sparge water? • **Sparging and Lautering Equipment—Your System** • Plastic bucket systems • Fitting the picnic cooler • Stainless steel lauter-tuns

BOILING THE WORT   136

Extracting hop bitterness • Protein coagulation • Evaporation of wort • Boilovers • **Catch the Heat—Boiling Equipment** • Stove-top boiling, gas and electric • Outdoor propane cookers • Immersion heaters • Brewing kettles

TRUB AND HOP REMOVAL   142

Removing hops • Trub and its removal • How much trub? • Trub: Its influence on fermentation and flavor • Trub: How to remove it • Trub, whirlpools, and equipment • When to go the distance

TRANSFERRING EXTRACT AND WORT   149

Gravity and pumps • Spigots and valves

CHILLING EFFECTS: COOLING YOUR WORT   152

The principles of wort chilling: Why and how • The principles of heat exchange • **Equipment and Techniques for Extract and Mash-Extract Homebrewers** • Chilling concentrated worts • Full wort boils: Extract and all-grain brewing • Pot-immersion method • Using ice • Coil immersion • Counterflow systems

FERMENTATION   160

Lager and ale • Before yeast metabolism begins • Choosing the yeast strain • Adequate yeast • Aeration • **Yeast Metabolism and Fermentation** • Single-stage fermentation or two-stage fermentation: Which is best? Again, it all depends • Stuck fermentation • Lagering, storage, and ale cellaring

FERMENTATION EQUIPMENT FOR THE HOMEBREWER   168

Aerators • Fermenters • *The 200-Year-Old Burton Union "Blow-off" System* • **Controlling Fermentation and Lagering Temperature** • Keeping it warm

• Keeping it cool • **Suck-Back and Fermentation Locks** • **Transferring Beer from Here to There**

BEER RECIPES   223

BEER EVALUATION: What Am I Tasting and Why Is It in Beer?   379

FOREWORD

TO THE FIRST EDITION, 1994

by Professor Michael J. Lewis*

I have never homebrewed, though I've been around homebrewing a long time. I first seriously observed the sport in the days of Pabst Blue Ribbon malt extract plus four pounds of sugar and baker's yeast. They were rough and ready times. Homebrewers consumed their product, of course, if they got to it before it exploded into the butter, but I'm not sure they could ever "relax and have a homebrew"! In those days—the early 1960s—I was already brewing at the University of California at Davis on a rather sophisticated 5-gallon pilot-scale brewery as part of my teaching and research responsibilities, and I began to use that experience to teach courses about the homebrewing art. I like to think those courses made a difference, and of course, our university extension program has grown hugely since then, but nothing can compare to the sea change in the life of homebrewers wrought by Charlie Papazian and the Association of Brewers and its numerous offshoots, including the American Homebrewers Association and Brewers Publications. This book adds to Charlie's incomparable contribution to the field.

Homebrewers are among my favorite people. They have a passion for beer and brewing that few other groups can match, and a thirst for information that borders on the fanatic. Ideas are rapidly taken up and tried, and stand or fail on

*Professor Emeritus Michael J. Lewis is an internationally recognized brewing scientist, now retired. He developed the program in Brewing Science at the University of California, Davis, and taught it for more than thirty years, until 1998. He now continues in brewing education as the academic director of Brewing Programs at the University of California Davis Extension where he primarily organizes and teaches (with colleagues) the seminal Master Brewers Program. Graduates of this program often win the prestigious J. S. Ford Prize on the diploma examinations of the Institute of Brewing and Distilling; graduates are especially well represented throughout the American craft brewing industry. Professor Lewis has been awarded the Award-of-Merit of the Master Brewers Association of the Americas, the Recognition Award of the Brewers Association; has been elected a Fellow of the Institute of Brewing and Distilling (London); is a Life Member of ASBC, MBAA, and IBD; and has won the Distinguished Teaching Award of the University of California. He continues to give papers at national meetings of the industry, especially MBAA and CBC, which are occasionally offered for publication; he has published three books.

Professor Lewis closed his consulting practice years ago but remains fascinated by all things brewing and welcomes communications from those developing new ventures.

their intrinsic value; and information travels quickly. We now teach home-brewing to a very different clientele than formerly: The passion and fascination remain the same, but the level of sophistication is much higher now than be-fore, and so are the expectations for success. So is the willingness to invest in equipment and knowledge and good raw materials, such that there is very little these days the determined homebrewer cannot achieve. Charlie Papazian wrote this book with such homebrewers in mind. Any book is a compendium of what an author knows, what he has read and learned, what his experience has taught him, and how he thinks and what he thinks about. Charlie excels in all of these categories and brings it all to this book.

Homebrewing is a hobby like any other, in which one needs to invest time and money and thought; but that is where similarities end. Homebrewing is not stamp collecting or bird-watching, because there is an actual end product that meets the creative needs of an individual. One might say the same is true of arts or sports hobbyists—but surely amateur musicians or painters or golfers must inevitably fall so far short of satisfying their own expectations that their hobbies must be more frustration than satisfaction. It's different for homebrew-ers. Homebrewers, perhaps, are more akin to those whose hobby is cooking or quilting or some other useful pastime. But even here the analogy is not exact—after all, one must eat and stay warm whether the meal is from scratch or Stouffer's. A homebrewer (oddly) makes something that can totally satisfy his or her need to create and yet can be entirely done without; it therefore qualifies as an act of love—self-love, perhaps, but love nevertheless.

Is that why the hobby generates the kinds of passions and enthusiasms that it does? Why do people homebrew? Many years ago there was some legitimacy to the argument that one could choose between Budweiser on the one hand, and homebrew or perhaps imports on the other. These days the commercial brewing industry (including the microbrewery and brewpub industry) provides such an extraordinary range of beers that it seems hard to justify homebrewing on the basis that one's sensory expectations cannot be met somewhere between Budweiser and Big Foot. But the naissance of the microbrewing industry, far from preempting the homebrew hobby, seems to have acted as a spur to it. Though more and more people can now enjoy without much effort a wide range of beer products, for some odd reason they want to make these products for themselves or they want to further expand on what is available.

The dollar cost of specialty beers (including microbrewed products) might spur some to homebrewing, but I don't meet many poor homebrewers. Most homebrewers are clearly in it for fun and pleasure, and saving a buck is of sec-ondary importance—at best a thin disguise akin to a fly fisherman justifying his sport by the price of fish. No! Homebrewers just enjoy making beer, enjoy tasting the beer they make, delight in reaching out through these ancient pro-cesses to centuries of craft brewers who went before, are fascinated by the technology, history, and science of the craft, and love to meet others with the same passion. Homebrewing is intriguing and it's fun, and this book will add to both aspects of the hobby.

Making beer at home no longer need be a hit-or-miss operation, and an excellent presentation is not only achievable but expected. All homebrewers should know precisely how they made a beer and exactly what they would do in practical terms to improve or change it. Once a beer has been improved to the point where it satisfies the taste buds of its creator, the brewer should then be able to reproduce that beer at will. Though slavish consistency is not a necessary part of homebrewing, I have never quite understood the point of making a different beer at every brewing. Surely a brewer should work steadily and logically at improving a few beers that each meet a particular desired taste profile; without this logical and developmental approach, every brew is a crapshoot. Though Charlie offers many recipes in this book, they are (or should be) beers *he* likes best; that is a useful starting place for making those *you* like best.

I have never much enjoyed the company of those homebrew aficionados who crave original gravity without good purpose and who worship excessive consumption of alcohol, or those who never tasted a beer they didn't like (except any domestic major) or boast loudly of beer-drinking feats *extraordinaire* in places far away and of products curious. I prefer the company (and usually the beers) of those who realize that beermaking and beer drinking are a matter of taste. It's not a macho thing. It's okay not to like some beers; it's okay to eschew bitterness/blandness; it's okay not to like black beer, or brown or pink; it's okay to know what you like and to say so. It's *not* okay to discount others' preferences, however extreme or peculiar or ordinary they might be. And it's okay not to win prizes. The crucial essence of homebrewing demands you make exactly what you individually like best, and appreciate what you create and have fun while doing both. This puts a premium on information—hence this book.

Homebrewers don't like too much bad beer happening too often—it costs money and time and effort and occasionally damnable pride. In my experience folk can only "relax and have a homebrew" if the beer tastes good and tastes the way the brewer intended. That's why we now teach nine homebrew courses each year, and why I heartily welcome this new book.

PREFACE: BEER IS MY BUSINESS AND I'M LATE FOR WORK

I remember walking over and accepting a taste of beer from my uncle Paul (a close family friend), who was sitting in the stiff-backed living room chair. It was Ballantine beer and I liked it. That was in Cranford, New Jersey, 1954. I stood less than belt-buckle tall and I vividly recall liking the stuff. But my parents successfully discouraged any more sips, and as any five-year-old would have done, I went back to playing with my brand-new Lionel train set circling our brightly lit Christmas tree.

I went through the next thirteen years of growing up without a drop of beer. But boy oh boy, I remembered how good it tasted.

I was too young to harbor thoughts of sneaking a bottle or two. Besides, my parents rarely drank beer, and there never seemed to be any around unless my uncle Paul was visiting.

In 1958 we moved to Warren, New Jersey, and I continued my quiet forbearance and led a life of go-carts, cowboys and Indians, touch football, model rockets, airplanes, stamp collecting, Cub Scouts, Little League baseball, and secret clubhouse meetings. (We called ourselves the Red Devils. We never did much except dig a secret escape tunnel just in case.)

In 1967 I graduated from Watchung Hills Regional High School. I never ever got higher than a C grade in English, and I recall my English teacher recommending to my parents that I become a science student; no hope in the liberal arts for me. These things never worried me and somehow it seemed appropriate to celebrate graduation with beer. My high school buddy, Bob, had a few connections through his older brother, and we found ourselves with a six-pack between the two of us. I don't remember much except that the beer tasted downright awful and that the effect of three cans totally disoriented me at the imperfect moment of climbing over a split-rail fence—headfirst and head down. We spent half the night sleeping off our inebriation in the parking lot of the Union Village Methodist Church.

I don't think my parents ever suspected my illegal indulgences until the time I got Bob arrested along with myself, four other underage rascals, and a case of beer. We were all nineteen or twenty at the time. After a $240 fine and the bad taste of beer still lingering, I continued to modestly indulge in store-bought beer during my first few years of nuclear engineering studies at the University of Virginia in Charlottesville.

The truth of the matter was that throughout my early college years I had not enjoyed the taste of beer since I had taken my first sip from Uncle Paul.

Then George Conner walked into my life, or rather came to play marbles at our own Whoop Moffitt Memorial Marbles Tournament. My roommates and I got to know George more and more. After long days of work at his own Arbor Hill Preschool and day-care center, he'd saunter down for a game of Go or dissertations on the state of our lives.

George was a beer drinker, and it wasn't too long before he suggested that we go visit his beermaking neighbor. We had never heard of such a thing as "homebrew" before. With little hesitation we found ourselves trying a neighborly brew. The novelty of making one's own beer intrigued me much more than the taste of what I now recall as fizzy, cidery, and alcoholic-tasting prohibition-style homebrew.

We found ourselves walking away buzzed, inspired, and with the following cryptic recipe written on a 3 × 5-inch card:

> 5 gallons warm water
> 1 can Premier Blue Ribbon malt (light or dark)
> 1½ cans full sugar, white or black, more or less
> Mix
> Add 1 cake bread yeast when cool
> Ferment until bubbling stops (7 days to 5 weeks depending on your sugar
>   content and temperature). Best at 45 degrees F.
> Tip [sic] bottle.

My first three 10-gallon batches of dump-and-stir (I stirred with a short-handled wooden spoon and my forearm) homebrew kept the sewer rats happy. The stuff was undrinkable. Being somewhat persistent, I managed to discover corn sugar, beer yeast, and that washing my arm mattered. Consequently, up from the 8 × 8-foot dirt-floored basement of George's preschool emerged many an infamous palatable brew.

I still can't figure out how I managed to enjoy the stuff, but enjoy it, I did. I somehow acquired a taste for those brews, as did most of our acquaintances; even those who disliked commercial beer found "Charlottesville pleasure" in every bottle. Perhaps we drank in secret sympathy for those original thirty orphaned gallons. Actually for the state that 1970 to '72 was in, it tasted damned good.

I continued my education through five years. I abandoned an invitation to continue with the naval ROTC at the beginning of my fourth year but did persist to achieve a bachelor of science in nuclear engineering in 1972.

After graduation and a third consecutive summer working at Pine Island Camp in Belgrade Lakes, Maine, pure whimsy brought me to Boulder, Colorado, that same year. Nuclear engineering became unclear engineering, and within a year I found myself starting my teaching career as a preschool teacher and a born-again homebrewer. A kindergarten through eighth grade teacher, I remained through 1981, taking off each summer to hitchhike and backpack across the United States and British Columbia, as well as having extended backpacking ventures in the Hawaiian Islands, Fiji, Bali, and Central America. And yes, I sampled beer—homebrewed, village-brewed, and commercial—whenever I could afford it.

It was in 1973 that I figured I knew enough about making beer (which was hardly anything at all, but the results were legendary) to teach a beer-brewing class through Boulder's Community Free School. It was in these first class sessions that I actually boiled my first wort. I soon discovered many ways to improve on beer and developed a taste for what I'd call quality beer, an experience I had never known before. Yes, I've had my failures and memorable brews; who present could ever forget the original and legendary "Goat Scrotum Ale" or "Barkshack Ginger Mead"?

Through those years from 1973 to 1983 I taught over 1,000 people in the Boulder-Denver-Front Range area of Colorado how to make and enjoy great beer. My mimeographed six-page class curriculum evolved to a funky but inspirational self-published, self-typed forty-page book titled *The Joy of Brewing* (1976). Four years later I self-published the ninety-page *The New, Revised and More Joy of Brewing* (1980). Three years later I signed a contract with Avon Books to write *The Complete Joy of Home Brewing* (1984) and later revised that book several times, ultimately leading to *The Complete Joy of Homebrewing, Fourth Edition* (2014).

Meanwhile most graduates of my class became avid homebrewers and beer enthusiasts. In 1978 they inspired the formation of the American Homebrewers Association (AHA) and its magazine, *Zymurgy*. In fact, one of the four students in my very first class, Charlie Matzen, along with a bottle of April Morning Honey Spruce Lager, was the principal catalyst for inspiring the idea of a newsletter for homebrewers. I recall the moment quite vividly. It was Easter Sunday and we had just finished a few bottles of homebrew in the Utah desert in the area surrounding Lake Powell; Colorado River Canyon country. There was a thunderstorm approaching from a distance. We relaxed and had another homebrew. Lightning zigzagged across the sky. Curiously, the brightest flash streaked from one cloud to another as the letter Z. The rain never came, but we had another homebrew and knew the Z stood for "zymurgy," the last word in the dictionary, meaning the science and art of yeast fermentation. Later that evening we also saw a vision of the Easter Bunny walking across Lake Powell—but that's another story. Homebrew has been responsible for many inspirations in my life. *Zymurgy* magazine and the American Homebrewers Association were two of them.

The nonprofit educational association was founded in 1978 with the contribution of three years of volunteer help from dozens of local Boulder homebrewers, along with $4,000 in personal loans that eventually got repaid about five years later. In 1981 I left teaching (though I still enjoyed it) to take on the one full-time position at the AHA, drawing and living off a salary of $300 per month. By 1987 the AHA and *Zymurgy* had evolved to serving as a separate yet joined division of the Association of Brewers (now called the Brewers Association). At year end 2013 the AHA had over 43,000 members.

In the 1980s other divisions of the Brewers Association emerged or were created to meet the growing interest in information about beer and brewing. The Institute for Brewing Studies and its magazine the *New Brewer* were created in 1983. They served the informational and professional needs of persons interested in small-scale commercial microbrewing. Keep in mind that in 1983 there were only a dozen microbreweries in North America; ten years later there were over 400 and now in 2014 we call them "craft brewers." There are over 3,000 small and independent craft brewers in the United States with nearly 2,000 in the planning stages.

In 1981 it was not homebrew but perfect pints of real ale at the Great British Beer Festival that inspired me to initiate the first Great American Beer Festival (GABF) in 1982. The first GABF was a small event with three microbrewers, seventeen large or regional brewers and about 700 Boulder beer enthusiasts. Thirty-plus years later it features 500 American breweries, nearly 3,000 beers, and 50,000 festival attendees from all over the world. There was always too much to learn, and Brewers Publications (established in 1986), the book publishing division of the Association, was also inspired by many bottles of great homebrew. It publishes a few books per year on the subject of beer and/or brewing.

In 2005 the Association of Brewers merged with the Brewers Association of America, retaining all the activities of the Association of Brewers and the now-unified support of most of America's small heritage and craft brewers. The Association has about fifty full-time employees. As president of the Brewers Association, I continue to manage, write, guide, and travel. Brewing remains a priority and I still continue to brew twelve to eighteen batches of beer and mead a year. I'm "on the road" two to three months per year, attending brewing events, visiting breweries, and listening to and talking with amateur and professional brewers worldwide.

When I'm not traveling on business you may find me camping, cycling, gardening, fishing, relaxing in my hammock, or somewhere out of the ordinary.

Keg tossing? Well, whatever I do, I take great care not to spill any beer.

I enjoy traveling sight unseen to developing and third world countries to learn more about people, myself, and the way we are and have been. Naturally I drink the local beer, but I mostly enjoy just drinking it in interesting and lively environments and not necessarily having to talk about it, just like most other beer drinkers.

Through the years I've brewed thousands of gallons of mostly good beer. Thousands of times I've heard first-time homebrew drinkers say, "Hey, this stuff is good." I've heard as many times, "I like this, and I don't usually like beer." I get these responses from men and women, young and old. It almost seems as though no one dislikes well-brewed homebrew and the company of good people. There is something inherently likable about good beer. It's appreciated, and the taste for it naturally develops.

Now you'll have to excuse me. . . . I've got to go. . . . Beer is my business and I'm late for work.

INTRODUCTION

You've been homebrewing for fifteen years, or five years, or three years. Perhaps you've been brewing for less than a year. Whoa-ho, there are many of you who have been at it for six months and have already brewed over twenty batches. Somehow you've found the means, the mind, and yourself with this book in hand. You've come to the profound realization that WORK IS WORK . . . PLAY IS PLAY . . . BEER IS BEER . . . BUT HOMEBREW IS THE BEST.

Ladies and gentlemen, you are out of control—and that ain't bad, is it?

10 REASONS WHY YOU BOUGHT THIS BOOK

Whether you consider yourself a beginner, intermediate, or advanced home-brewer, you've come to realize there are a lot of variables that can influence the character of your beer.

1. You are enjoying beer as you've never enjoyed beer before.
2. You have learned to recognize, respect, and appreciate beer in ways you had never imagined.
3. You're a hobbyist at heart, and the art of homebrewing has revealed a means to tap into your creative instincts.
4. You've found the results rewarding and worth the distinction of sharing with friends. Mesmerized by bubbles rising from the bottom of your glass of homemade brew, you've dwelled on the mysticism of it all.

5. As brewers have done for 10,000 years, you've sipped, quaffed, and conceded thirst for the beers of your creation.
6. A bit of masterfulness has crept into your everyday life.
7. With a bounce in your step and bubbling in your fermentation locks, you move forward in your daily life knowing that there is a full fermenter in your home brewery.
8. Bottles and kegs condition themselves with the proper effervescence and will soon debut. You measure your days knowing that while your beer ferments or ages life is improving in your home.
9. You've begun to plan for your next batch, while always on the lookout for new ideas, new techniques, and new beers.
10. You may even be thinking of going professional and are wondering how much more complicated, creative, and life-changing can beer making get.

THE GOLDEN RULE

The Golden Rule of Homebrewing is: "Relax. Don't worry. Have a homebrew." Without a doubt the single and most dramatically significant thing that can spoil the taste of your beer is . . . worrying. Remember that whenever you brew or enjoy a glass of beer.

You have strived to Relax. You have pursued the fine art of Not Worrying. And indeed you've had a Homebrew. You often wonder what the world could be like if more people brewed their own beer.

You are a brewer. You appreciate quality beer. You have this book in hand. Have you already jumped to the recipe section in search of a recipe for your favorite kind of beer? Perhaps you thumbed through the ingredient section investigating whether there was anything new to enliven your curiosity. What does this book say about lagering? You wonder, having flipped to the index in search of techniques that enable you to keep up with the creativity that's rampant in the craft brewing world and to brew more types of beers like those you'd be willing to pay money for.

You're at the beginning of another book on brewing. What worthy advice might this writing offer? Yes, "Relax. Don't worry. Have a homebrew" is still the Golden Rule of Homebrewing. Yet another quite profound truth of brewing beer is that it is an art. Beer is fashioned with the tools of knowledge and experience. Science is a valuable tool, but the artistic elements of brewing cannot be reduced to a scientific process. Be wary of the scientification of brewing.

Science is temporary rule, order, and an attempt to explain why the world behaves as it does. It is a set of laws and statements about phenomena observed and verified repeatedly. Throughout history science agrees on sets of rules for relatively short periods of time. Then we change the rules and laws, because someone else has observed new and different things, and new rules are based on more current experience. Scientific knowledge can help us make better beer.

But science alone can never create the experience of producing fine beer. Our own experiences are absolute and essential. Your heart, mind, and soul become part of the beers you create. Your senses are your most valuable tool. Taste your ingredients, your fermentation, and your premature beer. Watch it ferment. Note the aromas. The difference in the sound that bubbles make in hot water and cold water tells you something.

Brewing is not just a recipe and a set of important procedures and measurements in your brewing logbook. You must observe your beer and note what it is telling you. The development of the art of brewing takes time. For all of us who brew, it continues. The purpose of this book is to help enhance the spirit of creativity, to explore new tools for brewing, and above all to help advance your wonderful journey in homebrewing.

The Homebrewer's Companion, Second Edition is not about how to chill your wort—it is about how heat moves. It's not about trub separation—it is about the behavior of liquids. It's not about reactions in brewing—it is about dancing with enzymes and ions. It is not about culturing yeast—it is about creating life and soul. It is not about beer styles—it is about people and the environment in which we enjoy beer. It is not about maximum yields and efficiencies—it is about personal priorities.

The Homebrewer's Companion, Second Edition is not about homebrewed beer—it is about yourself.

THE HOMEBREWER'S
COMPANION

First Few Thoughts

Work is work. Play is play. Beer is beer. Homebrew is the best.

The Homebrewer's Companion, Second Edition is for intermediate and advanced homebrewers. Before we move ahead to a somewhat orderly and advanced presentation of brewing ingredients, process, equipment, and style, this first brief section offers a few reminders. Let's just be sure that you're not forgetting a few basics before advancing your skills. You may already have your homebrewery in order, but just in case, grab a homebrew and cruise through these first few thoughts.

Improve Your Water. Improve Your Beer

If you are using a municipal water source, there is one simple thing you can do that can help improve the quality of your beer. Purchase and install a sink-top bacteriostatic activated-carbon water filter. It's simple to install, and you can configure it so that you only use it for water that you consume. Your investment will range from about $50 to $200, but over the long haul it runs about 2 cents per gallon. Unlike boiling, activated charcoal will remove chlorine and chloroamines from your water supply. These chemicals combine with organic compounds to create harsh, undesirable flavors, barely perceptible to some but annoying to others. The advantages of filtering are twofold: It is simple to do and it will markedly improve the taste of your water.

Siphoning Sense

Transferring beer from one container to another is an essential step for every homebrewer. There are many ways and means to simplify this process, but there is one principle that must be kept in mind whenever handling fermented beer: Avoid aerating the beer once it has finished fermentation. The introduction of oxygen to finished beer will accelerate the staling process and render beer oxidized and unpalatable.

Preventing the spoilage of good finished beer is easy. Avoid splashing the beer when siphoning by placing the outspout of the siphon at the bottom of the receiving vessel. This is a simple and very important principle you can keep in mind to help maintain beer freshness.

DO YOU HAVE A PROBLEM?

It tastes funny, but you're not quite sure why. Was it the ingredients, the yeast, the process, the temperature, the bottles? For a new brewer, it can be quite frustrating knowing that your beer isn't exactly what you would like it to be, but not knowing why.

There's one simple observation you can make that will almost always indicate whether or not you have a bacterial contamination that has affected the flavor of your beer. Hold a bottle of beer up to a bright light and carefully examine the fill line in the bottle's neck or any part of the surface where beer and glass are in contact. Is there a deposit adhering to the glass in the form of a ring or small dots? If so, you can be 100 percent certain that you have a bacterial contamination, whether you like it or not and even whether you like the beer or not. It's time to investigate your sanitizing process and get out the household bleach. At least now you know what kind of problem you have and you can seek advice on how best to get back to clean brewing. Don't give up. Don't worry. Every brewer confronts this problem several times a lifetime. And solves it.

SANITIZING CONTAMINATORS

Many homebrewers use a wire mesh strainer to strain hot wort from spent grains. Due to their weave, wire mesh strainers are impossible to sanitize with chemical solutions such as bleach and water. Bacteria and other contaminating microorganisms evade chemical solutions by lodging themselves in the microscopic world of nooks and crannies. For the price of a paper clip and a bit of forethought, one can use the brewpot and the boiling wort to heat and sanitize the strainer. Immerse the strainer in the boiling wort during the final 15 minutes of boiling. Configure a paper clip as an extended handle and hook it on the lip of the pot to prevent the strainer from falling completely into the boiling liquid.

Do you use a saucepan to ladle hot wort from the brewpot into your fermenter? Does the saucepan have seams that hide and protect bacteria? If so, your saucepan needs a heat treatment as well. This might best be done directly on your stove top.

WASH YOUR HANDS

Didn't your mother tell you this? Before handling equipment coming into contact with wort or fermenting beer, wash your hands with soap and water. But please don't get overly compulsive about this. Have a homebrew and think about the sense it makes.

CHEAP SANITATION

At less than $2 per gallon, household chlorine bleach is about as cheap a sanitizer as you can get. It will make over 300 gallons of sanitizing solution. It works well and, with a few hours of soaking, even removes stains and bacterial deposits on the inside of contaminated beer bottles. One ounce of bleach mixed with 4 gallons (15 l) of cold water will last for weeks in a cool environment. It is easily rinsed with hot tap water. (For brewing purposes, hot tap water is essentially sanitized water, so no need to worry here.) It works on plastic hoses, funnels, fermenters, glass; there is really no justification for contaminated beer because of ineffective sanitizing solutions. Caution: With prolonged contact it does corrode stainless steel and other metals.

TASTE IT

It takes a lot of practice, but taste your beer. Taste your unfermented wort. Taste it while it is fermenting and at bottling time. Taste your malt ingredients. Chew every kind of grain. Crush, squeeze, and feel hops between your fingers. Smell the perfume they emit. Slowly learn the difference between fresh ingredients and stale ingredients, between fresh beer and old beer.

Use your senses of sight, smell, touch, taste, and hearing to experience your ingredients, your beer, and the brewing process. If you take the time to do this, you will learn the art of brewing in a way no book or technical measuring instrument can convey.

Participate in beer evaluations as a learning apprentice or as a judge or for fun. In the company of others there is a lot to learn about beer, yours and those you buy.

What does the rest of this book offer? It's presented in hopes of fulfilling your expectations with thought-provoking ideas, information, and resources to help you discover more ways to brew the kind of beer you like.

Ingredients, Process, and Equipment—and Beer!

Malt, hops, yeast, and water; these are the basic ingredients of beer. But ingredients alone do not beer make. The manner in which the ingredients are processed and the kind of equipment used to process the ingredients are as essential as the ingredients themselves.

- Ingredients
- Process
- Equipment

These are the fundamental factors that provide the basis for structure from chaos. The chaos of a thousand variables, all harmonizing into dynamic relationships resulting in the final character of beer. Ingredients, process, equipment; they are variable beyond your wildest imaginations. They affect one another in ways mysterious and obvious. Their dynamics inspire an appreciation for things created.

The art of brewing is about appreciating these relationships and appreciating the necessity of being master of ingredients, process, and equipment; the substance, action, and tools.

The brewmaster is one who may observe and understand or who observes and does not understand—but observes nonetheless and is willing to learn. An open mind, flexibility, intuitiveness, and the willingness to adapt are all essential in achieving the final expression:

- Beer

Read about ingredients. Read about process. Read about equipment. Know that only when they are conceived and respected as a whole can beer be made by a brewmaster.

MALT

MALT EXTRACT

Most homebrewers owe the success of their brewing hobby to the satisfaction of having made their first batch of beer from malt extract. Over 90 percent of home-brewers continue to use malt extracts for their brewing endeavors. Malt-extract brewing clearly has its advantages over more time-consuming (and more reward-ing for many) all-grain full-mash brewing. In less than 2 hours a homebrewer can easily brew 5 gallons (19 l) of quality beer using a minimal amount of equipment.

As the hobby matured and became increasingly more popular, malt-extract brewing became more rewarding and increased its ability to match the quali-ties all-grain brewers seek with their beers.

Sometimes beer made from malt extract syrups or powder has been considered less appealing than beer made from all grains. This difference may be due not to extract versus all-grain factors but rather to other important brewing variables.

In the mid-1980s England's Campaign for Real Ale (CAMRA, a watchdog organization for Great Britain's consumer beer interests) taste-tested three dif-ferent beers made from the same full-grain mash. One was made from wort drawn directly off the mash. Another was made from malt extract syrup that had been processed from that mash with tap water added. The third was made from the same malt extract syrup with distilled water added. Being proponents of full-grain mashing, the CAMRA panel members admitted to being biased against extract-brewed beer. But they found in a blind tasting that they pre-ferred the malt-extract-and-tap-water-based beer over the distilled-water-based brew and found no characters in the full-grain brew to solicit a preference for or against the extract-based brew.

Yet the panel and other participants in this experiment still realized that many extract-based beers brewed in the pubs left something to be desired. They

could not identify what it was other than describing homemade pub-brewed extract beer as "nearly always having a characteristic (and indifferent) flavor that we think of as 'malt extract.'"

The panel concluded:

1. Freshness of product was one factor contributing to the excellent quality of the beers they tasted in this experiment.
2. The quality of yeast used in the experiment was thought to be a significant factor.
3. A knowledgeable and well-trained brewer brewed the experimental beers under controlled conditions. This may have been a factor in the overall good quality of all the beers.

Their conclusions were astute and bear remarkable insight as to what was to transpire almost ten years later in the American homebrewing hobby.

DOES FRESHNESS REALLY MAKE A DIFFERENCE?

Today in America the popularity of the hobby clearly is an advantage to home-brewers because they can be more assured of fresher malt extracts. This is particularly important with malt extract syrups, less so with dried extracts. While malt extracts in their package will not spoil, syrups tend to get darker with age and develop flavors that are contrary to the fresh flavor we expect in beer. Lighter malt extract syrups are more sensitive to these changes.

Dried malt extract, whether bought in bulk or in typical 3-pound (1.4 kg) packages, can be conveniently stored and measured. Store unused dried malt extract in double plastic bags in a cool, dry place. If you don't, you will create a unique product called "rock malt." Rock malt is best processed with a home-brew in one hand and a hammer in the other. The smashed pebbles can be dissolved in cold water overnight and then brought to a boil in the brewing process. But enough about rock malt.

The growing popularity of homebrewing has helped to move products on and off the shelves more quickly. Currently it is rare to find stock that has been sitting for over one year on the shelves.

KNOWLEDGE IS YEAST? YEAST IS KNOWLEDGE?

The quality of the yeast used in the CAMRA experiment was thought to be a significant factor. In the late 1980s American homebrewers were first introduced to a wide variety of liquid yeast cultures. The variety and availability of these cultures continue to increase, and their quality continues to be excellent.

In more recent times it can be said that the technology for both culturing and drying yeast has led to dramatic improvements in the quality, viability, and availability of dried yeast. Technology has even overcome the past challenges of producing dried pure-culture lager yeasts. But as mentioned in *The Complete Joy of Homebrewing, Fourth Edition,* one should stick with trusted brand-name yeasts rather than generic unidentified dried yeast packaged in plain white foil packets. Perhaps the one disadvantage of quality dried yeast is that variety is somewhat limited, but even this continues to improve as homebrewers and small craft brewers grow and create demand worldwide. Why the lack of choice? The technology and process for culturing and drying viable yeast cultures is expensive. A greater amount of any one type of yeast needs to be processed and sold in order to keep costs down. As demand increases, more varieties may become available.

Quality yeast has definitely improved the quality of beer made from malt extracts. American homebrewers now have access to the same quality of yeast used by professional brewers all over the world.

KNOWLEDGEABLE BREWING

The knowledge that American homebrewers have and the information they have access to are unsurpassed in the history of homebrewing. Magazines, journals, newsletters, judging groups, Websites, and knowledgeable homebrew shop personnel have guided hundreds of thousands of homebrewers in the right direction. Homebrewers are now able to avoid pitfalls common in a more distant past.

Malt extract always is the first thing to be wrongly (usually) blamed for low-quality beer. In commercial settings, such as pub breweries, there is an inclination to believe that with malt extract one does not need to know as much about brewing, and that a skilled brewmaster is not necessary. This gross misconception has always led to the demise of malt-extract pub breweries. In most cases it may take an even more knowledgeable and trained brewer to assure that the extract produces beer comparable to that made with full-grain mashes. If cost is a factor in brewing, in the end malt extract costs more than grain malt, and an advanced and skilled brewmaster costs more as well. That is why one doesn't encounter too many successful malt extract pub breweries. But for a homebrewer, malt extract has all the advantages of time savings, quality beer, flexibility, and satisfaction. The comparative cost differential is minimal at the homebrewing level.

THE WELL-ATTENUATED BODY

The popularity of homebrewing has inspired an absolutely astounding and be-wildering array of malt extract products. Hop-flavored specially formulated malt extracts with yeast are sold as kits intended to brew specific kinds of beer. Then there are malt extract syrups and dry powdered malt extracts. There are hundreds of malt extract products to choose from, produced principally in Aus-tralia, Belgium, Canada, Germany, England, Ireland, the Netherlands, New Zealand, Scotland, and the United States. It isn't by accident that these malts are produced in nations that have a notable brewing tradition.

Choosing the color of malt extract for a desired style of beer is a relatively easy exercise, but choosing a type of malt extract that will result in a beer with the correct fullness or thinness of body is not quite so simple. If you want a light-bodied Pilsener, then a malt extract should be used that is known to at-tenuate well, that is, be more fermentable and containing less full-bodied car-bohydrates such as dextrin. If you seek a full-bodied sweet brown ale or "chewy" stout, a malt extract that does not ferment as completely should be your choice. Brands of plain malt extract are generally consistent in their fer-mentability. Experiment with the dozens of brands to determine for yourself which brands are more or less fermentable. Keep good notes and don't forget to drink the beer.

Malt extracts come and go, and products are sometimes reformulated based on current conditions and demand. Check out brand reviews on the Internet to determine what other homebrewers and homebrew supply shop owners are say-ing about these products.

RECIPE CONVERSIONS

Recipes are starting points for all homebrewing formulations. They can be fol-lowed exactly as presented, knowledgeably varied, or altered because you have no choice. You will often be forced to choose another ingredient because of the unavailability, temporary or otherwise, of desired ingredients.

One of the simplest substitutions that can be made is malt syrup for dried malt and vice versa. Most malt syrup is about 80 to 85 percent solids and 15 to 20 percent water. For simplicity, use an 85 percent conversion factor when substituting dried malt for syrup. Thus, if 1 pound of malt syrup is called for in a recipe, you can substitute 0.85 pound of dried malt. Likewise for the reverse conversion, approximately 1.2 pounds of syrup will substitute for 1 pound of dried extract. Specific malt extracts will contribute specific characteristics to a beer. Substituting dried extract for syrup or vice versa will result in a variation of the beer's intended final character, but it will be a close approximation and may be a desired discovery (and another recipe worth repeating).

Malt extract brewers are often introduced to beers brewed by others and consequently inspired to brew themselves. But sometimes you may discover that that great taste of homebrew was based on a recipe calling for mashing grains. Good-quality malt extract can be substituted for grain malt in any recipe, giving results that can resemble (but not duplicate) the original beer. If you wish to convert an all-grain recipe to an extract recipe, you can substitute 0.65 pound (0.3 kg) of light dried malt extract or 0.75 pound (0.34 kg) of light malt extract syrup for every pound (454 gm) of pale malt (malted barley grain). If the grain recipe calls for lager malt (a lighter type of pale malted barley), try choosing an extralight or extrapale malt extract made from lager malt.

Some specialty malts such as crystal (sometimes referred to as carastan or caramel), chocolate, and other roasted black malts and roasted barley do not need to be processed through mashing. They offer extract brewers a simple option for enhancing a beer's flavor and color. Extract brewers who choose not to use any grains in their recipes can substitute colored malt extracts such as amber, dark, and extradark malt extract for specialty grains and produce similar results. Here are some examples portraying simple conversions:

> Specialty malts are crushed, and 1 cup (237 ml) equals approximately
> ¼ pound (113 g)
> 5 pounds (2.27 kg) amber
>   malt extract = 5 pounds (2.27 kg) light malt extract + 2 cups (474 ml)
>   crystal = 5 pounds (2.27 kg) light malt extract + ½ cup
>   (119 ml) black, roasted, or chocolate malt
> 5 pounds (2.27 kg) medium brown
>   malt extract = 5 pounds (2.27 kg) light or amber malt extract + 1 cup
>   (237 ml) black, roasted, or chocolate malt + (optional)
>   1 or 2 cups (237 or 474 ml) crystal malt
> 5 pounds (2.27 kg) very dark
>   malt extract = 5 pounds (2.27 kg) light or amber malt extract + 2 or
>   3 cups (474–711 ml) roasted, black, or chocolate malt

The versatility of light malt becomes apparent when you realize that you can combine it with different specialty malts to produce malt extract of any color.

GRAIN MALTS

A lot has changed on the American brewing scene since the birth of modern-day quality homebrewing in the 1970s, and there is every indication that these progressive trends will continue. These changes continue through the efforts and the grass-roots enthusiasm of homebrewers and their appreciation for diversity and quality in beer. Much of the change has been economically driven by the commercial small and independent craft brewers throughout America. They have created a market for specialty craft beers—beer styles other than typical light American-style lager beers. Small breweries have created a demand for a wide variety of imported and made-in-America specially malted grains.

Homebrewers have always been the grassroots-tier customers of the malt companies. The distribution system for homebrewing supplies chooses the malts it makes available to the hobby from the larger production batches of malts made for the commercial craft brewers.

With the continued popularity and growth of small brewery specialty products and the growing popularity of homebrewing, the homebrewer wins, especially the all-grain brewer. Homebrewers also benefit from the commercial brewing industry's research and development efforts to grow better barley (and hops) for brewing.

Pale malted barley (pale malt) is a generic tag used to designate many types of very light-colored malted barley, which usually makes up the majority of the grist (total amount of crushed grains, malted or otherwise). The term *specialty malt* refers to types of malt that usually are not the major portion of the grist but are added in relatively small quantities to influence the character of a beer's aroma, flavor, color, head retention, or mouthfeel. But you can't always use the specialty malt designation as such. There are exceptions, sure as there are homebrewers enjoying one of their own homebrews right this very moment as you read or reread this paragraph. There are some beer formulations whose grist will take on a major proportion of specialty malts. In these cases usually the lighter specialty malts are utilized.

USING SPECIALTY MALTS WITHOUT MASHING

Many specialty malts must be fully mashed with the rest of the grist, but as previously mentioned, there are exceptions. Black malt (sometimes referred to as black patent malt, named after an eighteenth-century process of roasting malt patented as British patent number 4112), chocolate malt, various crystal and caramel malts, and roasted barley are the principal malts available to homebrewers that do not require a mashing regime to convert nonfermentable carbohydrates to fermentable carbohydrates. These malts can contribute color, roasted flavor and some degree of flavor stability to the character of beer. Crystal and caramel malts also can contribute to the perception of final unfermentable sweetness.

For ideal extraction of the favorable qualities of any malt, the crushed grain should never be brought to a boil. Some beginning recipes and procedures guide beginning brewers to bring these specialty malts just to a boil and quickly remove them from the heat source. This is a simple procedure designed to encourage their use by first-time brewers. For those who desire to improve the quality of their beers with a small additional investment in time and attention, the grains should not be steeped in water whose temperature exceeds 170 degrees F (77 C). The extraction of undesirable tannin and astringent characters is minimized with a lower-temperature steep.

A procedure that works very well is to mix the crushed grains with water and maintain temperatures at 150 to 155 degrees F (66–68.5 C) for 30 minutes. The grains and water are mixed in a ratio of 1 pound (0.45 kg) to ½ gallon (1.9 l). Add the liquid strained and extracted from this "steep" to malt extract and continue the brewing process with a vigorous boil, adding hops and more water as needed.

THE ESSENTIAL KERNEL: ALL ABOUT MALT

If you've ever wondered why there isn't one book that neatly and concisely compiles all you'd ever want to know about malted barley, then you've never done any real research yourself. There is good reason why a comprehensive overview does not exist. The diversity of information and of individual brewers' needs is enough to drive you to making your own homebrew with whatever ingredients are available and coming to the conclusion that yours is some of the best you've ever had.

Almost all of the dependable information on malt originates from professional literature. Commercial brewers' needs are diverse. The equipment, the recipe formulations, the processes, and crop quality vary tremendously. Brewers must adapt to *whatever is the best quality of malted barley they can get.*

*After an initial 48-hour water steep, barley kernels sprouting rootlets while growing
acrospire emerge from beneath husk. Sprouted and dried barley kernels become malt.
From top: rootlet development after one day of germination; rootlets begin to wither after
five days of germination and acrospire length is about full length;
kilned and cleaned malt.*

Two-row, six-row, highly modified, undermodified, high-enzyme, low-enzyme, lager malt, ale malt—they have all been quite thoroughly explained in several books, including *The Complete Joy of Homebrewing, Fourth Edition*. The best advice I can offer to someone who wishes to understand "all about malt" is to read no fewer than ten authors/resources/books about malt and its influence on beer. Stock your refrigerator with several of your own beers in order to maintain contact with reality. Take notes. Do take notes! Divide them into two groups. Make a list of points that every source usually agrees on and generally trust those rules, facts, statements, and opinions. Also make a list of the points that either contradict or don't match other sources. Then seek out discussions with "experts" and begin to understand why these sources disagree or facts don't match. When you are through drinking all of your beer and have completed this research, *you* will be an expert.

How can the subject of "all about malt" be approached in a book such as this with a limited number of pages? The question was seriously considered. After much perusal of literature and a 12-ounce bottle of six-year-old homebrewed barley wine ale, I arrived at an answer: Get practical. What are some of the more common problems or challenges homebrewers might face when brewing all-grain recipes—particularly when brewing light lagers or pale ales, when the choice of malt can be influential? Let's examine some practical information about the characters of malt.

A KEY TO UNDERSTANDING MALT

There are many specifications by which malt is measured. These include but are not limited to:

Beta-glucan
Color of wort, clarity, and viscosity
Diastatic power
    Alpha amylase activity
Extract
    Coarse-grind extract (dry basis)
    Fine-grind extract (dry basis)
    Coarse-grind–Fine-grind difference
Growth of acrospire
Percent moisture
Protein
    Percent total protein
    Percent soluble protein
    Percent soluble/total protein ratio
Sieve (size) assortment

Beta-glucan—A gumlike substance that can cause commercial brewers problems with stuck runoffs and wort filtration if the beta-glucan level is too high. From 75 to 150 ppm is a range that is acceptable for malted barley.

Color of wort, degree of clarity, and measurement of viscosity—This is additional information that may be provided by the manufacturer of malt.

Diastatic power (includes alpha amylase activity)—A measure of potential enzyme "energy" that a malt has. We can be assured that all pale and lager malts have more than adequate enzyme power to convert their own soluble carbohydrates to fermentable carbohydrates plus about 10 percent adjunct starch. High-enzyme malts such as many varieties of American 6-row and newer varieties of 2-row have a surplus of power, allowing them to convert 40 percent extra adjuncts. Diastatic power is measured in degrees Lintner. A typical high-enzyme American six-row will be 150 to 180 degrees L, while an American two-row may be about 80 to 140 degrees L. European pale and lager-type malts have developed primarily 2-row barley malts for a wide range of uses but in general diastastic power ranges are notably lower than American grown barley malts. European units of diastatic power are expressed in degrees W-K (Windisch-Kolbach units).

$$\text{Degrees (W-K)} = (3.5 \times \text{degrees Lintner}) - 16.$$

Generally if the average total degree Lintner (diastastic power) of the grist is 60 to 70 or above, full conversion will occur. For example if a grist has 80 percent of 100 Lintner pale malt and 20 percent of 0 Lintner rice, full conversion would be expected:

$$0.8 \times 100 + 0.2 \times 0 = 80 \text{ Lintner} = \text{average overall diastastic}$$
$$\text{power of grist}$$

Extract—A measure of the soluble carbohydrates that can be extracted by the mashing process. It is measured by the ratio of the weight (dried) of the soluble material to the initial weight of the malt and is expressed as a percentage. For example, one year's crop of typical two-row lager malt coarse-grind extract may be about 79 percent, while a six-row lager malt may be 75 percent. This number can help estimate the total weight of solubles in a given volume of water, thus making it possible to calculate degrees Balling, Plato, or specific gravity.

Coarse-grind extract (dry basis)—imitates typical mash conditions.

Fine-grind extract (dry basis)—gives an idea of maximum yield given certain conditions.

Coarse-grind–fine-grind difference—partial indication of degree of modification. Larger differences indicate less modification; smaller differences, more modification. How it works is that fine grind will tend to give a maximum yield regardless of modification, while coarse grind/brewery grind yields will be influenced by degree of modification.

Growth of acrospire—A measure of the growth of the acrospire inside the outer husk layer of malt, indicating degree of modification of the malt. If the acrospire is less than half the length of the kernel, the malt is undermodified. If it is three-quarters of the length up to the full length, it is considered normally modified. Overmodified malt has an acrospire that sometimes grows the full length of the kernel or more. The degree of modification helps indicate the protein character of malt. More modification increases soluble proteins.

Percent moisture—Pale malts are usually 2 to 4.5 percent moisture. Roasted and mild malts have less moisture. If moisture gets too high, storability decreases.

Protein—Excellent beer can be made from less than ideally ground malt, low- or high-enzyme malt, undermodified or highly modified malt, and malt of varying color and viscosity, but when your protein goes haywire you may have problems unless you compensate for it in your brewing process. But first you've got to know what is not ideal and begin to understand its impact on the character of your beer.

Total protein content is expressed as a percentage of the total weight of the malt. Almost all of the nitrogen content of malt is bound in protein. Nitrogen is about 16 percent of the total weight of protein. Analysts measure the weight of the total nitrogen in malt (% N) and multiply by (100/16), which is equal to 6.25, to get total percent protein. Got it? Total percent protein $= 6.25 \times$ % N and is usually expressed as total percent protein. A range of 9 to 11 percent would be considered ideal by many brewers, but 6-row malts of this type are rarely available. Eleven to 12 percent is typical for American two-row, and 12 to 13 percent is typical for American 6-row. High protein contents must be carefully considered in the brewing process. If not compensated for, they may create problems in the character of the beer.

Soluble protein is a measure of proteins that act as a yeast nutrient. Solubility is a measure of the protein that can be expected to dissolve in the final wort. It is also an indication of proteolytic enzyme activity, since this activity helps break down some proteins into solution.

If, as a practicing homebrewer, you have reason to care or be concerned about malt quality (don't worry, please), then the single most telling and useful specification is that of soluble protein content. While the entire brewing process and other ingredients must be considered, protein content of malt can have a significant impact on many qualities of beer. The key words here are *can have*, because the malt you used and how you handled it may or may not have been crucial to your individual beer's character.

Sluggish fermentation, poor head retention, excessive diacetyl production, excessive chill haze, collodial haze (a permanent haze), and unstable beer (beer whose freshness deteriorates) can all be the result of out-of-bounds soluble protein content or improper handling of malt.

The study of proteins is a very complex and involved science. At the risk of oversimplifying their involvement in the brewing process, I'll explain some basic principles. Proteins in malt start out as very long chains of molecules. These long chains are made up of building blocks called amino acids. Amino acids are the smallest of the proteins. The longest chains of proteins are susceptible to breaking apart into medium-sized chains of proteins. Certain enzymes at specific temperature ranges break the longest chains into medium-sized chains. Then there are other types of enzymes that work at another temperature range to break the medium-sized proteins into the smallest amino acids. (If this sounds similar to mashing and breaking down long chains of carbohydrates into their constituent glucose molecules through the use of diastatic enzymes, you're right—and you deserve a homebrew.)

It is desirable to degrade proteins to varying degrees with the aid of protease enzymes that are in the malt. If the longest chains of soluble and insoluble proteins are carried over into the beer in excessive amounts, their presence will result in turbidity, destruction of head retention, and flavor instability. The medium-length chains of protein are born from the first breakdown of long chains. A certain amount of these medium-chain proteins is desirable for good head retention and mouthfeel. Finally, the smallest chains or building-block proteins are the result of the breakdown of medium-chain proteins. They are terrific yeast nutrients and essential, in proper proportion, for healthy fermentation, and good attenuation.

In summary, about 50 percent of the original long-chain proteins must be removed or broken down to create a reasonable balance of other types of proteins in order to optimize head retention, clarity, attenuation, healthy fermentation, and flavor stability.

Here are some additional generalizations you can consider. Six-row malts generally have higher protein contents. Higher protein contents are an indication of higher enzymatic power. Higher protein contents coincide with lower extract yields from the malt.

It is worth noting that high-protein, high-enzyme malts are often used with 20 to 40 percent starch adjuncts such as corn and rice. With 30 percent adjuncts in the grist and a 13.5 percent total protein malt, the total grist has an effective total protein of 9.5 percent. This effectively reduces the overall wort protein content to a level that does not create the same problems that would arise if these malts were used when brewing all-malt beer.

What is the relationship of soluble protein produced in highly modified malts and yeast nutrition? Fully or highly modified malts such as English two-row pale malt have had adequate yeast nutrients (amino acids) created during the malting process so final wort protein is not as dependent on the mashing process for these nutrients. Some brewers argue that English two-row malts benefit from a protein-degrading regime, creating better head retention and beer stability.

Here are a few other beer characters that all-malt homebrewers may relate to.

Some brewing researchers claim diacetyl levels in the final beer can be influenced by protein content and mashing procedures. When brewing all-malt beers and using normally modified malts (less soluble protein) with an infusion mash, there is a greater likelihood of excessive diacetyl (butterscotch flavor/aroma) in the final beer. Highly modified malts (more soluble protein) in an infusion mash tend to result in comparatively less diacetyl in the final beer.

Dimethyl sulfide (DMS) is a sulfur compound that smells and tastes like cooked sweet corn. When noticed, its impact on the character of beer is satiating and almost always undesirable. When DMS is evident and at a perceptible level in beer, it is the result of either bacterial contamination or the way the malt was processed. Lager malts are the lightest of malts due to their low kilning temperature. This process inherently leaves behind compounds in the malt that are precursors to DMS. If the malt is not properly processed with a vigorous one- to two-hour wort boil and rapid chilling before fermentation, detectable levels of DMS can form. English pale ale malts are kilned slightly darker than lager malts; consequently, as with other colored malts, the precursor compounds are "driven" off, thus offering little risk of DMS character contributed by the malt.

Sieve assortment—A measurement of the uniformity of the malt kernel size. This is important when setting malt mills to grind a consistent and uniform grist for maximum yield of extract.

Get the picture? How you can deal with all of this information and make at least some small improvements without risking anxiety will be explained in the section on mashing and boiling the wort.

SPECIALTY MALT FRENZY

Have you ever visited a full-service homebrew supply shop? They'll often carry twenty or more different kinds of grain malts. Thanks again to the popularity of specialty beers in America, many choices are now available to homebrewers. But what about all of these malts? What flavors will they contribute to beer? What kind of extract can one anticipate? If a certain color of beer is sought, how will one know how much to use?

The challenge seems quite bewildering at first. Relax. Remember you're a homebrewer. You have the opportunity to play around with these malts in relatively small amounts and get a genuine feel for what games they will play with beer character, flavor, and aroma.

All malt is made by allowing barley to go through a series of water steeping and draining to allow moisture uptake by the barley seed. The barley is then allowed to germinate under controlled conditions to a specified degree. The amount that the barley is allowed to sprout is called *modification*. This process is quite similar for all malts up to this point. It is during the drying process that malts take on their special character. All commercially available malt is dried in kilns. The character of the malt is determined by three main variables: the moisture content of the malt, the temperature at which the malt is kilned, and the time the malt spends at any given temperature. Some malts will be processed through a series of time and temperature kilnings to create their unique appearance, color, flavor, and aroma character.

Touch the malt. Examine its appearance. Are the grains more or less uniform in size? Are they plump or wrinkled? Break open a grain. Does it appear glassy (an indication of undermodification), or mealy or floury (an indication of well-modified malt)? Does the endosperm appear white, orange, light brown, reddish, dark brown, or black? Chew it. Taste it. Is it hard or "steely" (indicating possible kilning irregularities)? Is it friable (crunches easily)? Does it taste mildly sweet and malty? Does it have a toasted malt character? Is it toffee or caramel-like? Perhaps it's flavorless. What is the aroma like? Does it have a smoky, caramel-like, roasted, biscuit-like, or toasted aroma that may contribute to the aromatic character of the beer it is used in?

Using your senses as a tool to assess malt is an essential first step in understanding the character of beer made from malts. With practice you will develop your own data bank of information, more valuable than anyone else's assessment.

Experimentation is the most enjoyable way of discovering the character of these malts and what they contribute to beer, and you'll have plenty of great beer to share with friends. Alas, your resources of time and money may crimp this style of discovery. So, presented later in this section is a table of malt data and specifications. This essential information will be the foundation for reasonably calculating the color and original gravity of any beer that uses grain malt or malt extract in its recipe formulation. It is also the basis of recipe-formulating software.

COLOR

Color of beer is expressed in SRM units (Standard Reference Method). SRM is very close to the old degrees Lovibond method, and for practical purposes they are interchangeable. Predicting the final color of beer is a tricky endeavor. Using data that indicate the original color of the malts used is at best a reasonable approximation. Malt color is not the only variable that affects the final color of beer. Wort boiling promotes some degree of caramelization, darkening the beer. Water with high pH (high alkaline) can extract more than usual color from malt grains. Filtering beer can remove some color. Oxidation can increase beer color. Commercial brewers are much more sensitive to these influences and resulting variations because they are trying to produce a beer whose color is identical from batch to batch. For homebrewers the priorities are entirely different. Even if you are trying to match a color for a certain style of beer, there is variation within the style to allow at least plus or minus 1 to 2 degrees SRM. Homebrewers can get good results when blending different malts to achieve a given character and color if they use malt color as the sole factor in predicting beer color.

Each malt is assigned a color rating expressed in degrees Lovibond. In America these color ratings correspond with the color that 1 pound (0.454 kg) of malt will contribute to 1 U.S. gallon (3.8 l) of beer. For example, if we have a Vienna malt rated at 5 degrees L and we use 5 pounds (2.3 kg) in 5 gallons (19 l), the predicted color of the beer will be about 5 degrees Lovibond:

$$\frac{(5 \text{ degrees L} \times 5 \text{ lb.})}{5 \text{ gallons}} = 5 \text{ degrees L or SRM}$$

If 10 pounds (4.54 kg) are used in 5 gallons (19 l), then:

$$\frac{(5 \text{ degrees L} \times 10 \text{ lb.})}{5 \text{ gallons}} = 10 \text{ degrees L or}$$

The beer will have 10 degrees color.

If one were to use metric units to calculate color of beer from colored malt, the formula would be:

Degrees Lovibond malt $\times$ (kg malt/liters of beer) $\times 8.36 =$ color of beer

When different malts are combined in a recipe, the formula is extended as such:

$$\frac{[(°L \text{ malt}_1 \times \text{lb. malt}_1) + (°L \text{ malt}_2 \times \text{lb. malt}_2)]}{\text{gallons of beer}} = \text{color of beer}$$

PREDICTING EXTRACT AND ORIGINAL GRAVITY

Extract potential of malt is indicative of the maximum amount of sugars and unfermentable carbohydrates a brewer can expect to extract from malt. A key point to understand is that the figures given in malt analysis specifications or the following table is the maximum you can achieve. What really is achieved is dependent on the efficiency of your mashing system and other processes and techniques. Inevitably there will be extract left behind in the lautering system, during trub removal after boiling the wort, and even during the sparge of hops. And, oh yes, what about boilovers? Let's not even consider this for now. The point is that most homebrewers can predict what kind of final extract they will achieve by factoring about 70 to 85 percent mashing efficiency. This is dependent on your system, and you will be able to figure your efficiency rating by calculating a predicted extract based on 100 percent efficiency and comparing it with the actual. For example, if 100 percent efficiency predicts an extract resulting in an original specific gravity of 1.048 (12 B) and your actual reading is 1.036 (9 B), then the efficiency of your system is:

$$\frac{\text{Actual original gravity}}{\text{Maximum predicted gravity} \times 100}$$

or

$$\frac{36}{48} \times 100 = 75 \text{ percent}$$

(assuming your targeted volume is achieved).

There are three ways in which extract potential is expressed. If you read a specification sheet from a maltster, you will note that extract is expressed as a percentage indicating the ratio of dried soluble extract to the total original weight of the malt. As explained earlier in this section, this percentage can be converted to degrees Balling (or Plato) and thus specific gravity in a given volume of wort.

One degree Balling (or Plato) is equal to 1 pound of extract dissolved in 100 pounds of liquid (or 1 kg dissolved in 100 kg). If extract is expressed as 75 percent, this means that 1 pound of malt will yield 0.75 pound of extract. Dissolving this into 1 gallon of water will result in about 8.7 degrees Balling (or Plato) because the weight of the water plus extract will weigh about 8.6 lb.:

$$\frac{0.75 \text{ lb.}}{8.6 \text{ lb.}} = .087$$

Multiply by 100 and we get 8.7 degrees Balling (or Plato)

or

$\times 4 =$ abbreviated specific gravity 35 more accurately expressed as 1.035

The preceding conversion from percent (expressed as a whole number) to degrees Balling (or Plato) or specific gravity is expressed:

$$(\text{Percent extract} \div 8.6) = \text{degrees Balling for 1 gallon}$$

or

$$(\text{Percent extract} \div 8.6) \times 4 = \text{specific gravity (shorthand)}$$

The above degrees Balling or specific gravity is referred to as "extract potential."

Converting these expressions into useful formulas for estimating potential initial specific gravities for given volumes of beer gets simplified to:

$$\frac{\text{Pounds of malt} \times (\text{percent extract} \div 8.6)}{\text{volume of beer in gallons}} = \text{potential degrees Balling}$$

or

$$\frac{\text{Pounds of malt} \times (\text{percent extract} \div 8.6)}{\text{volume of beer in gallons} \times 4} = \text{potential specific gravity (shorthand)}$$

The metric equivalent is:

$$\frac{\text{Kilograms of malt} \times (\text{percent extract} \div 1.03)}{\text{volume of beer in liters}} = \text{potential degrees Balling}$$

or

$$\frac{\text{Kilograms of malt} \times (\text{percent extract} \div 1.03)}{\text{volume of beer in liters} \times 4} = \text{potential specific gravity (shorthand)}$$

When we know the extract potential (EP, either in degrees Balling or specific gravity shorthand) for a variety of malts, and these malts are combined in the formulation of recipes, estimating the maximum potential gravity of the beer is as simple as:

$$\frac{(\text{Pounds of malt}_1 \times EP_1) + (\text{Pounds of malt}_2 \times EP_2) + (\text{lbs. of malt}_3 \times EP_3)}{\text{gallons of beer}} = \text{potential original gravity}$$

If you were to use:
5 lb. of lager malt rated at 35
1 lb. of crystal malt rated at 20
1 lb. of dried malt extract rated at 45
you would calculate:

$$\frac{(5 \times 35) + (1 \times 20) + (1 \times 45)}{5 \text{ gallons}} = 48 \text{ or } 1.048 \text{ maximum potential gravity}$$

When you know the efficiency of your system, simply multiply that percentage by the maximum potential to arrive at the actual expected gravity. For example, if your calculated maximum potential is 48 or 1.048 and the efficiency of your system is 80 percent, then: $.80 \times 48 = 38.4$ or 1.038 predicted actual gravity.

Now let's take a moment to get real. Of course you aren't going to do all this math every time you formulate a recipe. That would seriously cut into your homebrew enjoyment time. In reality, if all this interests you, you'll invest in some great recipe formulation software. All these formulas are built into the program and all you really have to do is be knowledgeable enough to plug in the various malts and, with a bit of trial and error, figure out which kinds of malts to use in order to make the beer you like.

Whichever methods you use, refer to the Malt Table on pages 30–37, get knowledgeable, and have at it.

STORAGE OF MALT

The best way to store malt is to combine it with water, hops, and yeast, ferment, and then bottle it.

But if you must find short-term alternative means, you should consider that moisture, insects, heat, and age are the primary factors that will cause malt to become unusable.

Moisture will cause spoilage by promoting molding. This type of spoilage is characterized by a musty aroma and flavor as well as a gray, dusty appearance.

Insects will eat the grain, bore holes throughout, lay eggs, and defecate in the malt. Appearance will be obvious. Aroma can be cheeselike and the flavor ugly.

Age will make malt progressively more rancid. Heat will accelerate this process. This is essentially oxidation. Malts with higher moisture content are more susceptible to this problem. Malts such as crystal or dark malts are drier and don't show signs of this effect for quite some time.

Properly stored malt can last for a few years. Store in a cool, dry, airtight environment. Use two food-grade plastic trash bags if prolonged storage is anticipated. If you live in an area where insects are a problem, malt should be stored in a lidded, airtight plastic bucket. If insect contamination is suspected, place a piece of dry ice in the bottom of the container of malt. Make an allowance to vent the carbon dioxide as it evaporates from the dry ice. This will create an oxygen-free environment that will kill or at least seriously inhibit insects and their larvae.

Keep your storage area free of crumbs, spills, and malt dust. Be tidy, relax, don't worry, and have a homebrew.

Malt Table

Extract Potential
1 lb. in 1 gal. (final volume)

MALT	DIAS. POWER= DEGREES LINTNER	PERCENT PROTEIN= TOTAL DRY BASIS	PERCENT YIELD= COARSE GRIND DRY BASIS (OR FINE GRIND FG)	DEGREES BALLING (OR PLATO)	SPECIFIC GRAVITY	COLOR SRM (EBC)	CHARACTER/ SUGGESTED UPPER LIMIT PERCENT
Light Pale Malts							
American 6-row[1]	180	12	76	8.8	1.035	1.8	≤100%
American 2-row[1]	140	12	79	9.2	1.037	1.8	Higher protease activity; more soluble protein than English 2-row; ≤100%
Belgian pale ale[2]	>70	11	80*	9.3	1.037	3.2	≤100%
Belgian Pilsener[2]	105	10.5	79	9.2	1.037	1.8	≤100%
Bohemian pale malt[5]	>100*	11.5	79	9.2	1.037	2	≤100%

MALT	DIAS. POWER= DEGREES LINTNER	PERCENT PROTEIN= TOTAL DRY BASIS	PERCENT YIELD= COARSE GRIND DRY BASIS (OR FINE GRIND FG)	DEGREES BALLING (OR PLATO)	SPECIFIC GRAVITY	COLOR SRM (EBC)	CHARACTER/ SUGGESTED UPPER LIMIT PERCENT
English 2-row lager[6]	70	10	81	9.4	1.038	1.6–2 (3–4)	≤100%
English 2-row pale	>70	10	81	9.4	1.038	2–3 (5–6)	≤100%
German 2-row Pils[5]	110*	11	81	9.4	1.038	1.6 (3.0)	≤100%
Light-Colored Specialty Malts							
English mild	53	10.6	80	9.3	1.037	3–4 (≤6.5)	≤100%
American mild[1]	65	11.5	77	9	1.036	4–6	≤100%
English wheat malt[6]	143*	2	85	10	1.040	2	≤80%
Midwest wheat malt[1]	170	12.5	82	9	1.038	2.5	≤50%
German wheat malt[5]	95*	11	81	9.4	1.038	2 (4)	≤50%

(continued)

Malt Table (continued)

MALT	DIAS. POWER= DEGREES LINTNER	PERCENT PROTEIN= TOTAL DRY BASIS	PERCENT YIELD= COARSE GRIND DRY BASIS (OR FINE GRIND FG)	DEGREES BALLING (OR PLATO)	SPECIFIC GRAVITY	COLOR SRM (EBC)	CHARACTER/ SUGGESTED UPPER LIMIT PERCENT
Belgian wheat malt[2]	74	11.5	81	9.4	1.038	1.8	≤50%
American rye malt[1]	105	10.5	80(FG)	9*	1.036*	3.7	≤15%
German rye malt[5]	N/A	N/A	81	9.4	1.038	2–4	≤15%
English rye malt[6]	62	1.4	86	10	1.040	7.6	≤15%
English oat malt[6]	17	2.1	76	8.8	1.035	7.6	≤15%
American Vienna[1]	130	12	77	9	1.036	4	≤100%
German Vienna[5]	95*	11	80	9.3	1.037	3 (6)	≤100%
English 2-row Vienna[4]	50	11	78	9.1	1.036	3–4	≤90%

MALT	DIAS. POWER= DEGREES LINTNER	PERCENT PROTEIN= TOTAL DRY BASIS	PERCENT YIELD= COARSE GRIND DRY BASIS (OR FINE GRIND FG)	DEGREES BALLING (OR PLATO)	SPECIFIC GRAVITY	COLOR SRM (EBC)	CHARACTER/ SUGGESTED UPPER LIMIT PERCENT
American Cara-Pils®[1]	0	13.2	74	8.6	1.034	1.3	for added foam and head retention; ≤20%
Belgian Cara-Pils[2]	9	11.5	78	9.1	1.036	8 (18)	≤80%
American Munich[1]	40	12	77 (FG)	8.6*	1.034*	8–12	≤60%
German Munich II[5]	72*	11.5	78	9.1	1.036	8–10 (16–20)	≤80%
Gambrinus Honey Malt[8]	50	11	80	9.3	1.037	22 (44)	≤80%
Belgian Munich[2]	50*	11	80	9.3	1.037	10 (20)	≤80%

(continued)

Malt Table (continued)

MALT	DIAS. POWER= DEGREES LINTNER	PERCENT PROTEIN= TOTAL DRY BASIS	PERCENT YIELD= COARSE GRIND DRY BASIS (OR FINE GRIND FG)	DEGREES BALLING (OR PLATO)	SPECIFIC GRAVITY	COLOR SRM (EBC)	CHARACTER/ SUGGESTED UPPER LIMIT PERCENT
Crystal, Caramel, Carastan Malts							
American caramel – 10[1]	0	NA	75	8.7	1.035	10	≤20%
American caramel – 20[1]	0	NA	75	8.7	1.035	20	≤20%
American caramel – 60[1]	0	NA	74	8.6	1.034	80	≤20%
American caramel – 120[1]	0	NA	72	8.4	1.033	120	≤20%
English crystal– 20–30	0	11	77	9	1.036	25	≤20%
English Caramalt[4]	0	11	77	9	1.036	20–37	≤20%

MALT	DIAS. POWER= DEGREES LINTNER	PERCENT PROTEIN= TOTAL DRY BASIS	PERCENT YIELD= COARSE GRIND DRY BASIS (OR FINE GRIND FG)	DEGREES BALLING (OR PLATO)	SPECIFIC GRAVITY	COLOR SRM (EBC)	CHARACTER/ SUGGESTED UPPER LIMIT PERCENT
Belgian crystal[2]	0	NA	78	9	1.036	55 (145)	≤10%
Dark-Colored Specialty Malts							
American Victory[1]	(Low)NA	NA	70	8.1	1.033	28	toasted; ≤15%
Belgian Biscuit[2]	(Low)NA	NA	77	9	1.036	25 (50)	≤10%
Belgian "Aromatic" malt[2]	(Low)NA	NA	78	9.1	1.036	26 (55)	≤10%
English Brown[4]	0	11	71	8	1.033	52–65	≤10%
English Amber[4]	0	11	71	8	1.033	30–42	≤20%
Belgian Special "B"[2]	0	10.4	76	8.8	1.035	95–130 (300)	≤10%

(continued)

Malt Table (continued)

MALT	DIAS. POWER= DEGREES LINTNER	PERCENT PROTEIN= TOTAL DRY BASIS	PERCENT YIELD= COARSE GRIND DRY BASIS (OR FINE GRIND FG)	DEGREES BALLING (OR PLATO)	SPECIFIC GRAVITY	COLOR SRM (EBC)	CHARACTER/ SUGGESTED UPPER LIMIT PERCENT
American, Belgian, English Chocolate	0	NA	50–60	5.8–7.0	1.023–28.0	325–500	≤10%
American, English, Belgian Black Roast	0	0	50–60*	5.8–7.0	1.023–28.0	475–1000+	≤7%
Unusual Specialties							
Roasted Barley[1]	0	0	38*	4.5	1.018	300–500	≤7%
American (Cherrywood) smoked[5]	140	12	80	9.3	1.037	5 (10)	≤65%

MALT	DIAS. POWER= DEGREES LINTNER	PERCENT PROTEIN= TOTAL DRY BASIS	PERCENT YIELD= COARSE GRIND DRY BASIS (OR FINE GRIND FG)	DEGREES BALLING (OR PLATO)	SPECIFIC GRAVITY	COLOR SRM (EBC)	CHARACTER/ SUGGESTED UPPER LIMIT PERCENT
German (Beechwood)[5] smoked	NA	11.5	77	9.3	1.037	2–4 (4–8)	≤100%
Malt Extract							
Dried malt extract	varies	varies	97	11	1.045	varies	≤100%
Malt extract syrup	varies	varies	80	9.3	1.037	varies	≤100%

[1]Briess Malting Company, Chilton, Wisconsin; [2]Castle Maltings, Belgium; [3]Great Western Malting Co, Vancouver, Washington; [4]Hugh Baird & Sons, England; [5]Weyermann Malt, Germany; [6]Crisp Malting, England; [7]Liberty Malt Supply, Seattle, Washington; [8]Gambrinus Malting, B.C., Canada; *Estimated data.

NOTE: The values for diastatic power, protein, and yield may vary from year to year and batch to batch. The values represented in this chart are from actual or average data.

The data will vary slightly from year to year, crop to crop. This table of data is a good indicator of specifications. Current specifications for the malts listed in the chart above plus more than a hundred other types of malts are readily available on the Internet at the following Websites:

www.briessmalting.com
www.weyermann.de/eng
www.gambrinusmalting.com
www.rahr.com
www.castlemalting.com
www.crispmalt.info
www.brewerssupplygroup.com
www.greatwesternmalting.com
www.bairds-malt.co.uk
www.countrymaltgroup.com

FERMENTABLE ADJUNCTS

In the early and mid-1970s there was a distinct reason why Americans became interested in brewing their own beer. Virtually all the beer that was available was a typically light-flavored American-style adjunct lager. Heineken, Becks, and occasionally Guinness Stout were the hard-to-find alternatives. Homebrewers were primarily interested in fuller-flavored all-malt beers. If you wanted one, you had to make it.

Since then, the hobby has changed dramatically and continues to evolve for the better. Beer innovation has become unleashed and in many cases unhinged! What began as a slow unzippering of beer knowledge has reached ripcord proportions. Hobbyists have embraced diversity in the interest of creating an unending variety of beers. At the same time homebrewers have eagerly sought beer knowledge through reading and experience. In short you and your friends have become true beer enthusiasts nurturing a great deal of respect for beer and the brewing process. Yes of course we are talking about you!

In the mid-1970s it was unimaginable that there would be significant numbers of homebrewers who, though it may not have been their preference, respected the character of light-flavored adjunct beers. On the opposite end of this, commercial brewers of those light-flavored adjunct beers have also developed a great deal of respect for fuller-flavored all-malt beers.

With a greater understanding of the brewing process and with the availability of quality lager yeasts, the skilled homebrewer can brew quality light or full-flavored adjunct beers. Grain adjuncts can contribute some distinctive and positive characters to beer. They are worth experimenting with for producing very traditional American light lager-style beers or to see what unusual contributions they make or effects they have in brightening some of the characters of typically fuller-flavored ales and lagers. Finally there are unusual reasons to use cereal grains other than barley in brewing beer, such as duplicating indigenous beers from other parts of the world or substituting other grains in order to circumvent allergic reactions to specific grains.

A thorough discussion regarding the processing and use of unmalted grains in beer is in *The Complete Joy of Homebrewing, Fourth Edition*. Formulating recipes with unmalted grains can be done even more easily with the additional information supplied in the table on page 41.

BEER AND ALLERGIES

Buckwheat, amaranth, and quinoa are unique among common cereal grains in that they are not of the grass family. Persons with allergic reactions to certain grass cereals may find that alternative beers may be brewed from these grains. Other potential alternatives for persons with allergies to cereal grains are "heirloom wheats" called spelt (also known as dinkel, *triticum astivum spelta*) and

Malting Your Own Grains: A Basic Procedure for Survival

Malt is simply a grain that has been allowed to germinate and then has been dried. The process degrades proteins into more desirable types of proteins and develops starch-to-sugar converting enzymes, soluble starch and some sugar.

When malting individual varieties of grain, some experimentation will be necessary to approach optimal results. But adhering to these basic procedures will allow you to brew the simplest beers next time you find yourself on an extended sojourn to a remote village in the Himalayas, the Andes, the African bush, or an island without beer.

Clean the grain by rinsing and soaking in water, removing the chaff and other material that floats to the surface. Soak the grains in five to seven changes of water over a period of 30 to 40 hours or until the grains take on 40 to 45 percent moisture. (They'll weigh 40 percent more than dry weight.) Germinate in a relatively cool area (ideally at 55 to 65 degrees F [13 to 18 degrees C]) until the growing acrospire is about three-quarters or equal to the full length of the grain. (Ideal length will vary with different types of grain.) You will need to mix the germinating grains and rinse them with fresh water to prevent molding. This process generally will take two to six days.

Dry the malt by any means you have available—dry roof in the sun, low-temperature oven. Of particular convenience for brewers at home is a clothes dryer. Tie the malt into a large pillowcase or sack, set the heat on "delicates" or "permanent press" and tumble dry. The ideal temperature for your basic pale lager barley malt is about 122 degrees F (50 C) and upward to 221 degrees F (105 C) for more strongly flavored malts. Good luck and may we share a brew in Leh someday.

Fermentable Grain Adjuncts Extract Table

Extract Potential
1 pound in 1 gallon

ADJUNCT	TOTAL PROTEIN	PERCENT YIELD	DEGREES BALLING (OR PLATO)	SPECIFIC GRAVITY (1.0XX)	CHARACTER
Barley, raw or flaked	13%	65–74	7.5	30–34	High in haze-producing protein. Soluble protein is about a third that of malted barley. Protein rest in mash recommended for lighter beers. Helps head retention.
Corn/maize, flaked	9–12%	84	9.8	39	Very soluble low protein. Pleasant very mild corn/grain flavor. Moderate use can brighten hop flavors and aromas. Gluten-free.
Corn/maize, grits	9–12%	80	9.3	37	Very low soluble protein content. No or very mild grain/corn flavor. Moderate use can brighten hop flavors and aromas. Gluten-free.
Millet/sorghum, raw	8–11%	80	9.3	37	Very low soluble protein. Gluten free.
Oats, raw or flaked	9%	70	8.1	33	Adds fullness/creaminess to mouthfeel. Promotes good head retention. Protein rest recommended.
Rice, raw or flaked	9%	82	9.5	38	Very low protein. Neutral flavor. Moderate use can brighten hop flavors and aromas. Gluten-free.
Rye, raw or flaked	11.3%	77	9.0	36	Small contribution to robust flavor. Finished crisp, somewhat "spicy," and clean. Protein rest recommended.
Wheat, flaked	13–15%	70	8.1	33	Flaked more soluble than raw.
Wheat, raw	10–11%	80	9.3	37	No husk, therefore no contribution as husk astringency. Foam-promoting proteins available. Protein rest recommended.
Wheat, torrified*	11%	76	9	35	Heat-treated wheat allows for rapid hydration and starch and protein conversion. Mild toasted flavor.

*Tef, dinkel (spelt), Kamut, buckwheat, amaranth, and quinoa are other grains worth considering as brewing adjuncts, but brewing-related data are not available, and little is known regarding their contribution to beer character.

Other Fermentable Adjuncts Extract Table

Extract Potential
1 pound in 1 gallon total volume

ADJUNCT	PERCENT YIELD	DEGREES BALLING (OR PLATO)	SPECIFIC GRAVITY	CHARACTER
Agave syrup	100	8.5	34	Mostly fructose sugar and very fermentable. Lends a degree of light caramel flavor and aroma. Reports of less fermentability when used in quantities of more than 20% of the wort extract.
Belgian candi sugar	100	11.5	46	Lightens flavor and body. Will contribute to cider-like character in lighter beers. Usually used in full-flavored ales to lighten or enhance character and drinkability. Moderate use can brighten hop flavors and aromas.
Cane sugar	100	11.5	46	Lightens flavor and body when substituted for malt. Can contribute to apple- or cider-like character, especially when not cold-fermented. Moderate use can brighten hop flavors and aromas.
Corn sugar, dextrose	80	9.2	37	Approximately 20% of weight tied up as water molecules.
Corn syrup	—	—	—	Extract varies considerably depending on type. Avoid those with preservatives.

ADJUNCT	PERCENT YIELD	DEGREES BALLING (OR PLATO)	SPECIFIC GRAVITY	CHARACTER
Honey	65–75	7.6–8.8	30–35	Approximately 25% to 35% of weight tied up as water. Nearly 100% fermentable. Can lighten flavor and body when substituted for malt.
Maple sap	2–3	0.2	1.009	Sap is 1.009 ± .003 (0.2 ± .05 B), pH 6.8, hardness 250 ppm.[1]
Maple syrup	65	7.5	30	Will vary with type.
Molasses	77	9	36	Can contribute strong butter-like and wine-like flavors if added in excess. One cup or ½ pound per 5 gallons noticeably affects character.
Rapadura (Brazilian dried sugarcane juice)	86*	10	1.040	Amber to very dark. Used in moderation (½–1 lb. [225–450 g] per 5-gallon [19 l] batch); mild, complex, molasses-like character.
Rice extract	73	8.5	1.034	Excellent adjunct to lighten flavor of extract beers. Neutral in flavor.
White sorghum syrup (Briess)	79	9	38	Light, mild flavor; it provides proteins and amino acids necessary for yeast nutrition, head retention, and body along with color.

[1]"How to Make Maple Sap Beer," by Morgan Wright, *Zymurgy* magazine, Winter 1988.

*Estimated.

Kamut (*triticum polonicum*). Spelt and Kamut are ancient wheats that have not been hybridized. A significant percentage of persons normally allergic to wheat-based foods could possibly use spelt as an alternative. Spelt may be malted just as any other wheat and subsequently used as the basis for beer. Spelt is about 30 percent higher in protein than modern wheat. Kamut is higher in lipids. (See Speltbrau, page 291.) Sorghum is another grain from which beer can be made. Consult your physician before experimenting.

RECIPES IN THIS BOOK USING ADJUNCTS

HONEY

OTHER SUGARS

CORN

WHEAT

OATS

RICE

RICE EXTRACT

MAPLE SAP

FRUITS, HERBS, SPICES, ROOTS, AND THE GALAXY

Fruit.   Fruit in beer? Originally discussed in *The Complete Joy of Homebrewing, Fourth Edition* as perhaps an oddity, fruit remains a popular ingredient in beer, but is no longer considered an oddity. Wonderfully refreshing or complex beers can be brewed with the addition of fruit, its juice, or extract.

When you add the fruit during the beer-making process does indeed make a difference. Heat and fermentation will change the character of the fruit to varying degrees. Heat is discussed later in this section. If you do not want vigorous yeast fermentation altering the delicate and bright flavors of fruit, then add the fruit in the secondary or aging vessels, when there is minimal yeast activity. It's worth experimenting with adding the fruit just before fermentation; sometimes desirable flavor transformations occur. Your decision and process will be a personal preference based on what you like.

Generally speaking, the intent of adding fruit to beer is to have its flavor evident in the beer character. Fruit flavors are usually enhanced in beer when the bitterness levels are kept very low and are accompanied by a degree of residual sweetness, body, and in some cases a bit of acidity. Fruits have their own natural sugars. We are most accustomed to fruit flavors with the support of sweetness. Without some sweetness, the fruit flavor may not be familiar to most people and, as such, may not be preferred.

The addition of crystal and dextrinous malts will contribute sweetness and body. High-gravity brews or high-temperature mashes will also elevate sweetness and body.

Let your own preference be your guide. If you disagree with the preceding, hey, no problemo. Dry, light body, refreshing, and fruity might be your thing. That's why you're a homebrewer—to brew the kind of beer you prefer.

Boiling fruit will set pectins and result in a pectin haze that is sometimes slow in clearing. One method of preparing fruit as an ingredient for beer is to pasteurize it at about 140 degrees F (60 C) for 20 to 30 minutes. This can easily be accomplished by turning the heat off and adding the crushed fruit to boiled wort from which the majority of hops have been removed by scooping with a strainer. Pasteurizing fruit helps assure the brewer that most wild yeasts and other uninvited microorganisms will not reach the fermenter alive. Usually some microorganisms survive, but with the introduction of a healthy yeast culture, their influence is minimal. They are often evident as a light film on the surface of bottled beer and are relatively harmless.

Heating and then fermenting the fruit during primary fermentation will drive off some of the more delicate fruit flavors and aromas. (Caution: if you are using glass carboys as fermenters, the total volume of wort should not exceed 75 percent of fermenter capacity.) Heat reduces some flavors, and fermentation's carbon dioxide gas very effectively "scrubs" or "bubbles" desirable fruit volatiles out of the wort. As discussed previously, when yeasts are actively fermenting they can also digest fruit flavor compounds and alter the end perception of nuanced fruit flavors—this may be a desirable or undesirable outcome depending on your preference.

An option that works well with relatively clean fruit, juice, wine concentrates, and naturally made concentrated extract is to add the crushed fruit or juice (in whatever form) to the secondary stage of fermentation. At the secondary stage most of the fermentation is complete. You will inevitably be introducing some bacteria and wild yeast if using fresh or frozen fruit, but they will be greatly inhibited at this stage by the influence of alcohol, low pH, and hops. Brewers using this method who are able to relax and not worry will find a brightness and greater degree of desired fruit character in the finished beer. As an option you may add the crushed fruit to a small amount of water and pasteurize the mush at 140 degrees F (60 C) for 15 to 20 minutes to minimize contamination before adding the fruit to the secondary. After the addition, fermentation will become active once more, but usually not as vigorously as during primary fermentation. The fruit will become impregnated with carbon dioxide and float to the surface, where most of it will stay. The skilled home-brewer-siphoner *extraordinaire* will be able to siphon mostly beer from just below the floating fruit while transferring it to another vessel for further storage, lagering, or bottling. About one week in contact with the fruit is adequate. Certainly don't worry.

The skins of dark fruits will add color to the beer. Juice alone does not affect color as much. More often than not, edible fruit skin will have a good deal of tannin, which can contribute varying degrees of astringency if left in contact with the beer too long. The astringency will decrease with age and may be desirable or undesirable depending on your preference. Similarly red wine astringency develops into complex characters over time.

When using fruits whose skins will make only a minimal contribution to color, removing the skin of the fruit will be to your advantage. Unbruised fruit is almost sterile under the skin. The skins from such fruits as apricots and peaches are very easily slipped off if the fruit is immersed in boiling water for 15 to 30 seconds. It can be frozen in new freezer bags or used immediately.

Fresh fruits usually must be crushed or mashed before adding to the ferment. Thawed frozen fruit will not require mashing because the action of freezing and thawing has already ruptured the skin, allowing the juices to flow out and the yeast to impregnate it.

Related Recipes: The Horse You Rode in On Apricot Honey Spiced Ale (page 281), Unspoken Passion Raspberry Imperial Stout (page 268), Return to Innocence Mountain Juniper–Cherry Bock (page 279), Frumentacious Framboise (page 289), Ruby Hooker Raspberry Still Mead (page 355), Aloi Black Raspberry Still Mead (page 354), A Taste of Happiness Sparkling Apple Cyser (page 350), and Waialeale Chablis Mead (page 349).

Vegetables.   While beers made with vegetable adjuncts are not quite as popular, there is certainly one worth mentioning because of its place in American history. The pumpkin was used by early settlers as a base for "beer" when other more typical ingredients were not available. The pumpkin beer recipe in this book is a wonderfully palateful brew that deserves serious consideration.

Related Recipes: Cucurbito Pepo (Pumpkin) Ale (page 287), Mr. Kelly's Coconut Curry Bavarian Hefeweizen (page 249), Someplace You Gotta Go Coconut Porter (page 259), and Mile High Green Chile Ale (page 283).

Herbs, Spices, and Roots.   This list could go on forever. There are several popular herbs and spices discussed in *The Complete Joy of Homebrewing* (coriander, ginger, heather, juniper berries, kaffir lime leaves, licorice, orange peel, spruce tips, yarrow). Whenever possible, use fresh or freshly ground dried whole herbs, spices, and roots. Preground herbs, spices, and roots should only be considered as a very last resort; the decreased flavor and aroma brightness is quite significant.

Freshly ground with a mortar and pestle, coffee grinder, or blender, these ingredients can be added during various stages of the boil, to the secondary

fermenter or at bottling time. Just as with fruit, some of the more delicate volatiles of herbs and spices are lost if boiled, heated too long, or vigorously fermented.
This will vary with each type of spice. An effective way to enhance beer with
spices is to add half during the final 5 to 10 minutes of boiling (or steep) and
half to the secondary. But it is very difficult to generalize, as the optimum method
of extraction for desired character for each herb essence is different.

If you wish to experiment and are not quite sure what effect a new idea will
have on your beer, don't sacrifice an entire batch of beer. Teas can be made by
boiling water and allowing the herbs to steep. Dose a glass of beer that you
happen to be enjoying and you'll get an idea of how the flavor will influence the
beer. Remember the flavor of the herbs in water will not be similar to the flavor
of herbs added to fermenting beer. Why? Because alcohol extracts certain
character from herbs and fermentation can digest and alter herbal character.
This is an important point to keep in mind. Remember hops are an herb too
and you know how playing around with various points of addition can dramatically affect hop character in beer. With herbs you can add a desired amount of
cooled (but not reaerated) herbal tea (concentrated teas are recommended) to a
portion of beer you wish to bottle with that flavor. This is the cautious method
and allows some reassurance on your part that everything will be okay. We
know it would anyway, but what the hey.

Here are a few ideas that warrant consideration.

Cardamom Seed.   A unique and strongly aromatic herb often used in East
Indian cooking and tea (chai). Bought as a dried pod with dark seeds or as podless seeds. The preground seed has a different character, possibly attributable
to age and oxidation. A half teaspoon (2 g) of podless seed boiled in wort for the
entire boil will contribute a very subtle flavor, but notable to a 5-gallon (19 l)
batch of beer. The subtle flavor is reminiscent of the character of Pepsi-Cola.
Two grams (½ tsp.) freshly crushed and added to the secondary fermentation
will contribute a strong aromatic character to the beer.

Coriander Seed. This flowery and aromatic spice is commonly used in certain styles of Belgian white (wit, wheat) beer. The coriander plant is also known

as cilantro or Chinese parsley and is used in Asian and Latin American cooking. The flavor of the seed is a world apart from the root and plants. Corianders of different origins (Asian, Latin American, African, etc.) have unique and distinctive secondary flavors worth exploring. Obtain whole seeds and crush them as you need them. Add 1 to 2 ounces (28 to 57 g) of the freshly crushed seed to the final 10 minutes of the wort boil for a 5-gallon (19 l) recipe. This will create an assertive and distinctive flavor and aroma. An additional ½ ounce (14.2 g) added to the secondary stage of fermentation, allowed to steep for at least one week, will have an equally intense but more delicate effect. Hop bitterness of medium to low intensities are recommended for coriander beers.

Related Recipes: "You'll See" Coriander Amber Ale (page 244) and The Horse You Rode in On Apricot Honey Spiced Ale (page 281).

Cubeb Berries.   Like small peppercorns with stems in appearance, these berries contribute an unusual eucalyptus-like character to brews in the smallest of doses. One gram in 5 gallons crushed and added to the secondary fermentation will do nicely.

Ginseng.   You've got to enjoy the flavor of this as a tea if you are going to consider it for your brew. The very expensive root can be made into a tea, or extract can be used. Ginseng has a bitter character, so it may be wise to reduce the hop level and increase the sweetness of the beer by using caramel or crystal malts. Consider combining it with other things such as gingerroot. The combination may prove to be synergistic.

Star Anise.   About the size of an American quarter, these attractive seed pods contribute a licorice-like character to beer. Two to 3 ounces (57 to 85 g) of whole pods and seeds can be added to the wort for at least a 30-minute boil. The pods are woody in nature, so a longer boiling time is required to extract their essence. The licorice-like aroma is intense in the wort, but mellows out in the character of the final beer. Crystal or caramel malts added for sweetness will positively balance the flavor of star anise. For more subtle character ½ to 1 ounce (14.2 to 28.4 g) is recommended. Do not grind.

Related Recipe: Topple Over Anise-thetic Brown Ale (page 285).

Szechuan Peppercorns.   These are NOT the same as chile peppers. These peppercorns are a combination of pods and seeds that have an extremely unusual mouth-numbing menthol-like hotness. They are available at Oriental food supply specialty stores. A half ounce to 2 ounces (14.2 to 57 g) of freshly ground Szechuan peppercorns will absolutely create conversation and some converts at your next beer tasting.

Related Recipe: Love's Vision—Honey and Pepper Still Mead (page 353).

See *The Complete Joy of Homebrewing, Fourth Edition,* pages 105–111 (hops, herbs, and spices, etc.). An excellent resource for brewing with herbs is Stephen Buhner's 500-page book, *Sacred and Herbal Healing Beers* (Brewers Publication, 1998).

MISCELLANEOUS ODDS AND ENDS

Smoked Malt.   Unusual and delicious enough to include in this section. Smoked flavor in beer can be a wonderful complement if in balance with other beer characters and you enjoy smoked foods. Smoked malt is easily found at home-brew supply shops. German beechwood, American cherrywood, and Scottish peat smoked varieties are the most available. If you can't find the kind of smoked malt you are looking for, it is a relatively simple matter to make your own. Smoked malt can be added to recipe formulations in amounts of a few percent to 100 percent depending on what type of malt you are using and the balance you seek.

You will need a kettle-type barbecue grill (such as a Weber) and a clean brass screen to fit over the grill. First, burn off all of the grease from the grill. Clean with a wire brush. Soak whole pale malted barley in cool water for five minutes. Start with and light a *small* amount of charcoal briquettes (10 to 13). Place apple, maple, birch, hickory, alder, oak, cedar, juniper, pear, cherry, mesquite, or other desirable smoking wood on the hot charcoal. Replace the grill. Lay the screen atop the grill and spread the grain over the screen. Cover securely with the lid and open vents to allow maximum smoking. Inspect every 5 to 10 minutes and stir frequently. Remove grains when dried. A cooler fire will prevent darkening of the malt. This is a warm-hot-smoke method of smoking grains. A cool smoke method uses cool smoke in contact with malt in a chamber somewhat removed from the heat of the fire.

Low bitterness levels and high malty character are recommended for beers brewed with smoke-flavored grains. Full-bodied malty porters and Oktoberfest styles work exceptionally well.

Related Recipes: Rogerfest Cherrywood Lager (page 329), For Peat's Sake "Scotch" Ale (page 277), A Return to Innocence Mountain Juniper–Cherry Bock (page 279).

Artificial Sweeteners?   Personally my advice would be to forget it. Aspartame, sorbitol, stevia, and saccharine contribute the peculiar character and aftertaste of artificial sweeteners to beer as well as soft drinks. Furthermore, some concoctions made from these artificial sweeteners such as Equal (which contains Nutrasweet [which is aspartame] and dextrose, among other things) are fermentable. I've tasted beer brewed with artificial sweetener. The brewer loved it and so did others. I usually don't interfere with discussions about my preference, but count me out.

HOPS

Finesse. Exotic, complex, subtle, whimsical, boisterous, evocative. The small, wondrous flower-like hop cone impassions many a brewer and beer enthusiast with so very little. At 8 milligrams (0.00028 oz.!) per bottle of beer, the "stuff" of hops imparts all the wondrous character that beer enthusiasts have come to appreciate.

We know that hops contribute bitterness, flavor, aroma, and stability to the beer and a calming effect to the beer drinker, though it appears that this calming effect is sometimes counteracted by an excitement about all things beer. Hopheads and lupomaniacs are often known to discuss life in terms of "the lupulin effect."

If there is one principle to remember about hops and their use, it is that their freshness should always be considered. Fresh means that the hop has not gone stale, or become old or oxidized to a degree that negatively impacts the character of beer. Minimal oxidation or staling is desired of bittering hops. They are best at their freshest. However, some degree of aging and oxidation is essential for the best-quality hops used for flavor and aroma. Flavor-active components of the essential oils of aroma hops are low in fresh hops. These flavors and aromas increase with about three to six months' aging after harvest at ambient to cool conditions. There is some deterioration of bittering resin during this time, but a balance is determined and achieved by the skilled hop merchant.

In this discussion, fresh does not imply freshly picked, nor does it imply whole hops rather than hop pellets. Fresh simply means that the hops, whatever dried form they are in, have been maintained and stored with care and have not deteriorated to an unusable degree. The entire art of using hops cannot get any more essential than this. Have a homebrew and think about this.

While you're contemplating, let's sneak in one other significant point. Bitterness and hop flavor are relative. When discussing hop bitterness and flavor

we must always bear in mind that we are referring to bitterness and flavor *in beer*. While this may seem to be a trivial point, many a brewer has gone temporarily astray by making comparisons of hop bitterness and flavor in other aqueous solutions, such as teas, hot, cold, or otherwise. Assessments of hop teas, though of limited instructional value, cannot, should not, and must not be seriously correlated to predictive characters in beer. It just ain't the same.

THE PERCEPTION OF BITTERNESS IN BEER

Bitterness is not always what meets the tongue. At the 2010 Slow Food Salone del Gusto held in Turin, Italy, I participated in a workshop about the perception of bitterness and how it relates to beer led by Mirco Marconi and Professor Paulo Gasparini (University of Trieste). Paper "taste strips" were distributed to all attendees who were then asked to register their experience. A show of hands revealed that about ten percent of people experienced a disgusting and rather objectionable taste sensation. About sixty-five percent perceived bitterness but did not think it objectionable. Twenty to twenty-five percent perceived nothing. The audience was mostly European with perhaps a fifteen percent mix of individuals from other parts of the world. Wow. This many people did not experience bitterness? Professor Gasparini who has done extensive genetic and cultural research on this subject conceded that the show of hands was not surprising. "Your ability to sense bitterness is genetic. You can blame your mothers and fathers for not being able to fully appreciate some of the beers we will taste during this session."

Whether we love, hate, tolerate, or balance them, hops are infused into our life as brewers. So, what are some of the dynamics surrounding bitterness and hop character in beer? Here are a few thoughts and truths that will offer you perspective as you pursue hoppiness in your life.

Brewers often indicate bitterness units as a calculated measure. Calculations serve well as an indicating measurement, but are only an approximation. Analytical measurement is the only true indication, but keep in mind the following points:

- Hop bitterness is a measure of a specific hop-derived compound. This hop bitterness reaches saturation depending on the qualities of the wort, somewhere below 100 BU.
- There are other compounds that contribute to beer bitterness derived from other ingredients, vegetal matter of hops, malt, and grain-derived compounds.
- The addition of hop oils by late- and dry-hopping will dramatically alter perception of bitterness, often tricking the mind.
- The balance of beer's malt sugars and alcohol will affect perception of bitterness.

Millions of Americans enjoy a thousand brands and hundreds of thousands of homebrewed formulations of hop-delirious India Pale Ale. Maybe, just maybe, a significant percentage of IPA drinkers really do not perceive bitterness at all, but they love the flavors of IPA and are just as enthusiastic as the lupomaniacs. Is this a reason why some excessively hopped brands appeal to a small portion of beer enthusiasts, while more balanced IPAs appeal to those who perceive but aren't offended by bitterness? And for those who do not like bitterness, it can be blamed on genetics. Genetic percentages are likely going to be different with various ethnic groups, perhaps explaining resistance in some cultures to certain characters in beer.

One last thought: People who say they do not like bitterness often don't understand what they have an aversion to. Many of these "I don't like bitterness" people often enjoy IPAs, which are high in hop aroma and flavor; hop oils are known to suppress or mask the perception of bitterness. Yeast-derived flavors will also suppress hop bitterness to some degree.

How about a little respect? India Pale Ales are not just bitter beers. They are hoppy beers and full of complexity coming from a variety of hop utilization during the mashing, brewing, fermentation, and serving processes. They come from a variety of hops. Bitterness does not define IPA.

HOP VARIETY: DOES IT MATTER?

Short answer: Yes, it does matter. Knowing that some hops are more bitter than others and that a long boil extracts and introduces only bitterness to beer, many homebrewers are misled to think that if bitterness is all you want from hops, then it doesn't matter what kind of hops you use. Not true. The kind of hops you use as bittering hops does indeed influence the character of beer. One only has to sample the empty bitterness of any homebrewed kit or commercial beer (and there are many) made with alpha acid hop extract. These brews lack complexity and depth of flavor.

Another example to illustrate this point is to compare three beers, the first boiled 1 hour with 2 ounces (57 g) of 5 percent alpha-acid-rated Kent Goldings hops, the second with 1/3 ounce (~9 g) of 15 percent alpha-acid-rated Magnum hops, and the third with 1/3 ounce (~9 g) of 15 percent alpha-acid-rated Columbus hops, all boiled 1 hour. Bitterness will be theoretically equal, but the resulting beers will be notably different in character. Some residual nuanced flavor differences will be perceived and the sharpness, aggressiveness, and overall sensation of bitterness will be markedly different. One is often led to believe that hop flavor comes only from the volatile oil components of hops and is completely lost if the hops are boiled for 30 minutes or longer. While it is true that nearly all flavors from hop oils are lost during short periods of boiling, distinct flavor characters from bitter hop resins will remain with the beer. Levels of different hop compounds will create different sensations of bitterness.

Having some degree of knowledge about hop "anatomy" will help in developing an understanding of how many different ways hops can contribute to the bitterness, flavor, and aromatic character of beer.

HOP ANATOMY: WARNING, THIS MAY GET UGLY

The female hop plant produces flower-like hop "cones." These can be seedless or seeded, depending on the variety of hop. The contribution that seeds impart to beer is not significant. The hop cone consists of petal-like "leaves." At the base of the leaves are tiny yellow glands called lupulin glands. The "leaves" contribute some tannin during the wort boil and help facilitate the precipitation of malt proteins out of the wort. The lupulin glands contain waxes, oils, and resins.

Resins.   There are two kinds of resins: hard and soft. Hard resins are believed by hop scientists to contribute very little, if anything, to the character of beer. Soft resins are primarily responsible for bitterness and some flavor character.

The soft resins are categorized into three groups: alpha acids, beta acids, and "other." When alpha and beta acids oxidize they fall into the "other" group. When hops are fresh the "other" resins do not contribute significantly to the

character of beer. Beta acid's principal components are lupulone, colupulone, and adlupulone, none of which is very soluble. With fresh hops, beta acids do not contribute significantly to the bitter character of beer. Some hop analysts estimate that beta acids are one-tenth as bitter as alpha acids—when they are soluble. Beta acids become soluble with age and oxidation. Very old hops, besides having a host of other undesirable characters, will have little if any bitterness contribution from the principally bittering alpha acid. The bitterness old hops contribute is derived mostly from oxidized beta acids.

Life is not simple, nor is how beta acids influence the bitter character of beer. Beta acids do indeed contribute to the bitterness of beer. Research has shown that their contribution can be positively perceived by the beer drinker as a preferred milder-type bitterness. This effect is more pronounced with the use of aroma-type hops because the ratio of the beta fraction to alpha acids is higher in aroma hops. For example, if two beers had identical amounts of bittering units (BUs), but one beer's bitterness units were contributed to by a higher amount of beta acids, the bitterness character of that beer may be preferred over the beer whose bitterness contribution came more from alpha acids. Even though their bitterness units were measured to be equal.

Alpha acids' principal components are humulone, cohumulone, and adhumulone. These are the hummers that most significantly contribute bitter character to beer. They are insoluble except when treated to a vigorously boiling wort. Then they become partially soluble and some of the alpha acids go through a chemical change called isomerization. Milligram for milligram, isomerized alpha acids (iso-alpha acids) are more bitter than alpha acids. But nonisomerized alpha acids do not dissolve or, shall we say, "melt" into the flavor of the beer. So we can only count bitterness contributed by isomerized alpha acids. (If you're not on your second glass of beer by now, you might want to consider making a move to the refrigerator right now. I warned you it may get ugly. Relax, don't worry, and have a homebrew.)

Let's get back to the three components of alpha acid. The proportions of humulone, cohumulone, and adhumulone vary among hop varieties and with the yearly harvest. Hop scientists continue to investigate their proportional relationships and what they contribute to the flavor of beer. One discovery that is generally observed is that hop varieties with a greater proportion of cohumulone tend to manifest harsher or more robust bitterness in beer. Brewers Gold, Bullion, Cluster, Northern Brewer, Chinook, and Galena are a few hops that are considered to have relatively higher levels of cohumulone. Tettnang, Hallertau, Fuggles, Hersbrucker, and Saaz are hop varieties with lower levels of cohumulone. Because of the lower levels of cohumulone, an equivalent amount of bitterness from these hops would be expressed a bit more softly. Neither type has a general advantage over the other. The choice of hops is dependent on the style you wish to brew and, more important, your preference and perceptions. Any brewer who has

Hop Oils & Resins: Comparison of Mid-Range Cohumulone, Myrcene, Humulene Proportions in Aroma and Bitter Varieties of Hops

HOPS TYPE	(RESIN) COHUMULONE	(OILS AS % OF TOTAL OIL)	
		MYRCENE	HUMULENE
Higher-Alpha-Acid Bittering Varieties			
Northern Brewer (German)	30%	36%	40%
Brewers Gold (USA)	45%	38%	30%
Nugget (USA)	27%	53%	17%
Chinook (USA)	32%	37%	20%
Cluster (USA)	40%	50%	17%
Galena (USA)	37%	57%	13%
Galaxy (Australia)	35%	37%	0.2%
Lower-Alpha-Acid Aroma/Flavor Varieties			
Hallertau Tradition (German)	27%	25%	42%
Hallertau (American)	21%	39%	34%
Mt. Hood (American)	22%	35%	34%
Hersbrucker Pure (German)	20%	14%	30%
Saaz (Czech)	24%	33%	20%
Tettnang (German)	25%	27%	27%
Tettnang (American)	23%	40%	21%

used the hops listed in the Hop Oils & Resins table can appreciate the fact that the character of bitterness is different as cohumulone varies.

Hop Oils.   Hop oils are the principal contributors to hop flavor and aroma in beer. Many of the more volatile components evaporate completely within about 20 minutes' boiling time. Some components remain behind despite boiling. There are many different types of oils that are present in varying proportion, depending on the variety of hop and the particular harvest. Two significant oils worth mentioning in this discussion are humulene and myrcene. Hop scientists tell us hops with a higher proportion of myrcene contribute a harsher and more generally perceived unpleasant aroma and flavor. Bullion and Cluster were good examples and it is probably no coincidence that these varieties are hardly grown now. These types of hops generally are not favored as flavor or aroma hops. Hops with relatively higher levels of humulene are preferred as aroma and flavor hops because of their subjectively pleasant character. Hops such as Hallertau, Tettnang, and Saaz fall into this classification. Very interestingly, a certain amount of slow, low-temperature oxidation of humulene oils enhances the desirability of these types of hops as flavor and aroma hops. This oxidation could be considered a type of maturation or aging process.

One cannot have an American discussion of hop oils without at least mentioning what makes Cascade hops a unique hop. Geraniol and linalool (they sound like two characters from *The Hobbit* or *The Lord of the Rings,* don't they?) are primarily responsible for the citrusy and floral character found in Cascade hops. The Cascade hop is a poor storing hop and ages relatively quickly. These compounds increase to their highest levels soon after harvest.

Using Hop Oils

The addition of hop oils in parts per billion to beer can have a dramatic effect on the hoppy aroma and flavor of beer. Not usually carried by homebrew supply stores, they can be ordered by special request.

If used, hop oils should be added sparingly. The instructions provided by the manufacturer should be carefully followed. They can be introduced into beer much the same way that finishing hops are—at the end of the boil but best during or after fermentation or just before bottling.

Hop oils are difficult to use properly because they are not easily soluble in water or beer, therefore the oils must be dissolved in a solvent-like medium. An ounce or two of grain (ethyl) alcohol or high-proof vodka is perfect for mixing with a measured amount of hop oil. Then you add another cup of tasteless light beer to further disperse the oils (or use your own fermented beer). After it is mixed well, add it to the wort or beer. If hop oils are not predissolved, you will tend to get an oil "slick" on your beer and unpredictable intensities of flavor and aroma.

Consult the manufacturer's suggestions, but a rule of thumb with which to begin your own experimentation is to use hop oils at a rate of 10 to 50 parts per million (0.2 to 1 ml) when adding oils to 5 gallons (19 l) end volume of hot wort at the end of the kettle boil. Begin experimenting with adding hop oils at a rate of 1 to 10 parts per million (0.1 to 0.2 ml or about 1 to 2 drops from a glass pipette) when dosing 5 gallons (19 l) during postfermentation stages.

LOVE AND HATE TO THE BITTER END

All those good resins, and it's all a brewer can do to get hold of 30 percent of them. You are challenged every step of the beermaking way. The bitter hop resins are not only stubbornly soluble, they have a tendency to go by the wayside during the beermaking process. For simplicity many brewers take into account a kettle/wort boil utilization factor, but there are many other factors, though of lesser significance, that determine how much of the bitter stuff finally gets into beer. Though this subject is often discussed in basic books on brewing, it is worthwhile to review and list some of the more significant considerations that determine the development and utilization of hop bitterness.

In the kettle:

- Hop utilization decreases with an increase of wort gravity (see Hop Utilization Based on Density of Boiled Wort and Boiling Time on page 229). This is somewhat analogous to dissolving sugar in water; as the solution approaches saturation, it takes longer for the sugar to dissolve. Recall that alpha acids must be dissolved before they can become isomerized and affect measured beer bitterness.
- Hop utilization decreases with an increase of hop rate; the more hops added to the wort, the lower the utilization. Some brewers will choose to add bittering hops in stages to maximize their bitterness yield. (This also is a way of controlling or influencing oil component loss.)
- The same amount of hop pellets will be more utilized than whole hops. As an example, whole hops might be 28 percent utilized while, given the same conditions, hop pellets might be 33 percent utilized. While the difference in utilization is 5 percent, what this really indicates is that one must use 18 percent more whole hops than pellets if the recipe was formulated for hop pellets, and one must use 15 percent less hop pellets if a recipe was formulated for whole hops.
- Hop utilization increases with longer boilings up to about 1½ hours for normal worts and up to 2½ hours for very high gravity worts.
- Hop utilization levels off with very long boils. The iso-alpha acids you've

worked so hard to create begin to break down. The loss is about equal to the gain.

Stages elsewhere in the process that affect the overall hop utilization factor:

- Some hop bitterness can be lost during the fine filtration of finished beer.
- The loss of hop bitterness increases as fermentation temperatures increase. You will lose a higher percentage of hop bitterness with more bitter beers.
- Some hop bitterness can be lost to trub, hot and cold break material.
- Some hop bitterness can be lost to fermentation kraeusen foam expelled from the fermenter or adhering to the walls of the fermenter.
- Some hop bitterness can be lost to yeast sediment.
- Professional brewers have indicated that when increasing batch sizes dramatically, let's say from 5-gallon test batches to 10-barrel (310-gallon) production batches, hop utilization usually increases. Proportionally less hops are needed for the same amount of bitterness. At first this may seem as though the kettle configuration affects utilization, but by reviewing many of the preceding points, a crafty brewer should realize that there are many other factors that have changed along the wort's way to beer.

If all of this weren't enough to consider, think about this next factoid before taking another sip of your favorite brew. Water hardness and certain minerals can affect the *perception* of bitterness. Increased hardness will create a relatively harsher sensation of bitterness. Within reason, this could be desirable or undesirable. The unique bitter character of world-class beers such as the original ales from Burton-on-Trent can be attributed partly to the hardness of the brewing water. It is worth noting that classic Czech Pilseners are brewed with extremely soft water with very few minerals present. Their bittering rates and formulations would lead one to anticipate an extremely bitter beer, but the softness of the water helps create palatability, allowing these Pilsener beers to be highly hopped. Their flavor and aroma are enhanced by the combination of soft water and high hopping rate, though the perception of bitterness is generally perceived as pleasant and refreshing.

IBU, BU, AAU, HBU, MBU. WHAT'S GOING ON HERE?

First, let's review a few things. If you have been following my advice, you've had a few beers.

1. In the beer world bitterness is analytically measured as "bittering units" (BU) or "international bitterness units" (IBU). The numerical value is a

measure of a specific hop compound and will not consistently coincide with an individual's perception of bitterness intensity.

2. Due to genetics and other differences, individuals will have varying sensitivity to bitterness. Some will sense high-intensity bitterness, while others perceive no bitterness in the same beer. The descriptions of bitterness in beer style guidelines (see *The Complete Joy of Homebrewing, Fourth Edition*) are inclined toward representing average sensitivity to bitterness.
3. Other beer ingredients can contribute bitterness to beer.
4. The intensity and quality of hop flavor and aroma derived from oils, pellets, whole hops, or other hop formats can greatly alter the perception of bitterness intensity.

There are several ways to express bitterness and bitterness potential. International Bitterness Units (IBU) are also simply called Bitterness Units (BU). One BU is equal to 1 milligram of isomerized alpha acid in 1 liter of wort or beer. This is a system of measuring bitterness devised by brewing scientists and is an accepted standard throughout the world.

Homebrew Bitterness Units (HBU) are the same as what some of the early homebrewing books referred to as Alpha Acid Units (AAU), the system first devised by the late British homebrew author and pioneer Dave Line. One HBU is equal to a 1 percent alpha acid rating of 1 ounce (28.4 g) of hops. HBUs are calculated by multiplying the percent of alpha acid in the hop by the number of ounces of hops. Ten HBUs could be equal to 2 ounces (56 g) of a 5 percent alpha-acid-rated hop or 1 ounce (28 g) of a 10 percent alpha-acid-rated hop. MBUs are simply a conversion to metric units, using grams instead of ounces as a measure of weight. Approximately 28 grams = 1 ounce; 1 HBU = 28 MBU. Contrary to what BUs represent, HBUs, MBUs, or AAUs are *not* a measure of bitterness in beer. They are simply an indication of the amount of alpha acid called for in a recipe, which is a first step in figuring how much bitterness could end up in your beer.

Infrequently you may come across a professional recipe that specifies the amounts of bittering hops in terms of milligrams alpha acids/liter. This is not an indication of how bitter the beer is or of its BUs. It is used to devise a recipe for any given volume of beer. If the bittering hop amount is given in terms of mg/l alpha acid, first you must determine how many liters you are going to brew and multiply that amount times mg/l to determine how many total milligrams of alpha acid will be needed for the recipe.

Alpha acid rating of hops is expressed as a percentage of the total weight of the hop. For example, if you have 1 ounce (28.35 g) of 5 percent alpha acid hop, then you have .05 ounce of alpha acid. Multiply .05 times 28.35 to convert to 1.418 grams or 1,418 milligrams. Working the other way, you can determine that if you need 200 mg/l alpha acids and you wish to make a 19-liter (5-gallon) batch, then:

$$19 \text{ liters} \times 200 \text{ mg/l} = 3{,}800 \text{ mg of alpha acids} = 3.8 \text{ grams}$$

If a 5 percent alpha acid hop were used, then:

$$\frac{3.8 \text{ grams}}{0.5} = 76 \text{ grams } (2.68 \text{ oz.}) \text{ of hops}$$

Lupomaniacs and Freshly Picked Hops

Those who grow their own hops can't help but wonder if there is a secret advantage to using freshly picked hops (i.e., fresh off the vine and not dried) in brewing. In the U.S., hops are harvested from mid-August to early October, depending on the particular variety and where it is grown.

Harvest Beers (sometimes referred to as "freshop" or "wet hopped" beers) are a recently introduced type of beer. The "style" name "Harvest" has come to refer to using freshly harvested hops, whole and not dried hops, as an ingredient to beer. Direct from field to brewers' kettle, the hops are added "green and fresh" to infuse flavors and other character not otherwise found in dried hops. Many American craft brewers introduce their "harvest" ales in early autumn.

These beers usually have characters similar to a dried hop beer, but with the additional nuances of a green, almost chlorophyll-like character. To a degree the "fresh harvested hop" character diminishes with age. Unique character from "aged" fresh-harvest beers may emerge, but they have yet to be researched, identified, or discussed.

If you wish to experiment, here are some guidelines. Freshly picked hops are about 80 percent moisture. When dried they are reduced to about 8 percent moisture. Given this ratio, you would use by weight about ten times more undried hops than dried hops called for in a recipe.

Here's a hopbit: Interesting results were found by German hop researchers when they tested the stability of frozen undried hops. They found that the undried hops, when frozen, were significantly more stable than dried hops stored under identical conditions. Practically speaking, freezing ten times more water and dealing with increased volumes does not make this procedure commercially viable. But then, there are homebrewers . . . and they relax, don't worry, and drink homebrew . . .

HOPS, BEER DIVERSITY, BITTERNESS, FLAVOR, AND AROMA

Let's take a breather from science and the technical and review how hops have become an important driver of beer diversity.

Brewers have been making beer for well over 5,000 years, but amazingly hops have only been a main ingredient for the past few hundred years. Even more incredible is that hops have been utilized for their diverse aroma and flavor contributions for only the past decade or two. That's a split of a split second in terms of beer's timeline.

What's implied here is that American craft brewers have recently initiated the not-so-traditional flavor and aroma characters that beer drinkers generally have grown to like and perceive as floral, herbal, spicy, and fruity. But it's far more interesting than just this.

It may have begun with Michael Jackon's groundbreaking books in which he describes the spicy and herbal character of such traditional hops as German Hallertau and Czech Saaz. These are wonderful hops having fantastic herbal notes in flavor and aroma. But the issue for the beer-drinking renaissance originating here in the United States was that the levels of hop flavor and aroma were far below the levels that today's beer drinkers seek.

Along came Cascade hops in the 1970s. This was the original citrus "fruity" hop used by craft/homebrewers. Whether they knew what they were doing or not, they added these hops in different ways, creating hop aromas and flavors that were zealously welcomed by beer drinkers.

Higher alpha acid (more bitterness) hybrids followed such as Centennial, Chinook, Nugget—all adding to the American "citrus" hop revolution. Even in the late 1980s "aroma hops" as a term was used, and it was discussed in the original 1994 edition of this book. In the early 2000s, or perhaps as early as the waning years of the twentieth century, new American varieties were joined by unique hops from New Zealand. Hops, such as New Zealand Nelson B. Sauvin and Pacific Hallertau, joined American flavor and aroma varieties such as Mt. Hood, Amarillo, Simcoe, Columbus, Citra, Sterling, and many more. These new breeds of hops were often bred for their agricultural qualities and high alpha acid (bitterness) and not necessarily for their flavor and aroma.

But the unforeseen happened. American craft brewers began using these hops in late additions in the brewing process and dry hopping in the fermentation and aging process. Their procedures and methodology were equally diverse.

A new way of utilizing hops emerged. Not only did it emerge, it is now a major factor distinguishing American craft brewers' contributions to worldwide beer trends.

Grapefruit, tangerine, lemon, lime, rose, honey, nectar-floral, bergamot, passion fruit, red and black currant, gooseberry, banana, wine-grape bouquet, piney, woody, melon, lychee, geranium, apricot, peach, mango, mint, strawberry, blueberry, pineapple, watermelon, peppery characters from hops are just the tip of the tail that wags hop horticulture.

Hop growers are finally beginning to understand that there are a growing number of brewers and beer drinkers who not only desire but demand hop-character diversity in their beer. Furthermore, brewers are willing to invest in order to get hops that are not only grown with these characters but are, as crops, commercially sustainable. This is a complete topsy-turvy, upside-down way of thinking from the traditional hop growers' perspective. For decades hop growers were driven by large brewers' desires for high hop bitterness and a low price for that bitterness. Mostly it still is, but times are changing. In 2012 American craft brewers brewed only 6.5 percent of the volume of beer enjoyed in this country, but they used more than 50 percent of the hops grown in the U.S. Furthermore, American craft brewers (and that includes homebrewers) aren't just interested in plain bitterness from hops.

Hop breeding in the U.S. has been going on for decades. There has been increased attention paid to breeding for hop aroma and flavor, but more is needed—and fortunately progress is happening. Recently the German Society of Hop Research has recognized the important potential of hop flavor and aroma in their document "New Trends in Hop Breeding."

The German Society of Hop Research identifies key hop compounds such as:

- citronellol = citrus-like
- limonene = citrus-like
- linalool = citrus, flowery-like
- geraniol = flowery, rose-like
- 4-mercapto-4-methyl-pentan –2-one = black currant–like
- isobutyl isobutyrate = green apple–like
- 2-methylbutyl isobutyrate = apricot flavor

Hop growers and merchants recognize that knowing the above essential oils and their character portrayed in dried hop cones does not mean it is easy to predict aroma and flavor notes in beer. That is very true. Why?

Getting hop flavors and aromas into beer depends on many variables such as:

- When the hops are added
  - In the mash
  - In the kettle boil, middle stages or late stages
  - In the fermentation process

- Secondary fermentation
- Conditioning vessels
- Density or strength of the beer/wort
- Variables during the dry hopping period
  - Level of alcohol
  - Yeast in suspension (they interact with oils)
  - Beer style
  - Malt ingredients used
  - Temperature
  - Type of circulation
  - Time in contact with beer
  - Condition of hops and recognizing that qualities change with time

Blending hop varieties during the late or dry hopping additions can be quite an interesting and rewarding adventure. The combination of more than two different hops does not necessarily have an additive effect. Two plus two does not equal four. When certain hop flavors and aromas are combined, there is often a different aroma or flavor character that emerges. Usually what is perceived by the combination of hops is related to, but not necessarily indicative of, a pure single hop character.

American professional and homebrewing craft brewers have made hop flavor and aroma their legacy in beer and brewing history. Most of this science has yet to be researched. Meanwhile, perception and experience guide most craft brewers when it comes to choosing, using, and blending hops for their aromatic and flavor contributions.

These are interesting times for beer drinkers. The horizon looks promising, but it will take time for hop breeds to be ready for actual cultivation. Some varieties might have fantastic qualities but are susceptible to disease and agricultural pests. It takes time to develop new varieties. While beer drinkers anticipate new beer flavors, brewers will need to invest in research and development to support hop growers and make new flavors happen. Why? Because homebrewers and beer drinkers like you want these exciting characters in their beer.

FINESSE, FLAVOR, AND AROMA

As already noted, volatile hop oils are the principal contributors to beer's hop flavor and aroma; logically their infusion should come during the final 20 minutes or 2 to 5 minutes, respectively, of the wort boil. If the boil is stopped and the wort cooled as quickly as possible, volatile oils contributing to late hop flavor and aroma can be preserved through to the final product.

DRY HOPPING—GETTING PRACTICAL

Dry hopping is another means to infuse hop flavor and aroma into beer. British brewers use this method to give a special hop character to selected ales. The process involves adding selected aromatic varieties of hops to beer in cold storage, during the final stage of maturation. In Great Britain hops were traditionally added directly into the serving cask, where the hop oils were allowed to meld with the overall beer character.

Homebrewers can consider this traditional method of infusion but must plan to deal with loose hops clogging the draft/tapping system. A more practical approach for most homebrewers would be to add aroma hops at a general rate of ¼ to 1 ounce (7 to 28 g) for each 5 gallons of brew during secondary fermentation during the final one or two weeks before bottling or kegging. Separate the spent hops by careful siphoning.

This procedure often brings to question the risk of contaminating the beer with undesirable microorganisms. There are several reasons why this risk is not as great as it may appear. Dry hopping should be done in the secondary or lagering vessel and avoided during primary fermentation. By the time beer is in the secondary, the alcohol, lower pH (higher acidity), and lack of oxygen in the beer serve to inhibit bacteria that might be introduced during the early stages of fermentation. Beer spoilage organisms are not as likely to choose hops as a resting place, because hops themselves (particularly the beta acids) have antiseptic properties.

Cleanly packaged hops should be sought. Hop pellets can be used to great

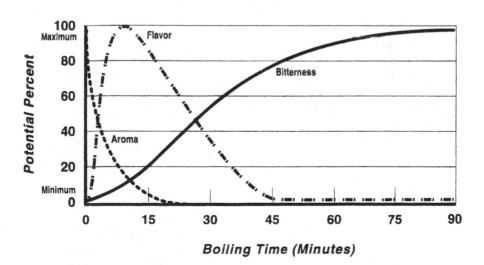

General Guide for Imparting Maximum and Minimum Potential Hop Aroma, Flavor, and Bitterness

Boiling Time (Minutes)

Lupomaniac immersed in a mountain of hops becomes momentarily dazed before becoming a brewer for life.

effect. Their use will minimize risk of serious contamination, though experienced brewers will argue both the pros and cons of the character they contribute compared with whole hops.

A final 2-minute steep of aroma hops in the wort boil, or the addition during secondary: Which is better? Dry hopping offers brighter and more vivid hop flavor and aroma. Hops added during the final stage of boiling is a more subtle accent that may be desirable with certain types of beer. You're a homebrewer. Try both methods.

HOP MADNESS. HMMMM

Now that we've come this far, you have two choices. You could become obsessed and try to do something about everything that affects hop utilization or you could get practical and have a homebrew.

Yes, you now have a feeling and an understanding of what the art of using hops is all about. You don't just have to believe what someone else tells you, but rather you can consider it from your knowledgeable perspective and decide what to do. If and when you change brewing equipment or procedures, you'll

have an idea of what to expect. Or maybe you'll be surprised, but then you'll be able to either pursue the difference or recover easily.

Practically speaking and from one homebrewer to another, don't get bogged down in obsessive details. After all, the very truth of the matter is that no matter how fresh your hops are, they are going to vary as much as 20 percent (i.e., plus or minus 10 percent) from the alpha acid rating you've been told they are. (Note: That's plus or minus 10 percent difference, not plus or minus 10 percent alpha acid weight.) Why? Because a hop plant grown on one side of the ditch may have received more water than a hop plant grown on the other. Perhaps the sample bale that the hop company based their analysis on was the one in the middle of the room and not the one you got your hops from (which was stored up against an outside wall). Maybe your hop cones were harvested on a Tuesday and the analyzed sample was harvested on Friday. Perhaps the shipment to your shop took eight days rather than three days.

To put things in a clearer and more practical perspective, consider for example that a 0.5 percent alpha-acid swing in an alleged 5 percent alpha-acid-rated hop is 10 percent (i.e., 0.5 is 10% of 5). Now what? Establish your own procedures and determine your own overall utilization factor. Be consistent, and the law of averages and the errors of misplaced precision will be in your favor.

EXTRACT BREWERS' TIP

Be careful when converting all-grain recipes to extract recipes that use a concentrated wort boil. Remember, hop utilization decreases with concentrated wort boils. While a 60- to 90-minute boil of an all-grain recipe may get 30 percent utilization, the same boiling time of 6 pounds (2.7 kg) of extract boiled in 2 gallons (7.6 l) of water will result in 23 percent utilization. Do a little math and you will realize the necessity of adding 25 percent more hops to have the same contribution to bitterness.

Likewise, if extract brewers wish to convert their boiling procedures to full wort boils (see page 154), the reverse of this principle applies; you need to consider reducing bittering hops by 25 percent.

Converting from a concentrated wort boil to a full wort boil (or vice versa) and substituting hop pellets for whole hops (or vice versa) can lead to as much as a 30 to 40 percent difference in the amount of bittering hops called for in a recipe in order to match what the recipe formulator intended. That's quite startling if you've never considered it before.

Most homebrewing recipe formulation software takes these differences into account when calculating predicted end bitterness.

STORAGE OF HOPS

There's not much to say here, but what there is to say is absolutely essential. Keep the hops cold, at or around freezing. Keep them double-plastic-bagged or in an airtight container or jar. Many brewers do not appreciate the importance of sealed containers and minimizing contact with air. Compressed hops, sealed in a jar with minimal air and stored in the freezer, will keep for years. Slow oxidation of some aroma-type hops will even enhance their character. A nice household appliance to have in your home: a vacuum bagger and sealer—it vacuums air out of a bag of hops, compressing them, and then seals the plastic bag. You can keep hops in the freezer for years. Oh yes, the appliance can be used for food too.

Interestingly, the more prized the hop, the poorer stability it has at room temperature. This is particularly true with the aroma-type (sometimes referred to as Noble) hops such as Hallertau, Tettnang, Saaz, and their hybrids such as Mt. Hood.

Time for a beer? You betcha! But just in case you want to dream with hops, check this next essay out:

DREAMING WITH HOPS—BED HOPPING

Hops have uses other than in beer. Call it the lupulin effect if you wish, but regardless of what you name it, hops do have a calming effect on the nerves, so much so that herbalists will recommend hop tea as a remedy for insomnia. More strangely, the smell of hops is said to help induce sleep. Usually hops and other herbs are combined as ingredient stuffing to make a "dream pillow." When slept with, the pillow not only induces deeper sleep but promotes vivid dreams. Most people are skeptics about this effect, but I have found through personal experimentation that these dream pillows work very well. So, for all the lupomaniacs and hopheads, here is a recipe for making your personal dream pillow.*

The following mixed ingredients will stuff two 8 × 6-inch pillows:

2 ounces (56.8 g) of your favorite dried whole hops
2 ounces (56.8 g) dried chamomile flowers
2 ounces (56.8 g) dried rosebuds, crushed
1 ounce (28.4 g) dried mugwort
1 ounce (28.4 g) dried lemongrass
½ ounce (14.2 g) benzoin (this is a natural preservative)

*Recipe by Barbara Wakshul, reprinted from the Summer 1980 issue of *Zymurgy* magazine.

Bag this mix in double-layered cheesecloth. Sew together an outer pillow from material that is attractive and tightly woven. Sleep with this dream pillow near your bed pillows, and be warned that your dreams may be so intense that you may decide to go back to having a beer before bedtime instead.

POISONED! AFTER BREWING BEER, USED HOPS CAN KILL YOUR DOG

Brewers and beer drinkers love them, but spent hops can kill your dog.

It's sweet, smells good, and you may put it into your compost. But be careful. If hops are eaten by a dog (yours or the neighbor's) it will likely result in death. If you are a homebrewer be aware and take precautions.

Brewers call the used hops and grains "spent hops"and "spent grains." The spent grains go to the farmer as protein-rich feed. The spent hops are composted at best.

Spent grains are wonderful for bedding and as composting material for the garden. So are hops. But if they are not dug into the ground or composted properly, wandering dogs may be attracted to the aroma and flavor.

I did a bit of Web research and found this excerpt from Workingdogs:

> Hops *Homulus* [sic] *lupulus*—the spent hops from the home brewing of beer presents a new danger to dogs. Since 1994, the National Animal Poison Control Center has been consulted on five dogs, only one of whom survived. The dogs present with panting, restlessness, and signs of increasing pain. The most significant symptom is a rapid increase in temperature called malignant hyperthermia. Treatment includes gastric lavage, charcoal slurry, coldwater baths and IV sodium bicarbonate to reverse metabolic acidosis. Hops contain a variety of biologically active compounds, the most suspect however is an uncharacterized alkaloid.

ADDITIONAL HOP-RELATED REFERENCES

Zymurgy magazine 1990, volume 13, number 4, Special Hops and Beer Issue. Articles include "History of Hops," "Development of Hop Varieties," "Hop Varieties and Qualities," "Assessing Hop Quality," "Processing Hops into Bales and Pellets," "Hop Products," "Hop Oil: Aroma and Flavor," "Growing Hops at Home," "Propagating Hops," "Factors Influencing Hop Utilization," "Calculating Hop Bitterness," "Matching Hops with Beer Styles."

Hops, by R. A. Neve, Chapman and Hall, 1991. Comprehensive book on hop cultivation.

Homegrown Hops, by David Beach, David R. Beach, 1988. Practical advice and procedures for home cultivation.

Using Hops, by Mark Garetz, Hop Tech Books, 1994. Practical and thorough discussion for the small-scale brewer.

See also *The Complete Joy of Homebrewing, Fourth Edition,* pages 18, 62–75, 76–87 (Hop Variety Guide), 301, 417 (hops, herbs, and spices, etc.).

WATER

MINERAL MAGIC

As a freshman in college at the University of Virginia in 1967, I aspired to become a chemical engineer, that is, until I took a course in chemistry. Every science and art has its own language and ways of explaining reality. I never could quite comprehend the logic of chemistry. That is why I switched into the university's nuclear engineering program, and five years later, after a lot of seemingly more logical math, physics, mechanics, thermodynamics, and a smattering of what seemed to be science fiction (the required electrical engineering courses were part of another science I couldn't quite fully grasp and barely escaped with passes), I received my B.S. degree in nuclear engineering.

Researching this chapter on water, I couldn't help but reflect on the struggles I had with chemistry in college. If only the introduction to college chemistry had been approached by relating it to some reality, such as beer and water chemistry, perhaps the lives of college freshmen could be more meaningful. As a freshman, I had no knowledge whatsoever about the qualities of beer and beer styles, but college should be inspiring, shouldn't it? Beer and water—how much more profound can chemistry be?

With limited knowledge of chemistry and microbiology, brewers over a century ago developed beer styles indigenous to their regions. Perhaps the single most influential factor in determining the style of beer brewed in an area was the mineral quality of the water. The unique bitterness quality of the pale ales and bitters of Burton-on-Trent (the home of the original and once iconic Bass Ale) was profoundly influenced by the high concentration of calcium sulfate in the water. The sweeter milds of Northern England were brewed with water with relatively higher concentrations of sodium and chlorides (sodium chloride). The porters of the south of England, the stouts of Ireland, and the dark beers of

Munich resulted from having to formulate brews using water high in carbonate. The qualities of the famous light Pilsener beers from the town of Pilsen in the Czech Republic were only possible because of the very soft, almost mineral-free water of that area.

Dissolved minerals in water and the chemical reactions during the beermaking process are two of the principal driving forces determining beer's quality. Minerals in water influence the flavor, aroma, color, head retention, clarity, alcohol content, and stability of beer. They also influence the performance of yeast, which in turn influences the flavor, aroma, and mouthfeel of beer.

Calcium, magnesium, sodium, chloride, sulfate, and carbonates (Ca^{+2}, Mg^{+2}, Na^{+1}, Cl^{-1}, SO_4^{+2}, HCO_3^{-1}) are the most important mineral ions/compounds brewers measure and balance in their brewing water. There are many other minerals and compounds influencing the health of fermentation and also may be monitored to ensure that the water is safe and will not negatively affect brewing and fermentation.

Practically speaking, if water is suitable for drinking and tastes great, then good beer can be brewed with it, but there are exceptions. Knowing the influence that water and mineral chemistry can have on beer engenders a more artistic approach to the beermaking process, even when the brewer chooses to do little about adjusting water. With a bit of knowledge and understanding, you give yourself a choice and are better able to brew the kind of beer *you* like.

With regard to the mineral content of water, it can be grossly generalized that naturally occurring "soft" water low in minerals is the most versatile of all brewing water. Not only will it allow one to brew a reasonable rendition of most beer styles, its mineral content can be added to with relative ease. Very hard water, high in permanent hardness, high alkalinity, and usually having a pH in the mid-7s, is the most frustrating to use. It is best suited for dark beers because of the neutralizing effect of the more acidic roasted dark malts. If high carbonate is not used for dark beers, it is best not used at all unless you are able to modify the water.

Water with temporary hardness is salvageable and can be relatively easy to adjust. It can be used for accurately brewing most styles of beer. By their nature, bicarbonates can be easily precipitated out of temporarily hard water by boiling, letting the precipitate settle, and decanting off the softer water. This is as simplified as mineral and water chemistry gets.

Malt extract brewers do not have to be as concerned about minerals as all-grain brewers do. However, permanently hard water can have an effect on healthy yeast fermentation, hop utilization, and the flavor character of hop bitterness. Malt extract brewers would always do better to avoid the use of very hard (permanent type), carbonate water and boil temporarily hard, bicarbonate water to remove the calcium carbonate precipitate.

Now it's time for a homebrew and a brief review of chlorinated water treatment and nitrates before we delve into the details of water chemistry and its influence on the brewing process and beer character.

Note: In the context of brewing, water chemistry parts per million (ppm) is considered to be nearly equivalent to milligrams per liter (mg/l). Water analyses will often express content in mg/l rather than ppm.

CHLORINE, CHLORINE, NASTIEST STUFF YOU MIGHT HAVE EVER SEEN

Added to virtually all municipal water supplies in minute amounts, chlorine is a necessary evil that helps assure that municipal water sources are free from other, more dangerous health-threatening microorganisms. The dose of chlorine in water supplies will vary with seasons and other circumstances to prevent the risk of contamination.

This very powerful disinfectant can combine with the organic ingredients in beer to form very powerful flavor compounds called chlorophenols. They can be detected as threshold flavors and aromas by many people at concentrations of a few parts per billion. If your beer is affected by this reaction and you can perceive it and you wish to do something about it, you can.

Boiling water can remove some of the chlorine compounds. It does not remove them all. The most efficient means of removing chlorine is to pass all of the brewing water through an activated charcoal (carbon) filter. Simple sink-top versions should be bacteriostatically rated. (There is a silver compound included with the carbon that prevents bacteria from surviving within the filter when not in use.) Filters cost from about $50 to over $200, but over its life a filter will produce water at a cost of about 2 cents per gallon. And it does make your drinking water taste remarkably better.

When using household chlorine bleach to sanitize equipment, be careful when the sanitizing solution concentration exceeds 10 ppm. Prolonged contact with metal will cause damaging corrosion.

NITRATES AND NITRITES

As the use of nitrogen-based fertilizers has increased, so have nitrates in water supplies. In some areas the problem is much more serious than in others. With regard to their effect in beer, some research has indicated that nitrates (NO_3) themselves do not affect the beermaking process. However, when nitrates are metabolized by some types of bacteria, either prior to or during the beermaking process, then nitrites (NO_2) are produced. Experiments have shown that they have a negative effect on the fermentation process at levels as low as 25 ppm.

MINERALS MATTER!

Mineral salts have shape, form, and substance until they are dissolved in water. As dry salts they are easily quantifiable, measurable, and visually real. However, when they are dissolved in water their ion components dissociate or separate from one another; they're still real, but you can't see them. These ions are charged either positively or negatively and attract one another when not in solution to become compound salts. Minerals in brewing water are dissociated ions floating in solution, ready to react with other matter given the right opportunity and conditions. Their reaction with this other matter is what the brewer is concerned about. The "other matter" is malt, yeast, hops, and our taste buds.

PRIMARY IONS

There are seven ions that have a substantial influence on the beermaking process. As you will soon realize, their influence must be understood as a whole; they have a complex relationship with one another and with the beermaking process.

Calcium (Ca^{+2}).   This is perhaps the single most important ion. It reacts with phosphates naturally present in malt to acidify the mash. The acidification is a crucial step in creating an environment in which protein-reducing (proteolytic) enzymes and starch-reducing (diastatic) enzymes work best. The reaction of calcium ions with phosphate compounds releases hydrogen ions (H^+) into solution, thus increasing acidity, corresponding to a decrease in pH.* An absence of calcium ions would also detrimentally result in the precipitation of oxalate salts in the finished beer, causing haze and gushing. Sparge water with an appropriate amount of calcium helps inhibit color increase (for light beers), decreases pickup of tannins (tannins contribute to chill haze and astringent phenolic flavor), and helps maximize the amount of sugar extract that can be rinsed or sparged out from mashed grain. The presence of calcium during the boil enhances protein coagulation. Its presence during fermentation enhances yeast health. An ideal concentration of calcium ion in the brewing water is in the range of 50 to 100 ppm. The calcium ion dissociates from calcium sulfate ($CaSO_4$), calcium chloride ($CaCl_2$), or calcium carbonate ($CaCO_3$) when these compounds are added to brewing water.

Sulfate (SO_4^{-2}).   Sulfate does not participate in any important brewing reactions but makes more of a stylistic contribution to the end flavor character of

---

*pH is a measure of the acidity or alkalinity of a solution on a scale of 1 to 14. Distilled water is neutral; it is neither acid nor alkaline. The measure of neutrality on the pH scale is 7.0. A pH of less than 7.0 is acidic, while a pH greater than 7.0 is alkaline (or called basic). The scale is a logarithmic scale. The numerical measures are not based on a linear scale. Simply speaking, the difference between 6 to 5 is ten times greater than 7 to 6.

beer. It draws increased bitterness from the hop during boiling and contributes a drying bitterness to the beer flavor. Sulfate is a source of sulfur if yeast or bacteria are given the opportunity to produce hydrogen sulfide (H_2S). In excess of about 450 to 550 ppm, sulfates promote undesirable types of bitterness sensation. When added to brewing water, calcium sulfate ($CaSO_4$) or magnesium sulfate ($MgSO_4$) will dissociate, providing a source of sulfate ions.

Magnesium (Mg^{+2}).   The magnesium ion promotes reactions similar to calcium but to a much lesser degree. In very small amounts (malt has it) it is beneficial to yeast metabolism. Its presence should never exceed 30 ppm. In excess it will contribute a sour-bitter-salty sensation.

Chloride (Cl^{-1}).   Chloride's contribution is stylistic—it contributes a fullness to the flavor of beer, accentuating the malty character. It does not participate in any important brewing reactions. It has a synergistic effect with sodium (Na). Chloride's effect on flavor becomes evident at about 200 to 250 ppm.

Sodium (Na^{+1}).   This ion has no chemical benefit in beermaking, though in conjunction with chloride, it accentuates a malty-sweet fullness in beer. Its effect can be stylistically desirable when concentrations are between 70 and 150 ppm. Above this amount, a salty character begins to interfere with the overall desirability of the beer.

Water softeners reduce hardness in water, but in doing so, they replace calcium ions with sodium ions, usually in amounts unsuitable for brewing.

Carbonate (CO_3^{-2}).   Carbonate inhibits crucial chemical reactions in the beermaking process as well as secondarily influencing beer character. It is alkaline in nature and neutralizes acids. In doing so, it counteracts the beneficial and necessary effects of calcium. When calcium mash reactions are inhibited by carbonates, malt yields are lowered during the mashing process. Carbonates contribute to an increase in color extraction during sparging (undesirable for light-colored beers). Carbonates also contribute a harsh character to the flavor of beer by extracting excessive tannins from grain husks. A beer with high pH is less stable and more susceptible to spoilage organisms. Carbonate concentrations in excess of 50 ppm will begin to create undesirable brewing conditions. However, dark-roasted malts and lactic "soured" German pale *sauer* malt, because of their acidity, help neutralize some of the effect of carbonate; thus, high carbonate water can successfully be used to brew dark beer. Or, with the addition of *sauer* malt, light-colored beers can be successfully brewed. Sulfates also help to neutralize carbonates. If carbonates exceed 200 ppm, then only dark beers should be brewed or *sauer* malt should be used.

Bicarbonate 2 (HCO_3^{-1}).   By way of reacting with carbon dioxide (CO_2) and water (H_2O), a carbonate ion can add a hydrogen ion to produce a bicarbonate ion. In normal mashes, ion-for-ion bicarbonate has twice the buffering capacity of carbonate. What this means is that a concentration of 50 ppm of bicarbonate has the same neutralizing power as 100 ppm carbonate and the same effects as described for carbonate. But although bicarbonate is a stronger alkaline, it is less stable and can be removed from water by simply boiling water and aerating. Boiling brings on a chemical reaction that liberates carbon dioxide (CO_2) and steals some calcium ions to combine with carbonate ions to form a compound that precipitates out as a solid. The water, now more suitable for brewing, is decanted off of the sediment. Because of the instability of bicarbonate, its contribution to water is called *temporary hardness*. If not dealt with, then bicarbonates will have the same effect as carbonates, only twice as powerful.

SECONDARY IONS

There are several ions that are often involved in brewing matters, though they are usually present in amounts that do not significantly contribute to beer flavor and aroma. If maximum amounts are exceeded, however, they can create havoc.

Iron (Fe^{+1} or Fe^{+2}). Its presence in water must be kept below .05 ppm or a blood-like, metallic flavor will dominate the flavor of beer. A very small amount of iron will enhance the quality of beer foam while adding to head stability; with high iron content this becomes excessive.

Copper (Cu^{+1}). A very small amount is needed for proper yeast metabolism. Professional texts cite trace amounts of about .01 ppm and recommend that levels be kept below 0.1 ppm. Ten ppm will prove toxic to yeast. It is best to avoid even approaching the theoretical "bang you're dead" limit. If copper kettles and beer equipment have been properly passivated by a weak acid solution, there will be very little copper pickup during the brewing process (see section on copper equipment).

Silicate (SiO_3^{-2}). This is present in very small amounts in almost all water. It really does not interfere with the brewing process, but does appear as scale on the inside of commercial brewing kettles and requires removal at regular intervals.

Zinc (Zn^{+2}). As a trace element, zinc is essential for proper yeast metabolism. Amounts should not exceed 0.2 ppm. In excess it is toxic to yeast and will impart a metallic flavor to beer.

Manganese (Mn^{+2}). Trace amounts less than 0.2 ppm are desirable for proper yeast metabolism. Amounts greater than this should be avoided.

MINERAL SALTS

A variety of mineral salts is commonly utilized by brewers to add desired ions to the brewing water. The accompanying table lists them with concentration information. In salt form, magnesium sulfate and calcium sulfate have water molecules attached to them, which affect weight, percentage, and ppm calculations. This has been taken into consideration for the data in the table.

Mineral Table

MINERAL SALT	ION COMPOSITION PERCENT BY WEIGHT	1 GRAM SALT IN 1 GALLON (3.8 LITERS)	1 GRAM SALT IN 5 GALLONS (19 LITERS)
Calcium Sulfate ($CaSO_4 \cdot 2H_2O$) *Common name: Gypsum*			
calcium (Ca^{+2})	23%	62 ppm	12 ppm
sulfate (SO_4^{-2})	56%	148 ppm	30 ppm
Calcium Chloride ($CaCl_2 \cdot 2H_2O$)			
calcium (Ca^{+2})	27%	72 ppm	14 ppm
chloride (Cl^{-1})	48%	127 ppm	26 ppm
Magnesium Sulfate ($MgSO_4 \cdot 7H_2O$) *Common name: Epsom Salt*			
magnesium (Mg^{+2})	10%	26 ppm	5 ppm
sulfate (SO_4^{-2})	39%	103 ppm	21 ppm
Sodium Chloride (NaCl) *Common name: Table Salt*			
sodium (Na^{+1})	39%	104 ppm	21 ppm
chloride (Cl^{-1})	61%	160 ppm	32 ppm
Calcium Carbonate ($CaCO_3$) *Common Name: Chalk*			
calcium (Ca^{+2})	40%	106 ppm	21 ppm
carbonate (CO_3^{-2})	60%	159 ppm	32 ppm

NOTE: Numerical data are rounded off to the nearest whole number.

GETTING IT! pH, ALKALINITY, AND HARDNESS

This is where water analysis can get hopelessly confusing for those who do not abide by the Golden Rule of Homebrewing. Get a homebrew, relax, stop worrying, and reread the section on bicarbonates once again. Pause (||).

Now that you're back, consider what follows.

In the United States water hardness is expressed as parts per million calcium carbonate (CaCO$_3$). Calcium is a main source of permanent hardness (in the old days "hardness" was an indication of how easily soap lathered), and magnesium is usually a secondary source. An important point to remember here is that ppm hardness is expressed *as if it were* calcium carbonate, not that it really is. Well then, if calcium indicates permanent hardness, so does sulfate, because it is usually associated with calcium in the form of calcium sulfate. Then what does carbonate indicate? Alkalinity? Yes, the amount of carbonate is related to alkalinity. As we've discussed earlier, bicarbonates are an even more powerful indicator of alkalinity. But bicarbonate is also a measure of temporary hardness, because when it is boiled it reduces hardness by combining with calcium and precipitating out as calcium carbonate. As calcium carbonate precipitates out, alkalinity is also reduced because carbonate is leaving the solution.

As a curious homebrewer, you should obtain an analysis of your water and determine its suitability for brewing beer. If it is soft water with hardness less than 50 ppm and pH of near 7.0, consider yourself fortunate. You can brew just about any type of beer, using easy adjustments if called for. For beer styles that call for brewing water with increased minerals, it is a relatively simple matter to add mineral salts to increase hardness to the desired levels.

If your water is high in hardness and pH is near a normal 7.0, you have lots of permanent hardness. Referring to the mineral needs of certain beer styles, you will be doomed to brew styles of beer such as classic Burton-style ale or Dortmund-style export. There is nothing to prevent you from formulating a Pilsener style of beer, but the results will have the characters that sulfates, sodium, chloride, and magnesium contribute to the overall character of the beer. A practical alternative is to find another, more appropriate water source for those styles or blend deionized, mineral-free water with yours in appropriate proportions.

When parts per million hardness increases and pH also increases, homebrewers will need to employ increasingly difficult procedures in order to make their water suitable for the style of beer they wish to brew.

Water with 150 to 250 ppm hardness and pH in the 7.2 and higher range will have quite a bit of detrimental carbonate temporary hardness, but boiling and the addition of some gypsum will remedy the situation to a great degree.

A pH higher than 7.5 and hardness greater than 250 ppm indicate that the water has a lot of temporary carbonate/bicarbonate hardness. Only some of it will precipitate out with boiling because there won't be enough calcium to combine with the carbonates to form calcium carbonate as a precipitate. Furthermore, there won't be enough calcium left for necessary reactions during the mash. In this case brewers usually calculate how much food-grade acid (such as sulfuric acid, phosphoric acid, or lactic acid; lactic acid would be the safest to use as a homebrewer) to add to the wort in order to neutralize the carbonates

without sacrificing excessive calcium. In some cases calcium sulfate may need to be added.

There is another alternative used by those who wish to brew more naturally and without additives. A portion of the mash is acidified by mashing at a temperature of 120 degrees F (49 C) for one or two days. At these temperatures lactic acid is formed by naturally present *Lactobacillus* bacteria. Principles of brewing chemistry are used to measure the acidity, and the correct proportion of this mash is added to the full mash in order to neutralize alkalinity created by carbonates. Another option available is to use German-made *sauer* malt, a specialty malt found at homebrew supply shops. For those homebrewers who do not wish to deal with this in-depth chemistry, finding another source for water is the best alternative.

Excellent beginning references to a more thorough discussion of water chemistry and brewing science are *Principles of Brewing Science,* by George Fix (Brewers Publications, 1989); *An Analysis of Brewing Techniques,* by George Fix and Laurie A. Fix (Brewers Publications, 1997); *The New Brewing Lager Beers,* by Gregory Noonan (Brewers Publications, 1986, 1996); and *Water,* by John Palmer and Colin Kaminski (Brewers Publications, 2012).

MINERALS AND BEER STYLES

There are certain characters that each mineral may contribute to the final character of beer. The presence of some minerals makes it impossible to brew certain types of beers with their traditional characters. We can surmise this from the information already presented in this section. What are the typical water qualities of certain styles? The ionic concentration chart that follows is a listing of what could be a typical water supply analysis from many of the great brewing areas of the world. Here is an important point that is easily overlooked: Before brewing chemistry was fully understood, brewing centers in the world were by and large stuck with the water they were able to get. Deionization and sophisticated treatment were not known. These brewing areas brewed types of beer that suited their water source. Munich, Dublin, Pilsen, Burton-on-Trent, and Dortmund are but a few examples of areas that developed certain styles primarily based on their water source. But the present-day situation is quite different.

For example, Munich brewers, using water with high carbonate concentrations, evolved a type of beer that was necessarily dark and malty. Now, with sophisticated acidification of the mash (lactic acid sour mashes), they can reduce the carbonate level low enough to allow the brewing of lighter lagers, so the dark

Approximate Ionic Concentrations (in PPM) of Classic Brewing Waters

(Variations can be expected to be ±25% in many cases, and sometimes more.)

BREWING AREA	CA^{+2}	MG^{+2}	NA^{+1}	CL^{-1}	SO_4^{+2}	HCO_3^{-1}	HARDNESS
Style of beer typifying heritage							
Pilsen *Light-colored lagers, zealously hopped*	7	2	2	5	5	15	30
Burton-on-Trent *Amber pale ales with distinctive sulfate-influenced hop character*	295	45	55	55	725	300	850
Dublin *Dark, malty ales with medium bitterness*	115	4	12	19	55	200	300
Edinburgh *Dark, malty, strong ales with low bitterness*	120	25	55	20	140	225	350
Dortmund *Strong, well-hopped amber lagers with full malty palate contributed to by sodium and chloride, and sulfate-influenced hop character*	250	25	70	100	280	550	750
Munich *Dark, malty lagers*	75	20	10	2	10	200	250
Vienna *Amber to brown malt-accented lagers with sulfate-influenced hop character*	200	60	8	12	125	120	750

Water chemistry at its best. Ultimately the character of the water really does affect the degree of enjoyment you'll find in every bottle of homebrew.

malts are no longer necessary to acidify the mash. A brewer wanting to brew a Münchner Helles style of lager should seek a noncarbonate, soft water, just as Munich brewers do.

In Dublin the famed Guinness Stout continues to be made with water similar to what was used a century ago. But brewers also make light lagers and ales. When an area brews a style of beer that does not typify its heritage, it is almost certain that the water is being treated in order to match a beer's profile.

In Dortmund, Germany, strong well-hopped amber lagers with full, sweet, malty flavor emerged due to high sodium and chloride ion concentrations in the water. Brewers found the very high carbonate level made it necessary to add (acidic) roasted malt to condition the water for a proper brewing balance and a pleasing beer flavor. High sulfate levels influenced hop bitterness character.

In Edinburgh, Scotland, the water is similar to Munich's and Dublin's, but with higher levels of sulfates. Dark malty strong ales with low bitterness are indicative of historic styles from Edinburgh.

Homebrewers who wish to adjust their water to match water from traditional brewing cities can simply subtract the ionic amounts in their own water from the desired amounts. The differences represent the amounts of ions that need to be added (or subtracted; not possible in some cases). Brewers with soft or distilled water are at a distinct advantage. Here is how a typical worksheet might be prepared:

	DESIRED WATER (MUNICH TYPE) (PPM)	YOUR WATER (PPM)	DIFFERENCE (PPM)
Ca	75	35	40
Mg	20	11	9
SO$_4$	10	18	−8
Cl	2	5	−3
Na	10	3	7
HCO$_3$	200	14	186

From the Mineral Table one can pick and choose what minerals to add in order to approximate the indicated additions (the "Difference" above) and come reasonably close to achieving the desired water character. Many recipe formulating software programs feature water adjustment calculators.

YEAST

In the high country of the Andes Mountains in Peru, local tribes continue the centuries-old tradition of brewing beer with available ingredients such as corn. The corn is not malted, but is chewed by the women of the village. Enzymes in the mouth are diastatic and break down carbohydrates to fermentable sugar. The "spittoon" is filled with "mouth mash" and allowed to ferment with indigenous yeast. The yeast is, you might say, very uniquely cultured. I have been told by a very dedicated researcher of indigenous old-world American fermentations that the special yeast culture is derived from the feces of unweaned infants. Tests of the culture have indicated that it was nearly a pure culture of *Saccharomyces cerevisiae,* or brewer's ale yeast. A bit startling? Relax. Don't worry. Have a, ahh, umm, er . . . home-poo . . . er . . . homebrew.

Fermentation opportunities for the American homebrewer are limitless. Most choose to ferment in a more traditional manner with more traditional yeast cultures. Malt (and other fermentables), hops, and water are all crucial to the character of a beer's profile. Yeast is an equal partner with its own unique influences on the qualities of beer. With the accessibility of dozens of yeast strains, the homebrewer can develop even greater flexibility in brewing.

Information, guidelines, techniques, and data are extremely helpful in developing one's brewing skills. The role that experience and experimentation have in helping develop the art of using and choosing yeast is absolutely essential. As with most homebrewing, the information and products available are of high enough quality that it is very unusual for an experiment or new endeavor to yield a brew that is anything less than drinkable. There are 50,000,000 yeast cells in one milliliter of beer during fermentation. Each single cell microorganism metabolizes fermentable carbohydrates and emits gas, alcohol, and the taste of beer one infinitesimal act at a time.

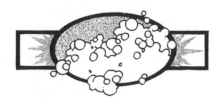

NAMES AND STRAINS

Technically speaking, all single-celled fungi yeasts are classified by genus, species, and strain.

The primary genus used by brewers is *Saccharomyces*, though other genera are used for some specialty beers. Of the *Saccharomyces* genus, there are two species principally used. They are *cerevisiae* and *uvarum* (sometimes called *carlsbergensis*). *Saccharomyces cerevisiae* is commonly known as ale yeast. *Saccharomyces uvarum* is lager yeast.

There are hundreds of strains of these two types of yeast. When used in a traditional manner, a particular strain of yeast will behave somewhat predictably, producing distinctive characters in beer. Particular strains of yeast have been catalogued and can be chosen to produce desired levels of estery/fruity character, alcohol types, sulfur compounds, diacetyl compounds (butterscotch or butter-like flavor and aroma character), and phenolic compounds (often described in German wheat beers and some Belgian ales as clove-like and/or smoky). Yeast strains are also chosen to minimize undesirable characters. Of note is the fact that one brewer's undesirable character is another brewer's desired character.

All ale yeasts are not the same. For example, one brewer may wish to accent the fruitiness of English-style ales. Another brewer may wish to brew strong ales with Belgian-style fruitiness. Two very different strains of ale yeast are used for these two styles. Brewers find strains of yeast particularly suited to replicating the character they seek in their ales and lagers.

Furthermore, some brewers may be brewing five-barrel batches while others ferment 100 or even 1,000 barrels at a time. The volume of liquid has an immense effect on the behavior and health of yeast. The pressure upon the yeast cell wall at the bottom of a 100-barrel tank is dramatically greater than that at the bottom of a homebrewer's 5-gallon carboy. Yeast under these various conditions will perform differently. One may not sediment well after fermentation is finished or may produce undesirable flavors and aroma due to the stress of pressure on the cell walls of the yeast. Another yeast may be affected by the osmotic pressure of too much sugar in solution (strong beers) and is not as capable of completing fermentation as effectively as another yeast.

Yeast varieties are capable of adapting to their environment and produce "house" character to a beer that may be desired by the brewer and beer drinker— you! Yeast is a living organism affected by many of the same stress factors as the human body: time, temperature, pressure, motion, nutrition, etc.

Lager yeasts are as temperamental as ale yeast. To maximize a certain character, brewers may choose strains that are capable of fermenting high-strength beer, that sediment cleanly, that produce few off or fruity characters at high temperatures, or are capable of resisting mutation over multiple generations of use. Lager yeasts, unlike ale yeasts, are capable of metabolic activity/fermentation at temperatures close to freezing. For most strains of ale yeast, the lower limit for dependable fermentation is about 60 degrees F.

Brewers are not simply content with lager and ale strains of yeast. The lambic traditions of Belgium and exotic fermentations of other beer cultures have inspired the use of "wild" strains of yeast often harvested from the ambient air. Wild yeasts can also be cultured; although that seems to be oxymoronic, it is effective. *Brettanomyces* strains are some of the most common wild yeasts today's brewers use for some of their specialty beers. These strains evolve beer character over many months of aging, sometimes years.

In summary, the strain of brewer's yeast used is perhaps a most critical consideration for the practical homebrewer. Strains of yeast are designated by any manner of names or numbers and are distinguished from one another by variations in their behavior. Different strains of yeast, whether they are ale yeast or lager yeast, will behave differently in some ways and similarly in others. The behavior of yeasts will affect wort attenuation, ester production, phenol production, fusel alcohol production, diacetyl (butterscotch character) levels, flocculation of yeast, alcohol production, and mutatability. Different strains of yeast are more or less susceptible to the influence of temperature, alcohol levels, mineral content, nutritional balance, atmospheric and osmotic pressure, and other factors.

Oh, and here's a question that inevitably gets asked. Can a brewer make an ale with lager yeast? Can you make a lager with an ale yeast? The answer, technically and traditionally, is no. But when all that matters is the perception of what you experience, the debate begins. Beers tasting like certain styles of lager beers can be made with ale strains of yeast, and beers tasting like certain styles of ale can be made with lager strains of yeast. You can do anything you want when you've got knowledge.

It is quite obvious that choosing your yeast by strain is crucial to the final character of the beer you wish to produce.

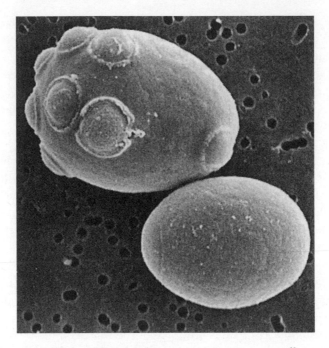

A *mother of all beers! Two* Saccharomyces cerevisiae *yeast cells imaged by a scanning electron microscope show the top cell with bud scars. The center scar is about 2 microns in diameter. It would take a string of over 5,000 yeast cells to equal an inch (2.54 cm).*

DRIED AND LIQUID YEASTS

Yeasts are available for use by the homebrewer in dried granulated form and various liquid forms.

Dried Yeast

By a long shot, dried packaged yeasts are the simplest to use. When a source of quality dried yeast is found, the brewer is doing well to consistently use it. A quality yeast is one that the brewer is pleased with, giving desired results. Quality ale and lager yeasts are dependably available in dried form. Their quality has come a long way since the 1980s. The best advice is to stick with brand names and avoid generic dried yeast that comes in plain white brandless packets.

For the hobbyist, dried yeast usually comes in 3.5-, 7-, or sometimes 14-gram packages. For a 5-gallon (19 l) batch, the addition of 7 to 14 grams of active dried yeast is recommended. Prior to pitching, rehydrate in ½ to 1 cup (118 to 237 ml) sterile water at about 100 degrees F (38 C) for 15 minutes to

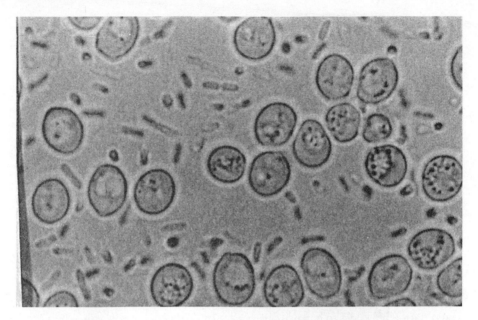

Not your beer—you hope! As seen through a laboratory microscope one yeast cell is about 5 to 7 microns in diameter. Saccharomyces cerevisiae *yeast cells are depicted here among rod-shaped* Lactobacillus *bacteria; bacteria you do not want in your beer (lambic styles excepted).*

activate viable yeast cells. The rehydrated slurry can be added directly to the wort at temperatures generally below 75 degrees F (24 C).

Before the yeast is introduced to the wort, it is crucial to oxygenate the wort to provide the yeast sufficient oxygen for its initial metabolic phases. During this lag phase yeast cells take up the oxygen and nutrients required for later growth and fermentation. When using dried yeast the lag phase is not as crucial because the dried yeast has gone through the lag phase during culturing and already possesses stores of oxygen and nutrients when it is packaged. This is one reason why dried yeast seems to "take off" within an hour or two when introduced to fresh wort. It jumps right into the growth and fermentation stages much more quickly.

"Wet" or Liquid Yeast

Using liquid cultures does not in any manner assure or increase the odds that the culture is clean and not contaminated. Actually, liquid yeasts are more susceptible to contamination than dried yeasts once they are handled by the brewer. Care must always be a top priority when using liquid cultures to help assure a maximum degree of purity. Yes, you still may abide by the Golden

Rule of Homebrewing, but an elevated degree of respect for the process of handling must be considered—while you are relaxing, not worrying, and having a homebrew. Remember, worrying can influence the flavor of beer more than anything else. It can influence the quality of yeast as well. Usually poor decisions are made when one is worrying about anything.

There are a few essential factors that must be considered when propagating or using liquid yeasts. They require a proper wort environment in order to successfully grow, thrive, and ferment. They need proper nutrition. This should never be a problem if the propagating medium or wort is all malt. If using over 30 percent adjuncts such as refined sugar, corn, rice, or other unmalted adjuncts, you will need to determine whether the nutrition (amino acid nutrients) requirements have been met. An equally important consideration is the requirement of oxygen. Whenever you're propagating yeast in any amount of sterile wort, it *must* be adequately aerated. Aeration by vigorous agitation in a sealed sterile container is often adequate. Temperature of propagation is another consideration that influences timely yeast growth and activity. You may find yourself in a situation propagating yeast at slightly higher temperatures than you'd normally expect to have during beer fermentation. This is okay when there is no alternative, but it may influence the behavior of the yeast.

Liquid yeasts can be derived from several methods or procedures:

1. from fermentation sediment, from agar slants,
2. from dormant yeast suspended or sedimented in small amounts of beer or fermented wort,
3. from your local craft brewer who is purging his fermenters of yeast slurry, or
4. the easiest and most dependable method: buying a homebrew-size culture from your local homebrew supply shop. The variety and strains available are of more types than you could brew in a year.

Reusing Yeast Sediment

Active yeast can be collected from the sediment from either the primary or secondary fermenter and added directly to fresh wort. Theoretically the best part of the yeast sediment to use is the middle layer of lighter, straw-colored yeast. This sits above trub and other organic material such as hop particulates. It is the most viable.

Four to 8 fluid ounces (125 to 250 ml) of yeast slurry should be used for pitching into 5 gallons (19 l) of wort, the upper limit being optimal. The practical homebrewer more often than not has less than ideal circumstances to work with. If the brewer is assured that the finished fermentation is not contaminated, excellent results are usually obtained with a slurry of yeast sediment poured out of a fermenter. Care should be taken to sanitize the mouth of the carboy by swabbing with disinfecting grain (ethyl) alcohol (or 150-proof cheap vodka) and flaming with a butane cigarette-type lighter.

Another source of yeast sediment is your friendly microbrewery or pub brewery. While most do not appreciate being bothered at the spur of the moment, many will accommodate the needs of local homebrewers if a regular schedule can be developed and there is one homebrewer contact or homebrew shop contact that will deal with the exchange. Use your imagination as a homebrewer when you reciprocate the favor, but keep in mind a professional brewer is not lacking for free beer.

If a slurry is taken and contained in a sterile jar, it can be kept relatively fresh and active for two to five days in the refrigerator. Don't seal the container. Fermentation can continue creating gas and dangerous pressure in a sealed container. The yeast's storability will depend on the strain.

CULTURING DORMANT YEAST IN SUSPENSION

A very practical means for culturing and storing yeast is the method outlined on pages 310 to 313 of *The Complete Joy of Homebrewing, Fourth Edition*. It is a simple method requiring very little specialized equipment and is accessible to virtually all homebrewers. It essentially cultures active yeast in mini fermenters: beer bottles, or pint or quart jars affixed with a fermentation lock. The yeast is cultured with real wort and is stored as a sediment under fermented wort, conditions most natural to beer yeast. Highly bittered wort is usually made in advance and stored in sterile jars or bottles. The highly bittered wort is an inhibitor of bacterial activity.

With this method, yeast may be cultured from any source. A yeast bank can be maintained easily. Yeast will remain viable for months at refrigerated temperatures. (I have had experience with a yeast that survived twenty-five years "under beer" and was recultured to brew an excellent light lager.) These cultures usually are more quick to grow than slants.

Commercial cultures are available to homebrewers as yeast suspended in sterile compartmentalized foil packages or in easy-to-use plastic vials. These yeast cultures can be used directly from the package as the directions indicate, but if you have the resource of extra time it's best to culture up to amounts sufficient for pitching into your volume of wort. Instructions are included with the packaging.

Practical homebrewers often find themselves pitching a less than ideal quantity of slurry (ideally: 1 cup [237 ml] for 5 gallons [19 l]). Don't worry; the smaller amounts will work. You can enhance the results and accelerate the growth of yeast in your pitched wort by holding the temperature of your wort at

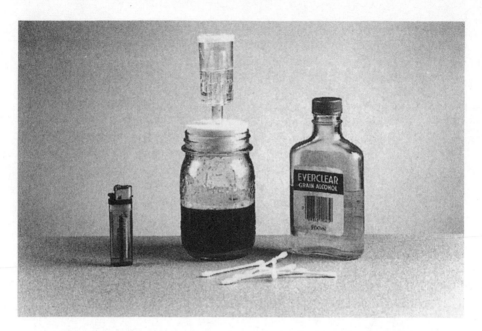

*Expose yourself to culture. Culturing yeast in sterile-prepared wort is quite a
simple process, requiring only a few precautions. Swabbing pouring surfaces
with grain alcohol-soaked cotton swabs helps reduce risk of contamination.
Flaming surfaces with a butane lighter further minimizes contamination.*

about 70 to 75 degrees F (21 to 24 C) until yeast activity is observed (usually
within 24 to 30 hours), then cooling to desired temperatures. The trade-off
here is that you may be encouraging a small degree of undesirable fruitiness at
these warmer temperatures when brewing lager beers. A wee bit of fruitiness is
reasonable considering the more deleterious effects of extended lag times,
which allow bacteria populations to gain a foothold in the wort before the yeast
cells sufficiently outnumber the bacteria and inhibit them by increasing the
acidity of the wort.

For homebrewers able to culture 1 cup (250 ml) of slurry, yeast can be pitched
into more appropriately cooled worts (50 to 55 degrees F [9 to 13 C] for lager)
with normal lag times and growth phases.

YEAST TYPES AVAILABLE

A sampling of just a few types of liquid yeasts available to homebrew shops
throughout the United States, Canada, Australia, Europe, and developing craft
brewing/homebrewing countries:

Ale Yeasts

German ale (both Alt and Kölsch) yeast
American ale yeast (often referred to as Chico or Sierra Nevada ale yeast)
Irish ale (Guinness Stout–type yeast)
British ale (from Whitbread brewery)
European ale
London ale
Scottish ale
Thames Valley ale
Bavarian wheat/Hefeweizen ale
Belgian Abbey, Saison, strong, wit, lambic blend, and other ale cultures

Lager Yeasts

Pilsen
Danish
Bavarian
Munich
Oktoberfest
Bock lager
Mexican lager
American
Bohemian (Czech origin)
California lager
Cry Havoc yeast (originally a lager yeast, but proved to be clean and
    produce reasonable amounts of ale-like fruity esters at warmer ale
    fermentation temperatures)

Culturing and Storing

Though it requires more equipment, training and practice, culturing yeast from slants is the preferred method of maintaining purity when storing yeast over long periods of time. Essentially, slants are test tubes with a small amount of gelatinized wort in them. Before the gelatin-like substance cools and solidifies, the test tube is tilted to allow the nutrient-rich wort to solidify with a greater surface area. The surface of the culturing medium is slanted relative to the tube. All procedures must be done under extremely sanitary conditions, using pressure cookers and high heat to sanitize everything that comes into contact with active surfaces.

Amounts of yeast invisible to the naked eye can be carefully transferred to the surface of these slants, usually with a sterilized wire that has been in contact with the yeast source. Within days the yeast will multiply under appropriate conditions and grow on the surface of the wort-gelatin, where they will remain dormant or slowly active for many months if kept refrigerated.

There are many excellent resources that explain in detail the process of making slants and similar petri dish mediums for the culturing, purifying, and storage of yeast. They are listed at the end of this section.

If you are using liquid yeasts from various sources, the opportunity will inevitably present itself when another brewer will give you a slant culture of a yeast that you'd love to try. The process of culturing from a slant is a lot simpler than making and maintaining slants. Relax. Don't worry, and have a homebrew AFTER you've transferred the yeast from the slant to the initial culture.

Here's how. You will need a test tube, sterile cotton (from the supermarket), an inoculating wire, a butane torch, and material you already have for propagating liquid yeast. Sanitize the test tube by boiling in water for 10 minutes. Cool and add about 3 to 5 milliliters (about 0.1 fl. oz.) of sterile, aerated, clear, and cooled wort, preferably at a specific gravity between 1.025 and 1.030 (6 and 7.5 B). Temporarily cover with a sanitized piece of aluminum foil and set aside.

Working in a dust-free, draft-free (that's not draft beer) environment, heat the wire to red-hot, burning off microorganisms. Cool the wire by touching the tip to the surface of slant media containing no yeast or dip into a small cap full of alcohol. (WARNING! Alcohol is very flammable. Do not immerse red-hot wire into a large container of alcohol.) Sanitize the mouth/opening surface of the test tube slant and test tube of wort by swabbing with a Q-tip soaked in ethanol (not methyl or methanol!). If you are using glass test tubes, you can briefly flame the opening with the butane torch. Hold your breath (seriously), open the slant, and use the sterilized wire loop to scrape off a bit of yeast from the surface of the slant. Immediately cap the slant, then open the wort-containing test tube and immerse the wire into the wort. Jiggle, remove the wire, and temporarily cover the tube with foil. Resume breathing and carefully replace the foil with a wad of sterile cotton. Place the test tube in an environment that is suitable for propagating yeast, upright at 60 to 70 degrees F (16 to 21 C).

Within 48 hours you should notice that the clear wort has a light sediment of yeast. Using similar procedures you will propagate the yeast by doubling the volume of wort in successive steps until you have a pint of fermenting wort, at which time you may consider pitching the sediment or the high kraeusen activity into your awaiting freshly brewed wort.

When is the appropriate time to pitch the propagation? You may do so at high kraeusen (when the yeast activity has created a foamy surface "kraeusen") or within 24 hours after the yeast has sedimented. Each method has its advantages and works well. The high kraeusen method seems to result in much quicker activity in the freshly pitched wort. The disadvantage is that you are

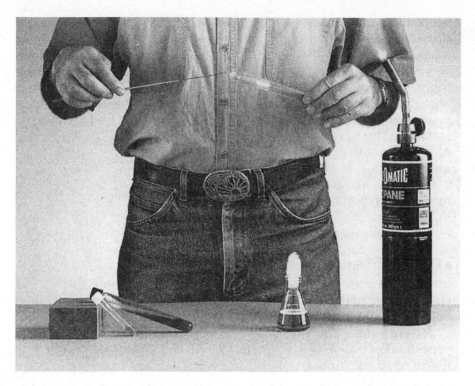

Step it up. Torched and sterile wire loop is used to scrape yeast cells grown on agar slant. These few yeast cells are introduced to a very small amount of sterile wort (small tube, left foreground) and allowed to ferment for two to four days. Later, double the amount of sterile wort to feed the yeast to continue fermentation. The beaker (right) of fermenting wort represents third step of "culturing up" yeast.

pitching, along with the active yeast, 1 pint to 1 quart (about 500 to 1,000 ml) of fermenting wort that may not match the carefully designed character of your freshly brewed wort.

For those who use highly bittered worts to propagate their yeast, pitching the sediment is preferred. The relatively clear fermented wort is poured off and only the yeast slurry and a small amount of propagating wort are introduced to the freshly brewed wort.

Tip: Before discarding the fermented wort atop your yeast sediment, pour a small amount in a glass and taste it. Yes, taste it. You will gain invaluable knowledge and experience on how freshly fermented yeast–cultured wort should taste—and shouldn't taste. If you taste off-flavors such as sour, phenolic, or sweet corn-like aromas, that may be evidence of a contamination brewing. Butterscotch flavors (which is technically called diacetyl) may be present in newly fermented wort. That should not worry you because in a real extended fermentation period, yeast removes diacetyl. But if the diacetyl is accompanied by sour flavors, well, then you may have a problem. Years of tasting fermented wort in this manner will make you an expert at knowing when your yeast is contaminated and that you should start over.

A note on sterile cotton: Handled with care, a wad of sterile cotton is an effective barrier to contaminating microorganisms. It is useful when actively propagating yeast. However, when storing yeast cultures, cotton is obviously not an effective barrier to evaporation or the oxidizing effects of air. Air locks should be utilized for long-term storage. A small piece of sterile cotton can be placed into the lower end of the lock to help assure that airborne contamination does not enter the stored culture if the water in the air lock inadvertently evaporates.

OTHER REASONS TO PROPAGATE YEAST

Introducing propagated yeast for primary fermentation is but one reason to propagate yeast.

KRAEUSENING

Kraeusening is the process of introducing a measured amount of freshly fermenting wort into finished beer in order to carbonate or condition it. True kraeusening methods rely on an introduction of wort that has just reached the kraeusen stage of metabolism/fermentation. This is usually just after the respiration cycle, when most of the fermentable carbohydrates have not yet been fermented. The yeast has passed through the lag phase, and uptake of energy-providing nutrients and oxygen is complete. At this point the yeast can be introduced into oxygen-free finished beer (you do not want to aerate finished beer) and be expected to complete the fermentation of the added wort.

Other, simpler methods of kraeusening work but are less than optimal. The addition of a measured amount of yeastless wort or malt extract at packaging time (bottling time) will provide fermentables, but a deficiency of oxygen will result in slow refermentation and long carbonation periods.

If corn sugar is added as a primer, the yeast cells are not sluggish, because the oxygen requirement for metabolizing corn sugar is minimal.

CHARGING EXTENDED LAGER

When homebrewers lager their beers for extended times (three to six months), the resulting beer is extremely clear. The reduced yeast count is a disadvantage if bottle-conditioning methods will be used to carbonate the beer. Culturing up a small amount of fresh yeast and adding it to the finished beer just prior to bottling will help carbonate the beer in a more reasonable amount of time. Another option for adding fresh yeast to well-aged or lagered fermentation is to rehydrate quality dried yeast, add this to the beer, and gently mix just before priming with sugar and bottling/kegging.

Out with One and In with Another

Classic Bavarian-style wheat beer is a great example of a beer brewed with two different yeasts, the second of which is introduced at bottling time. Typically the fresh original wort is fermented with a unique Hefeweizen strain of ale yeast that does not sediment well. When the fermentation is complete, Bavarian brewmasters and American homebrewers actually filter out the ale yeast, providing clear beer for bottling. Bavarian wheat beer is traditionally bottle-conditioned, and this is why well-flocculating/sedimenting lager yeast is propagated and added to the finished, filtered beer as a kraeusen.

Yeast Profiling

There is quite a bit of printed information on the qualities that various yeast strains contribute to the character of beer. The information is a great starting point and very helpful, but be cautious about generalizations: A particular strain of yeast will behave differently and produce different characters when used with individual brewing systems and different types of wort. For example, if a description of a yeast strain claims that it is well-attenuating, it may be—compared with other yeasts—but it most certainly will not be well-attenuating if proper nutrition hasn't been provided or a high-temperature mash has been used. Yeast can also differ from its stated description if mineral content varies from one wort to another.

You're a homebrewer. Take your homebrew in hand. Appreciate and note the variations of each brew. The best behavioral descriptions of yeasts are the ones you have made after using them in your brewery.

TRULY STRANGE YEASTS AND AFFILIATED CREATURES

BRETTANOMYCES

Yeast of the genus *Brettanomyces* is utilized in the production of certain beer styles, particularly inspired by certain types of Belgian ales. *Brettanomyces bruxellensis* and *Brettanomyces lambicus* are two yeasts that help produce the

very estery-fruity character of Belgian lambics and are sometimes used to create complexity in other ales, such as the Trappist beer Orval. Alone they do not produce sourness. These cultures are available to homebrewers through the same companies bringing you traditional lager and ale yeasts. If stored on slants, they must be cultured on wort that contains about 0.5 percent calcium carbonate. The yeasts produce enough acidity while in storage that they will eventually kill themselves when excessive levels are reached. The calcium carbonate neutralizes the acids.

Homebrewers can obtain very good results with these yeasts if a propagated culture is introduced during or after primary fermentation with normal ale or lager yeast. The *Brettanomyces* will ferment carbohydrates not normally fermentable by *Saccharomyces cerevisiae* or *uvarum* yeasts. They are slow fermenters but produce a great deal of perceptible esters and other complex character.

Brettanomyces yeasts and other wild microorganisms are found in the wild. In fact, when traditional Belgian lambic brewers inoculate their wort with yeast, they do not pitch cultured yeast but rather open the rafters and windows and let the autumnal breezes introduce a menagerie of yeasts and bacteria. When introduced to wort, these wild microorganisms create what is called "spontaneous" fermentation. Over a period of a year the bacteria and yeasts take their turn on feasting on the wort sugars, many dying off in the beer's transition to a more acidic/sour beer environment. The creation of Belgian lambics is a science but mostly an art.

Brewers worldwide who have been romanced by the complexity and intriguing characters of these beers have re-created their own versions of these "wild" beers by introducing the microflora of yeasts and bacteria literally in the air—in their neighborhood. This method is like gambling in Las Vegas, but the odds are a bit more in your favor that you can produce something that you or your friends might enjoy. Mind you, "odds . . . more in your favor" is not saying much about favorable success rate. Sometimes it works and sometimes it doesn't.

Another method of introducing wild organisms into beer is to age it in used wine or beer barrels. Once you've found a barrel that harbors a favorable balance of microbes, it can be reused with a degree of success, but there are no guarantees.

Have you ever made naturally fermented apple cider? If so, often you will create a cider with the interesting complexity of *Brettanomyces* fermentation, along with the work of other wild yeasts. *Brettanomyces* is commonly found on apple skins in certain environmental conditions. It can also be found on other fruits such as grapes. Some Italian Chianti will have character introduced by wild *Brettanomyces* yeasts initially found on the surface of Chianti grapes.

See the references listed on page 101 for more information on lambics, wild fermentations, and yeast.

"SCHIZO" YEAST

Not all yeasts reproduce by budding. There is one unusual yeast called *Schizosaccharomyces pombe* (*S. pombe* for short). It is the only yeast in the world that reproduces by fission, rather than budding. This means the yeast cell reproduces by dividing its body into two or more parts, each growing into its own entity. All other yeasts reproduce by producing lots of buds that grow onto themselves.

The sample that I was given was cultured from African millet beer brewed in the bush. It produced a beer from an all-malt recipe that resembled the estery character of beers brewed by some Belgian monasteries. Further discussion with brewing colleagues revealed that this yeast is dry-cultured for some of the wine industry. Evidently it has the ability to make passable wine from less than desirable grapes. The yeast tends to deteriorate (autolyze) rather quickly. If beer or wine made from this yeast is not racked off the primary in a short time, the autolyzed yeast imparts certain characters to the beer. I refrain from saying these characters are undesirable, because my experiment was not racked off and produced a beer that resembled certain kinds of Belgian ales that are desirable to many.

MORE INDIGENOUS YEAST

An experiment worth trying would be to brew a beer similar in nature to the beers first brewed by the Egyptians and Sumerians 5,000 years ago. They used barley or wheat along with available yeasts. There are heirloom wheats currently available at some specialty natural food stores. They are called spelt, Kamut, or dinkel and are ancestors of our hybridized modern wheat. Primitive malting and mashing procedures would produce a wort that may be very similar to the worts of 5,000 years past. This brew would not be authentic without heirloom yeast. Even this can be acquired. There is a company called World Sourdoughs from Antiquity—www.sourdo.com; P.O. Box 670, Cascade, ID 83611 U.S.A.—specializing in culturing and packaging sourdough yeast cultures from around the world. These yeast cultures are sure to include unique strains of *Lactobacillus* bacteria and wild yeast, and these mixed strains are likely what ancient brewers used. One of the nine varieties offered is Egyptian Red Sea Culture, said to be from one of the oldest ethnic bakeries in Egypt. It was found in the village of Hurghada on the shore of the Red Sea. The bread was actually placed on the village street to rise. It is one of the fastest cultures to rise and has a mild sourdough flavor. Another variety, Egyptian Giza culture, is said to be found in a bakery in the shadow of the Sphinx in the town of Giza. The bakery dates back to antiquity.

Brewing a batch? Use your imagination and drink while still fermenting, as likely did the ancients. The art of brewing will certainly be more meaningful, and if you stand in the sunshine with your second glass of homebrew and you cast a shadow of a sphinx . . .

AND DID YOU EVER NOTICE YEAST DUST?

I have sometimes noticed with curiosity a dusting of yeast adhering to one or perhaps all sides of a bottle of bottle-conditioned beer. It was a total mystery to me until I came across a summary of some research Belgian brewers had undertaken to unravel this aberrant behavior. They found that yeast is electrically charged the same as glass, and because the two have the same electrical charge, they repel one another. Sometimes if the yeast is deficient in certain nutrients, it will take on a different charge and become attracted to the sides of the bottle. Only the Belgians with their admirably wonderful world of unusual beers would undertake such research. A recent study proposes research dealing with the influence of transport conditions on adhesion of yeast to the bottom of the bottle. They wrote back in the early '90s, "Further studies of these aspects under zero gravity conditions are planned for the next Eurospace mission [1994]." Furthermore they conclude that these considerations of transport conditions "will be required to solve this important national problem." Right on, Belgium! Perhaps homebrewers might consider these questions as well. I believe they should.

REFERENCES FOR WILD BREWS AND LAMBIC

Three excellent books on the art and science of lambic, wild fermentations, and yeast are:

Yeast: The Practical Guide to Beer Fermentation, by Chris White and Jamil Zainasheff (Brewers Publications, 2010).

Wild Brews: Beer Beyond the Influence of Brewer's Yeast, by Jeff Sparrow (Brewers Publications, 2005).

The pioneering first English-language book on the subject, *Lambic,* by Jean-Xavier Guinard (Brewers Publications, 1990—out of print but may be found used).

REFERENCES FOR YEAST AND CULTURING

Zymurgy magazine, volume 12, number 4, 1989, Special Yeast and Beer Issue. Articles include "Homebrew Starter Cultures," "Yeast Biology and Beer Fermentation," "Wild Yeast," "Yeast Nutrients in Brewing," "Commercial Production of Dried Yeast," "Yeast Stock Maintenance and Starter Culture Production," "A Sterile Transfer Technique for Pure Culturing," "Collecting Yeast While Traveling," "Collecting and Reusing Live Brewer's Yeast," "Isolation and Culture of Yeast from Bottle-Conditioned Beers," "Running a Yeast Test," "Analysis and Evaluation of Commercial Brewer's Yeast," "Of Yeasts and Beer Styles," "Fleischmann's [aka Budweiser] Yeast," "Lambic: A Unique Combination of Yeasts and Bacteria," "The Hybrid Styles [of Beer]: Some Notes on Their Fermentation and Formulation."

Yeast Technology, by Gerald Reed and Tilak W. Nagodawithana (Van Nostrand Reinhold, 1991). Up-to-date developments in yeast genetics, analytical techniques. Sections on flocculation, nutrition, fermentation, wild yeast, killer yeast, and more.

Yeast Culturing for the Homebrewer, by Roger Leistad (G. W. Kent, 1983). How to culture and grow yeast at home in an easy-to-follow format.

MAKING BEER

EQUIPMENT AND PROCESS

EQUIPMENT

Are there other do-it-yourself hobbies besides homebrewing that inspire so many innovations? Whether you consider yourself a beginner, intermediate, or advanced brewer, the means to your end begins by choosing ingredients and follows with choosing the process and equipment. There are hundreds of options along the way. Many can be bought ready to go and off the shelf of your homebrew supply shop, or you may find yourself fashioning a brewery of your own design.

Throughout your homebrewing endeavors there is much likelihood that you will continue to learn and consider new ways of brewing; revising, upgrading, simplifying, diversifying, and relaxing and having a homebrew at every step of the way. It's the nature of homebrewing to create and to care about quality. It is also the nature of homebrewers to increase their respect for and enjoyment of beer.

There are no perfect systems for homebrewing. Individual needs will vary from one home to another. An apartment in New York City, a suburban home in Missouri, a houseboat in Florida or Seattle, a ranch in Texas, a farmhouse in Colorado, a condominium in Michigan, and a mobile home traveling cross-country all present unique circumstances. Financial resources and leisure time are also factors to consider when choosing and designing the home-brewery.

Whatever your current system, keep your mind open to new ideas and innovations. Change when you envision an improvement and your resources allow you to make it happen. Relax. Don't worry. Have a homebrew, and perhaps do something different just for the plain fun of it!

THE PROCESS

In the end you will be holding a glass of the best beer in the world—yours. Getting there involves a number of steps. For beginners the process is often

Out of control? Got the bug? How many batches of beer have you brewed in the last year?

reduced to a very unintimidating simple one, with very few choices to consider. Do you remember your first batch? Be honest. It was probably like going on your first starship mission through Wort-5 hyperspace—into the unknown. Nervous and not quite confident, you probably appreciated the beginning simplicity and few choices. Now you know better. Making beer? Hah. No problem. Let's brew. And brew, you have, becoming more confident and less intimidated with every new batch of great beer. You have learned to abide by the Golden Rule of Homebrewing.

So now you're ready to consider all manner of processes, equipment, ideas, ingredients, and gadgets. Perhaps you can pick up a few tips here and there without changing things too much and really improve your beer. But you pause because you thought it could never get any better than the one in your hand right now. Maybe . . . Thirsty? Have a homebrew.

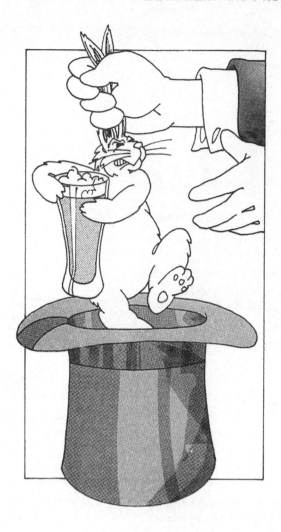

Let's have a look at the principles of the beermaking process and consider some equipment utilized to achieve your end: the best beer possible in your privileged situation as a homebrewer.

AN OUTLINE OF THE BEERMAKING PROCESS

MALTING BARLEY

Let's face it—most of the grain malt you'll use to make homebrew will be bought from your local homebrew supply store. The dependability and the quality of grain malt is as good as that available to commercial breweries. You can make your own, but the malting process is an extension of the hobby most don't consider, for reasons of inconsistency of product and loss of time to relax with a homebrew. (Hmmm . . . but it does take four to five days to sprout barley.)

However, someday you may be in a situation that forces you to develop your malting skills. The situation is called survival. Unfortunately there are a number of people who find themselves in that mode because they are allergic to barley, wheat, rice, corn, and other grains normally used in beer. Malting your own grains may give you an alternative.

Before considering any alternative grain-based beer due to health considerations, you should consult with your physician. Many persons who are allergic to cereals such as barley, rice, oats, corn, millet, rye, or tef, all from the grass family, may find hope in pseudocereals such as buckwheat, amaranth, sorghum, or quinoa. Another serious possibility is a triticum grain called spelt (also called khorosan [or the trademarked Kamut®] or dinkel). Spelt is an "heirloom" wheat or an ancient wheat that has not been hybridized. Sometimes, individuals who find themselves allergic to wheat are not allergic to spelt.

Buckwheat, amaranth, sorghum, quinoa, and spelt all have starchy endosperms that are ultimately fermentable if reduced by enzymes. One way to make these grains fermentable is to process them as though they were barley: malt them and mash them.

Malting is the simple process of germinating grain and then drying it: voilà! malt. Practically speaking, one soaks grains for 24 to 40 hours (depending on the grain), changing the water about every 8 hours. Then the grain is allowed to sprout until the growing acrospire is about the full length of the grain (this will vary depending on the grain). Then it is dried.

Drying is exceptionally easy. Put the wet "green malt" in a pillowcase. Tie it securely shut and place it in the clothes dryer until dry. Your lingerie setting will probably produce the lightest malt. Drying at a forced-air temperature of 180 to 220 degrees F (82 to 104 C) will produce malt similar to lager and pale malted barleys. Sounds outrageous? But hot damn—it really does work. When done, spread the malt on a flat surface and use a fan to blow away the dried rootlets and shriveled acrospires. You've got malt to experiment with. If you do this on a regular basis, you'll want to take careful notes of times and temperatures throughout the process to determine what gives optimal results.

If you want to make darker beers, simply roast a small portion of your homemade light malt in your oven at temperatures between 350 and 450 F (186 to 232 C), depending on the degree of roastiness you want.

Survival: Remember that sometimes your objective is not to get good yields but simply to make good beer—any beer!!!

See related recipe: Speltbrau, page 291.

MILLING: CRUSHING YOUR GRAINS

If you use any kind of malted grain in your brewing formulations, the first place you'll have to make a decision will be at the malt mill. Whether you are using crystal or roasted malts to jazz your extract brews or you are about to make an all-grain beer, you'll need to crush malt in order to begin the process of getting the good stuff out of the grain.

There are two points to consider when crushing grain. One is to grind the grain in a manner that optimizes the extract yield, and the other is to grind the grain in a form that will cause the developed sugars to flow and rinse easily from the grains and into the brewpot. If you don't crush at all, you get virtually no yield but terrific flow. If you crush into a flour, you get a most excellent yield but a clogged glutinous (no) flow. There's a balance somewhere in between as sure as there should be a glass of beer in your hand right now.

A good balance is achieved if you can crush the grains in a manner that removes the husk relatively intact. The milled husk should still look like it was a husk. The remaining endosperm should be about 50 percent grits and 50 percent rough to fine flour. Certainly the best way to learn what a good grind looks like is to examine freshly milled malt firsthand at an operating commercial brewery or get a sample from a brewery. Mix the crushed malt before taking a handful. Don't simply observe a pile of crushed malt. It will give false impressions of composition, since the lighter husks will tend to migrate to the top of the pile, and the flour to the bottom.

The best type of mill to grind grains through is a roller model. With this type of mill the grains are drawn through a very precisely measured gap between two rotating metal cylinders. Commercial brewing mills have cylinders about 8 to 12 inches (20 to 30 cm) in diameter and the "crushing" spacing between them can be set to accommodate different size grains and different grind requirements. These are very expensive to buy and beyond the resources of most homebrewers. For about $200 or less in supplies and a lot of mechanical know-how and skills, homemade roller mills can be built.* Small roller mills especially designed for homebrewing are also available to homebrewers. Check them out at your local homebrew shop.

The advantage of a roller mill over a "corona"-type grain/flour mill is usually a few percentage points of yield or a little less lautering/sparging time. Sacrificing a few minutes or a dollar's worth of yield is the choice most brewers make when they grind grains with the mill they find as a best buy. Corona flour mills are designed so that the malt is forced between two plates rotating against each other by the action of a large hand-turned screw-auger. The distance between the plates can be set so close together that they turn the grain into a powdery flour, or set so wide that the grains pass through uncrushed. The action of the plates can certainly crush the grain adequately. The disadvantage is that the husks have to pass a greater distance through this measured gap, so they begin to break down into smaller husk particles. Relax. Don't worry. Have a homebrew. Your beer will turn out terrific, whichever type of mill you use. In the final assessment, grain ground with a corona mill will cause a slower runoff during the mashing/lautering process than a good roller mill. You can do two things to help this situation: (1) buy an additional dollar's worth of grain to make up for the yield difference and (2) have another homebrew during the additional leisure time you've just created. Pretty nifty, eh?

Now, regarding those plates on the corona-type mill or the cylinder gap on your envy-of-the-neighborhood roller mill, you will need to adjust the spacing depending on the malt you use. Grain malt comes in varying sizes depending on harvest, variety, type of malt, etc. Ideally you should consider setting the gap for each individual type of malt if the grains appear to be significantly different in size. The fine-tuning of the grind often is achieved by only a quarter or half turn on an adjusting screw. There can be big size differences that you will see and feel between raw grains, pale malts, two-row and six-row, crystal

*Internet search on "build your own homebrew mill." Also see "Building a Roller Grain Mill," by Wayne Greenway and Russ Wigglesworth, *Zymurgy* magazine, special issue, 1992, published by the American Homebrewers Association, Boulder, Colorado.

and black malts. Be sure to put your hand under the mill as the crushed grain flows out. Examine the handful to determine whether more adjustments are needed. Don't examine the pile; the husks tend to "float" to the top and give a false impression.

You can turn your mill by hand, and that works fine if you're only grinding 2 or 3 pounds (about 1 or 1½ kg) at a time. But with all-grain 5-gallon (19 l) batches, most of you will figure out a way to harness your electric drill, spare bicycle, or spare electric motor by means of pulleys and/or reducing gears to power your grinder. In order to determine what to do, have a homebrew and contemplate your mill from a distance of about 3 feet. If that doesn't work, invite a mechanically minded friend over, give him or her a homebrew, and let this person observe the situation as you have. It works.

In summary, remember that you are a homebrewer and are usually brewing 5- to 10-gallon (19 to 38 l) batches of beer, not 3,000 gallons (11,400 l). Your grain bed will be 6 to 18 inches (15 to 46 cm) deep, not 4 feet (1.4 m) deep. Having less than optimal yields will cost you an extra dollar or two a batch, not hundreds of thousands or millions

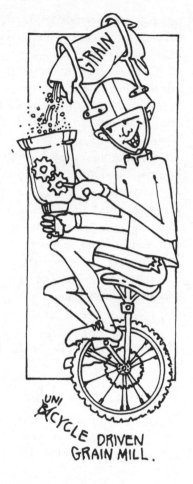

UNI BICYCLE DRIVEN GRAIN MILL.

of dollars a year. When used properly, roller mills are the best for optimizing yield and runoff. If you have access to one of them, that's terrific, but a properly used good old corona-type flour mill will always make terrific beer.

Coffee grinders, food processors, rolling pins, and blenders should be avoided because the pulverizing effect of the grind is exaggerated or inconsistent, causing frustration during the mashing process and disappointment in the quality of the beer.

MASHING

Master brewers have been combining art, science, skill, and experience for over 5,000 years. Perhaps nowhere in the brewing process is the delineation between art and science less certain than in the mashing process. Experience and a feeling for ingredients serve the brewer well for fine-tuning the end results. As in any stage of the brewing process, however, novices with the desire and time should be thoroughly encouraged to just brew it. All-grain mashing may seem intimidating at first, but brewing on a small scale in your home is very forgiving. Homebrewers have a lot of latitude during this process. Very good beer can certainly be made despite the theoretical demands of grain mashing. Just brew it.

For extract brewers desiring to add additional qualities and diversity to their brewing endeavors, a combination of mashed grains and extract offers most of the simplicity of extract brewing with a limited amount of mashing. The basic principles of all-grain mashing (and mash-extract brewing) can be found in *The Complete Joy of Homebrewing, Fourth Edition*. The following discussion will assume basic knowledge of these principles. But as a quick reminder: The purpose of mashing is to dissolve carbohydrates and activate various enzymes into solution in order to achieve a desired balance of various carbohydrates and prepare the wort for optimal fermentation.

PHYTASE AND THE ACID REST

Acidification of the mash is essential in order to optimize diastatic (alpha and beta amylase) and proteolytic (peptidase and protease) enzymatic activity. When water contains an adequate amount of calcium ions (50 to 100 ppm) and the pH of the water is below 7.2, acidification occurs at virtually any mash-in temperature by the reaction of the calcium ions with phosphates from the malt.

However, if very soft water is used, calcium is lacking in the water. The brewer may choose not to add calcium salt "additives." If this is the case, then acidification can be achieved by mashing in at 95 degrees F (35 C). At this temperature phytase enyzmes are optimally activated and convert malt phosphate compounds to acidic compounds, thereby acidifying the mash. The process takes 2 to 3 hours.

If the water is high in carbonates, development of acidity with this method will not be adequate, and alternative lactic acid "sour" mashes (see "Getting It! pH, Alkalinity, and Hardness," or "The Principles of Sour Mash Brewing" in *The Complete Joy of Homebrewing, Fourth Edition*) need be considered.

Enzyme Activity During the Mashing Process

ENZYME	EFFECTIVE RANGE IN MASH	APPROXIMATE TEMPERATURE RANGE FOR MAXIMUM ACTIVITY	BEST PRACTICAL UTILIZATION IN MASH	TYPICAL PH RANGE
Phytase	86–128 F (30–53 C)	pH dependent	95 F (35 C)	5.2–5.3
Peptidase*	113–122 F (45–50 C)	45 F (113 C) at pH=4.2	122 F (50 C)	4.2–5.3
Protease	122–140 F (50–60 C)	122–131 F (50–55 C) at pH 4.6 to 5.0	122 F (50 C)	4.2–5.3
Protease primarily for head retention		130–140 F (54–60 C) at pH 4.6–5.0	130–140 F (54–60 C)	4.2–5.3
Beta glucanase**	95–140 F (35–60 C)	104–113 F (40–45 C) and at 140 F (60 C)	122–130 F (50–54 C)	4.5–4.8
Beta amylase	126–144 F (52–62 C)	140–149 F (60–65 C)	145–157 F (63–69 C)	5.2–5.7
Alpha amylase	149–158 F (65–70 C)	155–158 F (68–70 C)	145–157 F (63–69 C)	5.2–5.7

*When brewing all malt beer, the peptidase rest may be bypassed in favor of developing better foam- and head-related proteins at higher temperatures. (There is adequate protein nutrient developed at slightly higher temperatures.)

**Seventy-four percent of glucanase activity is related to endo beta glucanase$_{1-4}$ at an optimum temperature range of 104 to 113 degrees F (40 to 45 C), and 26 percent of glucanase activity is related to endo beta glucanase$_{1-3}$ at an optimum temperature range of 140 degrees F (60 C).

PROTEASE, PEPTIDASE, AND THE PROTEIN REST

(See pages 22–23 for discussion of proteins and malt and their effect on beer.) The protein-degrading enzyme rests are a bit of an enigma. The degradation of long-chained proteins into medium-chained proteins occurs best at higher temperatures than are optimum for degradation of medium-chained proteins to the simple proteins. If we used optimum temperatures for long-chain degradation, we would deactivate the enzymes that are needed in the next step. Consequently 122 degrees F (50 C) is a compromise temperature where there is both protease and peptidase activity. (Protease breaks down soluble albumins and insoluble globulins into peptones and polypeptides, both important for foam stability. The reduction of albumins and globulin is important for reducing haze. Peptidase breaks down medium-chained peptones and polypeptides to peptides and amino acids, both important yeast nutrients.)

The protein rest is not necessary when using fully modified malts and especially overmodified English pale ale malts. The proteins in these malts are already adequately degraded.

The peptidase protein rest becomes essential for mashes with over 10 percent starch adjuncts in order to develop necessary protein-based yeast nutrients, absent in starch adjuncts.

During proteolytic activity the soluble protein albumin and insoluble protein can be acted upon by protease to help reduce chill haze in beer. The secondary protein products resulting from this degradation help foam stability. If yeast nutrition is of secondary importance (especially when all-malt beers are being made, since more than adequate nutrition is available even without a protein rest), then the protein rest can occur at about 130 to 135 degrees F (54 to 57 C) in order to maximize the foam-enhancing activity and reduce haze.

BETA GLUCANASE AND GUMS

The degradation of filter-clogging gums is usually not an issue for most homebrewers. Commercial brewers who filter the mash or have deep grain filter beds may have problems with gum content of low-temperature-kilned lager malts. The mash may be held at a special temperature for a beta glucan rest. A beta glucan rest is often monitored and considered during protein rests or a rest at a slightly higher temperature. Homebrewers should simply relax, not worry, and have a homebrew while a commercial brewer worries with furrowed brow about glucans.

DIASTASE AND MAKING SUGARS

The objective in choosing mash temperatures for diastatic activity is to achieve the best yield of desired fermentable sugars and dextrins. Compromises in temperature choices must be made due to the fact that alpha amylase produces the best yield at different temperatures than beta amylase. The activity of both is necessary to achieve the brewer's desired end.

Another important fact that the brewer must consider is that although maximum activity of diastatic enzymes is achieved at the upper limit of their temperature ranges, the activity is short-lived and does not produce the highest extract. When mashing at higher temperatures for fuller-bodied, dextrinous beers, you can expect a little less extract.

Highest fermentable yield is achieved at 149 degrees F (65 C). Highest extract is achieved between 149 and 155 degrees F (65–68 C). Highest dextrinous yield is achieved between 155 and 158 degrees F (68–70 C).

Assuming proper acidification of your mash, you can approximately expect:

- A mash at 158 degrees F (70 C) complete in 20 minutes
- A mash at 150 degrees F (66 C) complete in 45 to 60 minutes
- A mash at 145 degrees F (63 C) complete in 90 to 120 minutes

A thinner mash will increase extract yields by increasing the viability of the enzymes and the speed at which conversion takes place. (Note: Mashes that are too dilute will inhibit proteolytic enzyme activity.)

TYPES OF MASHING PROCEDURES

With the availability of quality commercial malts, any type of mashing procedure will most likely produce excellent homebrewed beer. Then why choose one mashing procedure over another? You may have to use a certain procedure because of the limitations of your brewing space and equipment. If your ingredients are substandard (this can happen in a poor barley harvest year), the yields and the final product could be improved by your choice of procedure. Mashing offers the homebrewer flexibility and more control over the quality of the beer.

There is a lot of potential for mashing terminology to be confusing, so let's begin by defining our terms. *Infusion* is the act of steeping one ingredient in another; in the case of mashing, it is malt in water. *Decoction* is the process of extracting by boiling.

There are various steps the brewer may implement in processing the mash. These choices are:

1. a low-temperature acidification step
2. a protein rest
3. a starch conversion

Brewers will raise the temperature of the mash through various steps by (1) applying heat to the mash, (2) adding (infusing) hot water to the mash, or (3) bringing a portion of the mash to a boil (decoction) and adding it back into the main mash. Applying heat directly to the mash to achieve large temperature gains is usually avoided due to the time it takes to get from one temperature to another. It is desirable to reach diastatic conversion from the previous stage as quickly as possible. That is one reason why infusion and decoction methods are employed. Heating the mash directly is a method often used when making fine temperature adjustments during starch conversion or when "mashing out" at 167 degrees F (75 C) to halt all enzyme activity. "Mashing out" is a step that is not essential but does stabilize the balance of fermentable and nonfermentable carbohydrates achieved during carefully monitored mash periods. It is an assumed step, so even though mash-out is utilized with all mash schedules, it is often not reflected in the number of steps the mash schedule is named after.

As you can see, it's time for a homebrew. Go get one.

There are many options, but the ones most utilized by brewers are:

The one-step infusion mash
The two-step infusion mash
The two- or three-step decoction mash

THE ONE-STEP INFUSION MASH

Crushed malt is infused with hot water at a temperature calculated to reach a desired equilibrium temperature when mixed with the malt. The mash bypasses the protein rests, achieving starch-converting temperatures immediately. This mash is best suited for highly modified and ideally crushed malts. English pale malts are particularly well suited for this system.

One-step infusion mashes can be used with mash-tuns (mashing vessels) that also serve as lauter-tuns (straining vessels). If you cannot apply heat directly to your mash vessel, one-step infusion mashes are a necessary convenience. In order to stop enzyme activity with this system, the initial 25 percent of the sparge water can be at 180 degrees F (82 C) to raise the temperature of the grain bed above 167 degrees F (75 C). The remainder of the sparge water should be about 170 degrees F (77 C), an occurrence that is reached naturally with homebrewing systems whereby a pot of water gradually cools at room temperature.

Single-Step Infusion

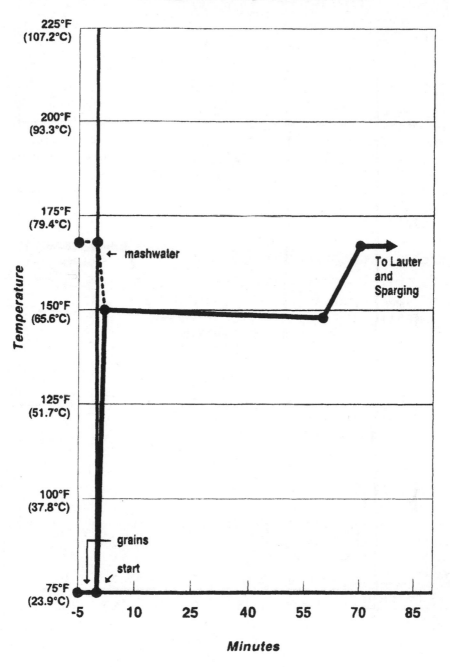

Temperature

225°F (107.2°C)

200°F (93.3°C)

175°F (79.4°C)

← mashwater

150°F (65.6°C)

To Lauter and Sparging

125°F (51.7°C)

100°F (37.8°C)

grains

start

75°F (23.9°C)

-5 10 25 40 55 70 85

Minutes

Simple Two-Step Infusion

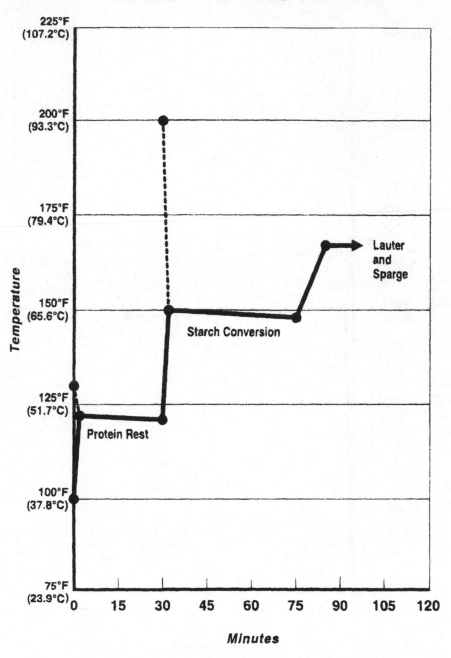

Step-by-step procedures, charts, and guides for infusion mashes are provided in *The Complete Joy of Homebrewing, Fourth Edition.*

TWO- OR THREE-STEP INFUSION MASH

The two-step mash goes through a protein rest and starch conversion and is particularly well suited to the music of Dwight Yoakam. Temperatures are raised with an infusion of hot water at calculated temperatures to reach desired equilibrium in the ranges of proteolytic and diastatic activity. Heat may need to be applied to the mashing vessel to adjust temperatures. If necessary, a third step may be added to this mashing schedule as an acid rest preceding the protein rest. In this case heat must be applied to raise the temperature from the acid rest to the protein rest.

The two-step infusion mashing schedule should be used if your malts tend to be higher in protein or not fully modified and/or you wish to improve head retention, reduce potential for chill haze, and help assure development of adequate yeast nutrients. If your malt is less than ideally crushed, the added soak time at lower temperatures will help assure solubility of the malt in the water. As you increase starch adjuncts in your formulation, step infusion procedures will be increasingly critical in developing necessary yeast nutrients during the peptonizing part of the protein rest.

This mashing regime is best suited for a lautering system separate from the mashing vessel because of the need to apply heat to the mash vessel. A stove top and a large stainless steel pot work very well. Without any insulation (at household room temperatures) a stainless steel brewpot can hold a mash containing 8 pounds (3.6 kg) of malt and water at conversion temperatures for 60 minutes with no more than a 2- to 3-degree F (1–2 C) drop in temperature. For all-grain, 5-gallon (19 l) batches, insulation is not critical due to the volumes you are working with. If necessary, heat may be applied at any point in time. If convenient, you can remove the pot from your stove top, place it on a safe surface, and wrap a few insulating towels around the pot to minimize heat loss.

Step-by-step procedures for two-step infusion mashes are provided in *The Complete Joy of Homebrewing, Fourth Edition.*

TWO- OR THREE-STEP DECOCTION MASH

In decoction mashing, a portion of the mash is removed, brought to a boil, and returned to the main mash to achieve temperature increases. Boiling water is added to achieve temperature for the initial acid rest and to maintain temperature during the diastatic rest.

Decoction mashing achieves a better yield from ingredients that are of less than ideal quality. With decoction mashing, undermodified malt or poorly ground malt will offer better yields than with infusion-type mashes. Boiling part of the malt mash increases yields by gelatinizing and bursting starch particles, making them available for diastatic conversion. Boiling also helps reduce chill haze by breaking down protein gums not otherwise affected by enzyme activity.

Decoction mashing schedules are common among German brewing companies. The tradition dates back to when undermodified malt was common and the thermometer was not yet invented. Decoctions served to develop consistency in methods for increasing temperatures of the mash. Germans use thermometers these days and their malt has improved in quality; however, decoction is traditional "old-school" and is still the preferred method of mashing. With regard to yields, the necessity is arguable, but with regard to flavor and beer character, the method is justified. These procedures have a positive effect on the character of German-style lager beer—the kind of character you can taste and are familiar with if you are a German-beer enthusiast.

For homebrewers, decoction mashing is a chore, to say the very least. It involves more time and closer attention to details during the mashing schedule than any of the other methods. The procedures are outlined here with charts and tables. For those who choose to employ a decoction method of mashing, a considerable investment in research and outlining your own procedures is necessary. You should begin by referring to the following excellent resource: *The New Brewing Lager Beers*, by Gregory Noonan (Brewers Publications, 1986, 1996).

KEY TO DECOCTION CHARTS

- A: Boiling water infused at a ratio of 0.625 quart per pound of grain (1.3 l per kg).
- B: If decoction is not used to raise temperature to the protein rest temperatures, an infusion of an additional 0.375 quart of boiling water per pound of grain (0.8 l per kg) will accomplish this.
- C: About one-third of the mash or about 0.4 quart per pound of malt (about 0.8 l per kg) is decocted. The thickest part of the mash should be removed for this decoction. Liquid should be left behind in the main mash. Vigorous stirring is required.
- D: About 0.5 quart per pound of malt (about 1.0 l per kg) is decocted. Again the thickest part of the mash should be removed for the decoction.
- E: Up to a total of 1 quart of boiling water per pound of malt (2.1 l per kg) can be added during any infusions to maintain diastatic conversion temperatures.

Three-Step Decoction Mash with Acid, Protein, and Starch Conversion Rests

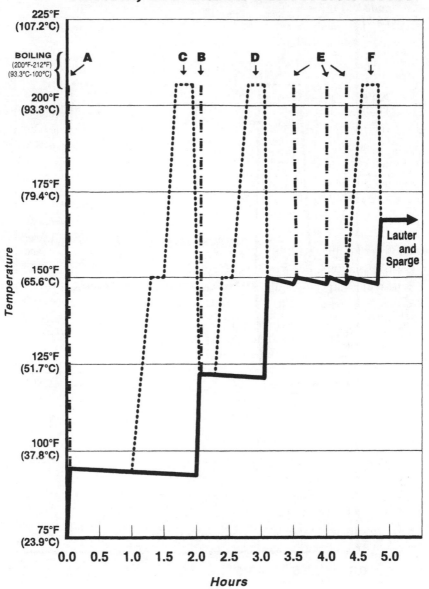

Two-Step Decoction Mash
with Protein and Starch Conversion Rests

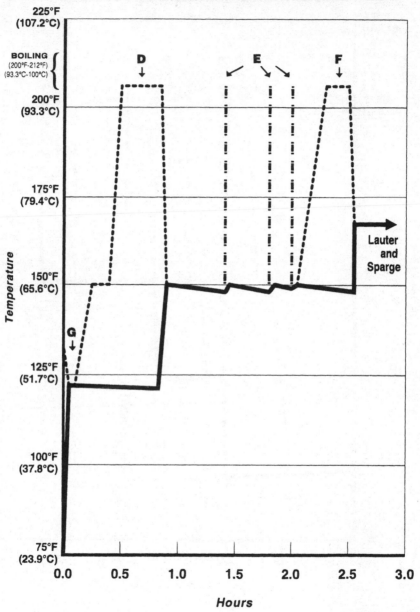

- F: About one-third of the mash (a fifty-fifty blend of thick mash and liquid) is removed for this decoction.
- G: If the acid rest is bypassed altogether, then adding 1 quart of water at 130 degrees F (54 C) per pound of grain (2.1 l per kg) will raise the mash temperature to 122 degrees F (50 C).

OPTIMIZING? WHAT ARE WE TALKING ABOUT HERE?

So what if we have reasonably good ingredients and we want to consider different methods of mashing to increase our extract yield or make our wort more fermentable (greater wort attenuation)? To what degree are we going to benefit? Let's refer to some research that has been done by professionals[*] and put things into perspective for the homebrewer.

Experiments were done using undermodified malt and well-modified malt in four different mashing procedures: two-step decoction, three-step decoction, one-step infusion, and three-step infusion.

The greatest difference in extract yield was between the well-modified malt mashed with a three-step decoction, yielding a high of 79.3 percent extract, and undermodified malt mashed with a one-step infusion, yielding a low of 76.2 percent extract. That is only a 3.1 percent difference in yield. That is equal to .0014 point of specific gravity (0.38 B) per pound of malt in one gallon of water (0.12 kg per l). If you were running a 10,000-barrel/year (11,700-hectoliter) brewery, your need for extra grains for the year would run about 15,500 pounds (7,032 kg). For a million barrels (1.17 million hectoliters), your needs would be an additional 1.55 million pounds (703,075 kg) of malt. But let's talk in homebrewing terms and consider a 5-gallon (19 l) batch of homebrew using 8 pounds (3.6 kg) of malt. You could make up the difference by adding 0.25 pound (0.11 kg) of malt. That's 30 to 40 cents' worth of malt. The 3.1 percent difference represents a loss of about 0.6 quart (0.6 l); let's just call it a pint of beer. Consider all of the other places you might lose one pint of beer: in sediment, during trub removal, through siphon waste, through hydrometer readings.

The greatest difference in wort attentuation was between the well-modified malt mashed with a one-step infusion, yielding a high of 67.5 percent wort attenuation, and undermodified malt mashed with a three-step decoction, yielding a low of 63.4 percent wort attenuation. That is only a 4 percent maximum difference. A 4 percent difference in attenuation is equivalent to about .002 point of specific gravity (0.5 B) in a 1.048 (12 B) wort.

For better yield and better attenuation, homebrewers must ask the question:

---

[*]*Malting and Brewing Science*, by Briggs et al., vol. 1 (Chapman and Hall, 1971), p. 287.

Is it worth it? Perhaps a more justifiable reason to consider different mashing schedules and procedures is the taste of the beer. Do different mashing processes affect the flavor and character of the beer? Of course they do, in various ways and to various degrees. The art of brewing is not simply considering numbers and statistics on paper. It is a blend of the science and the tasted results. Your tastes and your perceptions are an important individual factor. Remember, you're a homebrewer. Keep this in perspective if you ever find yourself reading technical research and recommended procedures for professional breweries.

MASHING VESSEL—THE MASH-TUN

The purpose of your mash-tun is very simple. It contains the grains and liquids during the mash and helps maintain heat. Other considerations are durability, cleanability, ease of operational procedures, and cost.

THE MASH-TUN/BREWPOT

The brewpot doubling as a mash-tun is a very simple and versatile system to consider. Although cost may be a factor, stainless steel is the most durable. A 10-gallon (38 l) pot is required for 5- to 7-gallon (19 to 26.5 l) batches. Four- or

5-gallon (15 or 19 l) brewpots can be used for mashing 8 pounds (3.6 kg) of grain or less for full wort boils of 4 gallons (15 l) or less.

Advantages: Simple. No extra cost if you already have one as a brewpot. Heat can be added to the mash if necessary. Can be used for any kind of mashing schedule. Holds heat well with some need for insulation (wrapping brewpot in large towel or blanket) for up to an hour for mashes containing 10 pounds (4.54 kg) of grain or more.

Disadvantages: Loses heat with mashes of less than 10 pounds; needs monitoring every 15 minutes for mashes containing 5 pounds of grain or less. Need to transfer mash to a lauter-tun (straining vessel to separate grains from liquid).

Types of mash: Well suited for any mashing schedule.

THE COOLERS

Food-grade insulated heat-resistant "picnic" coolers are popular choices for use as mash-tuns. Be sure they are heat-resistant. You will have material as hot as 180 degrees F in them. The cooler must have a drain for versatility as a lauter-tun.

Advantages: Maintains near constant temperature. Can be fitted with a straining system and double as a lauter-tun, eliminating the need for transferring the mash.

Disadvantages: Heat cannot be applied directly to the mash-tun. Less margin of error allowed when infusing water or decocting mash to raise temperatures. Difficult to mash out at 167 degrees F (75 C).

Types of mash: Very good for one-step infusion mashes. Can be used for two-step infusion or three-step decoction mashes if water and decoction temperatures and amounts are determined precisely.

PLASTIC BUCKETS

Five- and 6-gallon (19 and 23 l) white buckets used in the food industry are usable as mash-tuns. To prevent heat loss, they can be easily insulated with a variety of materials, including blankets, styrofoam shipping containers, and sleeping bags.

Advantages: Inexpensive. Easy to work with and can be fitted with spigots and straining systems.

Disadvantages: Needs some insulating material to help maintain heat during mashing process. Also see "Disadvantages" for coolers.

MASH TIPS

- The capacity of a 5-gallon (19 l) vessel for a mash is about 12 pounds (about 5.5 kg) of grain with the necessary water. For thicker mashes the amount of grain can be increased somewhat.

- Tincture of iodine is used as an indicator of starch conversion. The test must be done to cooled liquid to give an accurate indication of conversion. If the iodine turns purple-black, it is an indication of the presence of starch and incomplete conversion. If the color of the iodine remains unchanged, conversion is considered complete. When removing mash liquid for testing, place about a tablespoon of liquid on a cool white plate or bowl. Swirl the liquid so that it cools. An additional test can be pursued to indicate how complete the conversion is by removing a teaspoon of grains and squeezing the liquid out. Testing this liquid indicates how much of the soluble starches has been brought out of the grain into solution and converted. Large, poorly ground chunks of malt will take longer for extraction and conversion.
- Take care to minimize aeration of the hot mash. Oxygenation of the mash can be detrimental to the final quality of the beer. Mash oxidation occurs quite rapidly at hot mash temperatures. Oxidation forms precursor compounds contributing to accelerated staling in finished beer, if and when the finished beer is stressed by high or fluctuating storage temperatures, agitation, or extended aging periods. Don't worry. Simply keep this in mind. Avoid whipping up a froth when adding infusion water or making transfers. Oxidation in the mash stage can also darken the color of beer. Mash oxidation is usually of minimal concern to homebrewers, but it's good to know about.
- Here's a little gem that will help reduce chill haze and reduce some harshness: Add about 1 ounce (28 g) of finely crushed black malt to your light beers at the end of the mash. The addition will not affect color significantly but will adsorb some of the polyphenols, tannins, and long-chained proteins that cause chill haze and astringent character in beers. Some of the largest brewing companies in the United States have used this method for some of the lightest of their beers. You may have already noticed that chill haze is less of a problem—even nonexistent—in dark beers. Aha.
- Here's another gem of information that will help reduce mash oxidation and precursors causing finished beer oxidation. Add 2 teaspoons of ground cinnamon to the mash. Cinnamon is high in tannins and will adsorb and tie up polyphenols that could otherwise be involved with oxidizing reactions in the finished beer. This I learned from a retired Dutch brewing professor who also suggested other herbs could be used to achieve the same effect. The character of cinnamon will dissipate through the brewing process and not flavor the beer. For additional information on tannins as a clarifying agent, see "Gallotannins" in the "Clarifying Aids" section of *The Complete Joy of Homebrewing, Fourth Edition*.

LAUTERING AND SPARGING

You've made all of this good wort, on its way to becoming the next best beer you've ever made. Now it's time to separate the good liquid from the grains we extracted it from. The straining process is called *lautering,* and the vessel it is done in is called the *lauter-tun.* There's a lot of good stuff as well as some undesirable stuff impregnating these grains. The good stuff (called extract) needs to be rinsed away during the process called *sparging.* There are many points to be considered in order to get the most of the good stuff extracted and the least amount of the undesirable stuff left behind.

TEMPERATURE

The temperature of the mash at mash-out should be 167 degrees F (75 C). This halts enzyme activity and allows dissolved sugars to flow more freely from the grain. Temperatures higher than 170 degrees F (76.5 C) will begin to "cook" the grains into a gummy mess and cause difficulty during the lautering process.

FOUNDATION

If not already sitting atop a straining device, the hot mash must be transferred into the lauter-tun. However, before this is done, foundation water must be added to the lauter-tun to reach a level visibly above the straining "plate" or device. The water should be between 170 and 175 degrees F (77–79 C). This water provides a foundation upon which the mash can be suspended onto the straining interface. This prevents compacting of the grain bed and a clogged system.

FILTER BED

A poly-Posturepedic fully sprung mattress is best utilized for maximum somnambulism. Back up. Start over. Score one for me if I had you. If you didn't bite, then have a homebrew.

The broken and spent grains serve as a filtering medium for most of the particulate and insoluble material not wanted in the malt extract. When the flow of extract from the lauter-tun is begun, the first runoff will be cloudy and contain quite a bit of floating precipitate and particulate matter. This initial runoff should be recirculated by gently pouring it back onto the top of the grain bed. After a few minutes or a few quarts, the extract will run clear.

COLLECTING THE EXTRACT

The extract is drawn from the bottom of the lauter-tun and directed to the brewpot by means of a regulated hose. Regulation of the hose can be achieved by slipping a hand-pinched hose clamp valve onto the hose or a valve inserted in the exit of the lauter-tun. The outflow should be controlled as a slow flow and certainly not gushing out from the lauter-tun (more details on this later). Lautering a mash for a 5- to 10-gallon (19–38 l) batch should take about 30 minutes. The end of the hose should reach to the bottom of the brewpot so that aeration of the hot extract as it enters the pot is minimized.

BEGIN SPARGING

At least ¼ inch to ½ inch (6–13 mm) of liquid should be maintained on the surface of the grain bed during the lautering, as long as the supply of premeasured sparge water lasts. Sparge water should be maintained at 170 degrees F (77 C) and sprinkled evenly onto the grain surface as necessary. The formation of the grain bed should be disturbed as little as possible, though it is not critical at the top 2 to 3 inches (5–8 cm). The hot sparge water percolates through the grains and carries with it extract from the grains.

WHEN TO STOP

The quality of the extract changes as it trickles from the lauter-tun. The concentration of sugar decreases as the sparge water dilutes the runoff. Consequently the specific gravity of the runoff decreases. At the same time the pH of the runoff increases. When this occurs, undesirable compounds such as harsh-tasting polyphenols and tannins, haze-forming starch, and insoluble proteins are more easily extracted and brought out of the grain bed and into the extract.

Experiments by professional brewers and researchers provide information that gives us some indication of what the optimal point of ending the runoff might be.

For beers requiring a delicate and smooth finish, stop the runoff when the specific gravity falls below 1.008 (2 B) or pH is greater than 6.0 to 6.1, whichever comes first.

For more robust beers or beers not requiring extreme finesse, stop the runoff when the specific gravity falls below 1.002 to 1.004 (0.5–1 B) or pH becomes greater than 6.2 to 6.4, whichever comes first.

Generally the pH and the amount of undesirable materials begin increasing dramatically when the runoff is between 1.004 and 1.008 specific gravity. They really zoom when specific gravity drops below 1.004 (1 B).

By monitoring the pH and/or the specific gravity of the runoff, you can determine when to stop the lautering process. As head brewmaster, you should also be tasting the runoff at various stages to get a sense of what all these numbers mean in real life.

These guidelines all assume sparge water of low calcium hardness (0–50 ppm). Experiments have shown* that when the calcium content of sparge water is increased, the tendency of the late runoff to increase in pH is greatly inhibited. Additions of calcium to levels of 50 to 200 ppm will have dramatic effects, enabling the brewer to collect extract from a prolonged runoff. However, the increased calcium levels may alter the flavor profile and perceived bitterness of the hops if calcium sulfate is added to achieve these higher calcium levels.

Higher levels (50–200 ppm) of calcium in the mash also inhibit the increase in runoff pH, but the difference is not as great as the effect when adding calcium to sparge water.

SOME PRACTICAL CONSIDERATIONS

MEASURING THE RUNOFF

pH and specific gravity measurements must be done with extract between 60 and 70 degrees F (15–21 C). A half to ¾ cup (118–177 ml) of extract is all that is needed to fill the hydrometer flask and take a reading. A simple way of cooling the hot extract is to add it to a saucepan and immerse the saucepan in cold water. Simply swirl for 10 seconds to cool to appropriate temperature. pH is conveniently measured with pH paper strips rated for the range between 5.0 and 6.6 or thereabouts. More accurate pH measurements can be done if you invest in a pH meter. The choice is yours.

HOW FAST THE RUNOFF?

Lautering, sparging, and collecting the extract from an 8- to 12-pound (3.6–5.4 kg) mash will take about 20 to 40 minutes, but that doesn't mean lautering ten times the amount of grain will take ten times as long. The runoff is influ-

---

*"The Importance of pH Control During Fermentation," by David Taylor, *MBAA Technical Quarterly*, vol. 27, 1990.

enced by how deep the grain bed is and how quickly the dissolved sugar takes to migrate out from inside the saturated grain. To get the good stuff out takes patience because there is no benefit to speeding it along.

It requires patience because there is a limit imposed by the nature of the grain on how fast lautering can go. You want to avoid fast runoff, because that will result in a stuck runoff.

STUCK RUNOFF

Just as sure as you've had a boilover, you will also experience the occasional stuck runoff, set mash and the aggravation that comes with it. Stuck runoffs occur when the grain bed clogs the strainer interface or the filter bed compacts, thus restricting flow. The most common direct and controllable cause of a homebrewer's stuck runoff is impatience and allowing the flow from the lauter-tun to be faster than extract can percolate through the filter bed and strainer interface. When you remove more extract below the strainer than can be replaced by percolation, an air space is created below the strainer. Without the foundation water suspending the grains above the strainer, *whamo*—the grain compacts onto itself, enhanced by the slight vacuum below. Neither the situation nor the brewer is a pretty sight to behold at this point. Watch your language if your kids are around. Breathe deep and think, "Relax. Don't worry. Have a homebrew."

Other factors that increase the potential for a stuck runoff are gums from malt or unmalted grains such as oatmeal, rye, or wheat. Take great care in regulating the outflow. Don't let your impatience get the better of you or it will literally "stick it" to you. A glass of homebrew and patience are essential ingredients for this process. Every lautering system has its own tolerance. You will learn with experience.

Sometimes a gray "mud" will form on the surface of the grain bed. This insoluble material can form a barrier, preventing flow. The remedy for this is quite simple. Take a knife or fork and break this barrier by "raking" the surface to a depth of 1 to 2 inches (2.5–5 cm). If you have ever peered into a brewery mashtun you will notice their version of "knife blades" suspended over the mash, ready if necessary to cut through and break up the surface of the grain bed for the reason just described.

What to do if a stuck mash happens? First try making a wish. If that doesn't work, then sometimes "underletting" will help alleviate the situation. By forcing hot water back through the system in reverse, sometimes the compacted grains can be pushed away from the strainer grate. Let it sit for a while and slowly begin the flow again. Another option is to underlet with water and simply stir the mash, creating a new beginning for the filter bed and flow of extract. You'll have to recirculate the cloudy first-running extract once again to set up the filter. A last resort is to scoop out all the grains and start the lautering process all over again. It isn't a pretty sight, but very good beer can be salvaged from these unfortunate circumstances. Keep in mind that it happens to scalawags as well as to the best of us.

HOW MUCH SPARGE WATER?

The total volume of sparge water will vary with beer styles and mashing processes. Generally sparge water will equal about three-quarters to just over the total volume of water necessary for the mash process. It is better to have more than necessary and stop the runoff when indicated by pH, specific gravity, the volume of beer needed, or your taste experience.

It is sometimes the case that the total volume of extract wort is less than the total volume of beer anticipated. If the gravity of the collected extract is greater than expected, it is better to add water to make up the volume than it would be to continue the runoff. On the other hand, if the volume and gravity are less than anticipated, you have found yourself brewing less beer than you figured you would. Have a homebrew, cry a little, but don't let the teardrops fall into your brew—they will add sodium and chloride.

The mineral composition of the sparge water should be slightly acidic, containing 50 to 100 ppm calcium and not exceeding 100 ppm carbonates. Alkaline water high in carbonates will extract excessive color and the undesirable characters discussed previously.

SPARGING AND LAUTERING EQUIPMENT—YOUR SYSTEM

PLASTIC BUCKET SYSTEMS

The "Zapap" lauter-tun system discussed in *The Complete Joy of Homebrewing, Fourth Edition* is one of the most inexpensive and effective methods of lautering. This system has been improved with some additional equipment commercially available at homebrew supply shops. The system relies on the Zapap principles and integrates miniaturized elements of the sparging equipment used by commercial breweries. It is not only fun to use but impressive to observe. Manufactured by Listermann Manufacturing Company of Norwood, Ohio, one system uses a concave disk perforated with holes to replace the strainer bucket of the Zapap system. The advantage of this system is that it requires recirculation of only about 1 quart (1 l) of extract rather than 4 to 6

Flow of hot sparge water may be regulated with clamp or by positioning container of sparge water higher above lautering vessel and sparge arm outflow.

Action of exiting water causes sparging arm to rotate naturally. Holes are positioned and designed to maximize area sprayed.

Up to about 12 lb. (5.45 kg) of mashed grains fit into a 5-gallon (19 l) lauter tun.

Perforated disk serves as false bottom and strainer; it also suspends mashed grains.

Outflow draws strained liquid from beneath strainer.

Flow of sweet wort may be regulated with clamp. Aeration at outflow should be avoided. Initial cloudy flow can be recirculated through lauter tun by pouring back over grains in a lauter-tun.

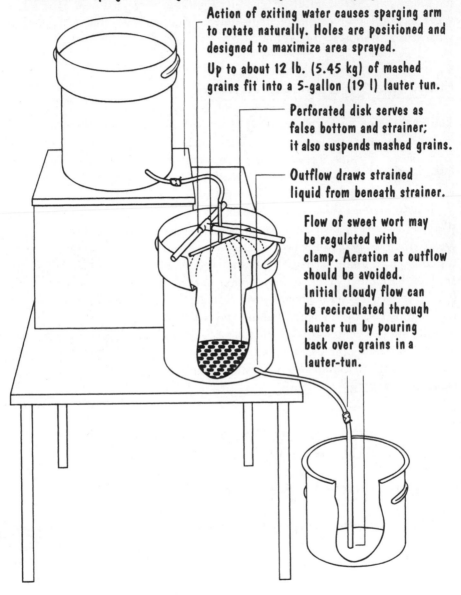

This ain't my kitchen, but you get the picture. One of many user-friendly commercially available lautering and sparging systems specially designed for all-grain homebrewing. Note leisure time to relax, not worry, and have a homebrew. (System courtesy of Listermann Mfg., Norwood, Ohio, and T-shirt courtesy of BrewCo, Boone, North Carolina.)

quarts (3.8–5.7 l) to clarify the runoff. Also because less foundation water is needed, the grain capacity of the 5-gallon (19 l) bucket is greater than with the Zapap system.

The sparging apparatus is the gem of the Listermann system. Fed by a gravity siphon or direct flow, hot sparge water enters a sparge arm that rotates under the power of water exiting the holes. The holes are precisely drilled and spaced so that the water covers the maximum area atop the grain bed. Flow can be regulated with a hose clamp. The system requires that the sparge water reservoir be about 3 feet (1 m) higher than the sparging arm's outflow. This system really allows more time to enjoy a homebrew.

FITTING THE PICNIC COOLER

Box-shaped picnic coolers are not easily fitted with a perforated false bottom. Instead, the straining and draining systems of picnic cooler lauter-tuns are often fabricated with slotted piping. Food-grade PVC or copper pipe is slotted by cutting about one-third of the way through about every ½ inch (13 mm) of the pipe's length. The pipe is assembled in a configuration so that it lies in three or four rows along the length of the cooler. The dead ends are capped and the opposite ends are junctioned to direct the flow out of the cooler. The slots are placed facing downwards. In this manner the extract percolates through the

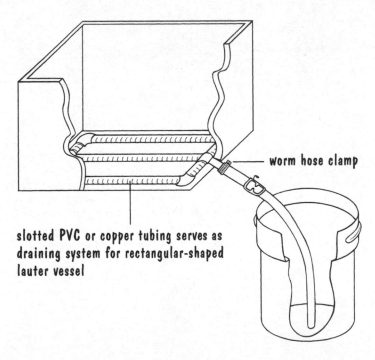

worm hose clamp

slotted PVC or copper tubing serves as
draining system for rectangular-shaped
lauter vessel

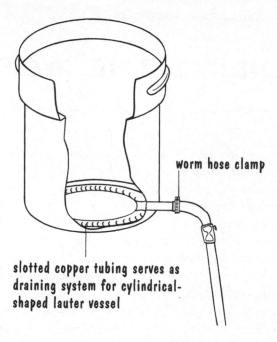

worm hose clamp

**slotted copper tubing serves as
draining system for cylindrical-
shaped lauter vessel**

grain into the slots on the underside of the pipe and flows out of the cooler. The pipe matrix should be designed so that it is removable for easy cleaning. Various methods of sprinkling hot sparge water onto the surface are employed. One of these is drilling a series of tiny holes in a capped-off length of pipe. As water flows by gravity into and through the pipe, the water is sprayed in tiny streams over the surface of the grain bed.

STAINLESS STEEL LAUTER-TUNS

A homebrewer with the right resources and friends in good places can fashion a lauter-tun from a stainless steel brewpot. These vessels are fitted with an "out" spout on the side near the bottom, from which extract can flow. Because of the cylindrical configuration of the vessel, straining and draining matrixes can be configured from slotted bent copper tubing in the same manner as described for the picnic cooler configuration, or with a perforated false bottom, similar to the concave disk of the plastic bucket system.

These systems are the most durable and are often fabricated by homebrewers who wish to make 10-gallon batches or who brew more often.

BOILING THE WORT

It's the time to really kick back, if you haven't already, with a favorite homebrew. The wort's boiling. The house smells great and there isn't much to do for the next 60 to 90 minutes, except maybe clean the mashing equipment and prepare the wort chillers and fermenters. Regardless, there's time for at least one brew.

There are four essential reasons to boil the wort: (1) to extract hop bitterness, flavor, and aroma; (2) to coagulate and precipitate out haze-forming proteins; (3) to eliminate compounds that could otherwise create undesirable flavors and other characters in your beer; and (4) to evaporate a portion of the wort when brewing higher-gravity beers.

More effective hop utilization, elimination of undesirable compounds, and protein coagulation are achieved with full-volume wort boils as opposed to concentrated malt extract boils.

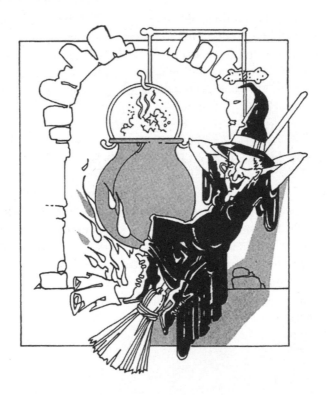

EXTRACTING HOP BITTERNESS

In order to impart a stable bitter flavor to beer, hop resins must be boiled to dissolve them and facilitate a chemical reaction called *isomerization* that enhances stable hop bitterness in beer. For optimal utilization of hops, the process takes at least 60 minutes with a vigorous full-wort boil. (Refer to pages 58–59, hop utilization in the kettle.)

The importance of a vigorous, rolling boil for maximum hop utilization cannot be emphasized enough.

PROTEIN COAGULATION

Certain types of proteins can be coagulated by boiling the wort. These coagulable proteins are primarily responsible for haze formation in the finished beer. However, boiling temperatures alone will not coagulate the proteins. It takes the action of the bubbles formed by vigorous boiling for both coagulation and precipitation to occur. Because these proteins are electrically charged molecules, providing a substance that is of opposite charge will enhance the coagulation. Irish moss (carragheen) is a seaweed that, when added in small amounts during the final 10 to 15 minutes of a rolling boil, helps attract coagulated proteins into clumps. About ¼ teaspoon (1 g) of Irish moss powder is adequate for a 5-gallon batch.

The importance of a vigorous, rolling boil for protein coagulation cannot be emphasized enough.

EVAPORATION OF WORT

The 60 to 90 minutes of boiling will typically evaporate 10 percent of the initial volume. If necessary, this volume can be made up with the addition of water prior to fermentation. Brewers of all-grain strong ales and lagers, however, may need to reduce the volume of the wort by evaporation to achieve targeted initial high gravities.

Evaporation also makes the house smell good to most sensible people.

BOILOVERS

No, the purpose of boiling is not to have boilovers! But they do occur every so often. Watched pots never boil, but unwatched pots boil over. Watch it and watch out. Care should be taken to *always* leave the lid ajar to reduce the risk of boilover. Never cover a boiling wort with a lid.

Boilovers usually occur during the first 5 to 10 minutes of the boil, because certain proteins have not yet been reduced during the boil. There's lots of "sudsing" during the first few minutes of boiling, so extra care needs to be given to watch the pot during this period. Gradually the hop oils and malt proteins are broken down and at a certain point, almost within a period of 10 to 20 seconds, you will observe the suds recede and the dense foaming stop. But securing a lid atop the kettle will surely re-create an atmosphere within the pot and result in a messy boilover. Never place a lid completely covering a boiling wort.

CATCH THE HEAT—
BOILING EQUIPMENT

Homebrewers use one of three types of heat sources to boil their wort.

STOVE-TOP BOILING, GAS AND ELECTRIC

Natural gas heating is the most friendly toward homebrewing. It is hot yet does not scorch the malt. Furthermore, because the pot is raised an adequate distance above the flame, the stove is less apt to be damaged by inadequate heat dispersal.

Electric stoves work well for volumes of 4 gallons or less. Wire trivets should be placed between the electric coil and brewpot to prevent direct contact with red-hot coils. The trivet will reduce scorching, caramelization, and darkening of the wort. For larger volumes and larger brewpots, use caution: Heat may not disperse into the pot of wort quickly enough, thereby overheating the coils and damaging the stove.

OUTDOOR PROPANE COOKERS

These outdoor burners are ideal for bringing large volumes of liquid to a quick boil. Fire one of these hummers up and you can bring 6 gallons (23 l) of wort to a boil in less than 15 minutes. Sometimes referred to as "Cajun cookers," which are used to deep-fry whole turkeys, these burners are rated as high as 200,000 BTUs and are available at many homebrew supply shops. Less powerful models rated at 25,000 to 35,000 are ideal for more casual firing up of the brewpot and are available at hardware stores.

These burners are also convenient for keeping the heat of cooking out of the house during warm summer days. Because they are fueled by propane, *they must be used outside*. Using these types of burners indoors will increase the carbon monoxide levels to a dangerous and sometimes fatal level, so don't use them in an enclosed area. Propane is heavier than air, and if there are leaks, the gas will migrate to lower areas of homes (like basement open-flame furnaces or water heaters) and can cause deadly explosions, adding to the danger of indoor use. The surface upon which the cooker sits must be nonflammable and heat-resistant.

For the more resourceful homebrewer, the heating unit from a discarded water heater makes an effective heat source for brewing. A stand must be built, and the fittings sometimes need to be converted from natural gas to propane.

Extreme care should be taken to keep children away from these cookers. Boilovers are more likely if not carefully monitored during the onset of boiling.

IMMERSION HEATERS

A less than desirable option for efficient wort boiling, these heaters should only be used when convenience dictates or other sources are not available. Electric immersion coils are placed in the wort. Caramelization of the wort and insipid boiling are common with most models.

BREWING KETTLES

A good brewpot is a joy to work with. It contains the wort during a rolling boil, is easy to clean, is affordable, and lasts a lifetime. Unfortunately all these attributes don't always find themselves in harmony.

ENAMELED BREWPOTS

This is the kind of brewpot that most beginning brewers use for their first wort. They are enamel-glazed steel pots more commonly used for canning and other lightweight kitchen uses. The enamel is essentially inert and does not react with the acidic wort. However, if these pots develop chips or cracks, the steel is exposed. Wort will react with the exposed metal, contributing to undesirable metallic flavors. With proper care they can last through quite a few brews, but a lifetime? Not. Every few years you will need to buy another. After going through three or four pots, you will have paid the same as if you had bought a stainless steel brewpot—once.

STAINLESS STEEL

Once you've bought one stainless brewpot, you'll never have to buy another, unless you want more of them. Sizes up to 3 gallons (11.5 l) are relatively inexpensive and can be quite affordable at homebrew supply shops or department stores. However, when you get to the 5- and 10-gallon (19 and 38 l) sizes, you're breaking the $100 barrier. For brewing 5-gallon (19 l) all-grain batches, a 10-gallon (38 l) stainless brewpot is essential.

Stainless steel kegs can be converted to brewpots and other brewing vessels—but there are some serious caveats to possessing these vessels. If you don't legally buy one either used from a brewery (with their knowledge) or obtain a legal document certifying that it is no longer owned by any brewery— you could find yourself in a lot of trouble and be criminally charged for possession of stolen property. Kegs are the property of breweries. It costs them upwards of $200 for a new keg. Brewers don't take kindly to homebrewers "stealing" and converting their property to make brewing systems. If interested in converting a keg, visit your local brewery and ask if they have some damaged kegs or ones no longer used. Getting them from a salvage yard is no guarantee at all that they are "free" to use; it's more likely they are stolen goods. Be sensible and don't create bad karma. Bad karma = bad beer. That's true anywhere in the world of beer and brewing.

Converting stainless steel brewery kegs into large brewpots is a job for your friendly neighborhood welder. Cutting off the top with special saws is no simple home project. Perhaps for a few dollars or a few bottles of beer in trade, you can get yourself a brewpot with handles safely and dependably welded onto the sides, and a lid thrown in for good measure.

Homebrew will get you through times with little money better than money will get you through times with no homebrew.

COPPER

Copper has been used for centuries as a material for fashioning brew kettles. There is often concern expressed that copper will react with wort and taint the beer with toxic amounts of copper. The dangers of using copper to prepare food products lie in alkaline food coming in contact with the metal, which causes copper ions to be leached into food. However, grain mashes, wort, and beer are all very acidic in nature. The acidity "passivates" the copper, coating the metal with a thin protective covering of oxide almost immediately.

If copper is ever scrubbed brightly clean, it should be passivated with a weak acid solution before using. Brewers will notice that when wort comes in contact with copper wort chillers, the surface becomes brighter. This brighter copper still has a protective oxide coating and in comparison is nowhere near as shiny as a brand-new copper penny (at least the shiny real copper pennies I grew up with).

Now, where are you going to find a homebrew-sized copper kettle that is not soldered with lead-based solder? Beats me. But if you do find one, use it if you wish. Inspect the goods carefully, and when in doubt, don't use it.

ALUMINUM AND OTHER METALS

Aluminum is rarely used in commercial brewhouse equipment. There are some logical reasons. Structurally, aluminum is not as strong as stainless steel. Caustic cleaning solutions (used in commercial breweries) must never be used to clean aluminum. A chemical reaction producing explosive hydrogen gas will result.

There is no reason why a homebrewer should avoid using an aluminum brewpot. The effect aluminum metal ions could have on the flavor and character of beer is negligible if it exists at all. The link of aluminum with Alzheimer's disease is inconclusive at this writing. If this risk is a personal concern, you should use your own better judgment.

Cast iron and mild steel should not be used in the brewing and fermenting processes. Iron compounds will create a variety of ill effects on the character of beer.

IMMERSION-TYPE ELECTRIC KETTLES

Available at homebrew supply shops are plastic buckets that are fitted with electric immersion heaters, either 110 or 220 volts. If you have a choice, get the 220-volt model; it will bring your wort to a boil in a reasonable amount of time. The drawback with both models is that they tend to caramelize the wort sugars, which darkens the beer and contributes a related flavor. If you're never going to be brewing really light-colored or delicately flavored beers, these "brew heats" are easy to use.

TRUB AND HOP REMOVAL

Both extract and all-grain brewers must remove spent hops before fermentation. Trub removal, on the other hand, is an option many homebrewers overlook. Hops are relatively easy to remove. For homebrewers, the removal of proteinaceous trub is not quite so simple and the relative benefits are debatable, but the potential for improving your homebrew makes it worthy of consideration.

REMOVING HOPS

Hops could simply be removed from the wort by passing the hot wort through a strainer on its immediate way to the fermenter, but simple straining is perhaps wasting an opportunity to remove the trub. More on this subject later.

A convenient method for infusing additional hop aroma and some flavor into the wort is to pass the hot wort and spent hops through a basketlike device to which fresh hops have been added. The basket, called a hop-back, also serves as a straining device for the spent hops. The effect of this configuration is to "hot-wort-rinse" hop oils from these hops. The aroma-producing oils find their way directly into the fermenter, where they add aroma to the finished beer.

TRUB AND ITS REMOVAL

Trub (pronouced *troob*) is mostly a tannin (polyphenol) protein compound precipitated out of solution during the vigorous boiling of wort or cooling of the wort. Its formation is the direct result of boiling malt (with its proteins) and hops (with its tannins, though malt has some tannins too). The heat and the vigorous boiling action cause precipitation. The trub formed during the boil is called the *hot break,* and trub formed at cooler temperatures, the *cold break.*

There is about three times more hot break than cold break formed, but amounts can vary considerably. About half of the trub is composed of protein.

The rest is bittering substances (some hop bitterness is lost to trub), polyphenols (tannins), fatty acids, and carbohydrates.

HOW MUCH TRUB?

The amount of trub that will precipitate out of wort is influenced by quite a few factors. In the boil it is desirable to precipitate out as much trub as possible. In all the brewing processes prior to the boil it is desirable to choose ingredients and processes that can minimize trub (without compromising desired beer character), whenever the advantages outweigh the disadvantages. Factors that can minimize the potential for trub in wort are: malt quality (poorly modified malt will increase trub), mash filtration (oversparging and pH contribute more polyphenols from the grain husks), grind and mill setting, and mash process (decoction mashing will reduce trub in boiling by formation and removal of trub during decoction boiling and mash filtration).

Factors that can maximize trub formation during the boil are: time of boil, density of boiled wort, amount of hops, use of Irish moss (or similar fining aids), degree of agitation, and pH of wort. After boiling, how quickly wort is chilled influences the amount of cold break that precipitates out.

Remember, if the compounds are in solution to begin with and the brewer does not take steps to precipitate them out, the compounds remain in the wort during fermentation and will affect the character of the beer to some degree.

TRUB: ITS INFLUENCE ON FERMENTATION AND FLAVOR

There has been no shortage of research and experiments performed by the commercial brewing industry and brewing institutions. Their concerns have addressed the needs of commercial interests and their very large-scale (larger than homebrewing) brewing systems and attention to fine differences. More on this perspective later, but for now, let's take a look at some of the conclusions reached.

Fatty acids in trub appear to serve as nutrients for vigorous yeast activity, increasing the rate of fermentation. The presence of trub decreases ester production, but increases fusel oil (higher alcohols) production by yeast. Trub can contribute negative flavor character to beer, darken the color of beer, decrease foam stability, and contribute polyphenols that can combine with other compounds to create staling. Trub can also interfere with or suffocate yeast activity when yeast is harvested for reuse, causing slower fermentation.

Interestingly, years ago it was found by researchers at Coors Brewing Company that oxygen had the same positive effect on fermentation rate as trub. When filtered trubless wort was fermented with a normal amount of oxygen, it took 30 percent longer to complete fermentation than the wort with trub and normal amounts of oxygen. Furthermore, it was found that filtered trubless wort with high oxygen fermented as well as trubed wort with low oxygen. From these and other observations the researchers partially concluded that the fatty acids (lipids in particular) in the trub provided the same type of nutrient energy as the oxygen effectively did in the filtered wort.

So what's a homebrewer to do? On one hand, trub seems to enhance fermentation, which is just what we want, but it also seems to negatively impact the flavor of the beer. Relax. Don't worry. Have a homebrew. Trub's influence is a relatively minor consideration for homebrewers. Keep in mind that there are many other steps in the homebrewing process that can enhance or inhibit the same effects—to a much greater degree. Keep things in perspective, and when you have the other process variables under control, consider trub and its removal more seriously. Don't worry about it, yet know you can continue to improve and fine-tune the quality of your homebrew.

The consensus in brewing literature encourages the removal of trub. With a homebrewer's needs and considerations kept in perspective, one would be doing very well to remove 60 to 80 percent of the trub. This can be achieved with some fairly simple techniques.

TRUB: HOW TO REMOVE IT

There are three principal methods that the homebrewer can employ to remove trub: settling, filtration, and whirlpooling.

Settling of the trub will occur when the wort, hot or cool, is allowed to sit quietly. The settling can be observed in a quiet brewpot or in a 5-gallon (19 l) glass fermenter of cooled wort. Transfer the top clear layer of wort to another container to separate it from the trub. Maintain very sanitary conditions when dealing with cooled wort.

A major problem with transferring clear cooled wort by siphoning or other means is that there is quite a bit of wasted wort, as much as 10 to 15 percent, because even though the trub has settled to the bottom, it is still suspended in fermentable wort. There are other alternatives, so please read on.

Filtration offers a very good means for removing most of the hot break if whole hops are used in the brew kettle. When used as a filter bed through which all of the hot wort must pass, the hops offer a natural means to catch much of the trub. When employed as a filtration bed in this manner, whole hops mustn't be disturbed once the flow of wort through them has commenced.

A simple strainer doesn't offer a very effective means to both collect the hops and utilize them as a filter. The ambitious homebrewer will need to fashion a hop-back. A lauter-tun can serve as a hop-back, but care should be taken to minimize aeration of the hot wort during transfer and it's essential to maintain sanitation during the entire process as the wort flows from the hop-back to the fermenters. As an assurance of sanitation, one could bring the filtered wort back to a pasteurization temperature of 160 degrees F (71 C) before transferring it to the fermenter, but by heating you will lose some of the nuance of hop flavors and aromas contributed by late hopping.

If you are using hop pellets, this method won't work, but the next one will.

Whirlpooling sets the hot wort into a circular whirlpool motion in a container. The heavier hop and trub particles will migrate to the center of the container because of the forces involved. Take a cup of tea with tea leaves in it and stir the cup in a circular swirling motion. Observe the tea leaves as they migrate to the center and into a conelike pile. This is exactly what happens to trub and hops in a whirlpool effect.

Commercial brewers and homebrewers with more sophisticated equipment will apply this principle to their brewpot or another tank and remove the wort from the side of the tank through an outlet.

TRUB, WHIRLPOOLS, AND EQUIPMENT

With a little ingenuity, homebrewers can use all three principles—settling, filtration, and whirlpooling—to their advantage with no more than a minimal amount of simply fashioned equipment. You will need a 3-foot (about 1 m) length of copper or stainless steel tubing. Use a tube bender to bend one end so that it forms a cane shape. Tie on a copper or stainless steel mesh cleaning pad to the straight end of the tube with some string, twine, or copper wire. This will serve as a partial filter and prevent hops from clogging the siphon tube-hose you are fabricating. Attach a 4-foot length of heat-resistant, food-grade plastic hose to the crooked cane end of the tube. Your siphon equipment is ready.

Stir your boiled wort in a vigorous circular motion, taking care to minimize aeration. This will take about 5 to 10 seconds. Replace the lid on the pot and let it sit for 5 to 10 minutes. The wort will partially clear and the hop and trub particles will tend to accumulate in a cone at the center and bottom of the pot. Fill your siphon hose completely with tap water and, while holding your thumb over the end of the hose, carefully place the copper-padded end of the tube in the bottom and side of the brewpot. Let 'er rip. Start the flow of the hot wort into an awaiting brewpot or two. Be careful to minimize aeration.

As the level of the wort decreases and approaches the bottom of the brewpot, you will be quite impressed at the entanglement of hops and gooey trub.

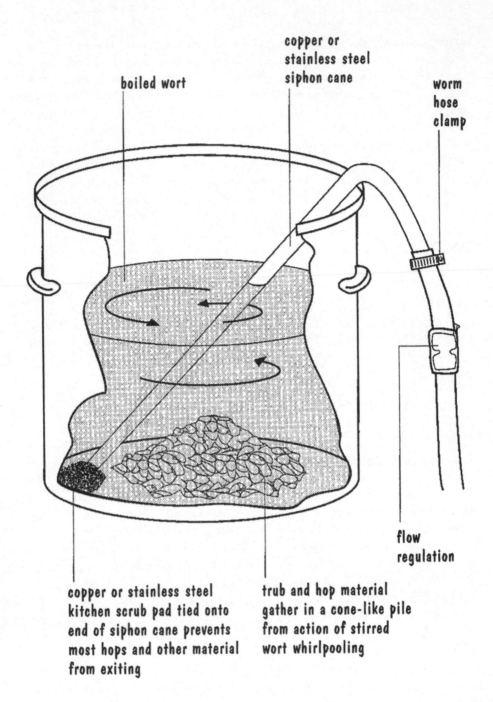

boiled wort

copper or
stainless steel
siphon cane

worm
hose
clamp

flow
regulation

copper or stainless steel
kitchen scrub pad tied onto
end of siphon cane prevents
most hops and other material
from exiting

trub and hop material
gather in a cone-like pile
from action of stirred
wort whirlpooling

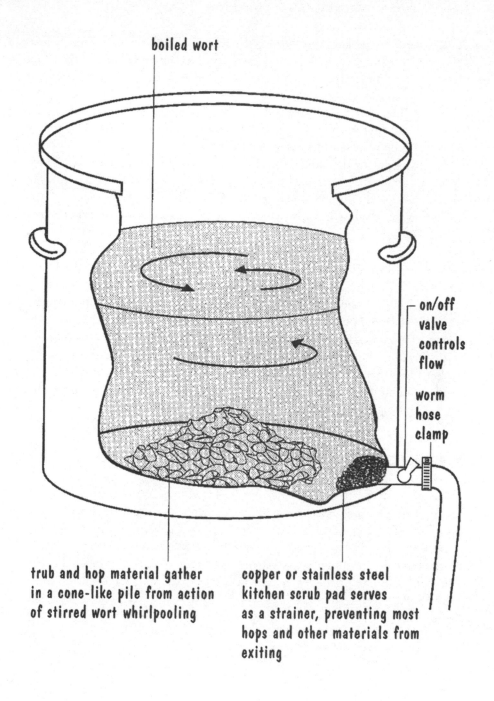

boiled wort

on/off valve controls flow

worm hose clamp

trub and hop material gather
in a cone-like pile from action
of stirred wort whirlpooling

copper or stainless steel
kitchen scrub pad serves
as a strainer, preventing most
hops and other materials from
exiting

Tilt the pot once the level gets close to the bottom in order to get as much good wort out as possible. Sparging with water is not recommended unless the water is acidic. Alkaline water will dissolve the precipitated trub and you will reverse all of what you've just accomplished.

Note: This siphon isn't necessary if your brewpot has an outflow on the bottom of the side where you can attach a valve-controlled hose. The copper pad can still be placed at the exit hole inside the pot.

At this point, while marveling at all that stuff you just filtered out, if concerned, you may bring the wort back to a boil for a very short time to sanitize it. Then proceed with chilling the wort and transferring it to the fermenter.

During the chilling process precipitation of additional tannin-protein trub occurs. The precipitate is called the cold break. The more quickly the wort is chilled, the greater the amount of cold break that will be formed. It will appear to be about 10 to 30 percent of what the hot break was. The principles of settling and whirlpooling are utilized by commercial brewers to remove the trub. However, most homebrewing methods do not offer the sanitary conditions required for additional handling of the wort during cold trub removal. Cold break accounts for about 15 to 30 percent of all the trub material precipitated during the boiling and chilling processes. If efforts have been made to remove most of the hot break trub, then you can relax and have a homebrew knowing that you've eliminated most of the trub. For homebrewers, the risk of contamination may not be worth the relatively minimal benefits gained by cold break removal.

WHEN TO GO THE DISTANCE

If you are brewing those perfectly finessed and superclean-tasting German, Czech, or American light lagers and Pilseners, you should consider maximizing the effects of trub removal. You will note improved clarity, less chill haze, better head stability, and a finer grin on your face. If you've found a way to remove most of the trub, be sure to oxygenate exceptionally well. And if perchance you notice an onionlike character in your beer, you may have removed too much trub. Some brewers claim that total trub removal results in an onionlike character in the beer. If you are concerned, be on the safe side and leave a bit in for good measure—I do.

TRANSFERRING EXTRACT AND WORT

There are several methods of getting the sweet extract or hopped wort from one place to another. Gravity or electric pumps can serve as the power. Hoses, coils, valves, and spigots can serve as conveyance. Whatever the methods, there are two very important considerations to always keep in mind. Minimize aeration of hot extract or hot wort. Sanitation of all equipment that comes into contact with cooled wort is of sacred importance.

GRAVITY AND PUMPS

Whenever possible, the natural and preferred way to move any liquid in the beermaking process is with gravity. It's cheap and quite dependable. However, with some brewing systems an electric pump can be a preferred alternative for moving liquid from one place to another. The prime considerations for using small pumps in a homebrewing system are that the pump is heat-resistant, that it does not infuse any air or oils into the flow, and that its internal components are made of food-grade materials.

SPIGOTS AND VALVES

After hassling with lively and misbehaving siphon hoses, one may be inclined to thoughtfully eye a container, homebrew in hand, and imagine, "Wouldn't it be nice if I could just cut a hole in the side and attach a spigot?" Well, yes, this can work rather nicely, but one must take into consideration a few things.

A spigot does not eliminate the need for hoses. Remember, you must avoid aeration of the hot wort. Once the hot extract or wort exits the spigot, it needs to be guided to the bottom of whatever container it's headed for with a length of hose. The hose's inside diameter should not be so large that it creates bubbles in the flow. As the liquid flows through the tube, it should fill the tube; in other words, no trapped air spaces during flow.

Spigots, their accompanying valves, and attached hoses are dandy for di-

Priming a siphon? Not exactly what I had in mind, but it is effective in getting one thing done.

recting mash runoffs. The flow can be regulated, and concern for sanitation is minimal at this point, since the extract has not yet been boiled. If a spigot and valve are to be used to help transfer cooled wort or hot wort on its way to be chilled, herein lies the challenge. Extreme care must be taken to sanitize the spigot and valve. Passing sanitizer and hot boiling water through them can greatly reduce the risk of contamination, but to minimize the risk even more, the valve and spigot should be disassembled and sanitized thoroughly. Sugars and bacteria from the last time you used the system are enjoying their dormancy in the crevices and interfaces within the valve. Plastic valves offer more of a challenge in that they are prone to scratching and scuffing. Don't underestimate the tenacity of beer-spoiling microorganisms. They want to get at your beer every bit as much as you do. You can relate to that, can't you?

THE SIMPLE HOSE

Hoses used as siphons equipped with external hose clamps are inexpensive and, with practice (more practice = more homebrew; oh, the price of getting it right), easy to use.

Siphoning cooled liquid offers few problems. Siphoning hot liquid requires some creativity, as the hose will lose its rigidity, buckle, and pinch the flow of liquid. When siphoning hot liquid or using a thin-walled hose it's necessary to use a heat-resistant racking or siphoning tube. This is usually a 2½- to 3-foot (0.75–1 m) length of plastic, copper, or stainless tubing bent to resemble a cane. The hose is attached (a clamp may be necessary for a watertight fit) and you are on your way.

How to start a siphon? Cheese and crackers, there must be a million ways. Here's one simple way. Wash your hands. Sanitize both the outer and inner surfaces of the hose. Coil the hose so that you can hold and control it all with one hand (your left one if you are right-handed). Rinse off the outside of the hose with warm tap water. Fill the hose completely with warm tap water and hold your thumbs on each end. Move away from the sink and uncoil the hose by untwisting it while keeping your thumbs on the ends. Empty about 12 inches (30 cm) of liquid from one end of the hose. Insert that end into the wort or beer and start the siphon by directing water into a bucket. When beer starts flowing, temporarily stop flow and direct it to the secondary vessel. This all takes about 37 seconds and eliminates the need for gargling with vodka and sucking on the hose.

There's a little trick needed for starting a siphon with a hose and cane. Attach the hose to the cane. Coil the hose. Point the tube straight up and then begin to fill the hose and cane with water. With careful guidance, the water will flow upwards into the cane, overflow, and rinse the sanitizer off the outer surface of the cane and hose below. With your thumb on the end of the hose, keep the filled cane pointed upwards and, when ready, quickly tip (don't get obsessive about the quickness; relax) and insert it into the hot wort (or beer if you're using a racking cane) and start the flow. If you don't hold the cane upwards while filling with water, you will have air bubbles residing in the tube and hose, which will cause aeration throughout the flow.

CHILLING EFFECTS: COOLING YOUR WORT

Whether you are a malt-extract, mash-extract, or all-grain brewer, the task of cooling boiling-hot wort down to yeast-pitching fermentation temperatures presents itself as an exercise in expediency. The methods range from simple, requiring no additional equipment, to complex, employing sophisticated equipment requiring an initial onetime investment of time and resources and great attention to sanitation. The method chosen depends on whether a full wort boil or concentrated wort boil is employed and whether the brewer has access to water cold enough to facilitate adequate cooling.

THE PRINCIPLES OF WORT CHILLING: WHY AND HOW

The primary reason for cooling wort is to reduce the temperature for optimal yeast activity and fermentation.

It is desirable to cool the wort as quickly as possible to minimize the time the wort is susceptible to contamination. Once the temperature of the wort falls below about 140 degrees F (60 C), the risk of contamination by spoilage microorganisms greatly increases. At temperatures between about 80 and 130 degrees F (27–54 C), most wort- and beer-spoiling bacteria thrive and are in their "groove," so to speak.

Also, some worts cooled slowly over more than an hour may develop compounds that will later result in excessive levels of DMS (dimethyl sulfide), undesirable flavor compounds reminiscent of the taste and aroma of sweet cooked corn. This is an increased factor when lager malt is used. English pale-type malt and other similarly higher-temperature-kilned malts do not present this problem.

Various methods, techniques, and equipment may be used to cool wort. They all employ various means of heat exchange, that is to say, taking the heat away. Let's briefly examine the principles of heat exchange in order to more fully appreciate what's going on and to allow yourself the opportunity for further creativity.

THE PRINCIPLES OF HEAT EXCHANGE

Time for a homebrew? Heat is a form of energy, and your hot wort has a lot of it. You can't make energy disappear, but you can convert heat energy to a different form of energy, remove it, or "dilute" it. Consider heat as an entity. It can travel. ("Cold" does not travel; only heat does.) In order for heat energy to be removed, it must be carried away. Cold water passing through the hot wort by means of pipes or tubes, or surrounding a hot pot of wort, will carry heat away. The cooler water must be moving away; otherwise, the heat removal will stop when that cool water is no longer cooler than the hot wort, because there's no reason for the heat to leave the wort. Got it?

There has to be movement to carry the heat away. It has to go somewhere. Now consider this: The greater the differential (that means "the difference" to nontechy types) between the hot wort and the cooling water, the *faster* the heat will leave your wort. Eventually the hot wort will reach "equilibrium" temperature with whatever it is in contact with. But remember, the greater the difference, the faster the cooling. To give you an example, 3 cups of 120-degree F (49 C) water will increase 15 degrees F in the same time 3 cups of 65-degree F (18 C) water will increase about 35 degrees F using identical heat sources. (I just did it!)

Commercial breweries use many different systems to cool wort. Some utilize large, shallow "pans" called cool-ships, where the wort fills to a depth of about 1 foot (0.3 m). These cool-ship rooms are ventilated with sterile air systems (or in the case of desired wild fermentations, ventilated to the outside ambient air). The hot break settles out of the hot wort while cooling to about 160 degrees F (71 C). Leaving the trub behind, the wort is drained and piped to counterflow-type (heat exchanger) wort chillers (discussed below) for cooling to fermentation temperatures. Other breweries will employ whirlpool tanks to receive the hot wort and then direct the hot flow out to a counterflow wort chiller. The system is completely enclosed and requires diligent cleaning and sanitation.

Homebrewers are very small craft brewers making big beers. Their wort-chilling techniques are home adaptations of the commercial systems.

EQUIPMENT AND TECHNIQUES FOR EXTRACT AND MASH-EXTRACT HOMEBREWERS

Sanitary procedures are essential through the 80- to 130-degree F (27–54 C) temperature range and until the yeast is pitched and begins to create an environment that inhibits the few microorganisms that find their way into the wort. (Absolute sterilization is impractical and highly improbable.)

CHILLING CONCENTRATED WORTS

For those employing brewing methods that boil concentrated worts, the process of chilling the wort is instantaneous and simple. Hot concentrated wort is passed through a sanitized strainer (sanitize the strainer by immersing it in the boiling wort during the final 15 minutes of boiling) to a fermenter containing adequate cold foundation water to reach fermentation temperature. In warmer climates the natural water source may not be cold enough to facilitate adequate cooling. In this case there are a few options for the homebrewer to consider.

Chill the foundation water in sanitized gallon jugs in your refrigerator. Utilize the cool-ship principle by immersing your covered brewpot of hot wort in cold water for 10 to 20 minutes. This will cool the wort to about 150 to 170 degrees F (66–77 C) within 10 to 20 minutes. It isn't essential to create a flow of water to carry the heat away, which will speed up the process. Between the two procedures of chilling the foundation water and/or partially cooling the wort, fermentation temperatures can easily be achieved.

FULL WORT BOILS: EXTRACT AND ALL-GRAIN BREWING

With a 5-gallon (19 l) batch you have all 5 gallons of boiling hot wort to chill. You want to chill it as quickly as possible and give careful consideration to sanitation. Let's consider the simplest ways first.

POT-IMMERSION METHOD

The pot-immersion method requires an investment in a long-handled stainless steel spoon. Use stainless steel because it can be effectively sanitized. Never use a wooden or plastic spoon. You will immerse your brewpot (with the lid securely on) in a flow of cold water, cooling the wort by the principle of heat exchange. Recall that the heat must be carried away. The flow of cold water facilitates this. As well, the hot wort must be stirred constantly for best results, but a stir every 10 or 15 minutes leaves a bit more time for relaxing with a beer; stirring carries the hot wort from the center of the pot to the cooler sides, where the heat is actually exiting through the walls of the pot.

The room where this is done must be draft- and dust-free. Roll up the sleeves of your shirt and wash your hands and arms before hovering over your pot while stirring. You don't need to churn your brew. With careful wort agitation, a slow flow of adequately cold water will drop the temperature to yeast-pitching level within 30 to 45 minutes.

The cooled wort may be transferred to the fermenter by ladling with a sanitized saucepan, through a sanitized strainer and a sanitized funnel if necessary. The strainer will remove spent hops (if still present). Aerate the cooled wort well as it splashes through the funnel and into the fermenter or after it is in the fermenter.

USING ICE

If you live in a climate where tap water isn't cold enough to chill your wort adequately, then sanitary methods of cooling with ice during the final temperature drop can be used. Never add ice directly to your wort. Water exposed to the air in your freezer will be contaminated with microorganisms and freezer flavors. Add 3 quarts (2.8 l) of water to an unused 1-gallon (3.8 l) Ziploc-type heavy-duty freezer bag. Employ sanitary procedures by double-bagging, inserting one bag inside another in order to protect the surface of the inner bag containing the water. Place the double-bagged water in a paper bag before placing in the freezer to reduce the risk of nicking and puncturing the plastic. Freeze the water solid. When you have reduced the wort temperature to about 80 to 85 degrees F (27– 29 C), add the bagged ice. Carefully remove the inner bag of ice from its protective outer bag. Immerse in the warm wort and let sit. Stir occasionally, but take great care to avoid puncturing the bag. Two one-gallon-size bags, each containing 3 quarts of 0- to –5-degree F (–18 to –21 C) ice, should reduce the wort temperature to 70 degrees F (21 C) with the greatest of ease.

If the ice bag method doesn't suit your fancy, you can add 80-degree F (27 C) wort to the fermenter and facilitate further cooling by wrapping the fermenter with a wet towel or large T-shirt. This works particularly well in drier climates and can reduce the temperature of the wort 10 degrees F (about 5 C) below room temperature. It takes a few hours, but a clean wort will wait without suffering too much.

COIL IMMERSION

The next-simplest method of wort chilling involves immersing a coil of copper (or stainless steel) tubing into the hot wort. Cold water flows in one end, and after heat transfer, warm flows out the other end of the coil. The heat of the wort travels through the copper coiling and into the cold water and is carried away.

Copper is easier and less expensive to work with than stainless steel. Fifteen to 20 feet (4.5–6 m) of ⅜- to ½-inch (0.95–1.27 cm) outside-diameter copper tubing is required. Form a coil by rolling the tubing in an 8- to 10-inch diameter (20–25 cm) cylinder of some kind. (Stainless steel soda [Cornelius] canisters [see sections on "fermenters," page 169, and "kegging," page 194] work well.) To reduce the risk of crimping the copper tubing while fashioning the coil, you can fill the copper tubing with water and temporarily seal the ends. When the coil is immersed in the brewpot, the ends of the coil must extend up and out of the pot. Bend the ends downwards in a U shape to prevent the attached plastic hoses from crimping. Attach hoses to both ends and secure with hose clamps. You will need to adapt the end of your "in with the cold water" hose to be able to connect with your water source. Adaptors will vary, but you can figure that out.

When using the coil-immersion method, care must be taken to minimize contamination. Immerse the washed, clean coil and stainless steel stirring spoon in the boiling wort during the final 15 minutes of boiling. This will sanitize the surface. Don't worry about the shinier appearance of the coil; everything is still copacetic.

Place the pot near your sink. Air drafts and dust should be absent or minimal in the room. Roll up your sleeves. Wash your hands and arms thoroughly. Attach the in-hose to your source of cold water. Begin flow, stir the wort con-

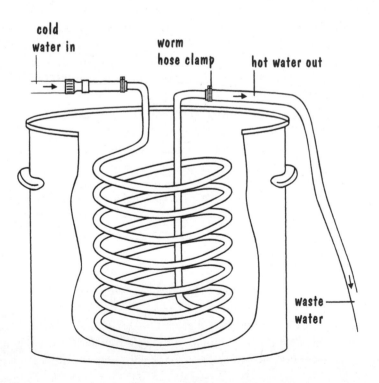

stantly, and don't sneeze into the wort or scratch your beard (or your nose) while peering into the stuff that will soon be beer. Aerate the wort with agitated stirring once temperatures fall below 110 degrees F (43 C). Monitor the temperature and quit once you've reached 60 to 70 degrees F (16–21 C). Carefully transfer the wort (and spent hops if still in the wort) through a sanitized strainer (sanitize the strainer by immersing in boiling wort during the final 15 minutes of boiling) to the fermenter.

For those living in warmer climates, with warmer tap water, ice bags or wet towels (as explained in the preceding section) may be employed to finish reducing the temperature.

COUNTERFLOW SYSTEMS

Requiring more time and/or expense in fabrication, the counterflow chilling system has advantages and disadvantages. This heat exchanger is designed so that hot wort passes through the *inside* of one coil (copper or stainless), while cold water bathes the outside of the hot wort coil and flows in the opposite direction of the wort (counterflow), carrying the heat away. Because the wort travels inside the coil, the care, cleaning, and sanitation of the coils must be given tremendous attention. Sanitizing solutions are often corrosive, so they cannot be in contact with the copper or stainless for any length of time. The coils, connections, and fittings require thorough rinsing with very hot or near-boiling water and must be cleaned both before and after each use. It has an advantage in that it is a closed system. If the system is sanitary to begin with, there is virtually no risk of contamination. The system requires that all of the

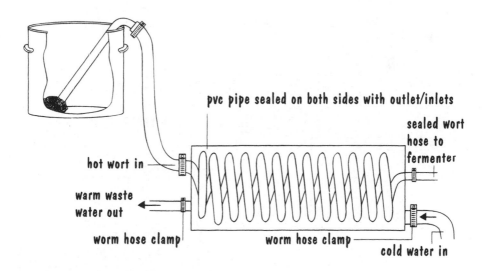

pvc pipe sealed on both sides with outlet/inlets

sealed wort hose to fermenter

hot wort in

warm waste water out

worm hose clamp

worm hose clamp

cold water in

spent hops be removed before the wort enters the system. Gravity (or a pump) can be utilized to siphon or move hot wort into the counterflow device and out directly into the fermenter.

There are several designs employed by homebrewers, using all types of fittings, adapters, tubes, and clamps. Two configurations are illustrated in these pages to seed your mind for more thorough development. The copper tubing usually used for these systems is about ¼ inch (0.64 cm) inside diameter.

The garden hose system calls for an approximately 15- to 20-foot (4.5–6 m) length of copper tubing to be inserted into a hose of slightly shorter length. The copper tubing's diameter is smaller than the inside diameter of the hose in order to allow water to flow through the hose and around the tubing. The tubing protrudes 3 to 5 inches (7.5–13 cm) out either side of the hose ends. The hose-tube is coiled for convenience. Additional short lengths of plastic tubing, T connectors, and hose clamps are configured at the ends to allow wort from the brewpot to flow into the copper tubing and exit to the fermenter, while cold water flows in the opposite direction into the hose and out as warm water that can be collected for cleaning or directed down the drain.

Another simple method utilizes ice chilling and is ideal for use in warmer climates where tap water is warm at best. Quite simply, hot wort passes into a coil of copper tubing that is immersed into a bucket or container of ice and water. The water-ice mixture is stirred constantly until the temperature of the cooled exiting wort reaches 70 degrees F (21 C). The flow of wort is temporar-

Detail—Attachment to Garden Hose

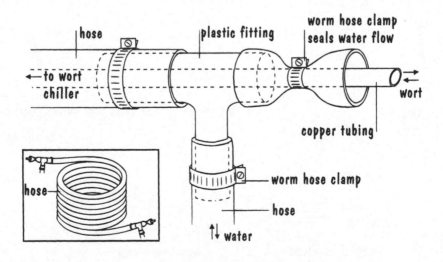

ily stopped while fresh ice and cold water replace the increasingly warmer water.

Be sure to clean, sanitize, hot-water-rinse, and drain these systems before storage. Place a piece of foil over each end to deter homeless spiders and roaches from loitering or seeking shelter.

FERMENTATION

If you're going to discuss beer fermentation with any degree of authority, there is one and only one definitive statement you can make about it: "It all depends . . ." That about sums up the whole process in a yeast cell. If you find yourself reading other books about yeast and fermentation, don't kid yourself into assuming that you've read something that will apply to all situations. It just ain't so. Never, ever, and forever. It all depends. Especially for the homebrewer.

An introduction to the basic principles of yeast metabolism and beer fermentation is presented in *The Complete Joy of Homebrewing, Fourth Edition*.

LAGER AND ALE

Whether you are using ale or lager yeast, the principal factors influencing yeast behavior are:

- The strain of yeast
- Their physical environment
    - temperature
    - pH
    - osmotic pressure (i.e., density of liquid)
    - head pressure (how tall is the volume of beer)
- Nutrients and food
- Oxygen
- Good initial health

There is no one perfect "schedule" of fermentation. The variables listed above are only some of the many that influence the life cycle of yeast, how yeast behaves, what compounds it consumes, and what compounds it creates on its mission of transforming wort to beer.

BEFORE YEAST METABOLISM BEGINS

There are a number of conditions that will evolve in the wort and with the yeast. Brewers have some control over this evolution, but it is the homebrewer's

first task to take a moment or two to appreciate the essential fact that yeast cells are living organisms and that they are in some ways more evolved than human beings. They can live in beer!

Only after developing this respect for yeast should the homebrewer proceed to consider what can be done to enhance conditions for the happiest and best fermentation.

CHOOSING THE YEAST STRAIN

It all depends . . . on the beer you're making and the fermentation conditions you anticipate. Of the hundreds of flavor-related compounds created during yeast metabolism, most are arrangements of carbon, hydrogen, and oxygen atoms. Remember, the food the yeast will convert to beer flavor is sugar, itself chains of carbon, hydrogen, and oxygen atoms. The yeast metabolize and rearrange these atoms into hundreds of other carbon, hydrogen, and oxygen chains, some of which are classified as

- Esters
- Alcohols (including fusel alcohols or fusel "oils")
- Diketones (including diacetyl)
- Aldehydes
- Organic acids
- Phenols
- Sulfur compounds (not strictly carbon, hydrogen, and oxygen atoms)

Every strain of yeast will behave differently and produce varying amounts of these products. And each one is also influenced by the conditions in the wort during fermentations. To highlight only one example out of thousands, studies have shown that the ester level of beer can be influenced by the presence of carbon dioxide during fermentation. The pressure at the bottom of a very tall fermenter is significantly greater than in a small fermenter; the more pressure, the more carbon dioxide remains in solution, thus affecting ester levels. Here's another informational gem. Research by brewers at the Guinness Brewery in Dublin indicated that prior to fermentation, ester levels can be affected by certain situations during lautering. For example, the amount of ethyl acetate esters can be influenced by the degree of filter bed compaction during lautering. Cutting the bed with rakes serves to loosen the bed, releasing more lipids into the wort and consequently suppressing ester formation during fermentation. On the other hand, long, clear runoffs from a compacted grain filter bed will reduce the amount of lipids (all relatively speaking, remember) making their way to the wort and thus tending to encourage ester production during fermentation. "It depends . . ." is an understatement.

There is often concern by homebrewers that some of the above-listed compounds are toxic. Aldehydes, some sulfur compounds, some types of alcohols (fusel alcohols) and esters can indeed be toxic. But toxicity is best defined by dose rather than by substance. The amounts of these compounds that can be naturally produced in homebrewed beer are at very low levels of concentration. One would have to drink two or three gallons of beer having high levels of the compounds every day to even have the remotest effect of toxicity. The "clean" alcohol (ethanol) would have more of an unhealthful effect on your body than any other trace compounds. Besides, any beers having perceptible levels of these compounds are most likely NOT going to taste like something you'll want to drink a lot of anyway. Much bigger problems can occur with moonshine. The distilling process concentrates these compounds, raising their levels thousands to millions of times higher than what you'd naturally find in homebrewed beer. By the way, high levels of esters, aldehydes, and fusel alcohols are culprits responsible for headaches and hangovers. Some people are more sensitive than others, and we all are certainly sensitive to abuse by overindulging.

ADEQUATE YEAST

Too little or too much yeast can affect fermentation. The beginning and intermediate homebrewer should consider the negative effects of underpitching, but certainly not worry about the effects of overpitching. The homebrewer striving for finesse will gain some advantage from knowing a few basics.

If inadequate amounts are used, the respiration cycle will be prolonged, and more reproductive cycles will need to occur to reach optimal yeast population.

If too much yeast is added, there won't be enough oxygen for all of them and on the average they will all be oxygen-deficient, resulting in some negative side effects.

How much is enough? If introducing liquid live yeast, about 6 fluid ounces (177 ml) of yeast slurry that is the consistency of a thick cream chowder is ideal for a 5-gallon (19 l) batch. There is little doubt that quality beer can be made if more or less yeast is pitched. Ask any practical homebrewer. But the possibility of making the best beer is increased if proper amounts of yeast are introduced.

AERATION

Once the wort has been cooled, it is essential that it be aerated in order to dissolve oxygen. Yeast must have oxygen to carry out the many tasks expected of it. But the amount of oxygen required varies . . . It all depends. Generally speaking, though, the required concentration will range somewhere between 4 and 14 mg/l (ppm). Recall the discussion of trub—you could conclude that if you are removing all of the trub or most of it, then your oxygen requirement will be on the high end of this range. If your trub is carried over into fermentation, then fatty acid/lipids will provide the yeast with compounds that help it synthesize the same energy it derives from oxygen. Thus your oxygen requirement will be less. These are only two variables to consider. Oxygen requirements will also vary with yeast strain. If insufficient oxygen is provided, a sluggish fermentation may be observed. Recall the discussion in *The Complete Joy of Homebrewing, Fourth Edition*—active dried yeast does not require as much dissolved oxygen from the wort, because before it was dried it was given enough oxygen to better proceed with healthy fermentation when rehydrated.

There is a downside to adding too much oxygen. Yeast tends to remain in the respiration cycle for a longer period and continues to reproduce, using more of the fermentable carbohydrates. There may be more undesirable flavor compounds that are produced during the respiration cycle in the finished beer. If the addition of oxygen is continued while the yeast is in the wort, there will be a tendency for the yeast to remain in the respiration stage (or even revert to the respiration stage if oxygen is added during fermentation), reproducing, and producing no alcohol. The flavor compounds resulting from this unnatural process are less than desirable. Some yeast strains do better at this than others, but so far, none have been found that will produce a good-tasting nonalcoholic beer using this process—yet.

When saturated with air at about 60 degrees F (16 C) by shaking, splashing or spraying, wort will pick up enough air to saturate to 8 mg/l of oxygen. This is usually adequate, especially considering that most homebrewers will not remove every bit of trub. If additional oxygen is desired, then sterile pure oxygen can be introduced to the wort to reach a maximum saturation of 40 mg/l of oxygen. (This will vary somewhat with wort density. Remember, it depends.) This amount is far in excess of proper levels. It is interesting to note that water at 60 degrees F (16 C) will hold more saturated air than wort at the same temperature, so it is possible to boost the levels of oxygen to some degree (but certainly not to an excessive degree) by adding cold water to the wort. This would be primarily a factor for malt extract brewers to consider. But don't get swell-headed and think you've found salvation. Just have a homebrew and appreciate it for what little it's worth.

YEAST METABOLISM AND FERMENTATION

Once yeast is added to the prepared wort, metabolic activity begins. There are dozens of different cycles that yeast can enter during their residency in wort and beer. There are several excellent references that go into much greater detail than this discussion does.* Remember all of these activities and flavor compounds that are produced are influenced by the type and strain of yeast as well as the condition of the wort and beer before and during the fermentation process. The general phases of yeast metabolism are:

1. *Lag Time*—A period of a few hours when yeast cells take up oxygen and nitrogen-based nutrients (protein amino acids) from the wort. This period is sometimes considered part of the respiration cycle.
2. *Respiration*—The period when reproduction occurs. Carbon dioxide, water, and flavor-related compounds are produced. No alcohol is produced.
3. *Fermentation*—The population of yeast is optimal and the metabolic cycles begin, whereby carbohydrates are converted to heat, alcohols, carbon dioxide, and other flavor compounds.

---

*Three excellent references are *Yeast: The Practical Guide to Beer Fermentation*, by Chris White and Jamil Zainasheff (Brewers Publications, 2010); *Principles of Brewing Science*, by George Fix (Brewers Publications, 1989); and *Zymurgy* special yeast issue, 1989 (American Homebrewers Association).

4. *Sedimentation*—Most of the conversion of fermentable carbohydrates is complete. Yeast enter a dormant life-preserving metabolic cycle and fall as sediment.

5. *Aging*—While not an actual yeast cycle, the aging process is a period in which flavor compounds produced by yeast can transform into other compounds, many considered favorable.

SINGLE-STAGE FERMENTATION OR TWO-STAGE FERMENTATION: WHICH IS BEST? AGAIN, IT ALL DEPENDS

Even though one-stage fermentation is the simplest, it should be considered only when the yeast strain you use does not autolyze quickly and impart yeast-bite or yeast extract–like flavors. Note that cooler fermentation temperatures can reduce the autolyzation process. Choose your yeast strains and fermentation conditions carefully if using single-stage fermentation. Generally if beer can be lagered or aged for short periods (less than three weeks) at below 60 degrees F (16 C), the single-stage homebrewer may be able to brew excellent beer without removing the beer from the primary fermentation yeast sediment. However, if warmer temperatures, longer aging times, or sensitive yeast strains are used, two-stage fermentation is needed to optimize the quality of your homebrew.

The two-stage process removes the beer from prolonged contact with the primary fermentation sediment. Long, cold lagering and postfermentation aging require that the beer be moved off any sediment for optimal quality development.

STUCK FERMENTATION

"My beer stopped fermenting before it was supposed to." This is a frantic statement best dealt with by having a homebrew and relaxing. Reading a recipe and assuming things are "supposed to" happen a certain way is not really homebrewing. Homebrewing is what you do and how your beer behaves. And it usually behaves the way *it* is supposed to, not the way a recipe concludes it should. Remember all of the variables. It all depends . . . Most of the time when a fermentation is apparently stuck, it is the result of a wort that is high in unfermentable carbohydrates. If you don't want a beer with such a high finishing gravity, you will have to look at all the variables you can change—the next time.

Sometimes a lack of oxygen or nutrients will result in a stuck, or more likely very slow, fermentation. Starting a new culture of yeast, waiting until it reaches high kraeusen (that is the phase when all the oxygen and nutrients have been taken up, the yeast is energized and the wort is frothy with foam), then pitching it into the stuck fermentation will help. Rehdyrating active dried yeast and adding it to the stuck fermentation is another, simpler option.

Be careful of carbon dioxide release foam-over, which occurs if the fermentation is cool and there is quite a bit of dissolved carbon dioxide in the stuck beer. Adding sugar or new fermenting beer with agitation may cause a sudden and messy release of carbon dioxide. Be prepared and cautious.

Some homebrewers will create conditions whereby complete fermentation will occur within 24 hours. It's possible, and you may be fooled into thinking that it prematurely stopped. A hydrometer reading will indicate the status of your brew.

LAGERING, STORAGE, AND ALE CELLARING

A period of cold storage often referred to as lagering enhances the qualities of bottom-fermented lager beers. Cold storage of ales is not as critical a factor in traditional ale flavor development.

LAGERING AND COLD STORAGE

A period of two weeks to several months can improve the quality of lager beers. The temperatures at which beers should be lagered will vary with different styles of beer and with different strains of yeast, though in general the temperature should begin at about 45 degrees F (7 C) and be slowly reduced to 32 degrees F (0 C). During this time several things happen.

1. Remaining yeast cells continue to break down fermentable carbohydrates.
2. The evolution of carbon dioxide purges (scrubs out) volatile undesirable flavor compounds such as hydrogen sulfide (H_2S) and dimethyl sulfide (DMS).
3. Yeast activity can reduce diacetyl levels.
4. Esterification (i.e., more esters are produced) occurs by the combination of organic acids and alcohols. Esterification during lagering is activated by enzymes produced by yeast. (Remember, "it depends"—different strains of yeast will produce different enzymes in various amounts.)
5. Oxygen-reduction reactions occur, affecting the flavor of the beer.
6. Yeast continues to settle out, clarifying the beer.
7. Chill haze is formed at very low temperatures. When beer is lagered for long periods, much of the haze will precipitate and sediment out. Commercial brewers have 10- to 50-foot-high tanks of cold beer for haze to fall out of. They can't wait *that* long, so many of these brewers filter.

A 5-gallon fermenter of homebrew at near freezing temperatures can drop out its chill haze in a reaonable time, resulting in clear beer.

An alternative to cold storage for long periods of time would be to bubble carbon dioxide gas through "green" beer for a period. The bubbling will purge many of the green flavors from the beer by scrubbing out the undesirable volatiles quickly. The disadvantage of bubbling carbon dioxide is that it also will purge desirable flavors and aromas. At the same time you aren't allowing adequate time to naturally minimize chill haze through precipitation and sedimentation. In summary, carbon dioxide bubbling is not recommended.

ALES AND SETTLING TIME

Cold lagering is not as necessary with ales. The warm-temperature fermentation will accelerate the evolution and dissipation of undesirable volatiles from the beer. Chill haze is not as serious a consideration if ales are served at their traditional temperatures (about 55 to 60 degrees F [13–16 C]).

Traditional English ale-brewing practices accelerate yeast sedimentation with the addition of isinglass finings. The beer is often served at its best within two weeks of brew day.

FERMENTATION EQUIPMENT FOR THE HOMEBREWER

One of the most innovative fermentation systems I have ever heard of included the use of a large, 10-foot-deep swimming pool. Tucson, Arizona, is not known for its cool weather. In the summer daytime temperatures regularly exceed 100 degrees F (38 C), and during the winter one can count on daytime heat in excess of 80 degrees F (27 C). Going underground is not an option. The geological formations of underlying hardpan rock prevent basements from being a standard home inclusion. Nonetheless, there are many homebrewers in Arizona. Cold beer goes down quite easily among the cactus, mountains, and good company.

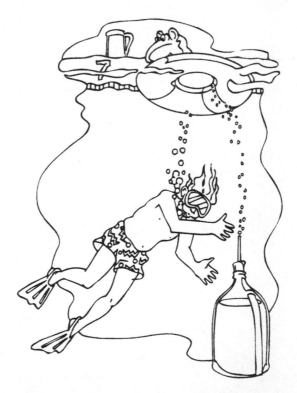

Air-conditioning is quite common, but for some it cannot satisfy the requirements of homebrewing. The logical solution for one homebrewer was to don a bathing suit and immerse the fermenting beer in the swimming pool. Carboy, fermentation lock, and beer were gently placed under 10 feet (3 m) of cool water. The brewer reported that checking the fermentation was a pleasure and the rising bubbles were very comforting. A natural Jacuzzi?

AERATORS

Yeast needs oxygen prior to fermentation. An adequate amount of dissolved oxygen is usually introduced into cooled wort as it enters the fermenter, with agitated shaking of the wort (in closed fermenters) or with the addition of cold tap water. However, some circumstances, such as high-gravity brewing, may warrant mechanical introduction of additional oxygen to help assure adequate levels of dissolved oxygen. Pumping ambient air into the cooled wort and allowing it to bubble through is a versatile and economic means of introducing oxygen into wort.

An aquarium (fish tank) aerator-bubbler is a simple and readily available piece of equipment that may be used for this purpose. The air pumped through this system can be purified by utilizing sterilized cotton as an air filtration medium. Insert a wad of sterile cotton into the tubing through which air flows from the air pump. Commercial filters can also be bought and attached to the system. The sterile cotton may be purchased wherever basic home medical supplies are sold.

To help disperse air into the wort, an aquarium aeration stone can be attached to the hose outlet. Using tubes and hoses is a convenient way of extending the system into the wort. Whatever method you use, it is absolutely essential that all pieces of equipment be sanitized before being immersed into the cooled wort. For porous material and fixtures with joints, disassembly and heat sanitation with boiling water is the best method to help minimize contamination.

Thirty minutes of aeration will be adequate to introduce the required oxygen into solution. Never introduce air once fermentation has begun.

FERMENTERS

Brewers use wood, plastic, glass, and stainless steel vessels to ferment beer.
Wood.   The use of wood has a long tradition in brewing, though it is rarely used today. Older breweries, offering unique products, are usually the exception. For homebrewers, wood should be considered only in the most desperate (or

creative) of situations, such as being stranded on an island in the South Pacific with a supply of water and a pallet of homebrew kits. No one would begrudge you fermenting in wooden barrels. Traditionally speaking, when beer is fermented in wood it does not usually come in direct contact with the surface of the wood. Brewer's pitch, a tasteless resin, is applied to the inner surface of fermenters, and with a great deal of care, is maintained every few months or as necessary. Fermenting beer in uncoated barrels should only be considered for some of the wilder styles of beer. Homebrewers have been known to brew excellent Belgian Flanders–style sour brown ales and masterfully made lambic-style beers in old sherry casks.* Aging certain types of beer in new or used wooden sherry, wine, or whiskey barrels offers creative options that can result in some very fantastic beer.

Plastic. Food-grade plastic fermenters are economical and offer the home-brewer ease in handling and cleaning. But their disadvantages eventually leave the homebrewer seeking a replacement after a fair amount of usage. Plastic stains and scratches easily and is more prone to the effects of abuse such as being used as a storage container for homebrewery equipment. Scratches, whether visible or invisible to the naked eye, will harbor bacteria and other undesirable micro-organisms partly responsible for beer spoilage. However, if plastic is well sani-tized (scratches and all) and a good healthy dose of yeast is added under optimal fermentation conditions, the cultured yeast will vastly outnumber any small bacterial populations hanging out in the cracks and crevices in the fermenter. Therefore, one should investigate less-than-ideal procedures when confronted with a spoiled beer that was fermented in plastic.

Open fermentation should rarely if ever be considered for the homebrewer. The home environment is much more contaminated with spoilage organisms than a clean brewery. In a word: don't. Plastic fermenters should be sealed with an airtight snap-fitting lid. Never, ever use a piece of plastic or towel as a cover. It is a 100 percent guarantee of contaminating the beer. Fermentation locks should be placed in a prebored hole in the secured lid. The lid should be sani-tized, and nothing should come in contact with the fermentation except the hose or racking tube you will use to transfer the beer into its prebottling vessel. Drafty rooms, dusty environments, careless breathing, and mucking about must be avoided whenever the fermentation is exposed to the outside air for transferring or bottling purposes.

When using plastic, single-stage ale fermentation is recommended to mini-

---

*For further reading see *Wild Brews: Beer Beyond the Influence of Brewer's Yeast,* by Jeff Sparrow (Brewers Publications, 2005); "Scratch Brewing the Belgian Way," by Michael Matucheski, in *Brew Free or Die* (Brewers Publications, 1991); "The Legend of Wild and Dirty Rose," by Michael Ma-tucheski, in *Just Brew It* (Brewers Publications, 1992); "Scratch Brewing the Belgian Browns," by Michael Matucheski, *Zymurgy* magazine, Summer 1989.

mize handling. Bottle when visually evident activity has stopped or after assessing the activity with a hydrometer. Because of the risk of oxidation, the beer should not be kept in plastic for more than a few days after fermentation is completed.

In summary, plastic requires more attention, care, and timing during the fermentation process but can give consistently adequate results for homebrewers who prefer this alternative for one reason or another.

Glass.   Glass is one of the most preferred fermenter materials. One-gallon jugs and 2-, 3-, 5-, and 6½-gallon (7.5, 11.4, 19, and 25 l) glass carboys offer a number of advantages to the homebrewer. The inner surface is not susceptible to scratching, is chemically resistant to most substances, and can be cleaned relatively easily. Perhaps one of the nicest advantages of glass is that you can watch the beer's fermentation activity.

Glass is unsafe if handled improperly. Always lift and carry with dry hands. Never lift or carry a carboy with wet hands. Obviously breakage can cause severe injury, but I had to say it anyway. Procedures to avoid pressure buildup in a glass carboy must be taken into consideration. Glass will break if subjected to drastic and sudden changes in temperature. Boiling wort should never ever be added to an empty, cool carboy.

Cleaning a glass carboy is a simple process of filling with cold water and 1 to 2 ounces (30–60 ml) of household bleach and allowing it to soak overnight. A light brushing with a bendable, long, wire-handled bottle brush will then remove all fermentation residues. A bottle washer of the type that screws onto your faucet and directs a stream of water upwards is an extremely useful gadget for rinsing glass fermenters.

With experience you will be able to determine when to bottle your beer by simply observing the fermentation activity through the clear glass. As a rule, when fermentation does not produce any surface bubbles and the beer begins to clear and appear darker, it is ready to bottle. The procedure for measuring specific gravity to assure completion of fermentation becomes unnecessary.

Whenever a blow-off fermentation system is employed, it is essential that all particulate material be strained out of the wort before it enters the fermenter. Large-diameter hoses (approximately 1⅛-inch [2.86 cm] outside diameter) can be affixed to the opening of the glass fermenter in order to minimize the risk of clogging, pressure buildup, and bursting. A simple option to consider when using glass fermenters is to completely eliminate the risk of pressure buildup in a carboy due to a clogged blow-off tube by only filling the fermenter to three-fourths of its capacity. This is essential if fermenting fruit beers in carboys. You may choose to top up to the full volume after fermentation is complete, but do so only with deaerated and sanitized water (boiled and then cooled).

Small glass carboys and one-gallon glass jugs offer convenience when brewing small batches or experimental brews. Be especially aware that fermentation activity and possible beer character can be significantly affected by the size and shape of the fermenter. Large commercial operations must consider these variables when scaling recipes and procedures up or down. Perhaps two of the most significant considerations for the homebrewer are the effects of convection-like circulation currents during fermentation and the effects of heat retention and dispersal during fermentation.

Heat is generated by yeast activity and is dispersed from the fermentation through the walls of the fermenter. Heat transfers to and from the brew in the fermentation room. The efficiency and speed of heat transfer are a function of the ratio of volume to fermenter surface area. What this means is that for smaller one-gallon fermenters, heat will travel in or out of the brew much more quickly. Detrimental ambient room temperature fluctuations are quicker to affect smaller brews, a factor particularly worth considering in homebrewing areas that are prone to temperature changes.

Stronger circulatory currents are set up in larger containers by the action of carbon dioxide production. These actions can affect flocculation, suspension, and other activities of the yeast, thus affecting the character of the beer.

Shove it in. Large-diameter hoses can be affixed to the opening of glass fermenters in order to expel kraeusening fermentation and minimize the risk of clogging, pressure buildup, and bursting more probable with smaller diameter hoses.

The 200-Year-Old Burton Union "Blow-off" System

For centuries, world-class top-fermented pale ale was fermented using the Burton Union System in the Burton-on-Trent area of England. That all stopped when brands and the century-old breweries were bought by large international global brewing companies. A combination of water quality, brewing technique, and yeast handling had helped one ale in particular achieve international recognition. Bass Ale was considered by many beer enthusiasts as a world classic and had been brewed with the same yeast for over 200 years. What once made Bass Ale even more distinctive was the method employed for fermentation and propagating the yeast, known as the "Burton Union System." Bass Ale is now only a "brand" of beer currently owned by Anheuser-Busch InBev and they no longer ferment Bass Ale (currently contract-brewed at other breweries) using the centuries-old method.

Simply put, the Burton Union System directs the yeast kraeusen-head produced during the initial stages of primary fermentation from the fermenters through a blow-off system into collecting troughs. The very flocculent strain of top-fermenting ale yeast was collected from these troughs and re-pitched batch after batch, year after year. As the fermenting head was blown off and collected in the system, there were three "phases" of brew that separated in the system. Some of the fermenting wort was allowed to flow back into the fermenters, while the settled yeast was collected by selective channeling of the liquid. The foamy head maintained itself in the "open" system and served as a barrier between the ambient air (full of contaminants) and the pure yeast below.

The brewers at Bass had determined that yeast harvested from the Union System was not only the purest but also the most healthy and viable. Yeast sedimented out of the fermenters was discarded or processed into other food products.

The Burton Union System was unique and was particularly well suited to the particular strain of yeast that was once used to make Bass Ale.

The best course of action here is to relax and have a homebrew. Remember—you are a homebrewer, and your beer much more often than not comes out great. Don't worry. Appreciate the many factors that *can* have an effect on the character of your fermentation and the flavor of your beer. Enjoy this diversity and the challenge of considering all this stuff while enjoying the results of your latest efforts. A homebrew in hand is quite helpful in keeping a perspective on your brewing endeavors.

Not your typical homebrew setup. The Burton Union System was used in the original Bass Ale brewery for centuries before being discontinued in the early twenty-first century. The Burton Union System was unique and crucial to the survival and purity of the original yeast.

Commercial brewers often have to consider the effect of pressure on the behavior of yeast and fermentation when fermenting in tall two- to four-story-high fermenters. The effect of pressure in small-scale brewing is virtually none. **Stainless Steel.** Used by commercial brewers the world over, stainless steel is the preferred material for fermenters. On a homebrewing scale the only serious disadvantage is cost—stainless can be expensive. Care needs to be taken when sanitizing with solutions of household bleach and water, as even dilute concentrations of bleach can cause corrosion. Bleach solutions, if used, must be thoroughly rinsed with warm water. Prolonged contact with bleach solution should be avoided.

There are ready-to-use prefabricated homebrew-size stainless steel cylindro-conical fermenters, sometimes called "uni-tanks," available for homebrewing. It is a closed system. The top portion is cylindrical and the bottom portion is conical. The vessel is easily used for both primary and secondary fermentation without transferring the beer. This is accomplished by opening the valve at the bottom of the cone, where all the yeast and sediment has accumulated,

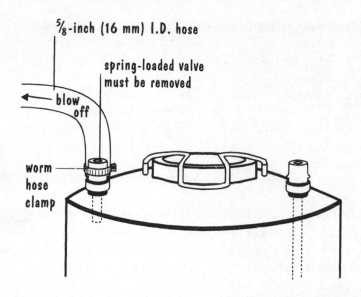

⅝-inch (16 mm) I.D. hose

spring-loaded valve
must be removed

← blow
off

worm
hose
clamp

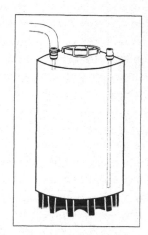

and allowing the sediment to exit the fermenter. Now the fermentation can continue at another temperature for either lagering or cellaring in the same vessel. It's a miniature version of what you see in most of your small local breweries.

Other, more accessible stainless vessels can be adapted as fermenters for homebrewing.

One reasonable source for stainless steel as a homebrewing fermenter is to adapt 2-, 3-, and 5-gallon (7.5, 11.4, and 19 l) stainless steel soda canisters (Cornelius, "Corny," tanks) for the job. The opening is large enough to allow easy cleaning. There are two fittings on the tops of these canisters. Usually marked "in" and "out," they normally dispense "out" soda (or beer) and take "in" carbon dioxide pressure to push the soda (or beer) out. (Using these canisters as homebrew kegs is discussed in the kegging section.) In order to use these canisters as fermenters, the "in" fitting is adapted to serve as the "blow-off" stream for primary fermentation. To accomplish this, examine the removed "in" fixture and notice the spring-loaded valve seated inside. Remove this valve so that there is a clear way through the fixture. Reattach the fixture to the canister and slip onto the end a 4-foot (1.3 m) length of ⅝-inch (16 mm) inside-diameter plastic hose and secure with a hose clamp. The hose should be inserted into a bucket of sanitized water during fermentation to catch the overflow and serve as a fermentation lock.

CAUTION: Fermentation should never be done in a sealed, closed container. Use all necessary precautions to assure that all particulate matter having a potential to clog the system has been strained out of the wort. Also use only tank lids that have a safety pressure relief system.

The versatility of these canisters as fermenters goes beyond primary fermentation. They can also be used as a secondary fermenter. After fermentation is complete, the spring-loaded valve on the primary vessel can be returned to its original placement, the fixture screwed back onto the canister, and the unit used as it was originally intended—to dispense liquid. Carbon dioxide is used to gently push the fermented beer out of the canister, but rather than dispensing the beer via a tap, at this time you are going to dispense the finished primary fermentation into another similar vessel to be used as a secondary fermenter. To do this, the end of the "out" hose on the primary is connected by a hose and fittings to the "out" fixture of a secondary canister fermenter. In this manner the beer is pushed from one tank into another, out through the exit tube of the primary and into the secondary by way of the *exit* tube of the secondary. This procedure leaves behind most of the sediment and transfers the beer into the secondary at the bottom of the vessel. One tip worth considering is to purge the air from the receiving fermenter and minimize oxygenating the beer during transfer by injecting about 10 seconds' worth of carbon dioxide. (Carbon dioxide is heavier than air/oxygen.)

In fashioning this transfer system, you may have to shorten the long "out" tube by cutting with a hacksaw. The principles are simple, but there are additional considerations that the brewer must deal with to get the system to work properly. A tank of carbon dioxide with regulators and hoses is necessary, along with extra hose to connect fixtures. Sanitation of all fixtures, tubes, hoses, and anything whatsoever that comes into contact with the beer is essential.

If all this weren't enough, you can take the whole system one step further by transferring once again into a final "keg" of beer (more on that later).

CONTROLLING FERMENTATION AND LAGERING TEMPERATURE

Don't immediately assume this discussion is only about maintaining cool lagering temperatures. Some homebrewers need to keep their fermenters from getting too cold.

Whether your goal is to keep your fermentation warm or cold, the essence of dependable, carefree temperature control is a thermostatic device that senses temperature and reacts by switching electricity on or off. These thermostats, complete with sensing probe and switches, are readily available. Devices adequate for homebrewers will generally run from $50 to $100.

KEEPING IT WARM

For homebrewers brewing in Alaska or through a cruel New England or Midwest winter, maintaining warmer ale fermentation temperatures or keeping your lager from freezing can best be accomplished by storing your fermenter in an small enclosed insulated area. The heat source can be as simple as a 100-watt incandescent lightbulb for small areas or a fire-safe convection or radiator-type electric heater for a closet space. Shield your fermentation from direct light. Connect your lightbulb or heater to a thermostatically controlled device that switches on whenever the temperature drops below a certain point. A spare closet or a large cardboard box lined with sheets of insulating Styrofoam will work quite well, while an unplugged refrigerator can also serve the same purpose while doubling as a cold lagering box in the warmer months.

Recall that fermentation produces heat. To a certain degree a very well-insulated and sealed compartment can hold heat created by vigorous primary fermentation to help maintain ale-fermenting temperatures in extremely cold environments.

Heat tapes used to help prevent pipes from freezing can be wrapped around carboys. Electric blankets or heating pads can also be employed, but be very aware that a more sensitve thermostatic device should be interfaced with the tapes, pads, or blankets to regulate when they turn on and off. Fermenters should not be placed on top of pads or blankets for safety reasons. Rather, these heat sources should be draped around the area of the fermenters in a manner that easily allows the heat to escape from the pad or blanket.

The temperature of the air is not always indicative of the temperature of the brew. Once you have your system established, take temperatures of the fermentation and the air. Note the difference and adjust your thermostatic controls accordingly.

Keeping It Cool

For homebrewers living in more temperate climates, an extra refrigerator will serve perfectly to lager or ferment your homebrew at controlled temperatures. A thermostatic device is simply plugged into the wall. The refrigerator is plugged into its thermostatically controlled switching device, and the temperature-sensing probe is placed inside the refrigerator. The device can be set for any temperature. Some more sophisticated thermostats can be programmed for a variety of temperatures over extended periods. Top-loading freezers can also be adapted with a thermostatically controlled device.

Another way to cool your fermentation is to employ the principles of evaporative cooling. This works well in particularly dry climates. When water passes from the liquid stage to an evaporated gas stage, it literally takes a lot of heat energy with it. (That's why when water vapor gas turns to liquid [rain] in a storm, there is a lot of heat energy reversibly released. That in part is what makes a storm.) Homebrewers can employ this principle by wrapping a wet towel (or heavy cotton T-shirt) around a fermenter and letting water evaporate from it. Keep the towel wet and your beer will be no fewer than 10 degrees F cooler than the air temperature. The effect can be exaggerated by blowing air on the wet-toweled fermenters with a small fan.

Wetness can be maintained by fashioning a means of dripping water on the towels or by placing the fermenter and towel in a shallow pan of water. The towel will wick water up to a certain level as it evaporates.

SUCK-BACK AND FERMENTATION LOCKS

When a fermenter is moved to a lagering environment, temperatures are often drastically reduced. If there is any significant amount of air space in the fermenter, a vacuum effect will be created as the air in the fermenter is cooled. If there is not sufficient fermentation gas still being produced by the yeast, then outside air can be sucked into the fermenter. This can create problems if contaminated air is brought into the fermenter or if contaminated water from the fermentation lock is sucked into the brew.

To minimize the risk of contamination by fermentation lock liquid, the liquid can be reduced to a level so that it isn't possible for the water to be sucked into the brew by the reverse action of the vacuum. The liquid can be replaced with neutral sterile spirits such as vodka just in case there's suck-back. Sterile dry cotton can be stuffed into the fermentation lock passages to act as a filter barrier. If this method is used, it is imperative that the cotton not become wet, otherwise the barrier will become a wet bullet sucked into the brew. For this reason the fermentation lock should be dry for 24 hours. As equilibrium is reached, pour liquid back into the lock.

With a good lager yeast and proper timing, lagering will continue to produce some carbon dioxide. This will purge any air from the vessel that was introduced through suck-back.

TRANSFERRING BEER FROM HERE TO THERE

There are many reasons to move beer from one place to another. The most important and most obvious transfer is the one from your glass to your lips. But that's the end of the journey. There are several transfers made during the fermenting, aging, and bottling (or kegging) process to help assure that the beer's final character is the best.

Usually beer is transferred from one vessel to another to remove it from sedimented yeast and other matter or to move it to a special environmentally controlled container such as a lagering tank. In some breweries and perhaps sophisticated homebrew systems a "unitank" system is employed whereby, rather than moving the beer off of sediment, the sediment is removed from the temperature-controlled tank. The bottoms of these tanks are usually conically shaped so that yeast removal is easier (as mentioned in the discussion of stainless steel fermenters; see pages 174–176). The tanks themselves are jacketed with an enclosed circulating refrigerant system.

All homebrewers will find themselves transferring beer from one vessel to another at one stage or another. There are three important factors to consider with any transfer system you employ: (1) Avoid the introduction of oxygen during transfer, (2) maintain sanitary conditions throughout the process, and (3) avoid sudden and drastic temperature changes in the environment.

Small electric pumps can be used by homebrewers, but as with any equipment, they must be maintained in sanitary condition at all times. The pump should be of the type that will not aerate or introduce air into the stream.

Using a hose siphon is the easiest and cheapest means to transfer liquid from one container to another (see pages 150–151). It is powered by gravity and requires little maintenance other than sanitizing the hose or occasionally replacing it with a new one. There are as many ways to start a siphon as there are homebrewers. Before any method is used, the number one step that must be taken is to thoroughly wash and rinse your hands before handling the siphon hose. Soap and water and a good rinse will be adequate for homebrewers' purposes.

The outflow from the transferring hose should be directed to the very bottom of the receiving fermenter so that splashing is minimized. The effects of splashing can be reduced by adding a layer of carbon dioxide to the receiving fermenter. Homebrewers with a carbon dioxide dispensing system can easily add about a 15-second stream of regulated carbon dioxide gas into the fermenter. Carbon dioxide is heavier than air and will layer itself on the bottom of the receiving fermenter. Any splashing will only aerate the brew with harmless carbon dioxide. This method can also be used when transferring beer into kegs. Hey—relax and don't worry if you can't add a layer of carbon dioxide to your receiving fermenters and kegs. Have a homebrew—there are plenty of more important things you can attend to that will make more of a difference.

CARBONATION, CONDITIONING, AND OTHER GASEOUS MATTERS

PRIMERS

Natural conditioning with the addition of a measured amount of fermentable sugar prior to bottling or kegging is the most common method used by home-brewers to carbonate beer. Three-quarters of a cup (178 ml) of dextrose (corn sugar) added to 5 gallons (19 l) of fully fermented beer will adequately carbonate bottled beer. For kegged brew and draft beer, about ⅓ cup (79 ml) of dextrose per 5 gallons (19 l) will create appropriate carbonation.

All-malt enthusiasts may substitute dried malt extract for dextrose. In this case, the process is called kraeusening. Use 1¼ cups (296 ml) of dried malt extract for bottling or ½ cup (118 ml) for kegging. Whether dextrose or dried malt is used, priming sugar should be dissolved and boiled for 5 minutes in about 1 cup (237 ml) of water before adding to the beer prior to bottling.

Malt extract will take comparatively longer to carbonate beer than corn sugar. There is a solid theoretical basis for this phenomenon. Yeast does not require dissolved oxygen to metabolize dextrose, but does require dissolved oxygen or the development of nutritional equivalents to metabolize most of the sugars in malt extract. Neither the fully fermented beer nor the added priming solution contains dissolved oxygen, thus time is needed to develop nutritional equivalents, resulting in slow carbonation. Patience and time are the easiest remedies, but it is perhaps truer to the tradition of kraeusening to expedite a normal bottle fermentation by introducing yeast to a well-aerated malt extract solution and letting it metabolize oxygen for 4 to 6 hours before adding it as priming. An alternative for those using dried yeast would be to simply add some fresh dried yeast to the batch along with the malt extract solution. Dried yeast has its oxygen requirement stored, having taken it up prior to being suspended in its dried state.

BATCH VS. BOTTLE PRIMING

Each has its advantages and disadvantages, though batch-priming methods help assure consistent and contamination-free results. Batch primers rack (transfer) the finished beer off of any sediment to another vessel to which all of the priming sugar is added and then evenly mixed. Bottle primers attempt to add a carefully measured amount of priming sugar to each bottle and bypass the extra transfer.

There are three significant problems that are likely to be encountered with bottle priming: (1) Without being dissolved and boiled in water, granulated dextrose may contain beer-spoiling microorganisms, (2) a 10 to 20 percent difference would not be visually noticeable but can have drastic effects resulting in under- or overcarbonation, and (3) adding slightly carbonated beer to dry sugar can cause foaming. Until someone produces sanitarily packaged, premeasured, and inexpensive dextrose pellets for bottle priming, batch priming is the preferred means of priming.

Other fermentable sugars may be used as priming. Some will contribute unique flavor. The following table shows equivalents.

Sugars for Priming

(Volume Measurements of Various Sugars
for Batch Priming 5 Gallons [19 l])

SUGAR TYPE	BOTTLES	DRAFT/KEG
dextrose	3/4 c. (180 ml)	1/3 c. (80 ml)
honey	1 c. (240 ml)	< 1/2 c. (100 ml)
maple syrup	1 1/4 c. (300 ml)	5/8 c. (130 ml)
molasses	1 c. (240 ml)	< 1/2 c. (100 ml)
brown sugar	2/3 c. (155 ml)	< 1/3 c. (70 ml)
cane or beet sugar	2/3 c. (155 ml)	< 1/3 c. (70 ml)
dried malt extract	1 1/4 c. (300 ml)	5/8 c. (130 ml)

NOTE: Milliliter equivalents are rounded off to the nearest whole number divisible by 5.

FLAT BEER?

If you brew enough, you may encounter the rare batch of beer that does not carbonate. You did add sugar. You did rinse out the sanitizer properly. You did everything correctly. But your beer never carbonated. Without ever finding an explanation, you can salvage your flat beer. You could blend it with carbonated beers at your next party. But more seriously, each bottle can be uncapped and a pinch of dried yeast or a drop or two of rehydrated dry yeast can be added. Quickly recap and briefly agitate the bottle, store at room temperature for another few weeks, and in most cases the beer will carbonate.

When particularly strong beers do not carbonate, it may be the result of the yeast's intolerance to alcohol. In these special circumstances wine or champagne yeast can be used to salvage carbonation.

"ARTIFICIAL" CARBONATION

Just as some breweries inject carbon dioxide gas into flat beer right before it is packaged, homebrewers with scaled-down techniques can also artificially carbonate their beer before or after the beer is packaged. This method is particularly convenient when you need 5 gallons of homebrew tomorrow and you only have 5 gallons of unbottled yet fully fermented, clear beer in your fermenter.

To artificially introduce carbon dioxide into your homebrew, you will need a carbon dioxide draft system complete with fixtures. The principle one takes advantage of is that carbon dioxide gas will dissolve into a liquid solution when introduced under pressure. The amount of carbon dioxide that can be dissolved into beer and the level of carbonation that will result are determined by time, the pressure applied, and the temperature of the liquid. Average carbonation levels for most German, American, or British styles of beer fall into a range of 2.0 to 2.7 volumes of carbon dioxide. British styles are on the low end of this range, German styles in the middle, and American styles on the high end. By referring to the Volumes of Carbon Dioxide table (page 184), one can choose a desired amount of carbon dioxide and then determine the temperature of the beer and required carbon dioxide pressure.

In practice, after the flat beer is chilled, the desired pressure is applied to the keg through the regulator, and the keg is shaken until equilibrium is achieved. If time is short, an extra few pounds of pressure can be applied for quicker dissolution of the gas into the beer. If time is on your side, the correct pressure can be applied and the keg left to sit over a period of a day or two with occasional agitation until equilibrium is reached; i.e., when no more gas is heard moving into the cold beer when it is shaken.

Volumes of Carbon Dioxide (CO₂)

Pounds per square inch (psi)

Beer Temperature (°F)	1	2	3	4	5	6	7	8	9	10	11	12	13	14	15	16	17	18	19	20	21	22	23	24	25	26	27	28	29	30
30	1.82	1.92	2.03	2.14	2.23	2.36	2.48	2.60	2.70	2.82	2.93	3.02																		
31	1.78	1.88	2.00	2.10	2.20	2.31	2.42	2.54	2.65	2.76	2.86	2.96																		
32	1.75	1.85	1.95	2.05	2.16	2.27	2.38	2.48	2.59	2.70	2.80	2.90	3.01																	
33		1.81	1.91	2.01	2.12	2.23	2.33	2.43	2.53	2.63	2.74	2.84	2.96																	
34		1.78	1.86	1.97	2.07	2.18	2.28	2.38	2.48	2.58	2.68	2.79	2.89	3.00																
35			1.83	1.93	2.03	2.14	2.24	2.34	2.43	2.52	2.62	2.73	2.83	2.93	3.02															
36			1.79	1.88	1.99	2.09	2.20	2.29	2.39	2.47	2.57	2.67	2.77	2.86	2.96															
37				1.84	1.94	2.04	2.15	2.24	2.34	2.42	2.52	2.61	2.72	2.80	2.90	3.00														
38				1.80	1.89	1.99	2.08	2.17	2.26	2.36	2.45	2.54	2.63	2.73	2.82	2.91	3.01													
39					1.86	1.95	2.04	2.12	2.21	2.30	2.39	2.48	2.57	2.66	2.74	2.83	2.92	3.01												
40					1.82	1.91	2.00	2.08	2.17	2.26	2.35	2.43	2.52	2.61	2.70	2.78	2.87	2.96												
41						1.87	1.96	2.04	2.13	2.22	2.31	2.39	2.48	2.57	2.65	2.74	2.83	2.91	3.00											
42						1.83	1.92	2.00	2.09	2.17	2.26	2.34	2.43	2.51	2.60	2.68	2.77	2.85	2.94											
43							1.88	1.97	2.05	2.14	2.22	2.31	2.40	2.48	2.57	2.65	2.74	2.83	2.91	3.00										
44							1.84	1.92	2.01	2.09	2.18	2.26	2.35	2.43	2.52	2.60	2.68	2.77	2.85	2.94										
45								1.88	1.97	2.05	2.14	2.23	2.32	2.40	2.49	2.58	2.67	2.75	2.84	2.93	3.02									
46								1.84	1.93	2.01	2.10	2.18	2.27	2.36	2.44	2.53	2.61	2.70	2.79	2.87	2.96									
47									1.89	1.97	2.06	2.15	2.24	2.32	2.41	2.50	2.59	2.67	2.76	2.85	2.93	3.02								
48									1.85	1.93	2.02	2.10	2.19	2.28	2.36	2.45	2.53	2.62	2.70	2.79	2.87	2.96								
49										1.90	1.98	2.07	2.15	2.24	2.32	2.40	2.49	2.57	2.66	2.74	2.82	2.91	2.99							
50										1.86	1.94	2.03	2.11	2.19	2.28	2.36	2.44	2.53	2.61	2.69	2.77	2.86	2.94	3.02						
51											1.91	1.99	2.07	2.15	2.24	2.32	2.40	2.48	2.57	2.65	2.73	2.81	2.89	2.97						
52											1.87	1.95	2.03	2.11	2.19	2.27	2.35	2.44	2.52	2.60	2.68	2.76	2.84	2.92	3.00					
53												1.92	2.00	2.08	2.16	2.24	2.32	2.40	2.47	2.55	2.63	2.71	2.79	2.87	2.95	3.03				
54												1.88	1.95	2.03	2.10	2.18	2.26	2.33	2.41	2.48	2.56	2.63	2.71	2.78	2.86	2.93	3.01			
55												1.84	1.91	1.99	2.06	2.13	2.21	2.28	2.35	2.43	2.50	2.57	2.65	2.72	2.79	2.87	2.94	3.01		
56													1.87	1.94	2.01	2.09	2.16	2.23	2.31	2.38	2.45	2.53	2.60	2.67	2.75	2.82	2.89	2.96		
57													1.86	1.93	2.00	2.07	2.14	2.21	2.28	2.35	2.43	2.50	2.57	2.64	2.71	2.78	2.85	2.92	2.99	
58													1.84	1.91	1.97	2.04	2.11	2.18	2.25	2.32	2.39	2.46	2.53	2.59	2.66	2.73	2.80	2.87	2.94	
59													1.83	1.90	1.97	2.04	2.11	2.18	2.26	2.33	2.40	2.47	2.53	2.60	2.67	2.75	2.81	2.89	2.96	3.03
60													1.80	1.87	1.94	2.01	2.08	2.14	2.21	2.28	2.35	2.42	2.49	2.56	2.63	2.70	2.77	2.84	2.91	2.98

Draw a line straight across from the temperature of the beer to the desired volumes of CO₂, then straight up to find the correct psi of your regulator.

Carbonated and sediment-free bottled beer is within the means of the homebrewer who wishes sediment-free or quickly carbonated bottled beer, but the methods are significantly more complex. The beer must be fully carbonated (artificially or otherwise) before it is transferred to the bottle. Homebrewers will begin with a kegged container of chilled and fully carbonated beer and then transfer the beer to bottles under pressure. Pressure is maintained throughout the transfer system of hoses, tubes, and the "counterpressure" bottling gadget so that the carbonated beer will not release any of its dissolved carbon dioxide. The system is referred to as a counterpressure system because the gas pressure exerted by the carbon dioxide in the beer is countered by artificial carbon dioxide pressure from a regulated carbon dioxide source.

The counterpressure bottling device is first placed atop a sanitized bottle, temporarily sealing it with a rubber-like stopper through which gas or liquid can enter or escape. The first step after temporarily sealing the bottle is to purge air out of the bottle by allowing carbon dioxide to flow in and displace the original air by exhausting it. This is accomplished by opening and closing different valves. After the air has been evacuated from the bottle, a valve is shut and carbon dioxide is allowed to continue entering the bottle under a pressure equal to that of the kegged beer, thus pressurizing the bottle at a pressure equal to the pressure of the kegged beer. Next a valve is opened, allowing beer to flow into the bottle, but because of equal pressure in the bottle and keg, there can be no flow until the carbon dioxide in the bottle is slowly evacuated (as the original air was) by opening a valve. Beer slowly flows into the bottle to the desired level. The vent and beer flow valves are shut, the device is removed and the bottle is quickly capped.

The operation is much simplified when four hands are employed. *Safety glasses should always be worn* when operating this device because of the risk of an imperfect or flawed bottle bursting under pressure.

If you have time to consume, an idle mind, and the hankering to try something different, counterpressure bottling may suit your homebrewing hobby. Hand-operated counterpressure devices can be purchased for as little as $75.

THE ZEN OF BOTTLING

Most homebrewers consider themselves slaves to bottling when it comes time to package homebrew. Bottling doesn't need to be a time-consuming chore, requiring extensive preparation time and scheduling. It can be a procedure as spontaneous as having another beer, taking less than an hour of your time.

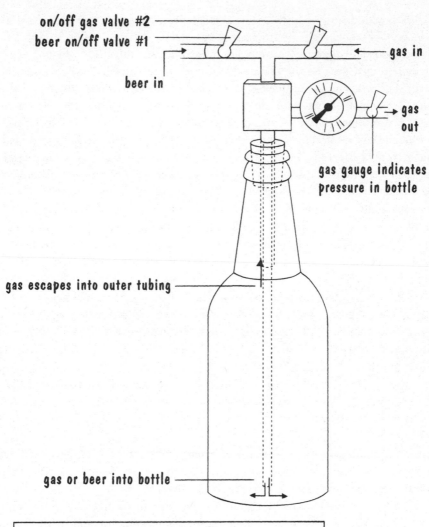

on/off gas valve #2
beer on/off valve #1

gas in

beer in

gas out

gas gauge indicates pressure in bottle

gas escapes into outer tubing

gas or beer into bottle

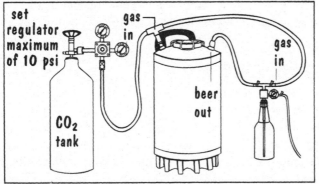

set regulator maximum of 10 psi

gas in

gas in

CO$_2$ tank

beer out

WHEN TO BOTTLE

Until you feel in touch with your fermentation, the trusted hydrometer will continue to give you a true indication of when to bottle. If you've brewed and bottled enough times, you will begin to realize that beer is ready to bottle when it appears a certain way. Easily observable in glass fermenters, an apparent darkening of the brew brought on by clarification and the cessation of bubbles are accurate indications that your beer is ready to bottle (or ready to move on to cold lagering). Hydrometer readings should be taken and recorded during the bottling process, but visual observation can serve well to indicate when the brew is ready to bottle. Practice and confirm with regular hydrometer readings until you are confident about making these judgments.

PREPARING THE BOTTLES

Contrary to the methods you may have been employing, all of your empty bottles should be ready to be filled with beer within a few moments' notice. How can this possibly be?

Between batches of beer, while the beer is fermenting and you have leisure time, take the opportunity to immerse your beer bottles in a 10- to 15-gallon (38–57 l) clean plastic trash can to which about ⅓ cup (79 ml) of household bleach and nearly a total volume of cold tap water have been added. It's a mindless task perfect for soothing a stressed mind numbed from a day's work. It will take all of 5 minutes to totally immerse two to four cases of empties in the sanitizing solution. Let soak overnight or until you are in the mood to take the next step. This could be days or a week later. Take about 15 minutes to drain all of the soaking bottles (do not rinse). Then simply affix a piece of aluminum foil atop them to keep dust and spiders out. Place the bottles in their boxes and store for weeks, months, or years until ready to use. Meanwhile immerse another round of empties in the pail and repeat only when you're good and ready. You'll find that the bottles will be sparkling clean, with stubborn stains vanished. If a particular bottle doesn't come clean, discard the bottle, as it isn't worth your valued time. Rubber gloves should be considered to protect your hands from the chemical and drying effects of the bleach solution.

When you've decided to bottle, simply remove the foil and give the bottle a quick rinse with hot tap water. A homebrew-type bottle rinser will complete this step in 3 seconds, enabling you to prepare and bottle 5 gallons (19 l) of beer as well as clean up within one hour.

Dishwashers are of little use for cleaning because they are comparatively high energy users and may not remove stains and bacterial deposits inside the bottles. There are other sanitizing chemicals that can be substituted for bleach, but they should be tested against the stain-removing capabilities of a dilute household bleach solution. Never mix bleach with other cleaning or sanitizing agents.

Iodine-based sanitizers are available and commonly used in the dairy industry and by many breweries. They are effective sanitizers. When diluted with water in proper proportions, they may be used to sanitize equipment without subsequent rinsing. However, the correct sanitizing proportion of 12½ parts per million (titratable iodine) represents very low concentrations and must be carefully measured. If concentrations exceed the recommended limit, the iodine residue will give beer an undesirable iodine flavor and will be toxic to yeast. A drawback of iodine-based sanitizers is that they stain equipment a yellow-orange color very easily, a stain that's probably impossible to remove.

MOVING THE BEER AND AIR SPACE

As discussed earlier, care should be taken to minimize aeration and oxygen uptake whenever transferring beer. To minimize the detrimental effects of oxidation in bottled beer, reduce the air space, which will reduce the amount of oxygen in the bottle. A half-inch (13 mm) air space is perfectly all right for all bottled beer.

The magical 1- to 1½-inch (25–38 mm) air space that we've become so accustomed to seeing in commercially bottled beer is dictated by high-speed counterpressure bottling machines. As commercial beer undergoes the counterpressure process of bottle filling, there is a brief moment in the assembly line when a filled bottle of beer is open to the air. It is during those split seconds that a needle-thin stream of sterile water is injected into the bottle. The agitated beer foams over perfectly, evacuating the space with carbon dioxide gas released from the beer. A sharp, light spoon-like tap on the outside of a bottle can produce the same effect. The bottle is capped as the "fob" barely oozes over the lip. When the foam subsides, there is that 1 to 1½ inches (2.5–4 cm) of air space.

A small amount of air space is required for proper bottle conditioning, while excessive air space increases the risk of the explosive effect of overcarbonated bursting bottles.

BOTTLES AND BOTTLING EQUIPMENT

Green, brown, or white; long-neck; stubby, returnable, not returnable, twist-off, or not; champagne, glass, or plastic; cap-able; swing-top or cork. These are your choices. Will your choice affect the character of your beer?

BOTTLE COLOR

Your choices will usually be brown, green, or white (clear). Brown bottles are the only type of bottle that offers any reasonable amount of protection from damaging strong light. When beer is allowed to sit in direct sunlight, a photochemical reaction takes place among the bitter-flavored hop molecules. In bright light it happens in less than a minute, and it smells and tastes like a skunk (polecat) smells. It isn't toxic, but for most people it does detract from the flavor. Commercial brewers cannot control how their beer is handled, and if it sits on a store shelf among the artificial lights for extended periods of time, the beer will be affected. Green bottles and clear bottles do not afford any protection whatsoever against damaging light.

As a homebrewer, you have the choice of relaxing, not worrying, and having skunk-free homebrew—from any colored glass bottle. There is no reason to even think about getting paranoid during the bottling process. Artificial light takes days and sometimes weeks to have an effect, if any at all. From your carboy into your bottles and into closed boxes in the quiet of your basement, storeroom, garage, or domestic cave, you've got complete control from bottle to glass. Don't hesitate to use whatever is convenient in terms of colored glass. Only if you plan on entering your beer into competitions should you consider bottling exclusively in brown bottles.

SIZES, SHAPES, AND LIFESTYLE

With proper batch priming, virtually any kind of bottle that has already had beer in it is fair pickings for recycling with homebrew. It is possible to use twist-off glass beer bottles, but one should seek twist-off-type caps to cap them. These special caps may not look much different, but they are thinner, and the more malleable metal is able to conform to the top of the bottle more easily. Regular caps work all right, though the occasional poor seal may result. The action of your bottlecapper will seal either cap to the extent that you probably won't be able to twist off the cap of your homebrewed beer.

Certain types of champagne and specialty beer bottles are well suited for homebrewed beer. All champagne bottles are usable, but some exotic types require a larger diameter bottlecap sometimes available through your local homebrew supply shop. You can always wire down a plastic champagne cork at considerably greater expense than a bottlecap calls for, but if you can afford that kind of champagne or beer, then the expense shouldn't matter.

PLASTIC

Sometimes a very convenient alternative for homebrewers is plastic PET bottles (the kind soft drinks are commonly packaged in). Commonly available in Canada, these bottles are "capped" with a reusable (a few times) plastic screw-on top, bypassing the need for a bottlecapper. The plastic is food-grade, light, easily sanitized, unbreakable, and particularly well suited for traveling and occasions where the risk of glass breakage is high. Over time, oxygen will slowly permeate through the plastic into the beer, but one to three months at cool temperatures with homebrewed care seems to have very little effect on the stability of beer. Aged barley wines and doppelbocks would do better in glass.

There are many laws of this universe. One of them is Boyle's law, which has to do with the observation that gases will seek equilibrium in the environment they are capable of inhabiting. What this all means to both PET bottler and bottlecappers is that though there is pressure in a bottle of beer and it seems that because of that outward pressure, no air would ingress into the beer, it doesn't happen that way. Why? Because the outward pressure is created by only carbon dioxide gas. There is no oxygen gas inside the beer pushing outward; consequently, it's as though the oxygen sees a void and thus it makes its way in, slowly. There is a very small amount of air ingress that bypasses the seal of a bottlecap as well. Seal your bottles securely. But don't worry.

SWING TOPS

Wired porcelain or molded plastic swing-top beer bottles are a great convenience for homebrewers. Porcelain caps are outlawed in some areas, due to the

*Swing-top bottles are particularly convenient while driving elephants through
the deepest of jungles. During my research and over rougher parts of the trail I found
that bottles could be sealed without spilling a drop.
Warning: Don't feed the elephants.*

detrimental effect porcelain has on the glass recycling kilns if inadvertently
mixed in.

These bottles must be sanitized just as any beer bottle, with special care to
assure that the gasket-seal is in good condition and sanitized as well. Removal
and sanitation of the gasket is added insurance against contamination, though
usually not necessary if the bottles are immersed in sanitizing solution for any

length of time. Replacement gaskets are available at most homebrew supply stores.

BOTTLECAPS

There are several types of bottlecaps available on the market. They all may be used for homebrewing with complete confidence. All are lined with a plastic material to help assure a proper seal. The lighter-gauged twist-off caps already discussed help assure better seals on twist-off bottles. There is one special type of cap worth considering usually described as an "oxygen absorbing" bottlecap. Its advanced inner liner creates a better seal against air ingress and also absorbs oxygen in the bottle. It is activated by moisture and best stored in a cool, dry environment. It seems especially perfect for those potentially old barley wines, strong ales, and doppelbocks. They cost more than regular caps, but at least you have the choice.

Here's a tip worth knowing when you intend to set aside beers for prolonged aging. If you are stashing precious beers (whether homebrewed or otherwise) for over a year and you truly intend to drink them, invert the bottle and dip the capped end in a pot of melted paraffin or sealing wax. They can then be stored upright. This works really well for homebrewers and minimizes air ingress into the bottle, thus preventing negative aspects of oxidation. I have tried twenty-five-year-old beers and meads that have held up well with minimal oxidation. This may not work as well in the commercial marketplace, because fluctuations in temperatures can cause wax coatings to crack or lose their seal. Homebrewers and beer collectors handle their stash in a more stable environment.

CORKS

The bottlecap was invented in the 1890s; not that long ago in the 5,000-plus-year history of beer. Closures such as the swing top and cork were often used in former times. Many specialty beers are still corked to this day. Wine corks and hand-operated "corkers" are available through most homebrew and winemaking supply stores. Corks can be sanitized to some degree in grain alcohol or high-proof vodka, though because of their porous nature, alien characters may develop in your beer. With cleanly packaged corks this problem is minimized. Though on occasion an earthen, cellar-like character can develop with corked beer. This may be desirable or undesirable depending on your personal preference. A well-brewed, clean beer should not be otherwise drastically affected.

Because of pressure, corks should be wired down with bottle wires available at home wine- and beermaking supply stores. Champagne-type or heavy-duty bottles are best suited for corking. It is also helpful to immerse the top seal of cork bottled beer into hot melted paraffin or sealing wax. This will help prevent the cork from drying out and losing its seal. For those beers you intend to age, you can still affix a bottlecap over the cork.

BOTTLECAPPERS

There are all manner of bottlecappers. Usually the more expensive they are, the more you are likely to enjoy the process of bottlecapping. Though more affordable than bench-style cappers, two-handed lever cappers are sometimes awkward to use and are prone to snapping the tops off of bottles, especially thin-walled bottles.

Hammercappers should be used as a last resort. If you don't know what I'm talking about, good—you don't need to know.

When choosing a good bench capper, you are investing in a lot of hassle-free bottling sessions and more time to enjoy your homebrew. Choose one that adjusts easily to all sizes of beer bottles and your standard champagne bottle. Though not as easy to find and in short supply, the antique models often found at flea markets are some of the best-designed cappers available. Keep your eye out for that perfect capper.

KEGGING AND DRAFT EQUIPMENT

The most obvious advantage that kegging has over bottling beer is that there aren't any bottles to wash. An additional, not quite as obvious, advantage is that properly kegged beer is less prone to oxidation. The air-space-to-beer-volume ratio is much smaller, reducing the effects of oxidation. Kegged beer—if stored properly—will keep its fresh character for a longer period.

Kegged beer and draft systems are a real treat for those with the resources of space and money to assemble all the necessary equipment to make it happen.

A few disadvantages are worth considering. It is far easier to take a few bottles of assorted homebrew to your friend's party or dinner event. Giving bottled beer as a gift is easier to cope with than giving kegs! Then there's the cost of setting the system up, but if that is not an obstacle, there are several convenient and pleasurable options available to homebrewers. The most common homebrew kegging systems (Cornelius "kegs" and PET plastic "kegs") are described and explained in *The Complete Joy of Homebrewing, Fourth Edition*.

SOME SAFETY AND QUALITY-ASSURANCE CONSIDERATIONS

Before disassembing any beer keg for cleaning, *always* take great care to release all pressure from within the keg. If you are sure you've already done this, check and do it once again. The explosive force of flying keg parts as they are loosened can be lethal. If there is any beer or sediment left over along with pressure, you could also be a prime target for a full-body beer soaking, never mind having to repaint the walls.

Valves, seals, and gaskets after much use will wear out and fail. To help assure yourself of a perfectly conditioned keg of beer, check all seals, valves, and gaskets by adding 5 pounds of carbon dioxide pressure to the just-primed and kegged beer. Work up a good lather of soap and water and smear this lather over all seals and joints or spray on a dilute solution of water and detergent. It's as if you were looking for a leak in a bicycle inner tube; look for air bubbles.

The smallest pinhole or crack in a gasket will result in flat, uncarbonated beer. If you do discover a leak, release all the pressure and attempt to reseat the fixture or seal. Reapply pressure and check again. Keep spare parts on hand to replace worn-out fixtures.

SEDIMENT-FREE DRAFT BEER

There are times when sediment-free draft beer is an option of choice, particularly when you will be traveling into the wilderness for days with only draft homebrew to sustain the spirits.

Sediment-free draft beer can be achieved in two ways, one of which was explained in a previous section dealing with artificial carbonation. A more natural method is not only very simple but inexpensive. A naturally conditioned sedimented keg of beer can be chilled (the closer to freezing, the better) and transferred from one keg to another by means of attaching the outflow fixture to the outflow fixture of an empty keg. Before the transfer, the empty keg is sanitized and purged of air by running carbon dioxide gas into the "out" valve. The tube inside will direct the gas flow to the bottom of the keg. As you release pressure from the "in" valve, air is evacuated and replaced with carbon dioxide. Similarly beer is pushed out of the full keg with carbon dioxide and into the "out" valve to the bottom of the awaiting keg. Releasing pressure from the "in" valve or safety release will allow the flow of sediment-free beer into your new keg. All that is required is an extra short hose and one extra valve fixture.

"ON DRAFT"—DISPENSING BEER

Having to walk to where your keg of beer is located is good exercise. It'll help keep you in shape. Now, why would I mention something like that? If you really get swept away with this hobby of homebrewing, things are likely to get a bit out of hand. It wouldn't surprise me if there is someone, somewhere out there, who has all his or her cold beer stashed in the basement with beer hoses running from a draft system to a bedroom headboard, a bathtub or shower stall, the kitchen, living room, dining room, and patio. It's all quite possible, and whenever homebrewers and possibilities intermingle, well . . . Need I say more?

Yes, much is possible, but when your beer lines are long, you'll need to be a bit more scientific and understand how keg pressure can be compromised with flow resistance, gains or losses in elevation, temperature changes, and a lot more. If you keep your beer lines short and dispense your beer within 3 feet (1 m) of the source, then the dynamics of pressure, flow, and resistance need not be seriously considered. But here are a few tidbits of information to prime your

*Canoe Brew? Sediment-free three-gallon stainless steel kegs are perfect for wilderness
canoeing and those long portages. Using a hand pump to dispense the beer,
I found that Canoe Brew made evenings perfect even when the fish weren't biting.
Pack it in and pack it out—they're ecologically smart, watertight,
and float when empty!*

thoughts if you ever consider putting together an elaborate draft system that runs throughout your castle, or if you want to appreciate the problems a tavern or bar has to deal with when installing a draft system.

- The hose through which beer flows will create varying resistance to flow depending on the inside diameter, hose material, and length. Increased resistance requires more pressure to push the beer from the keg through the hose and into your glass.
- An increase in elevation from the keg to the tap will create resistance to flow and require additional pressure to push the beer through the lines.
- When the pressure required to push the beer through the beer lines is more than the ambient pressure within the keg, then additional carbon dioxide is forced into the beer. The beer gains carbonation. Beer can lose carbonation if the reverse is true.
- The ambient pressure inside the keg is affected by how cold the beer is (refer to the Volumes of Carbon Dioxide table on page 184).
- If the beer lines are long and not insulated, beer can be warmed on its journey to the tap. Warmer beer releases carbon dioxide much more quickly and becomes overcarbonated or foamy.
- Unfortunately, relaxing and drinking lots of homebrew will not help you figure out how to put together a sophisticated system, but referring to other sources of information and doing a little scientific homework will. Here are several references that go into greater detail:
  - *Draught Beer Quality Manual* (Brewers Association)—current edition available online at www.draughtquality.org
  - "Setting Up Your Home Draft System," by Dave Miller, in *Just Brew It!* (Brewers Publications, 1992)
  - "Principles and Characteristics of Beer Dispensing," by Elton Gould, *The New Brewer*, vol. 5, no. 4, published by Brewers Association

The simplest of home draft systems requires a refrigerator, a carbon dioxide system (tank and regulator), a gas line with a fixture to attach to the keg, and a beer hose with a tap valve on one end and a fixture to attach to the keg. If smitten, you can drill holes through the walls of the refrigerator to accommodate hoses carrying pressurized carbon dioxide in and beer hoses out to a tap.

A less sophisticated method requires no adaptation of the refrigerator. Carbon dioxide can be applied only as needed to dispense a desired amount of beer. Simply open the refrigerator door, connect the tap line to the keg, and serve yourself. Add carbon dioxide as necessary. When you are using this method and are finished pouring for the day, top off your keg with about 10 pounds of pressure so that carbon dioxide is not lost from the beer when it attempts to equalize pressure in the air space in the keg.

If you have several kegs of homebrew on tap, a carbon dioxide manifold is a handy device to have. It allows you to split the gas lines and direct carbon dioxide from one tank to several kegs of beer at one time.

Serving cold beer from a warm keg can be done by means of a "jockey box." It allows you to chill only the beer that is actually being poured, saving energy or allowing for a quick and immediate chill. From a room-temperature keg, beer is pushed with carbon dioxide through a hose leading into an insulated box or chest. (Picnic-type coolers work well.) Inside the chest the hose is connected to a length of coiled copper or stainless steel from which the beer flows into a beer tap emerging from the side. Beer is chilled by means of ice and water inside the chest and surrounding the coils. Instant cold beer. Replace ice as needed.

Whenever using carbon dioxide gas for dispensing, *always use a properly functioning regulator.* Unregulated pressure can blow a keg apart and cause fatal injury. As a safety precaution, always turn the gas source off when it is not in use. Leaks can create their own hazards; carbon dioxide is heavier than air and can snuff pilot flames in water heaters and cause asphyxiation.

How long will a keg of beer last? If you dispense with carbon dioxide and have brewed a clean beer, homebrewed beer can last for several months and even a year, but only if you don't consume it in a hurry. The carbon dioxide does not hasten the deterioration of the beer, though with time the beer will naturally age and flavor character will change. For some styles of beer this may be desirable, while for others it may not.

If a carbon dioxide system is not practical or available, draft beer can still be enjoyed by pushing the beer out of the keg with a hand pump. Air is forced into the keg, and beer forced out. This method of dispensing beer is completely adequate as long as the beer is properly chilled and you plan on finishing the keg within the day. Beer will not maintain proper carbonation or its freshness when air is introduced. Air contains spoilage organisms that will eventually turn the beer sour over a matter of a few warm days. But prior to spoilage, much of the carbonation will be lost. Why? Even though you are putting a lot of air pressure into the keg to push the beer out, the beer does not "see" much carbon dioxide gas in the air. There is no carbon dioxide pressure being forced onto the beer and forcing the carbonation to stay in the beer. Even though there is pressure to force beer out, the beer's carbonation "instincts" see no pressure, so it equalizes the dissolved carbon dioxide pressure with the gas carbon dioxide pressure and slowly loses carbonation as the air space gets larger and you and your friends drink more homebrew. Hand-pumped homebrew is best served at colder temperatures.

AT THE TAP

When dispensing beer from a home tapping system, pull the "throttle" out full, even if your beer tends to be overcarbonated. Opening the tap partway only serves to agitate and spray the beer out, and much carbonation is lost. Pouring flat beer from an overcarbonated keg seems contrary, but it happens if you choke the throttle. You're better off pouring a full pitcher at full throttle and letting the foam subside. If you encounter an overcarbonated keg, you can reduce the carbonation by releasing carbon dioxide gas pressure from the safety release (on some kegs) or from the "gas in" valve. Release pressure every few hours or once a day until you can dispense beer with a reasonable amount of carbonation.

Five to 10 pounds per square inch of pressure is a normal range of regulated carbon dioxide pressure with which to dispense beer through a 3-foot-long draft line. Applying more than that may create overcarbonation or too vigorous a flow from the tap.

Your beer hoses and taps should be cleaned regularly. Run hot water and caustic beer cleaner solution through them. Wear protective eyewear. I always wear gloves and eyewear when using caustic! Getting caustic solution in your eyes or on your skin is a serious medical problem. Draft-line cleaning chemicals are available at homebrew supply shops. A perfectly good keg of beer can pick up moldy, sour, and other absolutely wretched flavors and lose all head retention from its quick trip through dirty beer lines. Commercial beer at your favorite beer bar or restaurant should be cleaned every two weeks, otherwise the beer's quality suffers—and you get cheated out of a great beer.

WHAT ABOUT THAT CREAMY GUINNESS HEAD?

It's the gas! For those of you who enjoy draft Guinness Stout, you can appreciate what a thick, creamy head really can be. Almost whipped cream or meringue-like, the head on draft Guinness Stout is created by injecting a mixture of nitrogen (N_2) and carbon dioxide gas into the dispensing system. Guinness and other beers infused with nitrogen are known as "nitro" draft beers. Nitrogen gas, when mixed with beer and agitated, creates very tiny bubbles. Because of the laws of physics, molecular behavior, and surface tensions, these bubbles of nitrogen and carbon dioxide break down very slowly, hence the long-lasting, dense head on draft Guinness and other nitro brews.

Homebrewers can duplicate the Guinness effect to some degree by using the simplest of methods. You will need a tank of nitrogen gas and a special regulator for high-pressure gas. (These are not cheap.) Prime your stout (or other beer) at a rate of ¼ cup (60 ml) of dextrose per 5 gallons (19 l). Apply 20 to 25 pounds pressure of nitrogen to the keg. Note that nitrogen does not dissolve very readily into beer, but it doesn't take very much to create a dense, creamy head. Because nitrogen does not dissolve into beer in great amounts, it is still necessary to carbonate with carbon dioxide.

When the beer is conditioned and chilled, serve as you normally would, but use mostly nitrogen to dispense the beer. Add some carbon dioxide to help maintain carbonation levels. The beer will be dispensed quite forcibly at 20 to 25 pounds pressure, but if it is served cold, once the foam has settled, you will get the head you've been looking for and the typically mild carbonation of a proper draft Guinness.

Another option is to simply purchase a Guinness tap. It comes designed with a flow restrictor for dispensing stout just like your favorite source of draft Guinness.

You can try this with any type of beer.

WHAT ABOUT THE LONG-LASTING, DENSE HEAD OF GERMAN DRAFT PILSENER?

If you ever go to Germany and intend to quickly follow your first glass of Pils with a second, order your second beer as soon as you get your first. You'll wait perhaps 5 to 10 minutes for each pour.

Classic German draft Pilsener is a slow pour. It takes time for the dense, rich head of foam to subside and the barkeep to top off your glass with a fair serving of beer.

Very cold fermentation, hopping with quality "noble"-type aroma/flavor hops, and decoction mashing help build the character of German draft Pilsener. The tapping system and regulation of pressure also have much to do with the quality of the head and carbonation. Pilsener is fully carbonated and dispensed with more than the usual amount of pressure. This practice creates a lot of foam in the glass. The foam is allowed to settle for a few minutes, then the glass is topped off with more beer. It is allowed to settle and then topped off again and again until the portion is correct. Draft Pils is not excessively carbonated, but it has a pleasingly long-lasting head that forms patterns of lace on the sides of your glass as you seek the bottom.

And while we're on the subject of head retention . . . as indicated above, cold fermentation enhances the ability of beer to maintain a head of foam. Warmer fermentations are more likely to create fusel oils (alcohols), which can have a negative impact on head retention.

CLEAR BEER WITH FILTRATION

The average beer drinker has been led to believe that crystal-clear beer is better beer. The clarity of beer can be an indication of its character, but it is not always true that the clearest beer will be the beer of preference. There are clear advantages and disadvantages of filtering beer. Knowing what they are and understanding the basic process will help you decide for yourself to what degree you want to clarify your brew.

You've brewed a batch and have observed its fermentation. With time the yeast has settled to the bottom of your fermenters, kegs, or bottles. And if you cold-lagered your brew for a good length of time, you've observed the formation of chill haze and its eventual settling out. You pour yourself a chilled bottle of clear enough beer, leaving most of the sediment behind in the bottle. You are a perfectly happy homebrewer. You've had a homebrew. You're relaxed. You're not worrying. Why bother with filtering? If this scenario has been your experience, read further with the intent of just knowing what clarity and filtration are about. You needn't read with the avid intent of designing your filtration system or considering the turn of every word as it flies off this page into your brain.

However, if you think it might be great to filter your beer, then consider the following with interest, but not necessarily commitment—yet. Have a homebrew.

Why bother? There are three main reasons why a beer might be filtered.

1. To make it visually more appealing (a subjective preference).
2. To make the beer more quickly suitable for consumption.
3. To help stabilize the character of the beer in some situations.

Brewers are most concerned with removing yeast, bacteria, and/or chill haze. Yeasts are the largest in size, bacteria smaller, and precipitated protein-tannin molecules (chill haze) the smallest. But in the process of removal, other beer characters can be affected. Depending on the circumstances and the brewer's filtration skill, color, hop flavor and bitterness, body (mouthfeel), and head retention all may be reduced. Oxygen or unwanted characters contributed by the filtration material or process can weasel their way into a perfectly brewed and fermented beer.

Beer undergoes filtration as it is forced through a porous surface. The porosity or size of the spaces that the beer passes through determines what remains behind and what is allowed through. "Rough" filtration or relatively more porous material may filter out yeast, but allow bacteria, chill haze, and most of the beer's other character to pass through. As the porosity decreases, the filtration is referred to as being "tighter," and smaller matter will be filtered out of the beer.

If you simply want to make clear, sediment-free beer, then filtration allows you to achieve this. However, if you are bottling filtered beer, you are bottling a beer without yeast. Without yeast, you cannot naturally carbonate beer in the bottle. You may add yeast (perhaps a different strain, as Bavarian wheat beer brewers do), prime, and referment in the bottle, but you will still have sediment. If sediment-free is what you aim for, then you have two choices: (1) Artificially carbonate and counterpressure in the bottle or (2) naturally carbonate your beer in a keg *before* filtration, though the entire filtration process must be done under counterpressure, complicating the process beyond most homebrewers' means, tolerance, and relaxedness.

If your beer has been properly brewed and matured in the fermenter, but the yeast has not had adequate time to settle out, filtration can clarify the beer and allow for artificial carbonation and ready-to-drink beer within hours. However, the temptation for some brewers is to filter and make beer ready before it has properly matured. There are dramatic flavor changes that occur over time with any beer. Some styles of beer will take less than a week to mature, while others may need months. If beer is filtered prematurely, you may indeed produce a clear, yeastless, and bacteria-free beer, but the "greenness" and immature character may be a real turnoff.

The principal reasons why commercial brewers filter their beer are to make it more visually appealing and to help stabilize the character of the beer. *Stabilization* can be a misleading term and is very relative to the process and the conditions under which the beer has been brewed and will be stored. Quality control and consistency are of top priority to commercial brewers. They brew their beer under some of the most sanitary conditions in the food industry. Their beer is in perfect order when it is time to be bottled. Their need for filtration is greater than homebrewers' because, after leaving the brewery, their beers will be transported, stored, and often handled under uncertain conditions. These conditions can be damaging to the character of the beer. Cold and sterile filtration can help stabilize the quality of their beer and minimize damage.

Most commercial brewers also pasteurize their beer before releasing it for consumption. Pasteurization is a process whereby the beer is heated in order to kill all living microorganisms in the beer. The beer can be pasteurized after it is bottled by passing row after row of bottles through hot water spraying in a

Finished beer's long journey to clarity through Enzinger filters at the Coors Brewing Co.

tunnel-like oven. This is called *tunnel pasteurization* and is the most common means of pasteurization. The beer's temperature slowly rises and slowly cools. Properly done, pasteurization will only subtly change the flavor of the beer. If done improperly, it can give the beer an unpleasant cooked flavor. Keg beer cannot be tunnel-pasteurized because of its mass. That is why almost all commercially made keg beer is unpasteurized (there are a few exceptions) and must be properly refrigerated.

Flash pasteurization is a process whereby beer is passed in stainless plumbing through a heat exchanger, where it is quickly heated to pasteurization temperatures, and then flows on to become very quickly cooled. This process is considered less damaging to beer's flavor than tunnel pasteurization, but there is an additional risk of recontamination during bottling or kegging. The pasteurized beer is fully carbonated, then bottled or kegged.

It is very interesting to note here that a small amount of living yeast in finished and fully conditioned beer will *help* stabilize the flavor character of beer. Some commercial breweries are known to add the smallest amount of live yeast back into their fully filtered and/or pasteurized beer just before packaging. Why? Because, in part, yeast scavenge for any available oxygen. Less oxygen in the beer, less oxidizing/staling activity in the beer.

Homebrewers have much more control over the storage conditions of their beer, so the need for filtration is not as urgent. Above all, filtration should never be a means to "fix" poorly brewed beer. Cleanly brewed beer should be much more of a priority than trying to stabilize an infected beer by removing bacteria or wild yeast through filtration. Forget it. You will not fix the beer, nor will you be able to brew a quality product. You may think filtration will extend the drinkable life of your beer by removing the inevitable few bacteria that are present in even the best-brewed beers. But in reality, other favorable beer characters are likely to change for the worse over that extension you thought you "bought." Furthermore, if your beer is that good, why not drink it or share it and brew some more? You and the world will be better off.

If removing tasteless chill haze is a concern, the beer must be chilled to 32 degrees F (0 C) in order to fully precipitate the chill haze. Beer freezes at about 28 degrees F (–2 C). Because chill haze molecules are so small, the tightest filtration is necessary. Unfortunately, with such tight filtration, other beer characters can be affected. Some hop flavor, bitterness, color, head retention, and mouthfeel will be lost in the process. In some cases it can leave the beer tasting empty, suggesting that something is missing. That's a very good thing if you are making American light lager styles of beer. But if character is removed to a degree that detracts from what you intended, you need to compensate by encouraging more of these characters during the brewing process. Experimentation with your particular system will determine to what degree you need to make adjustments.

If you've brewed a clean beer and have allowed the beer to settle its chill haze with cold lagering time, or if chill haze is not an issue for you (especially if you are brewing ales served at temperatures at which chill haze does not form), then a rough filtration will remove most of your yeast, while not affecting other beer characters.

It all may sound discouraging for the homebrewer, but it can be a joy to travel with sediment-free, clear beer. Filtration does have some legitimate uses for those special occasions.

FILTRATION EQUIPMENT

It's going to take some special equipment and a few extra dollars to put together your homebrew filtration system. If you hadn't figured that out by now, perhaps you're relaxing a bit too much. Never mind, though. Now you know. Have another homebrew and rest assured that if you really have the desire, it isn't all that complicated once you've invested the initial time in setting things up.

You'll need a filtering device, hoses to guide the flow of beer, stainless steel Cornelius kegs to hold and receive the beer, and a carbon dioxide system to force the flow of the beer through your filtration system. There are two types of filtration systems that are reasonably accessible to homebrewers. They are plate-type filters and cartridge-type filters.

PLATE-TYPE FILTERS

Costing less than $100 for the smaller models, plate-type filters are available to homebrewers through homebrew supply stores and mail-order outlets. They are constructed of plates of plastic alternately arranged with filter pads. The plates and pads are fitted parallel to one another and then sealed together by tightening wing nuts. There are channels in the plastic plates through which beer is allowed to flow. The beer flows through a series of usually two to five filter pads and is forced through with 5 to 20 pounds per square inch of carbon dioxide pressure.

The filter pads are compressed cellulose material impregnated with diatomaceous earth (also referred to as "d.e." or kieselguhr) and are offered in different porosity grades, depending on whether rough or tight filtration is desired. They are not reusable and must be replaced with new pads each time. Diatomaceous earth is calcified skeletons of microscopic-size diatoms. Their skeletal structure allows liquid to flow through, but not particulate matter.

Attention to sanitation is imperative. The filter pads and system are sanitized before use by first passing a sanitizing solution of ¼ teaspoon (1.2 ml) of household bleach diluted in 2 gallons (7.6 l) of cold water through the system. Then about 1 gallon (3.8 l) of hot boiled water is passed through to rinse off the sanitizing solution. It is important to use boiled deaerated water to rinse the sanitizing solution out of the system. Filter pads impregnated with aerated water will contribute undesirable dissolved oxygen to any beer that flows through the system.

Plate filtration systems are often wet and leaky and should be used in an area where wetness is not a problem. You must anticipate some beer loss. You'll need to discard the initial quart (0.95 l) of beer flow, for it contains a higher proportion of rinsing water and possible paper-like flavors from the filter pads. Leaks and drips will take their toll during the process. Two quarts (1.9 l) of beer loss is not too much to expect and is worth factoring into the overall efficiency of your brewing system. (Two quarts [1.9 l] out of a 5-gallon [19 l] batch is a 10 percent loss. If you were mashing and going to great lengths to achieve that extra 2 or 3 percent mashing efficiency, you may be compromising your earlier efforts during filtration.) You will increase your filtration efficiency as you increase the amount of beer you filter through this type of system. These systems have the potential of filtering more beer at one setup than the alternative system discussed later.

Beware of inexpensive plate-type filtration systems marketed as wine filters. Their design usually cannot withstand the higher pressures sometimes required to push beer through the system. Why? Wine is often quite clear by the time it goes through a filter. The system does not clog up as much and thus does not restrict flow and require additional pressure to push the liquid

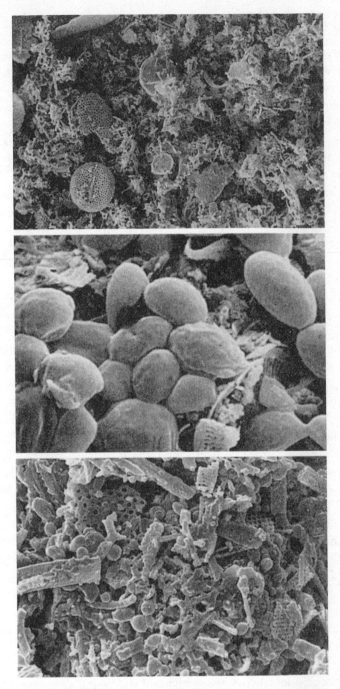

Fossils and yeast. Diatomaceous earth; microscopic skeletons of calcified diatoms provide barriers to yeast cells and bacteria while allowing beer to flow through. Trapped yeast are evident.

Filtration Ratings

POROSITY	TYPE OF FILTRATION	WHAT'S FILTERED
<0.5 micron	sterile, very tight filtration	yeast, bacteria, chill haze
0.5 micron	tight filtration, nearly sterile	yeast, bacteria, most chill haze
0.5–1 micron	medium filtration	yeast, bacteria
1–5 microns	rough filtration	some or most yeast

through. Wine filters or poorly constructed systems will rupture under excessive pressure.

CARTRIDGE-TYPE FILTERS

A cartridge filter system offers the most versatility and ease of operation for homebrewers who are only filtering one 5-gallon (19 l) batch at a time. Beer is pushed through the cartridge-type system with carbon dioxide. The beer enters the sealed cylinder and passes through the outside surface of a cartridge-like filtration device into the core of the cartridge. Once the filtered beer has made its way into the core, the flow is directed out of the cylinder through internal plumbing and an attached hose.

The cartridge filters are usually not reusable. The cylindrical filter housing with fixtures and keg connectors will cost between $50 and $80, while the filters will range in cost from about $5 to $10, depending on the size of the system and the type of filter cartridge you use.

The cartridges are made of inert porous polypropylene plastic. There are two main types of cartridges. Spun polypropylene is the less expensive type and is essentially a string of polypropylene wrapped tightly around a core. The pleated cartridge is more expensive, but is reusable, is easier to use and clean, and lasts longer. It is constructed with a polypropylene pad that is ridged like an accordion and surrounds a core.

Cartridges are available in various porosities, depending on how tight or rough your filtration requirements are. The systems are also rated for efficiency. If tight filtration is your goal, purchase systems that are rated at 99.9 percent efficiency.

The porosity of a cartridge rated for rough filtration can be made tighter with the addition of small amounts of a diatomaceous-earth-and-water/beer "slurry" in the entering beer stream. The tiny skeletons that make up the d.e.

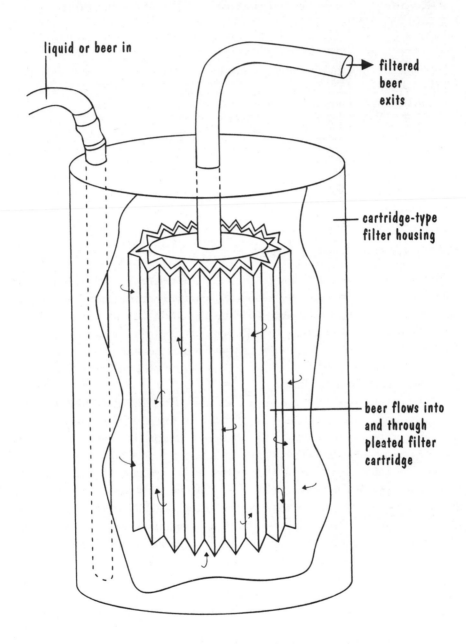

Cartridge-Type Filter

liquid or beer in

filtered
beer
exits

cartridge-type
filter housing

beer flows into
and through
pleated filter
cartridge

build up on the surface of the filtration cartridge and decrease the porosity. This method can also be used to increase the amount of beer you can filter through a limited system such as this. The surface pores of the main filter will eventually become clogged and restrict the flow of beer. If flow is allowed to continue, the filter will eventually become totally restrictive. The hazier the beer, the more quickly this will occur. By adding d.e. to the stream, you are slowly extending and building up the surface area. The cake of tangled microscopic skeletons continues to allow flow, while continuing to catch microscopic critters and chill haze molecules.

The system must be cleaned, sanitized, and rinsed before and after every use. After each use, back-flush the system by forcing hot water through in a reverse direction. Remove the cartridge and inspect it. You may need a forceful jet of water to remove surface material. The cartridge itself should be cleaned by soaking overnight in a caustic lye solution. About 2 tablespoons per gallon of water should be adequate. **Caustic lye can be an extremely dangerous cleaner to work with, causing blindness and/or skin burns if not handled properly. Use protective rubber gloves and eye protection, and carefully read instructions on how to mix it. Never, ever add water to caustic. (The reaction is explosive.) Rather, add caustic to water, slowly and carefully to dissolve it. If you feel slipperiness on your skin when using caustic, that means that your skin is being eaten away!**

After the caustic cleaning, rinse completely with hot tap water and then immerse the cartridge in a weak sanitizing solution of household bleach and cold water. Rinse and store dry in an airtight container. Before using the cartridge, sanitize and rinse it once again.

Once the system is assembled for use, then sanitizing solution followed by boiled deaerated water must be flushed through the entire system to help assure sanitized conditions. As with the plate filters already discussed, there will be a small amount of beer waste, as you will need to discard the first pint of filtered beer exiting the system.

The preceding is a relatively brief overview of how to filter your beer. The details are left up to your own ingenuity and inevitable trial, error, and success. Recall how you felt when you brewed your first batch of beer. The process of filtration may seem rather intimidating and complex at first, but as with any new endeavor, your efforts will become second nature and will reward you with exactly the kind of beer you want. If that's what you want.

MEASURING DEVICES

There are hundreds of ways to measure the hundreds of variables during the beermaking process. Most homebrew supply shops will stock the essentials for what you need to measure.

Here are a few additional hints to consider when measuring.

HYDROMETERS

Glass hydrometers measure specific gravity and/or degrees Balling/Plato. Most hydrometers are calibrated to be accurate at 60 degrees F (15.6 C). Readings must be adjusted if liquids are measured at warmer or cooler temperatures. The following table can be used as a reference.

For example, if your hydrometer indicated that wort at 100 degrees F was 1.030, you must add .006 to the reading to indicate the real 1.036 specific gravity.

Although conversions exist for temperatures above 120 degrees F (49 C), the measurement of hot liquid is neither practical nor safe with glass hydrometers. The temperature shock may stress the glass and cause it to crack. A more reliable and accurate means of measuring the specific gravity of very warm or hot liquid is to pour 1 cup (250 ml) in a saucepan, immerse the saucepan in a bath of cold water, and swirl for a minute. The liquid should be cooled enough to pour into your hydrometer flask and be measured accurately.

THERMOMETERS

Thermometers are used and abused throughout the brewing process. Glass thermometers are prone to break and respond slowly to temperature changes. A probe thermometer with a dial or digital readout is your best investment. Look for accuracy, quick response, and durability.

CHARISMATIC SPOONS AND DIPSTICK MEASURING

As if your brewing spoon weren't charismatic enough, it can also serve as a measuring device. For each brewpot you have in your galley, measure into it water in ½-gallon (2 l) increments. Immerse your spoon in the water and permanently mark (notch, carve, scratch, or otherwise deface) levels at this and each additional ½-gallon (2 l) increment. You can notch a few scales on different sides of the spoon. If your spoon doesn't have a long enough handle, fashion yourself a dipstick. Wood is fine, but never use it to measure cooled wort.

This method of measurement comes in quite handy when estimating evaporation from boiling wort or trying to determine whether what you have in the pot will fit in your fermenter. The time you save by using this device is equivalent to the time it takes to drink one tall, cool glass of homebrew. Now.

Hydrometer Correction

LIQUID TEMPERATURE DEGREES F (C)	CORRECTION TO SPECIFIC GRAVITY (DEGREES BALLING [OR PLATO])
50 (10)	− .0007 (negligible)
60 (15.6)	0
70 (21)	+ .001 (0.25)
78 (25.5)	+ .002 (0.5)
84.5 (29)	+ .003 (0.75)
90.5 (32.5)	+ .004 (1)
96 (35.5)	+ .005 (1.25)
101 (38)	+ .006 (1.5)
106 (41)	+ .007 (1.75)
110 (43)	+ .008 (2)
120 (49)	+ .010 (2.5)

COLOR

The exact color of beer is not of great concern if you are simply going to enjoy the process of making beer and drinking it. However, if you are fine-tuning your skills as a brewer and/or trying to match a beer or attempting to win in competitions, you may wish to consider measuring your beer color.

The color of beer is influenced by several factors during the brewing, fermenting, and handling process. Malt usually has the most significant impact on the color of beer; a discussion of malt and its effect on color is found on page 25.

There are two standard color measurements used by professional brewers. One is the American Standard Reference Method (SRM, nearly identical to the older degrees Lovibond system), and the other is the European Brewing Convention (EBC). Each uses different analytical procedures. It should be noted that each system has its limitations and does not actually measure the color, but rather the intensity of certain types of light. The systems do not recognize the difference between a coppery red beer, an amber, a gold, a yellow, or shades of redless brown.

There is not a dependably calculable relationship between EBC and SRM color units. However, the following relationship is reasonably accurate for gold- or straw-colored beers of about 4 degrees SRM or less. For colors darker than 4 degrees SRM, this calculated relationship is undependable. Doubling the numerical value of SRM to estimate EBC equivalence is the method used in this book. Even though it is quite unscientific, an estimate is better than nothing.

$$\text{degrees EBC} = (2.65 \times \text{degrees SRM}) - 1.2$$

or

$$\text{degrees SRM} = (0.377 \times \text{degrees EBC}) + 0.45$$

The equipment necessary to analyze color using standard methods is far from the means of even the above-average homebrewer. But a simple method of color analysis for beers whose color is less than or equal to 17 degrees SRM was developed by Roger Briess and George Fix. Their method is outlined here with their permission.

The standard for the method is Michelob Classic Dark, brewed by Anheuser-Busch. It is generally widely available and its color is consistently 17 degrees

SRM. The method is quite simple and compares the color of carefully measured dilutions of Michelob Dark with the beer being evaluated. The amount of distilled water it takes to dilute Michelob Dark to appear equal in color to the evaluated beer correlates to the color of beer in degrees SRM.

The authors of this method recommend that distilled water be used as the diluent. Both the Michelob standard and the test beer should be degassed by agitation because dissolved carbon dioxide can affect color. Reflected indirect light sources should be identical when observing samples.

The Color Intensity Curve

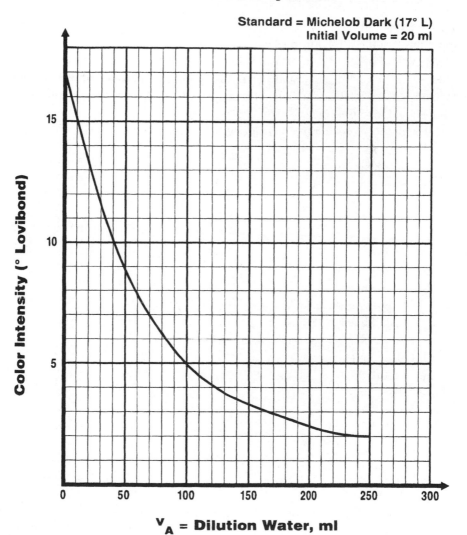

Clear "white" glass long-necks are convenient vessels to use for making comparisons. Syringes or pipettes should be used to accurately measure volumes of liquid. For reference, note that 1 cup = 8 fluid ounces = 237 ml; and 12 fluid ounces = 355 ml.

To make the evaluation, begin with 20 milliliters of degassed Michelob Dark. Add distilled water to the Michelob until it matches the color of the degassed sample. Refer to the chart to determine the color rating of the sample.

PERCEIVED COLOR OR MEASURED COLOR: WHICH IS BETTER?

The American SRM (Standard Reference Method) and EBC (European Brewing Convention) of measuring beer color measure the intensity of a certain wavelength of light. The numerical values assigned to measured "color" do not always coincide with our visual perception of hues, lightness, and darkness. When beers are evaluated in competitions and for enjoyment, the description of color should take priority.

Descriptors of color, ranging from lightest to darkest:

a. Very light
b. Straw
c. Pale
d. Gold
e. Light amber
f. Amber
g. Medium amber
h. Dark amber
i. Copper/garnet
j. Light brown
k. Brown/reddish brown/chestnut brown
l. Dark brown
m. Very dark
n. Black

BEER STYLE GUIDELINES

BACKGROUNDER ON BEER STYLE DEVELOPMENT

From the brewhouse come centuries of mystery, folklore, tradition, and the fine art of brewing, interpreted by each brewer. From modern brewing chemists come statistical and scientific data. Add to this spiritual alchemy, the demands from commercial sales departments calling for a market-oriented product, and the free spirit of the homebrewer—and the vagaries of beer styles become apparent.

American brewers are immersed in one of the most stylistically prolific periods ever. There is an outpouring and appreciation of styles not seen in this country and the world for decades. There are many reasons for the development of beer style guidelines, benchmarks. For one, it is a common language for evaluating beer and communicating about brewing endeavors.

Some brewers and beer enthusiasts believe that styles are defined a bit more than necessary. But in a competition, standards must be established in order to define what the awards represent. Beer style guidelines serve as guideposts or targets to help us direct our brewing efforts and achieve the kind of beer we want.

Furthermore, beer traditions are intertwined with the idea of beer styles. Both serve as a focus for developing and maintaining pride and history within a beer community. They help establish beer passion, respect, enthusiasm, appreciation, and responsible enjoyment. Stylistic awareness moves beer away from being viewed as simply an industrial commodity, a brand, or just another faddish, trendy alcoholic beverage.

Consider the alternative. If beer style education and knowledge were abandoned, all that would be left would be brands and brand culture. Beer brands are primarily driven by breweries. The concept of beer styles and tradition is what binds brewer to brewer and beer drinker to beer drinker. Brand building is an important factor in developing any business, but it is singular and self-serving. That's a good thing if you are running the business. But what about beer enthusiasts such as homebrewers? Beer style culture is a foundation that can be shared and grown by the entire beer community. Be cognizant of brands

and what they represent. Know and enjoy beer styles, their historic and culinary context. And love beer.

Many brewers and beer enthusiasts already appreciate this, but most beer drinkers worldwide have surprisingly little knowledge of the richness, diversity, and flavors of beer's culture. Beer style appreciation nurtures creativity, innovation, and tomorrow's stylistic beer kings.

Guidelines are just that: guidelines. They are a tool. They are not some kind of law or regulation. Their purpose is to help enhance our understanding and the quality of our beer. The art of establishing, changing, and using guidelines is a game we all play. In the end it is our participation as spectators that makes it all worth the playful and meaningful consideration. Glasses full of brew and enjoyment.

Developing beer style guidelines is not a simple endeavor.

Generations of past brewers stand guard over the styles they created and popularized. Modern beer enthusiasts taste traditional styles without the benefit of broad cultural experience. Furthermore, each new American brewer has, by virtue of his or her travels and homebrewing or professional experimentation, developed a personal creative process of recipe formulation.

In a broad sense of the term, there are over a hundred distinctly different ale, lager, and hybrid styles of beer popularly brewed in America. With well-researched information, guidelines serve to help brewers develop an understanding and appreciation for beer traditions. This knowledge can in turn enhance the beer's image and educate the beer drinker.

Furthermore, understanding beer styles is important to:

1. the brewer who endeavors to formulate recipes,
2. the salesperson who communicates beer traditions and culture to the customer,
3. the increasingly sophisticated beer drinker who develops an appreciation and respect for beer as an alcoholic beverage, and
4. federal and state regulatory agencies to help them make informed decisions and rules that are more beer-friendly.

The Beer Styles Table beginning on page 168 in *The Complete Joy of Homebrewing, Fourth Edition* is a detailed outline of data and descriptions of seventy-seven of the most popular beer styles commonly brewed and explored in America. The following information is provided for each style:

Original Gravity (Degrees Plato)
Final Gravity (Degrees Plato)
Percent Alcohol by Volume
Bittering Units
Perception of Hop Bitterness
Perception of Hop Flavor
Perception of Hop Aroma
Color (SRM and EBC)
Color Description

There are many other factors that can influence the character of beer not presented in the *Complete Joy of Homebrewing, Fourth Edition*'s Beer Styles Table. These details could fill another book. They include description and levels of esters, degrees of fermentation (attenuation), body, mouthfeel, carbonation level, pH, types of alcohol, sulfur compounds, a variety of hops, and yeast byproducts. These and many other factors help create a range of complexity within each beer style.

The table includes the following beer types:

ALES

PALE ALE

American Blonde or Golden Ale
Classic English Pale Ale

American-Style Pale Ale
American Wheat
English-Style Summer Ale
English-Style India Pale Ale
American-Style India Pale Ale

BITTER

Ordinary Bitter
Special or Best Bitter
Extra Special Bitter

SCOTTISH ALES

Scottish Light
Scottish Heavy
Scottish Export
Scotch Ale (see Belgian)

GERMAN ALES

Berliner Weisse
Kölsch
Düsseldorf-Style Altbier
Bavarian Hefeweizen/Weissbier (wheat beer)
Bavarian Dunkel Hefeweizen/Weissbier (dark wheat)
Weizenbock/Weissbock

AMBER ALES

Irish Red Ale
American Amber Ale
Imperial or Double Red Ale
Imperial or Double India Pale Ale
English Old Ale
English Strong Ale

BROWN ALES

English Brown
English Mild
American Brown

PORTER

Robust Porter
Brown Porter

STOUTS

Classic Irish Dry Stout
Foreign Export Stout
Sweet Stout
Oatmeal Stout
American-Style Stout
British-Style Imperial Stout
American-Style Imperial Stout

BLACK ALES

American-Style Black Ale

BARLEY/WHEAT WINE

British-Style Barley Wine
American-Style Barley Wine
Wheat Wine

SPECIALTY ALES

Smoked Ales

BELGIAN AND FRENCH STYLES

Belgian Blonde
Belgian Pale Ale
Belgian Pale or Dark Strong Ale
Dubbel
Tripel
Flanders Brown/Red
Scotch Ale
Lambic
Gueuze
Fruit Lambic (Framboise, Kriek, Pêche, Cassis)

Wit/White
French and Belgian-Style Saison
French Bière de Garde

LAGERS

LIGHT LAGERS

Pilseners
German Pilsener
Bohemian/Czech Pilsener
American Pilsener

Other Pale Lagers
Dortmunder/Export/Oktoberfest
Munich Helles

American Light Lagers
Low Carb/Calorie/Lite
American Lager
Australian, Latin American, and Tropical Light Lagers

AMBER LAGERS

American Amber
German Märzen
Vienna (Austrian)
German (Smoked) Märzen Rauchbier

BOCK BEERS (STRONG, DARK, OR LIGHT)

Dark Bock
Heller (Light) Maibock
Doppelbock

DARK LAGERS

American Dark
Munich Dunkel

Schwarzbier
Baltic-Style Porter

HYBRID BEERS/LAGERS, ALES

California Common
Cream Ale

BEER RECIPES

So tell me the truth, is this the first section you turned to upon first reviewing this book? Everyone appreciates recipes, even the master brewer. As it is with most master chefs, it is with master brewers—recipes serve as guidelines and a source of ideas. The skilled homebrewer will consult a recipe or perhaps a number of similar recipes and brew something that is actually an interpretation of the original.

By now we can all appreciate the incredible number of variables during the brewing and fermentation processes—ingredients, equipment, process, and handling—that are absolutely different with every brewer. A recipe can offer a meaningful target, but the nuances of your homebrewing system must be taken into consideration. Yours will be a different but similar beer.

If you've read this book from the beginning, you will read these recipes knowing how to tweak the hops, adjust the grind, control the temperature, culture your yeast, or adapt your water in order to maximize the efficiency of whatever brewing system you've put together. More or less, higher and lower, shorter and longer, this for that—you'll be taking into consideration a lot of information and applying the invaluable asset of your own brewing experience.

Use the recipes as they are or feel free to adapt them to your own situation. Whatever you brew will certainly serve as a homebrewer's companion during your next brewing session.

TABLE OF RECIPES

(continued)

TABLE OF RECIPES

TABLE OF RECIPES

A FEW ASSUMPTIONS

- Whole hops are used in all recipes, unless otherwise specified. If substituting hop pellets for whole hops, reduce hop amounts by 10 to 15 percent when considering bitterness contribution.
- All hops are American hops unless otherwise specified.
- Bitterness units will always refer to (International) Bitter Units and not Homebrew Bittering Units unless explicitly mentioned.
- A concentrated wort boil is done for all malt extract or mash-extract recipes. If a full wort boil is used, you may wish to reduce the hop rates to about 75 percent of the amount called for in the recipe when considering bitterness and hop utilization.
- Mashing systems are assumed to be about 75 to 80 percent efficient. For less efficient systems, more grain may be needed to match recipe yields. Extract ratings of your grain may vary from one purchase to another and especially from one crop to another. Anticipate a ± 5 percent deviation with small 5-gallon batch brewing.
- Dissolved minerals in brewing water can affect extract yield in mashing. Recipes assume the use of soft, noncarbonate water. Adjust amount of malt and lautering techniques if carbonate water is used.
- Dissolved minerals can affect the hop utilization and especially the perception of bitterness. Recipes assume the use of soft water unless otherwise noted. If minerals such as sulfate for Burton-type pale ales are added (or are present in your water), then adjust your hopping rates to compensate for the effect of the minerals.
- Relatively ideal fermentation temperatures are assumed in describing the character of beer resulting from each recipe. If you have less than ideal temperature control, you may wish to adapt by experimenting with yeast strains that minimize the effect of having less than ideal fermentation temperatures.
- A quality liquid or dry culture of ale or lager yeast is always assumed. Sometimes a specific strain will be recommended, but you should use your own experience to determine which strain will work best for you.
- Color is indicated in degrees SRM (and EBC in parenthesis).
- Original gravity (OG) and final gravity (FG) are in units of specific gravity (and degrees Balling/Plato).

Hop Utilization Based on Density of Boiled Wort and Boiling Time

In Percent Utilization for Whole Hops (and Hop Pellets)
(From The Complete Joy of Homebrewing, Fourth Edition)

Approx. Specific Gravity of Boil (B)	1.040 (10)	1.070 (17.1)	1.110 (25.9)	1.130 (30)	1.150 (34)
Pounds of Malt Extract per Gallon of Boiling Water	1 (0.45 kg)	2 (0.9 kg)	3 (1.4 kg)	4 (1.8 kg)	5 (2.3 kg)
Time of Boil					
15 minutes	8% (9.6%)	7% (8%)	6% (7%)	6% (7%)	5% (6%)
30 minutes	15% (18%)	14% (17%)	12% (14%)	11% (14%)	10% (12%)
45 minutes	27% (30%)	24% (29%)	21% (25%)	19% (23%)	18% (21%)
60 minutes	30% (30%)	27% (30%)	23% (27%)	21% (25%)	20% (24%)

ALES

ENGLISH- AND AMERICAN-STYLE PALE AND AMBER ALES (MODERATE STRENGTH)

Jack Union's Classic Pale Ale (All Grain)

Let's wave the real flag of Great Britain. English Fuggles and Kent Goldings on a field of amber waves of grain. Yes, that would be a flag we would all salute and toast to, whether we're loyal, royal, or Yank. Cheers! To a pint of tradition. True English malts and some of the finest heirloom varieties of hops blend to make Jack Union's Classic Pale Ale one of the most memorable English-style ales you'll ever brew. In the bottle, call it a pale ale. On draft, let's call it something a little bit more than ordinary. I prefer special bitter because it's homebrewed and every bit as close as you could ever be to English soil.

Ingredients for 5 gallons (19 l):

7½ lb. (3.4 kg)	English Marris Otter 2-row pale ale malt
1 lb. (0.45 kg)	English crystal or caramel malt (40–50 L)
1 oz. (28 g)	English Fuggles hops (boiling): 5 HBU (140 MBU)
½ oz. (14 g)	English Kent Goldings hops (boiling): 2 HBU (56 MBU)
½ oz. (14 g)	English Kent Goldings hops (10 minutes, flavor)
1 oz. (28 g)	English Kent Goldings hops (2 minutes, aroma)
2 tsp. (8 g)	gypsum (calcium sulfate)
¼ tsp. (1 g)	Irish moss powder
*	English-type ale yeast
¾ c. (175 ml)	corn sugar (dextrose) or 1¼ c. (300 ml) dried malt extract (for bottling); or ⅓ c. (80 ml) corn sugar (dextrose) for kegging

O.G.: 1.045–1.049 (11–12)
F.G.: 1.010–1.014 (2.5–3.5)
Bitterness: 36; Color: 13 SRM (26 EBC); Alcohol: 4.6% by volume

A one-step infusion mash is employed to mash the grains. Add gypsum to very soft water at a rate of 2 teaspoons (8 g) per 5 gallons (19 l) of water. Add 7 quarts (6.7 l) of 168-degree F (76 C) water to the crushed grain, stir, stabilize and hold the temperature at 152 degrees F (66.5 C) for 60 minutes. Then raise temperature to 167 degrees F (75 C), lauter and sparge with 3½ gallons (13.5 l) of 170-degree F (77 C) water. Collect about 5½ gallons (21 l) of runoff. The sweet wort ends in your brewpot.

Add the boiling hops, bring to a full and vigorous boil, and boil for 60 minutes. Add the flavor hops and Irish moss for the last 10 minutes of the boil. Add the aroma hops for the final 2 minutes of the boil.

After a total wort boil of 60 minutes, turn off the heat and place the pot (with cover on) in a running cold-water bath for 45 minutes. Continue to chill in the immersion or use other methods to chill your wort. Then strain and sparge the wort into a sanitized fermenter. Bring the total volume to 5 gallons (19 l) with additional cold water if necessary. Aerate the wort very well.

Pitch the yeast when temperature of wort is about 70 degrees F (21 C). Ferment at about 70 degrees F (21 C) for about 1 week or until fermentation shows signs of calm and stopping. Rack from your primary to a secondary and "cellar" the beer at about 55 degrees F (12.5 C) for about 1 week.

Prime with sugar and bottle or keg when fermentation is complete.

Tits Up in the Mud Best Bitter (Malt Extract)

This one has to do with remembering the joy of brewing your first malt extract beer. It was simple and easy. This extract recipe is a reminder of the quality that still can be brewed using quality malt extract and knowledgeable procedures. Pigs may never fly but they can be happy, and when they are they may begin to feel what we feel when enjoying a great beer. Tits Up in the Mud Best Bitter is exactly what you've tasted fresh at the local pub somewhere in England. There's a definitive dose of English hops that contributes to the crisp, clean, and delicious refreshment. It recalls the character of English bitter you're likely to find around London or in the southern hop-growing areas of England. The aroma, the appearance, the taste, the sound, and the quench of a thirsty throat will warm the cockles of your heart. Surely shut your eyes and feel as happy as a pig lying tits up in the mud.

Ingredients for 5 gallons (19 l):

5 lb. (2.27 kg)	light dried English malt extract or 5.9 lb. (2.7 kg) light malt extract syrup
½ lb. (227 g)	English dark crystal or caramel malt (20 L)

1½ oz. (43 g)	UK Challenger hops (boiling): 7 HBU (196 MBU)
½ oz. (14 g)	English Kent Goldings hops (15 minutes, flavor): 2.5 HBU (70 MBU)
½ oz. (14 g)	English Kent Goldings hops (2 minutes, aroma)
½ oz. (14 g)	English Kent Goldings hop pellets (dry hopping)
¼ tsp. (1 g)	Irish moss powder
*	English-type ale yeast
¾ c. (175 ml)	corn sugar (dextrose) or 1¼ c. (300 ml) dried malt extract (for bottling); or ⅓ c. (80 ml) corn sugar (dextrose) for kegging

O.G.: 1.045 (11)
F.G.: 1.008–1.012 (2–3)
Bitterness: 32 BU; Color: 13 SRM (26 EBC); Alcohol: 4.6% by volume

Place crushed grains in 1½ gallons (5.7 l) of 150-degree F (68 C) water and let steep for 30 minutes. Then strain out (and rinse with 3 quarts [3 l] hot water) and discard the crushed grains reserving the approximately 2 gallons (7.6 l) of liquid.

Add the malt extract and boiling hops, bring to a boil, and boil for 60 minutes. Add the flavor hops for the last 15 minutes of the boil. Add the Irish moss for the last 10 minutes. Add the aroma hops for the final 2 minutes.

After a total wort boil of 60 minutes turn off the heat and immerse the covered pot of wort in a cold-water bath and let sit for 30 minutes or the time it takes to have a couple of homebrews.

Then strain out and sparge hops and direct the hot wort into a sanitized fermenter to which 2½ gallons (9.5 l) of cold water has been added. If necessary add additional cold water to achieve a 5-gallon (19 l) batch size. Aerate the wort very well.

Pitch the yeast when temperature of wort is about 70 degrees F (21 C). Ferment at about 70 degrees F (21 C) for about 1 week or until fermentation shows signs of calm and stopping. Rack from your primary to a secondary and "cellar" the beer at about 55 degrees F (12.5 C) for about 1 week.

Prime with sugar and bottle or keg when fermentation is complete.

This style lends itself especially well to kegging. Use only ⅓ cup corn sugar (dextrose) or ½ cup dried extract if keg-conditioning.

Quite Contrary American-Style India Pale Ale (All Grain)

Mary Mary
Quite contrary
How does your garden grow?

I don't know what caused Mary to become contrary but I can relate. Home-brewers are missing out on an interesting and tasty opportunity if they refer to corn and rice as "cheap adjuncts." Think about it. Why do we revere the use of sugar in fine Belgian-style strong ales? Why do we celebrate the complexities of wheat beer? Why do we speak of the splendor of oats and unmalted barley in our stouts. When many beer enthusiasts hear that corn and rice are in their beer they get apoplectic, when they should get apHOPlectic. Okay, maybe you may not exactly cherish light lager beers using corn and rice that have had the flavor refined out of them. But why blame corn and rice?

So over the past two years, just like Mary, you too can become contrary. Corn and rice can be used in many styles of beer to actually enhance and brighten hop character.

I've brewed Pilsener-type lagers using ten to twenty percent rice, accenting the flavor and aromatic nuances of unusual and hard-to-find hops. Equally the lighter base which rice provides can also elevate the complex nuances of many specialty malts. In particular I've enjoyed complementing rice with aromatic-type malts.

Maybe Mary was a homebrewer? Maybe she brewed Quite Contrary, an IPA with rice flakes at a rate of ten percent. I have, and it has all the IPA hop bitter, flavor, and aromatic strength of world-class IPAs but with a subtle dryness and crispness that enhance malt and hop complexity.

Don't be surprised if your beer-loving friends applaud: "This beer is really good, what is it? I really like this beer. I'll have some more."

Ingredients for 5 gallons (19 l):

7 lb. (3.2 kg)	2-row Marris Otter malt
1 lb. (454 g)	crystal malt (15 L)
1 lb. (454 g)	rice flakes
6 oz. (168 g)	aromatic-type malt
9 oz. (252 g)	dark or amber *rapadura* (Brazilian dried cane juice; sometimes called Sucanat)
²⁄₃ oz. (18 g)	Simcoe or Australian Galaxy hop pellets (boiling): 12% alpha, 8 HBU (222 MBU)
³⁄₄ oz. (21 g)	Amarillo or Centennial hops (boiling): 10.5 HBU (294 MBU)
1¹⁄₂ oz. (42 g)	Cascade hops (30 minutes, flavor): 7.5 HBU (210 MBU)
1¹⁄₂ oz. (42 g)	Cascade hops (10 minutes, aroma, flavor): 7.5 HBU (210 MBU)
3 oz. (84 g)	Cascade hops (2 minutes, aroma)
2 oz. (56 g)	Citra hops (1 minute, aroma)

½ oz. (14 g)   Simcoe or Australian Galaxy or Columbus hop pellets
                (dry hopping)
¼ tsp. (1 g)   Irish moss powder
*   English- or American-type ale yeast
¾ c. (175 ml)   corn sugar (dextrose) or 1¼ c. (300 ml) dried malt extract
                (for bottling); or ⅓ c. (80 ml) corn sugar (dextrose) for kegging

O.G.: 1.054 (13.5)
F.G.: 1.014 (4.5)
Bitterness: 108 (calculated), tastes like 55–65 BU; Color: 10 SRM
    (20 EBC); Alcohol: 5.3% by volume

A step infusion mash is employed to mash the grains. Add 9½ quarts (9 l) of 143-degree F (61.5 C) water to the crushed grains and rice flakes, stir, stabilize and hold the temperature at 132 degrees F (53 C) for 30 minutes. Add 4.75 quarts (4.5 l) of boiling water and add heat to bring temperature up to 155 degrees F (68 C) and hold for about 45 minutes. Then raise temperature to 167 degrees F (75 C), lauter and sparge with 3½ gallons (13.5 l) of 170-degree F (77 C) water. Collect about 5½ gallons (21 l) of runoff.

Add the boiling hops and *rapadura* sugar, bring to a full and vigorous boil, and boil for 60 minutes. Add 1½ ounces of the Cascade hops for the last 30 minutes. Add the Irish moss and another 1½ ounces of the Cascade hops for the last 10 minutes. Add 3 ounces Cascade hops for the last 2 minutes. Add the aroma hops for the final 1 minute.

After a total wort boil of 60 minutes, turn off the heat and place the pot (with cover on) in a running cold-water bath for about 45 minutes. Continue to chill in the immersion or use other methods to chill your wort. Then strain and sparge the wort into a sanitized fermenter. Bring the total volume to 5 gallons (19 l) with additional cold water if necessary. Aerate the wort very well.

Pitch the yeast when temperature of wort is about 70 degrees F (21 C). Ferment at about 70 degrees F (21 C) for about 1 week or until fermentation shows signs of calm and stopping. Rack from your primary to a secondary and add the hop pellets for dry hopping. If you have the capability, "cellar" the beer at about 55 degrees F (12.5 C) for about 1 week.

Prime with sugar and bottle or keg when fermentation is complete.

Zymurgific English-Style Summer Ale (All Grain)

English summer ales are the Brits' answer to summer's on-again, off-again sun-shine and with a bit of rain to keep things green. It's an English-style wheat beer; a specialty beer refreshment traditionally brewed for the season. This recipe is brewed a bit on the hoppy side, for the American beer enthusiasts in-

clined for something hoppy. It's light straw to golden colored with medium-low to medium bitterness, light to medium-light body, and low to medium residual malt sweetness. Torrefied and/or malted wheat is often used in quantities of 25 percent or less. Malt character involves your mind with biscuit-like malt with a moderate level of English hop flavor and aroma. This one will refresh and quench. Terrifically Zymurgific!

Ingredients for 5 gallons (19 l):

5 lb. (2.3 kg)	English 2-row malt (Marris Otter if available)
¼ lb. (114 g)	aromatic malt
½ lb. (227 g)	wheat malt
¾ lb. (340 g)	torrefied wheat
½ lb. (227 g)	dark Brazilian *rapadura* "sugar" or other brown sugar
¾ oz. (21 g)	UK Northdown or UK Palisade™ hops (boiling): 6 HBU (68 MBU)
¾ oz. (21 g)	UK Goldings or UK WGV (Whitbread Goldings Variety) hops (10 minutes, flavor)

⅓ oz. (9 g)	UK Goldings or Crystal hop pellets (dry hopping, aroma)
1 tsp. (4 g)	gypsum (calcium sulfate) if your water has a low mineral content
¼ tsp. (1 g)	Irish moss powder
*	your favorite English ale yeast; Wyeast 1275 English Thames Valley or White Labs English Ale yeast are excellent
¾ c. (180 ml)	corn sugar (dextrose) or 1¼ c. (300 ml) dried malt extract (for bottling); or ⅓ c. (80 ml) corn sugar (dextrose) for kegging

O.G.: 1.040 (10)
F.G.: 1.010–1.012 (2.5–3)
Bitterness: 28 BU; Color: 8 SRM (16 EBC); Alcohol: 4% by volume

A step infusion mash is employed to mash the grains. Add 6½ quarts (6 l) of 143-degree F (61.5 C) water and gypsum to the crushed grain, stir, stabilize and hold the temperature at 132 degrees F (53 C) for 30 minutes. Add 3¼ quarts (3 l) of boiling water and add heat to bring temperature up to 155 degrees F (68 C) and hold for about 45 minutes. Then raise temperature to 167 degrees F (75 C), lauter and sparge with 4 gallons (15 l) of 170-degree F (77 C) water. Collect about 5 gallons (19 l) of runoff. Add additional water to bring total volume to about 5¼ gallons (20 l) for the boil.

Add the boiling hops and *rapadura* sugar, bring to a full and vigorous boil, and boil for 60 minutes. Add the flavor hops and Irish moss for the last 10 minutes of the boil.

After a total wort boil of 60 minutes, turn off the heat and place the pot (with cover on) in a running cold-water bath for about 45 minutes. Continue to chill in this immersion or use other methods to chill your wort. Then strain and sparge the wort into a sanitized fermenter. Bring the total volume to 5 gallons (19 l) with additional cold water if necessary.

Aerate the wort very well. Pitch your yeast when temperature of wort is about 70 degrees F (21 C). Once visible signs of fermentation are evident primary ferment at temperatures between 65 and 70 degrees F (18–12.5 C) for about 1 week or until fermentation shows signs of calm and stopping. Rack from your primary to a secondary and add the hop pellets for dry hopping. If you have the capability, "cellar" the beer at temperatures between 50 and 55 degrees F (10–13 C) for 7 to 10 days.

Prime with sugar and bottle or keg when fermentation is complete.

BaBaBa Bo Amber Ale (Malt Extract)

Crazy. Just crazy. Crazy about brew. That's how you began and you realize you still are. Here's a simple malt extract recipe as a reminder of how excited you were when you brewed that first great batch of beer.

So you like Scottish-style ales? You like them hopped, mild, tawny, or light. Pint after pint you've sampled the best, and there seems to be so much variation. You've come to the conclusion that you like them all; there isn't a best. It depends on your mood and the company. Indeed, there are so many great Scottish ales throughout the Scottish countryside. Somewhere and sometime you'll come across a Scottish ale akin to Bababa Bo Amber Ale.

The bitterness level in this homebrewed Scottish ale is somewhat lower than what you might find in traditional English bitters. With this Scottish ale the lower bitterness is balanced nicely with excellent hop flavor and aroma. A good dose of crystal malt lends a fresh caramel character that increases Bababa Bo's drinkability. A favorite that you will brew more than once—I am sure.

Ingredients for 5 gallons (19 l):

5 lb. (2.27 kg)	light dried malt extract or 5.9 lb. (2.7 kg) light malt extract syrup
1 lb. (0.45 kg)	crystal or caramel malt (20 L)
2 oz. (56 g)	chocolate malt
1 oz. (31 g)	Styrian, UK, or American Goldings hops (boiling): 6 HBU (168 MBU)
½ oz. (14 g)	Styrian Goldings hops (15 minutes, flavor): 3 HBU (84 MBU)
¼ oz. (7 g)	any type Goldings hop pellets (dry hopping, aroma)
¼ oz. (7 g)	Cascade hop pellets (dry hopping, aroma)
1 tsp. (4 g)	gypsum (calcium sulfate)
¼ tsp. (1 g)	Irish moss powder
*	English or American ale yeast
¾ c. (175 ml)	corn sugar (dextrose) or 1¼ c. (300 ml) dried malt extract (for bottling); or ⅓ c. (80 ml) corn sugar (dextrose) for kegging

O.G.: 1.048 (12)
F.G.: 1.010–1.014 (2.5–3.5)
Bitterness: 26 BU; Color: 16 SRM (32 EBC); Alcohol: 5% by volume

Add the crushed crystal and chocolate malts to 2 gallons of 150-degree F (66 C) water and hold for 30 minutes. Remove the grains with a strainer.

Add the malt extract, boiling hops, and gypsum; bring to a boil and boil for 60 minutes. Add the flavor hops for the last 15 minutes of the boil. Add the Irish moss for the final 10 minutes.

After a total wort boil of 60 minutes, turn off the heat and place the pot (with cover on) in a running cold-water bath for 30 minutes. Immerse the covered pot of wort in a cold-water bath and let sit for 30 minutes or the time it takes to have a couple of homebrews.

Then strain out and sparge hops and direct the hot wort into a sanitized fermenter to which 2½ gallons (9.5 l) of cold water has been added. If necessary add additional cold water to achieve a 5-gallon (19 l) batch size. Aerate the wort very well.

Pitch your yeast when temperature of wort is about 70 degrees F (21 C). Once visible signs of fermentation are evident primary ferment at temperatures between 65 and 70 degrees F (18–12.5 C) for about 1 week or until fermentation shows signs of calm and stopping. Rack from your primary to a secondary and add the hop pellets for dry hopping. If you have the capability, "cellar" the beer at temperatures between 50 and 55 degrees F (10–13 C) for 7 to 10 days.

Prime with sugar and bottle or keg when fermentation is complete.

Jokester Mild Ale (All Grain)

You're someplace hot and tropical. It's humid. There's an overhead fan circulating the heavy air. Palm trees and infinite green seem to extend beyond the monkey forest just across the street. Are you thirsty yet?

What kind of beer would you brew for a tropical climate? Perhaps it might be a brew that had more guts, more balls, more hops, more malt—yet at a refreshing 3.5 to 4.0% alcohol content. Sound familiar? Maybe not, but you can't beat the great robust flavor in the mildly alcoholic brews from England. There's no need for the planet to shortchange beer drinkers' access to truly legendary and great-tasting beers for tropical pleasure. You're a homebrewer, so if you're warm and thirsty, seeking flavor, go for Jokester Mild.

Jokester Mild Ale showcases the subtle flavors of some very distinctive malts and sugars. Used in moderation the malt character in this beer creates balance even with an elevated hop bitterness, flavor, and aroma. Nothing is overdone. Note the 50 BUs of bitterness. The number is deceiving. Yes that's quite a bit, but with the particular variety of hops used, and the moderate addition of specialty malts, balance reigns.

Use a pipette to add 2 drops of Styrian Goldings hop oil to the secondary fermenter or to the beer at bottling/kegging. No more. No less. If you can get your hands on some, it's worth experiencing. When the hop oil is used in moderation, the flavor and aroma become well integrated and are not "overexposed" in the beer.

Ingredients for 5½ gallons (21 l):

    5 lb. (2.3 kg)   Marris Otter pale malt
    1 lb. (454 g)   English brown malt
    ½ lb. (117 g)   crystal malt (10 L)

¼ lb. (113 g)	aromatic malt
3 oz. (84 g)	Belgian Special-B malt
8.8 oz. (250 g)	dark Brazilian *rapadura* sugar (or other dark sugars with caramel and molasses character)
1 oz. (28 g)	UK Fuggles or Willamette hops (boiling): 7.5 HBU (140 MBU)
½ oz. (21 g)	Goldings or Vanguard hops (boiling): 3.8 HBU (105 MBU)
1 oz. (28 g)	UK Kent Goldings hops (5 minutes, flavor/aroma)
2 drops	Styrian Goldings hop oil
¼ tsp. (1 g)	Irish moss powder
*	English-type ale yeast
¾ c. (175 ml)	corn sugar (dextrose) or 1¼ c. (300 ml) dried malt extract (for bottling); or ⅓ c. (80 ml) corn sugar (dextrose) for kegging

O.G.: 1.039 (10)
F.G.: 1.010–1.011 (2.5)
Bitterness: 50 BU; Color: 16 SRM (32 EBC); Alcohol: 3.8% by volume

A step infusion mash is employed to mash the grains. Add 7 quarts (6.7 l) of 143-degree F (61.5 C) water to the crushed grain, stir, stabilize and hold the temperature at 132 degrees F (53 C) for 30 minutes. Add 3½ quarts (3.3 l) of boiling water and add heat to bring temperature up to 155 degrees F (68 C) and hold for about 30 minutes. Then raise temperature to 167 degrees F (75 C), lauter and sparge with 3½ gallons (13.5 l) of 170-degree F (77 C) water. Collect about 5½ gallons (21 l) of runoff.

Add the boiling hops, bring to a vigorous boil, and boil for 60 minutes. Add the Irish moss for the last 10 minutes of the boil. Add the flavor/aroma hops for the final 5 minutes.

After a total wort boil of 60 minutes, turn off the heat and place the pot (with cover on) in a running cold-water bath for 45 minutes. Continue to chill in the immersion or use other methods to chill your wort. Then strain and sparge the wort into a sanitized fermenter. Bring the total volume to 5½ gallons (21 l) with additional cold water if necessary. Aerate the wort very well.

Pitch the yeast when temperature of wort is about 70 degrees F (21 C). Ferment at about 70 degrees F (21 C) for about 1 week or until fermentation shows signs of calm and stopping. Then prepare for racking/transfer to secondary.

Use a pipette to add 2 drops of hop oil to ½ ounce ethanol or high-strength neutral spirits in a clean and sanitized glass. Dissolve and disperse into solution and observe that it turns milky in appearance. Add 4 ounces of beer (pasteurized light lager works great) to this alcohol and hop oil mixture, mix well, and then add to secondary fermenter.

Rack from your primary to the "hop oiled" secondary. If you have the capability, "cellar" the beer at about 55 degrees F (12.5 C) for about 1 week.

Prime with sugar and bottle or keg when fermentation is complete.

BELGIAN- AND GERMAN-STYLE LIGHT, AMBER, AND BROWN ALES

Golden Valley (or Val) Epiphany Ale (All Grain)

There are some beers that are simply genius. This one is a clone of a Trappist ale brewed in Belgium's Villers-Devant Golden Valley. "Golden valley" loosely translated into a Flemish-French "mash-up" is *val d'or*, probably shortened to *or val* and yes this recipe is about replicating the spirit of world-famous Orval. It's a pale ale that transcends to heaven as time slowly passes. A most unusual of beers perfectly suited to the interests of homebrewers. When ready for your enjoyment it is a hoppy pale ale, complete with hop aromatics. As time passes the hop aromatics recede and the *Brettanomyces* yeast begin to transform the beer experience. A faint hint of the *Brett* character develops after 4 to 6 months. It eventually progresses to a complex, fruity, and *Brett*-induced brew through the years and then diminishes after it peaks, offering different experiences after a decade or perhaps two. I once had a twenty-five-year-old Orval, still in great shape but with little hop and very reduced *Brettanomyces* character left.

Here are a few Orval insights that were revealed to me by Orval brewmaster Jean-Marie Rock, over several beers at a hillside cafe/bar in the small village of Chiny:

- Orval yeast regimes will provide a desired 90 to 100 percent yeast attenuation over time.
- Sugar is used in the recipe formulation.
- Sugar is used as priming for bottle conditioning.
- The beer is dosed with *Brettanomyces* yeast at bottling.
- In some lambic breweries *Brettanomyces* is carefully cultured with oak wood chips in order to provide a sugar source (cellobiase hydrolyzes some wood compounds), which helps maintain health and consistency of performance. But Orval does only a simple propagation and adds a "mini" quantity at bottling.
- 50 EBC (about 20 SRM) crystal malt and Pils malt are used in the formulation.
- Original fresh-tasting Bittering Units are perceived (by me) to be at 37–42 BUs.

Orval brewmaster Jean-Marie once explained to me, "To make beer is simple . . . why make it so complicated . . . Americans want to make beer-making so complicated . . . Why do people want to copy Orval? They should make their own beer and keep it simple like I have." Great words of advice—brew your own beer!

Your Golden Valley ale will serve as your own epiphany of a road less traveled.

Ingredients for 5 gallons (19 l):

6½ lb. (3 kg)	Pilsener malt
½ lb. (227 g)	crystal malt (20 L)
1 lb. (454 g)	white sucrose sugar or candi sugar
½ oz. (14 g)	Tomahawk™ (or Columbus/Zeus) whole hops (boiling): 7.5 HBU (210 MBU)
½ oz. (14 g)	German Hallertau whole hops (boiling): 2.5 HBU (70 MBU)
½ oz. (14 g)	Styrian Goldings hop pellets (dry hopping, aroma)
¼ tsp (1 g)	Irish moss powder
*	High-attenuating healthy culture of English ale yeast such as White Labs WLP515 Antwerp Ale Yeast or WLP007 Dry English Ale Yeast or Wyeast 1335 British Ale II™
*	*Brettanomyces* yeast culture
½ c. (115 ml)	corn sugar (dextrose) (priming bottles)

O.G.: 1.052 (13)
F.G.: 1.005–1.011 (1.2–2.5)
Bitterness: 40 BU; Color: 6 SRM (12 EBC); Alcohol: 6.2% by volume

A step infusion mash is employed to mash the grains. Add 7 quarts (6.7 l) of 143-degree F (61.5 C) water to the crushed grain, stir, stabilize and hold the temperature at 132 degrees F (53 C) for 30 minutes. Add 3½ quarts (3.3 l) of boiling water and add heat to bring temperature up to 155 degrees F (68 C) and hold for about 30 minutes. Then raise temperature to 167 degrees F (75 C), lauter and sparge with 3½ gallons (13.5 l) of 170-degree F (77 C) water. Collect about 5½ gallons (21 l) of runoff.

Add white sucrose sugar and boiling hops, bring to a full and vigorous boil, and boil for 60 minutes. Add the Irish moss for the final 10 minutes of the boil.

After a total wort boil of 60 minutes, turn off the heat and place the pot (with cover on) in a running cold-water bath for 45 minutes. Continue to chill in the immersion or use other methods to chill your wort. Then strain and sparge the wort into a sanitized fermenter. Bring the total volume to 5 gallons (19 l) with additional cold water if necessary. Aerate the wort very well.

Pitch the yeast when temperature of wort is about 70 degrees F (21 C). Once visible signs of fermentation are evident ferment at temperatures of 70 to 75 degrees F (21–24 C) for about 1 to 2 weeks or until fermentation shows signs of calm and stopping. Rack from your primary to a secondary and add the hop pellets for dry hopping. "Cellar" the beer at temperature of about 55 degrees F (13 C) for 1 to 2 weeks.

Prime with sugar and your own measured dose of *Brettanomyces* yeast and bottle when fermentation is complete. Store at temperatures of about 70 degrees F (21 C).

Belgian Tickle "Dubbel" Honey Ale (Malt Extract)

The yeast makes every bit of difference in this formulation. This recipe could be a dandy strong English old ale if fermented with a typical ale yeast, but the use of a Belgian yeast culture will transform this wort into a romantically fruity and complex and well-attenuated Belgian-style dubbel. This ale ferments and ages well at room temperature of 70 to 75 degrees F (21–24 C). And the honey is our substitute for the Belgians' addition of candi sugar (sucrose), a dose of which lightens the body while tickling the alcohol content.

Fruity esters are fermentation-temperature dependent and can be quite dominant if the beer is drunk prematurely, but with age they'll mellow and blend with the malt and alcohol. With the correct Belgian yeast strains, this ale resembles full and fruity Belgian ales such as Chimay Red, brewed by Trappist monks. I use the word *resembles* because the finesse and character of Chimay is beyond duplication, unless, of course, you wish to take the same vows and become a monk, in which case perhaps there can be a similar movement of spirit. But then you may not be permitted to tickle. Belgian Tickle, anyone?

Ingredients for 5 gallons (19 l):

5½ lb. (2.5 kg)	light dried English malt extract
2 lb. (0.91 kg)	light honey
1 lb. (0.45 kg)	dark crystal or caramel malt (40 L)
1½ oz. (42 g)	Styrian Goldings hops (boiling): 7.5 HBU (210 MBU)
1 oz. (28 g)	Goldings hops (15 minutes, flavor): 5 HBU (140 MBU)
½ oz. (14 g)	Crystal hops (steeping, aroma)
¼ tsp. (1 g)	Irish moss powder
*	Belgian ale yeast culture such as White Labs WLP545 Belgian Strong Ale Yeast or Wyeast 3787 Trappist High

¾ c. (175 ml)   corn sugar (dextrose) or 1¼ c. (300 ml) dried malt extract
(for bottling); or ⅓ c. (80 ml) corn sugar (dextrose)
for kegging

O.G.: 1.066–1.068 (16.1–16.6)
F.G.: 1.012–1.016 (3.5–4.5)
Bitterness: 26 BU; Color: 15 SRM (30 EBC); Alcohol: 7.1% by volume

Add the crushed crystal malt to 2 gallons of 150 degree F (66 C) water and hold for 30 minutes. Remove the grains with a strainer.

Add the malt extract and boiling hops, bring to a full and vigorous boil, and boil for 60 minutes. Add the flavor hops for the last 15 minutes of the boil. Add the Irish moss for the final 10 minutes of the boil.

After a total wort boil of 60 minutes, turn off heat. Add the aroma hops and let steep while cooling. Immerse the covered pot of wort in a cold-water bath and let sit for 30 minutes or the time it takes to have a couple of homebrews.

Then strain out and sparge hops and direct the hot wort into a sanitized fermenter to which 2½ gallons (9.5 l) of cold water has been added. If necessary add additional cold water to achieve a 5-gallon (19 l) batch size. Aerate the wort very well.

Pitch your yeast when temperature of wort is about 70 degrees F (21 C). Once visible signs of fermentation are evident primary ferment at temperatures between 65 and 70 degrees F (18–12.5 C) for about 1 week or until fermentation shows signs of calm and stopping. If you have the capability, "cellar" the beer at temperatures between 50 and 55 degrees F (10–13 C) for 7 to 10 days.

Prime with sugar and bottle or keg when fermentation is complete.

"You'll See" Coriander Amber Ale (Mash Extract)

Many Belgian ales rely on very special strains of yeast for their unique character. Here's an ale that is enhanced with the classic and refreshing character of coriander seed. Some strains of Belgian yeast will contribute to this character, but you don't have to rely on the yeast for "You'll See," as you'll see. A relatively light and dry character is designed into the body of this brew, with hop bitterness taking a backseat to the zig-and-zag zing of freshly crushed coriander seed. But as any occupant of the backseat knows, this blend of noble hops from Germany and Czechoslovakia is definitely in the driver's seat.

Purchase whole coriander seeds and crush or grind them yourself. One ounce (28 g) is infused with the boil for deep flavor, and another ¹/₂ ounce (14 g) is added during secondary fermentation for aromatic effect.

Of all the coriander-flavored beers I've tasted over the years (both commercially made and homebrewed), I have observed hardly any oxidation even with three- or four-year-old coriandered beer. Might coriander have an unusual antioxidizing effect? Yes it does.

Ingredients for 5 gallons (19 l):

2 lb. (0.91 kg)	pale malted barley
1 lb. (0.45 kg)	crystal or caramel malt (40 L)
¹/₂ lb. (227 g)	wheat malt
3¹/₂ lb. (1.6 kg)	light dried malt extract or 4.1 lb. (1.9 kg) extra light malt extract syrup
³/₄ oz. (21.3 g)	Northern Brewers hops (boiling): 7 HBU (196 MBU)
1 oz. (28 g)	Czech Saaz hops (15 minutes, flavor): 4 HBU (112 MBU)
¹/₂ oz. (14 g)	German Hallertau hops (2 minutes, aroma)
¹/₂ oz. (14 g)	Czech Saaz hops (2 minutes, aroma)
1¹/₂ oz. (42.6 g)	freshly crushed coriander seed
¹/₄ tsp. (1 g)	Irish moss powder
*	neutral ale yeast; American Ale 1056 does very well
³/₄ c. (175 ml)	corn sugar (dextrose) or 1¹/₄ c. (300 ml) dried malt extract (for bottling); or ¹/₃ c. (80 ml) corn sugar (dextrose) for kegging

O.G.: 1.049 (12.5)
F.G.: 1.008–1.012 (2–3)
Bitterness: 28 BU; Color: 13 SRM (26 EBC); Alcohol: 5.4% by volume

Use a single-step infusion mash schedule for this recipe. Add crushed malts to 4 quarts (3.8 l) of 168-degree F (76 C) water. The mash will stabilize at 153 to 158 degrees F (67–70 C). Hold this temperature at the higher end for 60 minutes. Sparge with about 1½ gallons (5.7 l) of 170-degree F (77 C) water. Add more water (do not oversparge) to brewpot if necessary to make an initial extract volume of about 2½ gallons (9.5 l).

Add the boiling hops and dried malt extract, bring to a full and vigorous boil, and boil for 60 minutes. Add the flavor hops and 1 ounce of the freshly crushed coriander seed for the last 15 minutes of the boil. Add the Irish moss for the final 10 minutes of the boil. Add both aroma hops for the final 2 minutes.

After a total wort boil of 60 minutes, turn off the heat. Strain, sparge, and transfer the wort to a fermenter partly filled with about 1½ gallons (5.7 l) of cold water.

Aerate the wort very well. Pitch the yeast when the temperature of the wort is about 70 degrees F (21 C). Ferment at about 70 degrees F (21 C) for about 1 week or until fermentation shows signs of calming and stopping. When primary fermentation is complete, transfer the beer to a secondary and add the remaining ½ ounce (14 g) freshly crushed coriander seed to the secondary fermenter and let it sit with the beer for at least 1 week before bottling. Crush seed in a sanitary manner, minimizing the risk of introducing contaminating microorganisms. (Do not use your malt mill.)

Prime with sugar and bottle or keg when fermentation is complete . . . and you'll see.

Leftmalle Belgian-Style Dubbel (All Grain)

A while ago it never occurred to you that beer could really be enjoyable beyond belief. Now beer is your friend. But like everything in life you've developed preferences. Some beers you like more than others—and you could say the same thing about your friends.

Sure to be one of your friends' favorites is this strong dubbel style of Belgian ale, very similar in character to the dubbel brewed by the Belgian Trappists at Westmalle. There's an expression of interplay between creaminess and medium-light body. It is nutty, with gentle dryness of palate from the roasted malts; very low banana esters hang out in the disguised background. It has hop smoothness, balance of bitterness underlying hop flavor, and a sneaky alcoholic kick.

The Belgians have always enjoyed brewing outside of the box and so have you—remember, you're a homebrewer. So, Leftmalle Dubbel has quirky ingredients of its own to assure uniqueness of formulation (which Belgians would appreciate), yet the finale is faithful to the appearance, taste, and aromatic character of the original Westmalle Dubbel.

Instead of candi sugar (which is nothing more than crystallized sucrose), agave syrup and Brazilian dark *rapadura* sugar are added. Agave syrup is about 72 percent fructose, 25 percent dextrose, and 3 percent other sugars. The agave syrup serves to increase yeast attenuation and decrease the sensation of body. Specialty malts replicate the gentle fragrant aroma and flavor of sweet, caramelized, and roasted malt, which play an important role in this particular beer. Late hopping with Santiam serves to add a honey-like floral character. There's no citrus-hop aroma in this beer.

At 8 percent alcohol you'll take note, but won't feel the excessive heat of alcohol that other styles of strong Belgian ales often exhibit. Don't ferment this beer at too high a temperature. You want only subtle fruity esters in this brew. By all means if you wish to boost fruitiness, find a Belgian ale yeast you enjoy brewing with, but if it is in the direction of Westmalle Dubbel you wish to go, I'd recommend an ale yeast that evolves very low levels of esters.

Ingredients for 5¼ gallons (20 l):

7 lb. (3.2 kg)	Pils malt
½ lb. (227 g)	Belgian or other aromatic malt
½ lb. (227 g)	honey malt
½ lb. (227 g)	crystal malt (80 L)
6 oz. (168 g)	debittered black malt
2½ lb. (1.15 kg)	agave syrup
1 lb. (454 g)	dark Brazilian *rapadura* sugar (or ½ c. [120 ml] molasses and ¾ lb. [340 g] dark brown sugar)
1 oz. (28 g)	UK Fuggles or Willamette hops (boiling): 5 HBU (140 MBU)
½ oz. (14 g)	Santiam hop or Mt. Hood (30 minutes, flavor): 2.5 HBU (70 MBU)
1 oz. (28 g)	Czech Saaz or Sterling hops (20 minutes, flavor): 3.4 HBU (95 MBU)
¾ oz. (21 g)	Santiam hop pellets (1 minute, aroma)
¼ tsp (1 g)	Irish moss powder
*	Belgian Trappist yeast (use low-ester-producing type); White Labs Cry Havoc all-purpose yeast works very well for this recipe
¾ c. (175 ml)	corn sugar (dextrose) or 1¼ c. (300 ml) dried malt extract (for bottling); or ⅓ c. (80 ml) corn sugar (dextrose) for kegging

O.G.: 1.072 (17.5)
F.G.: 1.012 (3)
Bitterness: 25 BU; Color: 28 SRM (56 EBC); Alcohol: 8% by volume

A step infusion mash is employed to mash the grains. Add 9 quarts (8.6 l) of 143-degree F (61.5 C) water to the crushed grain, stir, stabilize and hold the temperature at 132 degrees F (53 C) for 30 minutes. Add 4½ quarts (4.3 l) of boiling water and add heat to bring temperature up to 155 degrees F (68 C) and hold for about 30 minutes. Then raise temperature to 167 degrees F (75 C), lauter and sparge with 3½ gallons (13.5 l) of 170-degree F (77 C) water. Collect about 6 gallons (23 l) of runoff.

Add the boiling hops, agave extract syrup, and *rapadura* sugar; bring to a full and vigorous boil and boil for 60 minutes. Add the Santiam or Mt. Hood flavor hops for the last 30 minutes of the boil. Add the Saaz or Sterling flavor hops for the last 20 minutes of the boil. Add the Irish moss for the last 10 minutes. Add the aroma hops for the final 1 minute.

After a total wort boil of 60 minutes, turn off the heat and place the pot (with cover on) in a running cold-water bath for 45 minutes. Continue to chill in the immersion or use other methods to chill your wort. Then strain and sparge the wort into a sanitized fermenter. Bring the total volume to 5¼ gallons (19 l) with additional cold water if necessary. Aerate the wort very well.

Pitch the yeast when temperature of wort is 74 to 76 degrees F (23.5–24.5 C). Ferment at about 74 degrees F (23.5 C) for about 1 week or until fermentation shows signs of calm and stopping. Rack from your primary to a secondary. If you have the capability, "cellar" the beer at about 55 degrees F (12.5 C) for about 1 week.

Prime with sugar and bottle or keg when fermentation is complete.

Nomadic Kölsch (Mash Extract)

Kölsch is a particularly refreshing, pale, light-bodied, subtly fruity, balanced traditional ale of Cologne (Köln), Germany. If there were ever such a thing, you might describe Kölsch as a low-bitterness "Pilsener-ale." Right. To some the mere suggestion that something could be a Pilsener-ale is blasphemous, but I'm enjoying my Kölsch no matter how I describe it. Are you?

Ale yeast is used for primary fermentation, with lager yeast added during cold lagering to help assure maximum attenuation.

Ingredients for 5 gallons (19 l):

2 lb. (0.91 kg)   pale malted barley
½ lb. (227 g)   wheat malt
¼ lb. (114 g)   Dextrine™ or Cara-Pils™ malt

3½ lb. (1.6 kg)	extra light dried malt extract or 4.4 lb. (2 kg) extra light malt extract syrup
¾ oz. (19.9 g)	Northern Brewer or Perle hops (boiling): 6 HBU (168 MBU)
1 oz. (28 g)	German Hallertau or Liberty hops (15 minutes, flavor): 4 HBU (112 MBU)
½ oz. (14 g)	German Spalt or Mt. Hood hops (15 minutes, flavor): 2.5 HBU (70 MBU)
½ oz. (14 g)	German Hallertau hops (2 minutes, aroma)
½ oz. (14 g)	Czech Saaz hops (2 minutes, aroma)
¼ tsp. (1 g)	Irish moss powder
*	German Kölsch ale yeast
*	lager yeast
¾ c. (175 ml)	corn sugar (dextrose) or 1¼ c. (300 ml) dried malt extract (for bottling); or ⅓ c. (80 ml) corn sugar (dextrose) for kegging

O.G.: 1.044–1.046 (11–11.5)
F.G.: 1.008–1.012 (2–3)
Bitterness: 34 BU; Color: 4–5 SRM (8–10 EBC); Alcohol: 5% by volume

Use a protein-developing step mash. Add 3 quarts (2.9 l) of 140-degree F (60 C) water to the crushed malt. Stabilize at 132 degrees F (55.5 C) and hold for 30 minutes. Then add 1½ quarts (1.4 l) of boiling water. Stabilize at 148 to 152 degrees F (64–67 C) and hold for 30 minutes. Add heat and mash out to 165 degrees F (74 C).

Sparge with about 1½ gallons (5.7 l) of 170-degree F (77 C) water. Add more water (do not oversparge) to brewpot if needed to make an initial extract volume of 2½ gallons (9.5 l). Anticipate evaporation of about ½ gallon (1.9 l).

Add the malt extract and boiling hops, bring to a full and vigorous boil, and boil for 60 minutes. Add the flavor hops for the last 15 minutes of the boil. Add the Irish moss for the last 10 minutes. Add the two aroma hops for the final 2 minutes.

After a total wort boil of 60 minutes, turn off heat and immerse the covered pot of wort in a cold-water bath and let sit for 30 minutes or the time it takes to have a couple of homebrews.

Then strain out and sparge hops and direct the hot wort into a sanitized fermenter to which 2 gallons (7.6 l) of cold water has been added. If necessary add additional cold water to achieve a 5-gallon (19 l) batch size. Aerate the wort very well.

Pitch your Kölsch yeast when temperature of wort is about 70 degrees F (21 C). Once visible signs of fermentation are evident primary ferment at temperatures between 60 and 65 degrees F (15.5–18 C) for about 1 week or until fermentation shows signs of calm and stopping. Then transfer the beer into a secondary fermenter, add an active culture of lager yeast and lager at 40 to 45 degrees F (4–7 C) for 3 to 4 weeks or until fermentation is complete.

Prime with sugar and bottle or keg when fermentation is complete.

WHEAT, RYE, AND SPECIALTY WHEAT ALES

Mr. Kelly's Coconut Curry Bavarian Hefeweizen (All Grain with Honey)

If you like the tantalizing flavors of a spicy Indian curry, you are sure to find this beer intriguing. I did, and I liked it, too. This recipe is slightly adapted from brew pal Brian Kelly, formerly of Denver, Colorado. He's a curry freak and an expert brewer, winning awards with a beer brewed from this recipe, a recipe he says is based on a Sri Lankan crab curry recipe. My hat is off to Brian and his creative success.

The beer? Well, it's a light-bodied Bavarian-style wheat beer with all the excitement of ginger, cayenne, coriander seed, cinnamon, lime leaves, and fenugreek. A refreshing pleasure—the heat of the cayenne is suggestive but not overwhelming. Hurry curry ishna?

Ingredients for 5 gallons (19 l):

5 lb. (2.3 kg)	malted wheat
¼ lb. (114 g)	rice hulls (necessary to help with lautering the huskless wheat malt)
1 lb. (0.45 kg)	American Victory malt
1 lb. (0.45 kg)	Munich malt
2 lb. (0.91 kg)	wildflower honey
½ oz. (14 g)	German Hallertau hops (boiling): 2.5 HBU (70 MBU)
½ oz. (14 g)	Czech Saaz hops (boiling): 2 HBU (56 MBU)
3 oz. (85 g)	grated fresh ginger
1 Tbsp. (8 g)	cayenne pepper
1 Tbsp. (8 g)	freshly crushed coriander seed
1 Tbsp. (8 g)	freshly ground fenugreek
3	inches (7.6 cm) stick cinnamon
4 c. (950 ml)	unsweetened shredded coconut
0.6 oz. (17 g)	lime leaves (or curry leaves)
¼ tsp. (1 g)	Irish moss powder
*	Bavarian-style wheat beer (Weissbier or Weizenbier) yeast and German lager yeast
¾ c. (175 ml)	corn sugar (dextrose) or 1¼ c. (300 ml) dried malt extract (for bottling); or ⅓ c. (80 ml) corn sugar (dextrose) for kegging

O.G.: 1.050–1.054 (12.5–13.5)
F.G.: 1.004–1.008 (1–2)
Bitterness: 16 BU; Color: 11 SRM (22 EBC); Alcohol: 5.5% by volume

Use a single-step infusion mash schedule for this recipe. Add crushed malts and rice hulls to 7 quarts (6.6 l) of 168-degree F (76 C) water. The mash will stabilize at 153 to 155 degrees F (67–68 C). Hold this temperature for 60 minutes. Sparge with about 3 gallons (11.4 l) of 170-degree F (77 C) water. Add more water (do not oversparge) to brewpot if necessary to make an initial extract volume of about 5 gallons (19 l).

Add all of the boiling hops and honey, bring to a full and vigorous boil, and boil for 60 minutes. For the last 30 minutes of the boil, add the cayenne, coriander, cinnamon, lime leaves (or curry leaves), fenugreek, 1½ ounces (43 g) of the grated ginger, and 2 cups (475 ml) of the coconut. Add the remaining 2 cups (475 ml) coconut and the Irish moss for the final 10 minutes.

After a total wort boil of 60 minutes, turn off the heat, add the remaining 1½ ounces of ginger (43 g), and place the pot (with cover on) in a running cold-water bath for 45 minutes. Continue to chill in the immersion or use other methods to chill your wort. Then strain and sparge the wort into a sanitized fermenter. Bring the total volume to 5 gallons (19 l) with additional cold water if necessary. Aerate the wort very well.

Pitch the yeast when temperature of wort is about 70 degrees F (21 C). Ferment at about 70 degrees F (21 C) for about 1 week to 10 days or until fermentation shows signs of calm and stopping. Rack from your primary to a secondary and "cellar" the beer at about 55 degrees F (12.5 C) for about 1 week. Prime with sugar and bottle or keg when fermentation is complete.

Tennessee Waltzer Dunkelweizenbock (Mash Extract)

All beers are brewed because they are inspired by someone or some event. If there is no inspiration, there is no beer. I'm sure you understand this as a homebrewer. Tennessee Waltzer Dunkelweizenbock was inspired by and made for those who love beer but not bitter beer. In the tradition of southern Germany and big bocks, the signatures of this brew are its rich maltiness and low hop bitterness.

Here's a beer that has about 20 percent wheat malt, rather than a more traditional 40 to 50 percent base of wheat. Hey, I'm a homebrewer, so please allow me to design my own wheat beer. Your inspiration may motivate you to redesign a bit. Here is a deceptively strong 5.5 percent alcohol lager, richly dark but not opaque, and immensely drinkable. Bavarians would suck this one up or down with no problem. You can add your favorite wheat beer yeast if you wish. Neutral ale yeast will result in a brew more reminiscent of lager bock than of a spicy wheat beer. I don't care for that clove-like wheat beer character, but you might.

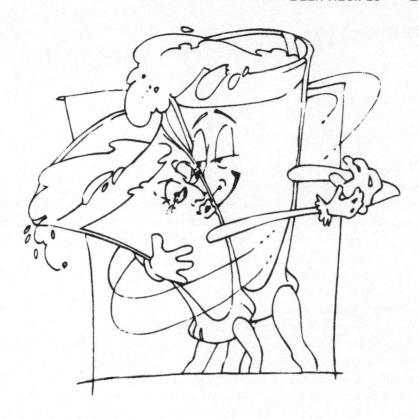

Ingredients for 5 gallons (19 l):

4 lb. (1.8 kg)	light dried malt extract or 5 lb. (2.3 kg) light malt extract syrup
1 lb. (0.45 kg)	Pilsener malt
1½ lb. (0.68 kg)	Munich malt (10–15 L)
1 lb. (0.45 kg)	German CaraMunich™ malt (75 L)
2 lb. (0.91 kg)	wheat malt
2 oz. (56 g)	rice hulls
¼ lb. (114 g)	roasted chocolate malt
¼ lb. (114 g)	roasted black malt
1 oz. (28 g)	Perle or Spalt hops (boiling): 9 HBU (252 MBU)
½ oz. (14 g)	German or American Hallertau or Mt. Hood hops (steeping, aroma)
¼ tsp. (1 g)	Irish moss powder
*	lager or ale yeast: Bavarian- or Munich-type lager yeast or American ale yeast

¾ c. (175 ml)   corn sugar (dextrose) or 1¼ c. (300 ml) dried malt extract
(for bottling); or ⅓ c. (80 ml) corn sugar (dextrose) for
kegging

O.G.: 1.064–1.068 (15.5–16.5)
F.G.: 1.016–1.020 (4–5)
Bitterness: 30 BU; Color: 33 SRM (66 EBC); Alcohol: 6.8% by volume

Using a protein-developing step mash, add 6 quarts (5.7 l) of 130-degree F
(54.4 C) water to the crushed malt. Stabilize at 122 degrees F (50 C) and hold for
30 minutes. Add 3 quarts (2.9 l) of boiling water. Stabilize at 152 to 155 degrees
F (66.7–68.3 C) and hold for 60 minutes. Add heat and mash out to 165 degrees
F (74 C). Sparge with 2½ to 3 gallons (9.5–11.4 l) of 170-degree F (77 C) water.
Collect 4 gallons (15.2 l).

Add the dried malt extract and boiling hops, bring to a full and vigorous
boil, and boil for 1 hour and 20 minutes. Add the Irish moss for the last 10 minutes of the boil. Evaporate about 1 gallon (3.8 l) during the initial boil, using
your visual assessment; in other words, "eyeball it."

Turn off the heat, add the aroma hops, and let steep 2 to 3 minutes. Then
immerse the covered pot of wort in a cold-water bath and let sit for 30 minutes
or the time it takes to have a couple of homebrews.

Then strain out and sparge hops and direct the hot wort into a sanitized
fermenter to which 1½ gallons (5.7 l) of cold water has been added. If necessary, add additional cold water to achieve a 5-gallon (19 l) batch size. Aerate
the wort very well.

If using lager yeast, pitch the yeast when temperature of wort is about
70 degrees F (21 C). Once visible signs of fermentation are evident ferment at
temperatures of about 55 degrees F (12.5 C) for about 1 week or when fermentation shows signs of calm and stopping. If you have the capability, "lager" the
beer at temperatures between 35 and 45 degrees F (1.5–7 C) for 3 to 6 weeks.

If using ale yeast, pitch the yeast when the temperature of the wort is about
70 degrees F (21 C). Ferment at about 70 degrees F (21 C) for about 1 week or
until fermentation shows signs of calm and stopping. Rack from your primary
to a secondary. If you have the capability, "cellar" the beer at about 55 degrees
F (12.5 C) for about 1 week.

Prime with sugar and bottle or keg when fermentation is complete.

Rye Not? (All Grain)

Rye malt is definitely worth involving in your ales and lagers. Be cautious. Too
much rye malt will most likely and unbearably set and stick your mash, stopping
runoff during the lautering. Attention must be given to flow from the lauter-tun.
You'll need rice hulls and a few glasses of homebrew for this one.

Rye contributes an austere crisp character to beer. Now, how's that for describing something I really don't know how to describe? Rye Not? is a smooth lager complemented with plenty of caramel malt character and is not overly hoppy.

Ingredients for 5 gallons (19 l):

4½ lb. (2 kg)	pale malted barley
1¼ lb. (0.57 kg)	crystal or caramel malt (20 L)
2 lb. (0.91 kg)	rye malt
¾ oz. (21.3 g)	Liberty or Vanguard hops (boiling): 4 HBU (112 MBU)
½ oz. (14 g)	French Strisselspalt or American Tettnang hops (30 minutes, flavor): 2 HBU (56 MBU)
¾ oz. (21 g)	Hallertau Hersbruck or German Saphir hops (10 minutes, flavor): 3 HBU (84 MBU)
1 oz. (28 g)	Mt. Hood or Santiam hops (steeping, aroma)
½ oz. (14 g)	Crystal or Hallertau hop pellets (dry hopping, aroma)
¼ tsp. (1 g)	Irish moss powder
*	ale yeast
¾ c. (175 ml)	corn sugar (dextrose) or 1¼ c. (300 ml) dried malt extract (for bottling); or ⅓ c. (80 ml) corn sugar (dextrose) for kegging

O.G.: 1.046–1.050 (11.5–12.5)
F.G.: 1.014–1.018 (3–4)
Bitterness: 24 BU; Color: 9 SRM (18 EBC); Alcohol: 4.6% by volume

A step infusion mash is employed to mash the grains. Add 8 quarts (7.6 l) of 143-degree F (61.5 C) water to the crushed grain and rice hulls, stir, stabilize and hold the temperature at 132 degrees F (53 C) for 30 minutes. Add 4 quarts (3.8 l) of boiling water and add heat to bring temperature up to 155 degrees F (68 C) and hold for about 30 minutes. Then raise temperature to 167 degrees F (75 C), lauter and sparge with 3½ gallons (13.5 l) of 170-degree F (77 C) water. Collect about 5½ gallons (21 l) of runoff. Sparge with about 3½ gallons (13.3 l) of 170-degree F (77 C) water. Add more water (do not oversparge) to brewpot to make an initial extract volume of 5½ gallons (21 l).

Add the boiling hops, bring to a boil, and boil for 60 minutes. Add the 30-minute flavor hops for the last 30 minutes of the boil. Add the 10-minute flavor hops and Irish moss for the final 10 minutes.

After a total wort boil of 60 minutes, turn off the heat. Add the steeping hops and place the pot (with cover on) in a running cold-water bath for 45 minutes. Continue to chill in the immersion or use other methods to chill your wort. Then strain and sparge the wort into a sanitized fermenter. Bring the total volume to 5 gallons (19 l) with additional cold water if necessary. Aerate the wort very well.

Pitch your yeast when temperature of wort is about 70 degrees F (21 C). Once visible signs of fermentation are evident primary ferment at temperatures between 65 and 70 degrees F (18–12.5 C) for about 1 week or until fermentation shows signs of calm and stopping. Rack from your primary to a secondary and add the hop pellets for dry hopping. If you have the capability, "cellar" the beer at temperatures between 50 and 55 degrees F (10–13 C) for 7 to 10 days.

Prime with sugar and bottle or keg when fermentation is complete.

DARK ALES—MODERATE STRENGTH

Brown Ales

Buzzdigh Moog Double Brown Ale (All Grain)

Double brown does not refer to the color! This beer is brewed to the tune of English-style sweetness. Buzzdigh Moog Double Brown Ale is high in hop character but balanced with a lot of malt. The richness of Munich, Vienna, and crystal malts combine for a deceivingly smooth and rich ale, complemented with the velvety chocolate-like character of roasted malts. The warmth of alcohol and fruitiness of strong ale mingle with the solemnly perceived Cascade hop aroma. This ale ages nicely and may take 4 to 6 months in the bottle to reach its peak.

Double brown is to English brown ale as doppelbock is to German bock, but I doubt you'll ever see this available in England—unless, of course, they have a copy of this recipe.

And what about "Buzzdigh Moog"? My grandparents used to call my brothers and me that when we were very small. In Armenian it kind of means "small, playful mouse." Not surprisingly, this ale may make you feel playful.

Ingredients for 5 gallons (19 l):

5 lb. (2.3 kg)	American 2-row lager malt
3 lb. (1.36 kg)	Munich malt
2 lb. (0.9 kg)	Vienna malt
1½ lb. (0.68 kg)	crystal or caramel malt (40 L)
¼ lb. (114 g)	black-roasted malt
¼ lb. (114 g)	chocolate-roasted malt
½ oz. (14 g)	English Palisade or Progress hops (boiling): 3.5 HBU (98 MBU)
1 oz. (28 g)	English Fuggles or Willamette hops (boiling): 5 HBU (140 MBU)
½ oz. (14 g)	Cascade hops (15 minutes, flavor): 2.5 HBU (70 MBU)

1 oz. (28 g)	Cascade or Chinook hops (1 minute, aroma)
¼ tsp. (1 g)	Irish moss powder
*	American ale yeast, such as American Ale 1056
¾ c. (175 ml)	corn sugar (dextrose) or 1¼ c. (300 ml) dried malt extract (for bottling); or ⅓ c. (80 ml) corn sugar (dextrose) for kegging

O.G.: 1.070 (17.1)
F.G.: 1.014–1.020 (2–2.5)
Bitterness: 38 BU; Color: 30 SRM (60 EBC); Alcohol: 7% by volume

A step infusion mash is employed to mash the grains. Add 13 quarts (12.4 l) of 143-degree F (61.5 C) water to the crushed grain, stir, stabilize and hold the temperature at 132 degrees F (53 C) for 30 minutes. Add 6½ quarts (6.2 l) of boiling water and add heat to bring temperature up to 155 degrees F (68 C) and hold for about 30 minutes. Then raise temperature to 167 degrees F (75 C), lauter and sparge with 3½ gallons (13.5 l) of 170-degree F (77 C) water. Collect about 5½ gallons (21 l) of runoff.

Add both boiling hops, bring to a full and vigorous boil, and boil for 60 minutes. Add the flavor hops for the last 15 minutes of the boil. Add the Irish moss for the last 10 minutes. Add the aroma hops for the final 1 minute.

After a total wort boil of 60 minutes, turn off the heat and place the pot (with cover on) in a running cold-water bath for 45 minutes. Continue to chill in the immersion or use other methods to chill your wort. Then strain and sparge the wort into a sanitized fermenter. Bring the total volume to 5 gallons (19 l) with additional cold water if necessary. Aerate the wort very well.

Pitch the yeast when temperature of wort is about 70 degrees F (21 C). Ferment at about 70 degrees F (21 C) for about 1 week or until fermentation shows signs of calm and stopping. Rack from your primary to a secondary and add the hop pellets for dry hopping. If you have the capability, "cellar" the beer at about 55 degrees F (12.5 C) for about 1 week.

Prime with sugar and bottle or keg when fermentation is complete.

Colorado Cowgirl's American Brown Ale (Malt Extract)

There are a lot of things American: apple pie, Thanksgiving, Canyonlands, hot dogs, baseball, Lyle Lovett, and homebrewing. I live in Colorado and I know that in the mountains and on the plains, Colorado cowgirls are out there. Doing what cowgirls do.

I sip my new simply and perfectly made brown ale. It's medium-bodied, brown, righteously bitter with a hoppy aroma and flavor. Nothing like an English-style sweeter brown ale. This is all-American to me. This is a style and type of beer that didn't exist until invented in the 1980s by American homebrewers who realized there were no limits when it came to using hops.

Its assertive bitterness will quench a dusty thirst.

Ingredients for 5 gallons (19 l):

6.6 lb. (3 kg)	amber malt extract syrup or 5.6 lb. (2.5 kg) dried amber malt extract
1 lb. (0.45 kg)	crystal or caramel malt (20–80 L)
5 oz. (0.142 kg)	chocolate malt
1 oz. (28 g)	Horizon hops (boiling): 12 HBU (336 MBU)
½ oz. (14 g)	Delta or Amarillo hops (15 minutes, flavor): 3.5 HBU (98 MBU)
¾ oz. (21 g)	Delta hops (1 minute, aroma)
¾ oz. (21 g)	Sorachi Ace or Citra hop pellets (dry hopping, aroma)
2 tsp. (8 g)	gypsum (if your water is soft; low in calcium and sulfates)
*	your favorite Far Western ale yeast
¾ c. (175 ml)	corn sugar (dextrose) or 1¼ c. (300 ml) dried malt extract (for bottling); or ⅓ c. (80 ml) corn sugar (dextrose) for kegging

O.G.: 1.054 (13.5)
F.G.: 1.010–1.014 (2.5–3.5)
Bitterness: 48–52 BU; Color: 20–30 SRM (40–60 EBC); Alcohol: 7% by volume

Add crushed crystal and chocolate malts to 2 gallons (7.6 l) of 150-degree F (66 C) water and hold for 30 minutes. Remove the grains with a strainer.

Add the malt extract, boiling hops, and gypsum; bring to a full and vigorous boil, and boil 60 minutes. Add the flavor hops for the last 15 minutes of the boil. Add the Irish moss for the final 10 minutes of the boil. Add the aroma hops for the final 1 minute.

After a total wort boil of 60 minutes, turn off the heat and place the pot (with cover on) in a running cold-water bath for 45 minutes. Add 2 gallons (7.6 l) of cold water to your sanitized fermenter. Then strain and sparge the wort into the fermenter. Bring the total volume to 5 gallons (19 l) with additional cold water if necessary. Aerate the wort very well.

Pitch the yeast when temperature of wort is about 70 degrees F (21 C). Ferment at about 70 degrees F (21 C) for about 1 week or until fermentation shows signs of calm and stopping. Rack from your primary to a secondary and add the hop pellets for dry hopping. If you have the capability, "cellar" the beer at about 55 degrees F (12.5 C) for about 1 week.

Prime with sugar and bottle or keg when fermentation is complete.

Wait a couple of weeks or so and then relax, don't worry, and toast a home-brew to some of the prettiest girls in all the land, Colorado cowgirls.

Saunders's Nut Brown Ale (Malt Extract)

My friend Michael Saunders once pleaded, "I want something like Samuel Smith's Nut Brown Ale. Can we make something like that?" Of course.

Caramel-like sweetness, relatively low bitterness, and the gentle nuttiness of roasted malts and barley. Could almost be your everyday session beer, no matter what kind of day you've had. Saunders's Nut Brown Ale will always be your friend. Cheers.

Ingredients for 5 gallons (19 l):

6.6 lb. (3 kg)	plain light English malt extract syrup or 5.6 lb. (2.5 kg) dried light malt extract
1½ lb. (0.68 kg)	dark crystal malt (60 L)
2½ oz. (70 g)	chocolate malt
2½ oz. (70 g)	roasted barley
¾ oz. (21 g)	Styrian Goldings, English WGV (Whitbread Goldings Variety) or English Bramling Cross hops (boiling): 6 HBU (168 MBU)
1 oz. (28 g)	English WGV (Whitbread Goldings Variety) or English Bramling Cross hops (10 minutes, flavor): 5 HBU (140 MBU)

½ oz. (14 g)   English First Gold or English Goldings hops (1 minute, aroma)

½ oz. (14 g)   English First Gold or English Goldings hop pellets (dry hopping, aroma)

¼ tsp. (1 g)   Irish moss powder

*   English ale yeast

¾ c. (175 ml) corn sugar (dextrose) or 1¼ c. (300 ml) dried malt extract (for bottling); or ⅓ c. (80 ml) corn sugar (dextrose) for kegging

O.G.: 1.058 (14.5)
F.G.: 1.014–1.018 (3.5–4.5)
Bitterness: 21 BU; Color: 29 SRM (58 EBC); Alcohol: 5.5% by volume

Add the crushed crystal malt, chocolate malt, and roasted barley to 2 gallons of 150-degree F (66 C) water and hold for 30 minutes. Remove the grains with a strainer.

Add the malt extract and boiling hops, bring to a full and vigorous boil, and boil for 60 minutes. Add the flavor hops and Irish moss for the last 10 minutes of the boil. Add the aroma hops for the final 1 minute.

MIKE SAUNDERS FINALLY
FINDS HIS BEER...

After a total wort boil of 60 minutes, turn off the heat and place the pot (with cover on) in a running cold-water bath for 45 minutes. Add 2 gallons (7.6 l) of cold water to your sanitized fermenter. Then strain and sparge the wort into the fermenter. Bring the total volume to 5 gallons (19 l) with additional cold water if necessary. Aerate the wort very well.

Pitch the yeast when temperature of wort is about 70 degrees F (21 C). Ferment at about 70 degrees F (21 C) for about 1 week or until fermentation shows signs of calm and stopping. Rack from your primary to a secondary and add the hop pellets for dry hopping. If you have the capability, "cellar" the beer at about 55 degrees F (12.5 C) for about 1 week.

Prime with sugar and bottle or keg when fermentation is complete

Porters

Someplace You Gotta Go Coconut Porter (All Grain)

If you like chocolate and coconut and haven't been "there" with a beer—then you gotta go. Coconut porter emerged as a bombshell when in 1998, Tokyo, Japan, homebrewer Ichiri Fujiura, entered a toasted coconut porter into the American Homebrewers Association's National Homebrewer Competition and won Best of Show/Homebrewer of the Year. His creativity has infected both American homebrewers and craft brewers. In 2012 the Hawaiian craft brewery Maui Brewery won the *Washington Post's* annual March "Beer Madness" taste tournament with their more subtle tasting Coconut Porter.

Unusual sounding? Yes. Does it taste great? Simply put, yes indeed. And it's easy to make. The secrets lie with lightly toasting your own unsweetened coconut flakes and going easy on the hops. Once you've been you'll wanna go back again and again. Rich and cocoa-like, balanced with a moderate amount of alcohol and a moderate amount of coconut character. Ramp the coconut amount up or down, depending on your preference. Great drinkability so that when one just won't do, another follows. Have at it and enjoy your own.

Ingredients for 6 gallons (23 l):

7 lb. (3.2 kg)	Marris Otter 2-row English malt
2 lb. (0.9 kg)	Munich-type malt
1 lb. (454 g)	English crystal malt (15 L)
½ lb. (227 g)	aromatic-type malt
½ lb. (227 g)	English chocolate malt
½ lb. (227 g)	Gambrinus honey malt
½ lb. (227 g)	debittered black malt
3 oz. (84 g)	English black malt

½ lb. (227 g)	unsweetened dried coconut flakes, toasted to golden (10 to 15 minutes in a 300-degree F [149 C] oven)
¾ oz. (21 g)	English Fuggles or Golding hops (boiling): 4 HBU (112 MBU)
½ oz. (14 g)	English Challenger hops (boiling): 3 HBU (84 MBU)
1 oz. (28 g)	English Kent Golding hops (20 minutes, flavor)
1 oz. (28 g)	Santiam hops (5 minutes, flavor/aroma)
½ oz. (14 g)	Santiam hop pellets (dry hopping, aroma)
¼ tsp. (1 g)	Irish moss powder
*	White Labs Cry Havoc yeast or Irish ale yeast
¾ c. (175 ml)	corn sugar (dextrose) or 1¼ c. (300 ml) dried malt extract (for bottling); or ⅓ c. (80 ml) corn sugar (dextrose) for kegging

O.G.: 1.054 (13.3)
F.G.: 1.014–1.018 (4.5–5.5)
Bitterness: 30 BU; Color: 40+ SRM (80+ EBC); Alcohol: 5% by volume

A step infusion mash is employed to mash the grains. Add 12 quarts (11.5 l) of 143-degree F (61.5 C) water to the crushed grain, stir, stabilize and hold the temperature at 132 degrees F (53 C) for 30 minutes. Add 6 quarts (5.7 l) of boiling water and add heat to bring temperature up to 155 degrees F (68 C) and hold for about 30 minutes. Then raise temperature to 167 degrees F (75 C), lauter and sparge with 4½ gallons (13.5 l) of 170-degree F (77 C) water. Collect about 6½ gallons (25 l) of runoff.

Add the two boiling hops, bring to a full and vigorous boil, and boil for 60 minutes. Add the flavor hops for the last 20 minutes of the boil. Add the Irish moss for the last 10 minutes of the boil. Add the flavor/aroma hops for the final 5 minutes.

After a total wort boil of 60 minutes, turn off the heat and place the pot (with cover on) in a running cold-water bath for 45 minutes. Continue to chill in the immersion or use other methods to chill your wort. Then strain and sparge the wort into a sanitized fermenter. Bring the total volume to 6 gallons (21 l) with additional cold water if necessary. Aerate the wort very well. Add the toasted coconut flakes.

Pitch the yeast when temperature of wort is about 70 degrees F (21 C). Ferment at about 70 degrees F (21 C) for about 1 week or when fermentation shows signs of calm and stopping. Rack from your primary to a secondary and add the hop pellets for dry hopping. If you have the capability, "cellar" the beer at about 55 degrees F (12.5 C) for about 1 week.

Prime with sugar and bottle or keg when fermentation is complete.

Slanting Annie's Chocolate Porter (Mash Extract)

First of all, I must confess: I cannot take credit for this sensuously creative and wonderfully balanced beer. I didn't brew it. But I watched it being brewed. I took care of it a little bit. I bottled it. But my brewing pal Tracy, inspired by her love of chocolate, waved the charismatic wooden spoon and created something that would endear itself to any chocolate lover: a chocolate-flavored porter.

Careful to take into consideration the bitterness of 1 pound of unsweetened chocolate, the formulation compensates by adding a moderate amount of hops for bittering and using a not ordinary amount of crystal malt and a dose of wheat malt. The caramel-like sweetness of crystal and the maltiness of wheat malt enhance the chocolate.

The results filled the kitchen with the aroma of chocolate brownies baking in the oven. Five weeks later I had in hand a chilled mug of deep, velvety, rich chocolate porter. Slanting Annie's Porter, that is.

Slanting Annie? Oh yes, she's a legendary character out of the old West from the small town of Creede, Colorado. One leg was shorter than the other, but she sure could deal a deck of cards. Or so the story goes.

Ingredients for 5 gallons (19 l):

1¾ lb. (0.8 kg)	pale malted barley
2¼ lb. (1 kg)	crystal or caramel malt (10 degrees L)
2¼ lb. (1 kg)	wheat malt
⅓ lb. (150 g)	black roasted malt
⅓ lb. (150 g)	chocolate roasted malt

3½ lb. (1.6 kg)	light dried malt extract
¾ lb. (340 g)	unsweetened chocolate (you can substitute 3 level tablespoons of cocoa powder for each ounce of solid chocolate to avoid the concern about cocoa butter; see Note)
1¼ oz. (42 g)	Willamette or English Fuggles hops (boiling): 6.3 HBU (175 MBU)
½ oz. (14 g)	Willamette or English Fuggles hops (15 minutes, flavor): 3 HBU (84 MBU)
½ oz. (14 g)	Willamette or English Fuggles hops (2–3 minutes, flavor/aroma)
¼ tsp. (1 g)	Irish moss powder
*	American or Irish ale yeast or White Labs Cry Havoc yeast
¾ c. (175 ml)	corn sugar (dextrose) or 1¼ c. (300 ml) dried malt extract (for bottling); or ⅓ c. (80 ml) corn sugar (dextrose) for kegging

O.G.: 1.064 (15.7)
F.G.: 1.018–1.022 (4.5–5.5)
Bitterness: 30 BU; Color: 32 SRM (64 EBC); Alcohol: 5.8% by volume

This uses a single infusion mash method and a full wort boil. Heat 1.75 gallons (6.7 l) water to 172 degrees F (77.5 C) and then add crushed grains to the water. Stir well to distribute heat. Temperature should stabilize at about 155 degrees F (68 C). Wrap a towel around the pot and set aside for about 60 minutes. Have a homebrew.

After 60 minutes add heat to the mini-mash and raise the temperature to 167 degrees F (75 C). Then pass the liquid and grains into a strainer and rinse with 5 gallons (19 l) of 170 degrees F (77 C) water. Discard the grains.

Add to the sweet extract you have just produced more water, bringing the volume up to about 6 gallons (23 l). Prepare the chocolate by microwaving it in a microwaveable container or slowly heat in a double boiler setup. This will soften the chocolate, making it easier to dissolve in the boil.

Add the softened chocolate, malt extract, and boiling hops; and bring to a boil and boil for 1 hour 30 minutes. (Anticipate evaporation of about 1 gallon [3.8 l].) Add the flavor hops for the last 15 minutes of the boil. Add the Irish moss for the last 10 minutes. Add the flavor/aroma hops for the final 2 to 2 minutes.

After a total wort boil of 1 hour 30 minutes, turn off heat and place the pot (with cover on) in a running cold-water bath for 45 minutes. Continue to chill in the immersion or use other methods to chill your wort. Then strain and sparge the wort into a sanitized fermenter. Bring the total volume to 5 gallons (19 l) with additional cold water if necessary. Aerate the wort very well.

Pitch the yeast when temperature of wort is about 70 degrees F (21 C). Ferment at about 70 degrees F (21 C) for about 1 week or until fermentation shows signs of calm and stopping. Rack from your primary to a secondary. If you have the capability, "cellar" the beer at about 55 degrees F (12.5 C) for about 1 week.

Prime with sugar and bottle or keg when fermentation is complete

Note: If using solid chocolate, you will notice very little if any kraeusen (those mounds of fermentation foam) during the primary fermentation. You will also note globs of hunka-hunka cocoa butter floating on the surface. Those globs of congealed cocoa butter create an oily surface that inhibits bubble formation. Don't worry. After 5 or 7 days of primary fermentation, transfer the fermentation to a secondary fermenter, siphoning, naturally, below the surface of the beer. Let the brew sit in the secondary until fermentation has stopped and signs of clearing appear.

When bottling, you will have siphoned a second time into your bottling vessel and a third time into your bottles, effectively siphoning oil-free beer from under the floating cocoa butter slick. Slanting Annie's Chocolate Porter will have a wonderful thick head, the rich aroma of chocolate, the subtle charm of hop flowers, and the taste of porter—a wonderful porter.

Stouts—Moderate Strength

Barrel of Monkeys Wheat-Oatmeal Nut Stout (All Grain)

Sometimes, if you're not careful to muster all your brewing skills and patience, your brewing session will not seem like a barrel of monkeys (i.e., not so fun). Oatmeal and wheat malt are a challenge and can help create stuck mashes. Take care and lauter slowly. Add rice hulls. Stuck mashes are an experience every all-grain brewer goes through at least once. It's like having your pot of wort boil over, every once in a while. Kind of a ritual, a rite of passage.

On the other hand, oatmeal does lend a dreamy smoothness to stout, and wheat helps head retention as well as contributing to a fuller malt flavor. Take care and you'll have a brew worthy of celebrating with a barrel of monkeys. The bitterness units may appear to be high on paper, but the blend of crystal, oatmeal, wheat, and high-temperature mash brings out a fullness that pleasantly balances this nutlike stout. This brew is especially terrific on draft!

Ingredients for 5 gallons (19 l):

6 lb. (2.7 kg)   English pale 2-row malt
2 lb. (0.91 kg)   wheat malt

1 lb. (0.45 kg)	crystal or caramel malt (10 L)
10 oz. (0.28 kg)	quick oatmeal
2 oz. (56 g)	rice hulls
½ lb. (227 g)	roasted barley
½ lb. (227 g)	roasted black malt
2 oz. (56 g)	Glacier or Goldings hops (boiling): 13 HBU (364 MBU)
½ oz. (14 g)	Mt. Hood or Vanguard hops (15 minutes, flavor): 3 HBU (84 MBU)
½ oz. (14 g)	Crystal hops or Mt. Hood hop pellets (dry hopping, aroma)
2 Tbsp. (16 g)	gypsum (calcium sulfate) if using very soft water
¼ tsp. (1 g)	Irish moss powder
*	Irish ale yeast
¾ c. (175 ml)	corn sugar (dextrose) or 1¼ c. (300 ml) dried malt extract (for bottling); or ⅓ c. (80 ml) corn sugar (dextrose) for kegging

O.G.: 1.056 (14)
F.G.: 1.016–1.020 (4–5)
Bitterness: 56 BU; Color: 45 SRM (90 EBC); Alcohol: 5.3% by volume

A step infusion mash is employed to mash the grains. Add 10½ quarts (10 l) of 143-degree F (61.5 C) water to the crushed grain, rice hulls, and gypsum (if needed), stir, stabilize and hold the temperature at 132 degrees F (53 C) for 30 minutes. Add 5½ quarts (5.2 l) of boiling water and add heat to bring temperature up to 155 degrees F (68 C) and hold for about 30 minutes. Then raise temperature to 167 degrees F (75 C), lauter and sparge with 3½ gallons (13.5 l) of 170-degree F (77 C) water. Collect about 5½ gallons (21 l) of runoff.

Add the boiling hops, bring to a full and vigorous boil, and boil for 60 minutes. Add the flavor hops for the last 15 minutes of the boil. Add the Irish moss for the final 10 minutes of the boil.

After a total wort boil of 60 minutes, turn off the heat and place the pot (with cover on) in a running cold-water bath for 45 minutes. Continue to chill in the immersion or use other methods to chill your wort. Then strain and sparge the wort into a sanitized fermenter. Bring the total volume to 5 gallons (19 l) with additional cold water if necessary. Aerate the wort very well.

Pitch the yeast when temperature of wort is about 70 degrees F (21 C). Ferment at about 70 degrees F (21 C) for about 1 week or until fermentation shows signs of calm and stopping. Rack from your primary to a secondary and add the hop pellets for dry hopping. If you have the capability, "cellar" the beer at about 55 degrees F (12.5 C) for about 1 week.

Prime with sugar and bottle or keg when fermentation is complete.

Pelhourino Stout—The Other Irish Stout (Mash Extract)

Not all stouts are created in the same image. Guinness comes to mind for most who know stout, and it is worthy of the highest esteem. Yet there are styles of stout, brewed even in Ireland, that are less pungent, less bitter, and just as smooth and equally stout.

Pelhourino Stout is brewed with as much roasted barley punch as a Guinness, but with a higher proportion of caramelized malt and less bitterness, to create an Irish stout reminiscent of Ireland's Beamish and Murphy's stouts. It's a super stout for those looking for a tad less bitterness yet the full nourishment of a true stout.

Ingredients for 5 gallons (19 l):

2 lb. (0.91 kg)	English pale malted barley
1½ lb. (680 g)	crystal or caramel malt (40 L)
¾ lb. (340 g)	roasted barley
⅓ lb. (150 g)	black roasted malt
3½ lb. (1.6 kg)	light dried malt extract
½ oz. (14 g)	Wye Target hops (boiling): 5.8 HBU (161 MBU)

½ oz. (14 g)   Goldings hops (20 minutes, flavor): 2.5 HBU (70 MBU)
¼ tsp. (1 g)   Irish moss powder
*   Irish ale yeast
¾ c. (175 ml)   corn sugar (dextrose) or 1¼ c. (300 ml) dried malt extract
                  (for bottling); or ⅓ c. (80 ml) corn sugar (dextrose) for
                  kegging

O.G.: 1.050–1.054 (12.5–13.5)
F.G.: 1.016–1.020 (4–5)
Bitterness: 22 BU; Color: 47 SRM (94 EBC); Alcohol: 4.5% by volume

Use a single-step infusion mash schedule for this recipe.

Add the crushed malts to 4½ quarts (4.3 l) of 168-degree F (76 C) water. The mash will stabilize at 155 to 158 degrees F (68–70 C). Hold this temperature at the high end for 60 minutes. Sparge with about 1½ gallons (5.7 l) of 170-degree F (77 C) water. Add more water (do not oversparge) to brewpot if necessary to make an initial extract volume of about 2½ gallons (9.5 l).

Add the malt extract and boiling hops, bring to a full and vigorous boil, and boil for 60 minutes. Add the flavor hops for the last 20 minutes of the boil. Add the Irish moss for the final 10 minutes of the boil.

After a total wort boil of 60 minutes, turn off the heat and immerse the covered pot of wort in a cold-water bath and let sit for 30 minutes or the time it takes to have a couple of homebrews.

Then strain out and sparge hops and direct the hot wort into a sanitized fermenter to which 2½ gallons (9.5 l) of cold water has been added. If necessary add additional cold water to achieve a 5-gallon (19 l) batch size. Aerate the wort very well.

Pitch the yeast when temperature of wort is about 70 degrees F (21 C). Ferment at about 70 degrees F (21 C) for about 1 week or until fermentation shows signs of calm and stopping. Rack from your primary to a secondary. If you have the capability, "cellar" the beer at about 55 degrees F (12.5 C) for about 1 week.

Prime with sugar and bottle or keg when fermentation is complete.

STRONG ALES—LIGHT AND DARK

Black Samba Imperial Baltic Porter
(All Grain with Malt Extract)

Baltic porter is a highly defined and rediscovered style of "lagered strong porter." It's a beer that is distinctly different in character from stout, other porters, and imperial stout. It is a smooth lagered beer with a velvety finish. Most American brewers have difficulty overcoming the American hop gene they carry within.

Baltic porters are not aggressively hopped, though dry hopping with floral hop aroma will enhance the malt emphasis of this very special beer.

In *The Complete Joy of Homebrewing, Fourth Edition* I introduced you to my original Baltic porter, called Heart of the Tide Imperial Porter. That brew has raised many eyebrows and reveals the truth about Baltic porters that most beer enthusiasts had never tasted. It is a strong black beer, lacking in hop and roast malt aggressiveness. Also surprising is the lack of ale-like fruitiness. Rare is the brewer, home or pro, that ventures in these directions. Be bold—brew strong.

Here's a revisionist version of traditional Baltic-style porter which would not have smoked malt, flaked corn, *rapadura,* honey, or agave extract. I tag this brew as an imperial porter as it goes outside the boundaries of tradition.

Black Samba is strong, black, and smooth but with added twists and the complexities of smoke and honey, the attenuated character of corn, the light caramel of agave extract syrup, and the eccentric molasses-like resonations of dark Brazilian *rapadura.*

Ingredients for 5½ gallons (21 l):

2½ lb. (1.15 kg)	dried light malt extract or 3.1 lb. (1.4 kg) light malt extract syrup
4½ lb. (2 kg)	pale malt
2½ lb. (1.15 kg)	Briess cherrywood smoked malt
1 lb. (454 g)	German CaraMunich™ malt (60 L)
1 lb. (454 g)	flaked corn
¾ lb. (340 g)	English roasted barley
¾ lb. (340 g)	debittered black malt
½ lb. (227 g)	honey malt
½ lb. (227 g)	Belgian aromatic malt
6 oz. (168 g)	English chocolate malt
2 lb. (908 g)	agave extract syrup
½ lb. (227 g)	Brazilian *rapadura* sugar
1 oz. (28 g)	Sterling or Santiam hops (boiling): 7 HBU (196 MBU)
1 oz. (28 g)	Glacier hops (30 minutes, flavor): 6.5 HBU (182 MBU)
1 oz. (28 g)	Mt. Hood or Santiam hops (15 minutes, flavor): 6 HBU (168 MBU)
2 oz. (56 g)	French Strisselspalt hop pellets (1 minute, flavor/aroma)
¼ tsp (1 g)	Irish moss powder
*	White Labs Cry Havoc yeast or Bavarian-type lager yeast
¾ c. (175 ml)	corn sugar (dextrose) or 1¼ c. (300 ml) dried malt extract (for bottling); or ⅓ c. (80 ml) corn sugar (dextrose) for kegging

O.G.: 1.089 (21.3)
F.G.: 1.020 (5)
Bitterness: 42 BU; Color: 60 SRM (120 EBC); Alcohol: 9% by volume

A step infusion mash is employed to mash the grains. Add 12 quarts (11.5 l) of 143-degree F (61.5 C) water to the crushed grain, stir, stabilize and hold the temperature at 132 degrees F (53 C) for 30 minutes. Add 6 quarts (6 l) of boiling water and add heat to bring temperature up to 155 degrees F (68 C) and hold for about 30 minutes. Then raise temperature to 167 degrees F (75 C), lauter and sparge with 3½ gallons (13.5 l) of 170-degree F (77 C) water. Collect about 6 gallons (23 l) of runoff.

Add the malt extract, agave extract, *rapadura* sugar, and boiling hops; bring to a full and vigorous boil and boil for 60 minutes. Add the 30-minute flavor hops for the last 30 minutes of the boil. Add the 15-minute flavor hops for the last 15 minutes. Add the Irish moss for the final 10 minutes of the boil. Add the flavor/ aroma hops for the final 1 minute.

After a total wort boil of 60 minutes, turn off the heat and place the pot (with cover on) in a running cold-water bath for 45 minutes. Continue to chill in the immersion or use other methods to chill your wort. Then strain and sparge the wort into a sanitized fermenter. Bring the total volume to 5½ gallons (21 l) with additional cold water if necessary. Aerate the wort very well.

Pitch the yeast when temperature of wort is about 70 degrees F (21 C). Once visible signs of fermentation are evident ferment at temperatures of about 55 degrees F (12.5 C) for about 1 week or until fermentation shows signs of calm and stopping. Rack from your primary to a secondary. If you have the capability, "lager" the beer at temperatures between 35 and 45 degrees F (1.5–7 C) for 3 to 8 weeks.

Prime with sugar and bottle or keg when fermentation is complete.

Unspoken Passion Raspberry Imperial Stout (Malt Extract)

Liquid sex in a bottle. This brew will leave you and your beer friends speechless. If you like the rich, creamy smoothness of a chocolate raspberry fudge cake or have ever imagined what raspberries dipped in semisweet chocolate could be like, then Unspoken Passion is a royal flush and you need to play your hand.

In the tradition of imperial stout, this ale is brewed with an alcoholic strength of 7.6 percent by volume and enough bitterness to offset the rich, heavy body contributed by the generous amount of malt. A blend of roasted barley, chocolate malt, black patent malt, and crystal malt contributes significantly to the character of the final brew.

The intensity of the raspberry flavor and acidity really comes through in the unfermented wort and at bottling; but with maturity the raspberry character

softens and melts into the full-bodied texture of a brew that will simply leave you and your friends speechless. Any bittering hop can be used, but high-alpha hops are most convenient, since 38 homebrew bittering units are called for in the recipe. For finishing, Cascade, Nelson Sauvin, and Citra hops are especially chosen because of their fruity/citrusy and tropical characters, a perfect complement to this brew.

Dare to brew something different and very special.

Best put up in small bottles and served in stemmed glassware. Serve cool in the winter months and, if it suits you (it certainly suits me), serve cold in warm weather as a rich, satisfying sipping refreshment.

The recipe is for 6½ gallons (24.7 l) because 5 gallons (19 l) just isn't enough and the beer ages extremely well.

Ingredients for 6½ gallons (24.7 l):

11 lb. (5 kg)	plain amber dried malt extract or 13 lb. (5.9 kg) amber malt extract syrup
1¼ lb. (0.57 kg)	crystal or caramel malt (20 L)
½ lb. (227 g)	debittered black roasted malt
¾ lb. (340 g)	roasted barley
½ lb. (227 g)	chocolate roasted malt
2½ oz. (70 g)	Chelan, Magnum, Newport, or Apollo hops (boiling): 38 HBU (1050 MBU)

1 oz. (28 g)   Cascade or Citra hops (steeping, aroma)
1 oz. (28 g)   New Zealand Nelson Sauvin hops (steeping, aroma)
2 tsp. (8 g)   gypsum (calcium sulfate) if soft water is used
11 lb. (5 kg)   red raspberries (crushed, unsweetened, fresh or thawed
                frozen)
*   Any ale yeast will do, depending on what fermentation
                character you may want to add to the character. If you want
                to accent malt, hops, and raspberries, use American Ale
                1056 or White Labs Cry Havoc.
1 c. (240 ml)   corn sugar (dextrose) or $1\frac{1}{2}$ c. (355 ml) dried malt extract
                (for bottling); or $\frac{1}{2}$ c. (240 ml) corn sugar (dextrose)
                for kegging
1   10-gallon food-grade plastic fermenter

O.G.: 1.080–1.084 (19.3–20.2)
F.G.: 1.022–1.030 (5.5–7.5)
Bitterness: 80–90 BU; Color: 40 SRM (80 EBC); Alcohol: 7.6%
    by volume

NOTE: A carboy fermentation primary fermentation. You need to use a clean, sanitized food-grade 10-gallon plastic vessel for primary fermentation. Allow at least 6 inches (16 cm) of head space in your fermenter so that the foamy kraeusen does not overflow. If you really wish to use glass carboys, split the batch between two $6\frac{1}{2}$-gallon (25 l) carboys.

Add the crushed crystal, black and chocolate malts, and the roasted barley to 3 gallons (11.4 l) of 150-degree F (66 C) water and hold for 30 minutes. Remove the grains with a strainer.

Add the malt extract, gypsum (if using very soft water), and boiling hops; bring to a full and vigorous boil and boil for 60 minutes.

Turn off the heat. Use a strainer to remove as much of the boiling hops as possible from the hot concentrated wort. Then add room-temperature raspberries and the steeping hops. Without adding any more heat, let steep at about 145 to 165 degrees F (63–74 C) for 30 minutes.

Add 4 gallons (15.2 l) of cold water to your sanitized fermenter. Add your hot wort, raspberries, and finishing hops to the fermenter and top up with cold water to make a total volume of 8 gallons (30.4 l). If you are using two glass $6\frac{1}{2}$-gallon (25 l) fermenters, add 2 gallons (7.6 l) of cold water to each and top with cold water to make two 4-gallon (15.2 l) batches.

Aerate the wort very well. Pitch the yeast when cool and let ferment for 7 to 10 days. You will notice that most of the raspberries and hops are pregnant with carbon dioxide and float to the surface. Do not disturb them.

On the seventh to tenth day siphon the fermentation to a $6\frac{1}{2}$-gallon (25 l) fermenter. Insert the hose between the floating layer of spent fruit and hops, and the bottom sediment. Relax. Don't worry about the few floating pieces of hops and fruit that may end up in your secondary.

Let fermentation go to completion, and bottle with 1 cup of corn sugar (dextrose). Be patient; carbonation may take a little longer because of the strength of this brew. If you plan on keeping bottles for more than a year, dip the capped bottles into melted paraffin or sealing wax to create a better barrier to oxygen.

Ohhh man, ohhh girl—it's gonna be a good one!

Gnarly Roots Lambic-Fringed Barley Wine Ale (Mash Extract)

Are you ready to try something really different? How about a strong 10 percent copper-colored ale with enough of a wild, fruity, and sour quirkiness to enhance the pleasure of an already wonderfully complex barley wine ale?

Using a barleywine ale recipe template, introducing and active cultures of *Brettanomyces bruxellensis* and *Brettanomyces lambicus* 1 week after the initial cultured yeast is pitched, creates a unique sensory experience.

The result is not a typical strongly soured Belgian lambic. Rather, the Belgian lambic character is obvious but gentle. Because of the high alcohol content

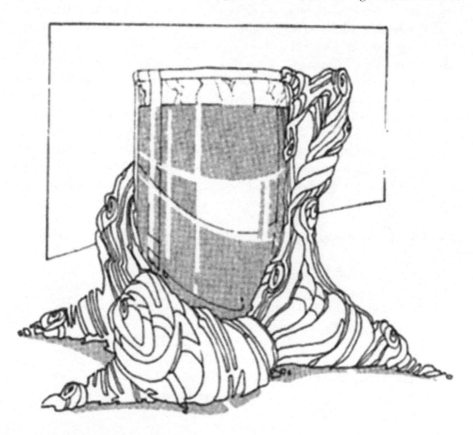

and the vigorous start of the cultured yeast, the *Brettanomyces* cultures are somewhat inhibited, but indeed survive.

This high-gravity barley wine is strongly hopped, but because of the high alcohol and relatively high final gravity, the bitterness is nicely balanced by the sweetness of the malt and by the fruity acidity of the lambic-type yeast by-products.

Let it age. Let it age. Let it age. Lagering at 60- to 70-degree F (15.6–21 C) cellar temperatures is perfect for this brew. It is best to rack the brew into a secondary closed fermenter because of the long storage time. The second fermenter is preferably glass so you can observe the disconcerting scum that forms on the surface of the beer as a result of the action of the *Brettanomyces* yeasts.

The *Brettanomyces* yeasts are wild and tend to break down and ferment some of the normally unfermentable carbohydrates. Be patient. I waited eight months to bottle my Gnarly Roots. And it tasted *soooo* incredibly good when I bottled it, I couldn't wait for it to carbonate. Unfortunately it may take several months to properly carbonate.

You will observe great clarity of the brew after eight months and wonder (don't worry) about the viability of the yeast. In order to minimize the possibility of worrying, add one package (14–21 g) of rehydrated dried lager yeast.

Since this is a long-lagered and well-aged brew, it is of utmost importance to reduce the risk of oxidation. When racking the brew from primary to secondary or from secondary to the bottling carboy, it helps to purge the air out of the receiving carboys with carbon dioxide. This can be accomplished with a ten- or fifteen-second shot of carbon dioxide from your regulated CO_2 tapping system or a couple of gumball-size pieces of dry ice added to the receiving carboy. When bottling, be careful not to aerate or splash the beer. The use of oxygen-absorbing barrier bottlecaps will enhance the life of this beer. Dip the capped bottles into melted paraffin or sealing wax to create a better barrier to oxygen.

Ingredients for 6½ to 7 gallons (25–26.6 l), because 5 gallons (19 l) isn't enough:

4 lb. (1.8 kg)	pale malted barley
1 lb. (0.45 kg)	crystal or caramel malt (10 L)
13 lb. (5.9 kg)	light dried malt extract or 15.3 lb. (6.9 kg) light malt extract syrup
¼ lb. (114 g)	Columbus/Tomahawk™/Zeus (CTZ), Australian Galaxy, Bravo hops (boiling): 60 HBU (1680 MBU)
1½ oz. (43 g)	Simcoe or Warrior hops (10 minutes, flavor)
1½ oz. (43 g)	Cascade or Citra hops (steeping, aroma)
¼ tsp. (1 g)	Irish moss powder

*	ale yeast: American Ale 1056 strain works well; White Labs Cry Havoc works well at both warmer and cooler temperatures
1	packet of dried Safale lager yeast for bottling
1 each	Cultures of *Brettanomyces lambicus* and *Brettanomyces bruxellensis*
1 c. (240 ml)	corn sugar (dextrose) or 1½ c. (355 ml) dried malt extract (for bottling); or ½ c. (240 ml) corn sugar (dextrose) for kegging

O.G.: 1.110 (25.9)
F.G.: 1.024–1.032 (6–8)
Bitterness: 80–100 BU; Color: 14 SRM (28 EBC); Alcohol: 10.8%
    by volume

A step infusion mash is employed to mash the grains. Add 5 quarts (4.8 l) of 143-degree F (61.5 C) water to the crushed grain, stir, stabilize and hold the temperature at 132 degrees F (53 C) for 30 minutes. Add 2½ quarts (2.4 l) of boiling water and add heat to bring temperature up to 155 degrees F (68 C) and hold for about 30 minutes. Then raise temperature to 167 degrees F (75 C), lauter and sparge with 3 gallons (11.4 l) of 170-degree F (77 C) water. Collect about 3½ gallons (13.3 l) of runoff.

Add the malt extract and boiling hops, bring to a full and vigorous boil, and boil for 1 hour 15 minutes. Add flavor hops and the Irish moss for the final 10 minutes of the boil.

After a total wort boil of 1 hour 15 minutes, turn off heat and add the steeping hops. Immerse the lidded pot of boiled wort in a tub of cold water for 30 minutes to help cool it. Change water after the first 15 minutes. Then strain, sparge and transfer the wort to a fermenter partly filled with 2 gallons (7.6 l) of cold water.

Pitch yeast when wort is about 70 degrees F (21 C). After 1 week of primary fermentation, add *Brettanomyces* yeasts to the fermentation. Rack into a secondary after one month. Allow to slowly ferment for 6 to 8 months at cellar temperatures of about 60 to 70 degrees F (15.5–21 C). (Note: Avoid disturbing the white scum covering the surface. As a barrier, it helps prevent oxidation.)

Bottle after six to eight months. When siphoning, draw beer from beneath the surface scum and most of it will remain behind or migrate and adhere to the sides of the fermenter as the level falls, but don't worry. At bottling time add a fresh slurry of rehydrated dried lager yeast to help assure proper bottle conditioning. And remember, you'll want to keep these bottles for prolonged aging. Dip the capped bottles into melted paraffin or sealing wax to create a better barrier to oxygen.

As a courtesy for your next brews, thoroughly sanitize all equipment that has come in contact with this batch of beer. Use chlorine bleach as a sanitizer.

Relax. You're in for a real treat. And if you ever run into me somewhere or someplace, I wouldn't turn down an offer to try your batch of Gnarly Roots Barley Wine Ale.

Here to Heaven Snow Angel Oktoberfest Wine Ale (Mash Extract)

American-style barley wine ales are a feisty lot. Some, approaching 10.5 percent alcohol by volume, offer sipping pleasure for those who enjoy the play of the intense bitterness of hops with the full-bodied sweetness of malt. Here to Heaven Snow Angel Oktoberfest Wine Ale is a departure from the Americanization of an English tradition, bringing into consideration the alacrity of Bavarian-style amber malts and a lower level of bitterness. The deep amber color reflects the warmth of the brewer's soul, as you will surely agree.

If bitterness units are calculated, one is led to believe there are about 130 units of bitterness in this brew. This will not be accurate because of the very high gravity of the boiled wort. The bitterness is indeed very high, but with proper aging, a balance is achieved with the rich combination of Munich and crystal malts.

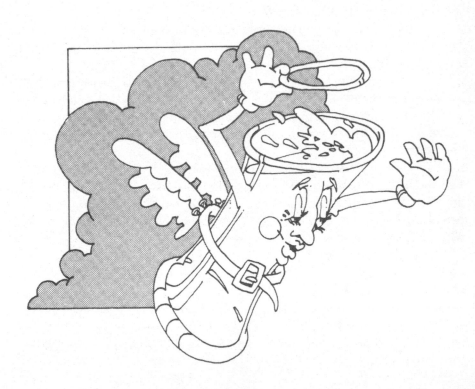

The actual original gravity will be slightly less than a calculated gravity due to the nonlinear nature of wort density measurements, as wort becomes very high in gravity.

The recipe is for 6½ gallons (25 l). It is a patient beer that ages well. It is well worth having 1½ gallons (5.7 l) more than your typical 5-gallon (19 l) batch.

Ingredients for 6½ gallons (25 l):

2 lb. (0.9 kg)	pale malted barley
3 lb. (1.36 kg)	Munich malt
1 lb. (0.45 kg)	crystal or caramel malt (20 L)
12 lb. (5.5 kg)	light dried malt extract or 15 lb. (6.8 kg) light malt extract syrup
¼ lb. (114 g))	Magnum or Newport hops (boiling): 60 HBU (1680 MBU)
1½ oz. (43 g)	German Hersbruck or Hallertau hops (10 minutes, flavor)
1½ oz. (43 g)	German Mittelfrüh, Mt. Hood, or Santiam hops (steeping, aroma)
¼ tsp. (1 g)	Irish moss powder
*	ale yeast, such as American Ale 1056 or White Labs Cry Havoc
1 c. (240 ml)	corn sugar (dextrose) or 1½ c. (355 ml) dried malt extract (for bottling); or ½ c. (240 ml) corn sugar (dextrose) for kegging

O.G.: 1.10 (25.9)
F.G.: 1.028–1.032 (7–8)
Bitterness: 80–100 BU; Color: 15 SRM (30 EBC); Alcohol: 10.8% by volume

A step infusion mash is employed to mash the grains. Add 6 quarts (5.7 l) of 143-degree F (61.5 C) water to the crushed grain, stir, stabilize and hold the temperature at 132 degrees F (53 C) for 30 minutes. Add 3 quarts (3 l) of boiling water and add heat to bring temperature up to 155 degrees F (68 C) and hold for about 30 minutes. Then raise temperature to 167 degrees F (75 C), lauter and sparge with 3½ gallons (13.5 l) of 170-degree F (77 C) water. Collect about 3½ gallons (13.3 l) of runoff.

Add the malt extract and boiling hops, bring to a full and vigorous boil, and boil for 1 hour 15 minutes. Add the flavor hops and the Irish moss for the final 10 minutes of the boil.

After a total wort boil of 1 hour 15 minutes, add the steeping hops and turn off heat. Immerse the lidded pot of boiled wort in a tub of cold water for 30 minutes to help cool it. Change water after the first 15 minutes. Then strain, sparge and transfer the wort to a fermenter partly filled with 2 gallons (7.6 l) of cold water.

Aerate the wort very well. Pitch yeast when wort is about 70 degrees F (21 C). Ferment at about 70 degrees F (21 C) for about 2 to 3 weeks or until fermentation shows signs of calm and stopping. Rack from your primary to a secondary. "Cellar" the beer at about 55 degrees F (12.5 C) for about 4 weeks.

Prime with sugar and bottle or keg when fermentation is complete.

Carla Vitoria's Barley Wheat Wine Ale (Mash Extract)

Formulated and brewed to commemorate the birth of our daughter. This barley wheat wine is a hybrid character of a classic English-style barley wine ale and a strong copper-colored Abbey ale (that happens to be famously Trappiste). The ester character is mild and is more English-like. The recipe has a deliberate blend of roasted and toasted malts: mild malt, aromatic malt, and Belgian Special-B malt. Age this brew slowly and patiently at cellar temperatures. It's a beer to be savored years from now.

Ingredients for 5½ gallons (21 l):

3 lb. (1.36 kg)	light malt extract syrup or 2.6 lb. (1.2 kg) very light dried malt extract
6½ lb. (3 kg)	Marris Otter malt
3 lb. (1.36 kg)	English mild malt
2½ lb. (1.15 kg)	wheat malt
½ lb. (227 g)	English crystal malt (10 L)
½ lb. (227 g)	Belgian aromatic
¼ lb. (114 g)	Belgian Special-B malt
½ lb. (227 g)	dark *rapadura* sugar
2 oz. (56 g)	Liberty hops (boiling): 9 HBU (252 MBU)
1 oz. (28 g)	Vanguard hops (30 minutes, flavor): 5 HBU (140 MBU)
1 oz. (28 g)	Mt. Hood hops (10 minutes, flavor): 5.25 HBU (147 MBU)
2 oz. (56 g)	Cascade hops (1 minute, aroma)
1 oz. (28 g)	Crystal hop pellets (dry hopping)
¼ tsp (1 g)	Irish moss powder
*	Wyeast Thames Valley Ale yeast, White Labs English Ale yeast, or White Labs Cry Havoc lager/ale yeast
¾ c. (175 ml)	corn sugar (dextrose) or 1¼ c. (300 ml) dried malt extract (for bottling); or ⅓ c. (80 ml) corn sugar (dextrose) for kegging

O.G.: 1.083–1.086 (20–20.7)
F.G.: 1.022–1.026 (5.5–6.5)
Bitterness: 50 BU; Color: 15 SRM (30 EBC); Alcohol: 8% by volume

A step infusion mash is employed to mash the grains. Add 13 quarts (12.4 l) of 143-degree F (61.5 C) water to the crushed grain, stir, stabilize and hold the temperature at 132 degrees F (53 C) for 30 minutes. Add 6½ quarts (6.2 l) of boiling water and add heat to bring temperature up to 155 degrees F (68 C) and hold for about 30 minutes. Then raise temperature to 167 degrees F (75 C), lauter and sparge with 3½ gallons (13.5 l) of 170-degree F (77 C) water. Collect about 5½ gallons (21 l) of runoff.

Add the malt extract, *rapadura,* and boiling hops; bring to a full and vigorous boil and boil for 60 minutes. Add the 30-minutes flavor hops for the last 30 minutes of the boil. Add the 10-minute flavor hops and Irish moss for the last 10 minutes of the boil. Add the aroma hops for the final 1 minute.

After a total wort boil of 60 minutes, turn off the heat and place the pot (with cover on) in a running cold-water bath for 45 minutes. Continue to chill in the immersion or use other methods to chill your wort. Then strain and sparge the wort into a sanitized fermenter. Bring the total volume to 5½ gallons (21 l) with additional cold water if necessary. Aerate the wort very well.

Pitch the yeast when temperature of wort is about 70 degrees F (21 C). Ferment at about 70 degrees F (21 C) for about 2 weeks or until fermentation shows signs of calm and stopping. Rack from your primary to a secondary and add the hop pellets for dry hopping. "Cellar" the beer at about 60 degrees F (15.5 C) for about 1 month or when fermentation is finished.

Prime with sugar and bottle or keg when fermentation is complete.

For Peat's Sake "Scotch" Ale (Mash Extract)

By no stretch of the imagination does this ale resemble Scottish-style ales or strong Scotch ales. It is a very interesting experiment to introduce to your palate. Going to the edge. It is a brew possibly for those who enjoy their single-malt scotch rich and smoky (as with Laphroaig).

For Peat's Sake "Scotch" Ale is balanced as a malty export Scottish-style ale, with one very important difference. Almost 30 percent of the grain bill is peat-smoked malt. The result is an intensely smoke-flavored ale—not the mellow smoke flavor of a Bavarian Rauchbier but an almost medicinal character unique to smoky peat moss. This ale mellows somewhat with age and will surely intrigue single malt scotch enthusiasts. For those not quite as enthusiastic, the peat-smoked malt could be cut back to 5 percent and the difference made up with English pale ale malt. But for now let's go on an adventure . . . if you dare.

Ingredients for 5 gallons (19 l):

3 lb. (1.4 kg)	light dried malt extract or 3½ lb. (1.6 kg) light malt extract syrup
2.2 lb. (1 kg)	peat-smoked malted barley
1 lb. (0.45 kg)	crystal or caramel malt
2 lb. (0.9 kg)	Vienna malt
1 oz. (28 g)	English or Styrian Goldings hops (boiling): 5 HBU (140 MBU)
1 oz. (28 g)	English Kent Goldings hops (15 minutes, flavor): 5 HBU (140 MBU)
¼ tsp. (1 g)	Irish moss powder
*	English- or American-type ale yeast
¾ c. (175 ml)	corn sugar (dextrose) or 1¼ c. (300 ml) dried malt extract (for bottling); or ⅓ c. (80 ml) corn sugar (dextrose) for kegging

O.G.: 1.052–1.056 (13–14)
F.G.: 1.016–1.020 (4–5)
Bitterness: 20 BU; Color: 10 SRM (20 EBC); Alcohol: 4.7% by volume

Use a single-step infusion mash schedule for this recipe.

Add crushed malts to 5 quarts (4.8 l) of 168-degree F (76 C) water. The mash will stabilize at 153 to 158 degrees F (67–70 C). Hold this temperature at the high end for 60 minutes. Sparge with about 2 gallons (7.6 l) of 170-degree F (77 C) water. Add more water (do not oversparge) to brewpot if necessary to make an initial extract volume of about 2½ gallons (9.5 l).

Add the malt extract and boiling hops, bring to a full and vigorous boil, and boil for 60 minutes. Add the flavor hops for the last 15 minutes of the boil. Add the Irish moss for the final 10 minutes of the boil.

After a total wort boil of 60 minutes, turn off heat and place the pot (with cover on) in a running cold-water bath for 45 minutes. Continue to chill in the immersion or use other methods to chill your wort. Remove the hops and transfer to a sanitized fermenter filled with 2 gallons of cold water. Bring the total volume to 5 gallons (19 l) with additional cold water if necessary. Aerate the wort very well.

Pitch the yeast when temperature of wort is about 70 degrees F (21 C). Ferment at about 70 degrees F (21 C) for about 1 week or until fermentation shows signs of calm and stopping. Rack from your primary to a secondary. If you have the capability, "cellar" the beer at about 55 degrees F (12.5 C) for about 1 week.

Prime with sugar and bottle or keg when fermentation is complete.

Return to Innocence Mountain
Juniper–Cherry Bock (All Grain)

This brew is all about finding your local mojo. Beer style guidelines offer reverence for tradition and inspiration for necessary and continued innovation. One frontier worth exploring in your own area is the marriage of ingredients of local origin and indigenous cultural processes. I've had the pleasure of tasting several specialty beers brewed by the poets of the brewers' world, Italian small craft brewers. Several brewers were striving to develop their beer with ingredients purely indigenous and identifiable to their community and environment. They presented for tasting a beer whose base foundation was a Belgian wit, but instead of the traditional coriander and orange peel, they added uniquely flavored tree lichen from the forest that surrounded their village. Another added a unique citrus fruit, grown only in the valley in which they lived.

Italians are not the only ones capturing the uniqueness of their community and environment. You are on the frontier. Alder-smoked beer and spruce-tip-flavored beer makes it for brewers of the Northwest. Perhaps it is hickory, mesquite, or maplewood smoked malt in other parts of the world. These are but a few simple examples. It's not just about using unique ingredients, but seeking the cultural process of your environment and blending them into the essence of beer formulation.

Go where no other has gone before. You and I likely have our standby brews of Czech-style light lager, pale ale, bitter, Belgian tripel, German Rauchbier, German Dunkel, IPAs, lambics, barley wines, or other everyday brews currently on tap. But every once in a while break out and find your local mojo. Your return to innocence, so to speak.

I made the mental effort to look around and look more closely at where I lived. The result: Return to Innocence Mountain Juniper–Cherry Bock. Along the mountain trail my wife, Sandra, and I harvested low-bush berry-laden mountain juniper. The month before Sandra had harvested 7 pounds of plump and flavorful chokecherries, freezing them for a future creation. I reminisced fondly about the birch-smoked malt and juniper-flavored Gotlandsdricka of Sweden (see *Microbrewed Adventures*) and wanted to brew something especially unique to my environment using local ingredients. The result is a bock-strength, subtly smoked cherry-juniper-flavored specialty that represents in part where I work, live, love, dance, and play.

Ingredients for 5½ gallons (21 l):

6 lb. (2.7 kg)	Pilsener malt
4 lb. (1.82 kg)	Munich malt
1 lb. (454 g)	smoked malt
½ lb. (227 g)	honey malt

½ lb. (227 g)	aromatic malt
¼ lb. (114 g)	German sauer malt
2 oz. (56 g)	chocolate malt
1 oz. (28 g)	debittered black malt
¾ lb. (340 g)	fresh-cut, fragrant, low-growing mountain juniper (*Juniperus communis*) branches with berries (the "berries" are actually classified as "cones")
¾ oz. (21 g)	Perle hops (60 minutes): 5.25 HBU (147 MBU)
1½ oz. (42 g)	Vanguard or Liberty hops (45 minutes, flavor): 5.25 HBU (147 MBU)
1¼ oz. (35 g)	Mt. Hood or Santiam hops (15 minutes, flavor): 7.5 HBU (210 MBU)
½ oz. (14 g)	Santiam hop pellets (dry hopping, aroma)
2 oz. (56 g)	Cascade hops (dry hopping, aroma)
7 lbs. (3.2 kg)	crushed chokecherries (or other available local cherries)
¼ tsp (1 g)	Irish moss powder
*	German or Bavarian-type lager yeast
¾ c. (175 ml)	corn sugar (dextrose) or 1¼ c. (300 ml) dried malt extract (for bottling); or ⅓ c. (80 ml) corn sugar (dextrose) for kegging

O.G.: 1.062–1.066 (15.2–16.1)
F.G.: 1.016–1.020 (4–5)
Bitterness: 40 BU; Color: 15 SRM (30 EBC); Alcohol: 6.1% by volume

A step infusion mash is employed to mash the grains. Add 12½ quarts (12 l) of 143-degree F (61.5 C) water to the crushed grain, stir, stabilize and hold the temperature at 132 degrees F (53 C) for 30 minutes. Add 6 quarts (5.7 l) of boiling water and add heat to bring temperature up to 155 degrees F (68 C) and hold for about 30 minutes. Then raise temperature to 167 degrees F (75 C), lauter and sparge with 3½ gallons (13.5 l) of 170-degree F (77 C) water. Collect about 5½ gallons (21 l) of runoff.

Add the boiling hops and juniper, bring to a full and vigorous boil, and boil for 60 minutes. Add the 45-minute flavor hops for the last 45 minutes of the boil. Add the 15-minute flavor hops for the last 15 minutes of the boil. Add the Irish moss for the final 10 minutes of the boil.

After a total wort boil of 60 minutes, turn off the heat and place the pot (with cover on) in a running cold-water bath for 45 minutes. Continue to chill in the immersion or use other methods to chill your wort. Then strain and sparge the wort into a sanitized fermenter. Bring the total volume to 5½ gallons (21 l) with additional cold water if necessary. Aerate the wort very well.

Pitch the yeast when temperature of wort is about 70 degrees F (21 C). Once visible signs of fermentation are evident ferment at temperatures of about 55 degrees F (12.5 C) for about 1 week or until fermentation shows signs of calm and stopping. Rack from your primary to a 6½-gallon (24.7 l) secondary and add the hops for dry hopping along with the crushed chokecherries. Continue secondary at 55 degrees for 2 to 4 weeks. Then rack from secondary to a third fermenter leaving behind the hops and chokecherry sediment. "Lager" the beer at temperatures between 35 and 45 degrees F (1.5–7 C) for 4 to 6 weeks.

Prime with sugar and bottle or keg when fermentation is complete.

SPECIALTY AND UNUSUAL ALES

The Horse You Rode in On Apricot Honey Spiced Ale (All Grain)

Yes, you and the horse you rode in on.

Now, after taking that, you deserve something very special! Jointly brewed from a recipe formulated by brew pal Tracy Loysen (she deserves the creative kudos for this one), this has got to be one of my all-time favorite fruit beers. If you enjoy the flavor and aroma of apricots and coriander, you will flip out over this indescribably amazing ale.

Light on the palate, light on the color, wondrously floral and fruity, blessedly acidic, perfectly balanced: malt, hop flavor, bitterness, body, and a colorful glow of gold. This ale will inspire the poet in you.

Ingredients for 5 gallons (19 l):

7½ lb. (3.4 kg)	American 2-row lager malt
1 lb. (0.45 kg)	Munich malt
1 lb. (0.45 kg)	wheat malt
¼ lb. (114 g)	crystal or caramel malt (40 L)
½ c. (120 ml)	honey (for just because)
1 oz. (28 g)	German Hallertau or Saphir hops (boiling): 5.2 HBU (145 MBU)
½ oz. (14 g)	American Tettnang or Mt. Hood hops (10 minutes, flavor)
1 oz. (28 g)	American Tettnang hops (2 minutes, aroma)
1 oz. (28 g)	freshly crushed coriander seeds
7 lb. (3.2 kg)	fresh or thawed frozen apricots, peeled (see Note)
¼ tsp. (1 g)	Irish moss powder
*	ale yeast, such as American Ale 1056
¾ c. (175 ml)	corn sugar (dextrose) or 1¼ c. (300 ml) dried malt extract (for bottling); or ⅓ c. (80 ml) corn sugar (dextrose) for kegging

O.G.: 1.055–1.059 (12–14)
F.G.: 1.008–1.014 (2–3.5)
Bitterness: 26 BU; Color: 7 SRM (14 EBC); Alcohol: 6.2% by volume

A step infusion mash is employed to mash the grains. Add 10½ quarts (10 l) of 143-degree F (61.5 C) water to the crushed grain, stir, stabilize and hold the temperature at 132 degrees F (53 C) for 30 minutes. Add 5½ quarts (5.2 l) of boiling water and add heat to bring temperature up to 155 degrees F (68 C) and hold for about 30 minutes. Then raise temperature to 167 degrees F (75 C), lauter and sparge with 3½ gallons (13.5 l) of 170-degree F (77 C) water. Collect about 5½ gallons (21 l) of runoff.

Add the honey and boiling hops, bring to a full and vigorous boil, and boil for 60 minutes. Add the flavor hops and Irish moss for the last 10 minutes of the boil. Add the aroma hops and ½ ounce (14 g) of the coriander seed for the final 2 minutes.

After a total wort boil of 60 minutes, turn off the heat and place the pot (with cover on) in a running cold-water bath for 45 minutes. Continue to chill in the immersion or use other methods to chill your wort. Then strain and sparge the wort into a sanitized fermenter. Bring the total volume to 5 gallons (19 l) with additional cold water if necessary. Aerate the wort very well.

Pitch the yeast when temperature of wort is about 70 degrees F (21 C). Once visible signs of fermentation are evident ferment at temperatures of about 55 degrees F (12.5 C) for about 1 week or until fermentation shows signs of calm. Rack from your primary to a 6½-gallon (25 l) secondary fermenter and add apricots and remaining ½ ounce (14 g) ground coriander seeds. Let the fruit and coriander sit with the beer for 1 to 2 weeks. If you have the capability, "lager" the beer at temperatures between 35 and 45 degrees F (1.5–7 C) for 3 to 6 weeks.

Prime with sugar and bottle or keg when fermentation is complete.

You may notice wild "surface" yeast on your bottled beer. This will not usually affect the character of your beer. Don't worry. The acidity and alcohol of your beer will inhibit the microorganisms you've introduced into the secondary with the fruit. Relax.

Note: Fresh apricots are easily peeled if immersed in boiling water for 30 to 45 seconds. The skins will slip off. This process can be done ahead of time or during apricot season and the skinned fruit (pits removed) frozen in unused, new freezer bags until ready to use. Wash your hands thoroughly before handling the fruit.

Mile High Green Chile Ale (All Grain)

Russ can certainly be credited with having brewed one of the first microbrewed chile beers in the country at the Wynkoop Brewery

The British would never dream of doing this to their pale ale. But American homebrewers and pioneer microbrewers couldn't resist. If you like roasted green chiles, then you won't be able to resist this beer either. My first pleasure of the combination of roasted green chile and ale was at Denver's Wynkoop Brewery, where the original brewmaster, Russ Scherer, added freshly roasted green chiles to a finessed pale ale formulation. This Mile High Green Chile Ale is a homebrewed version of what you can still experience at the downtown brewpub. It's both spicy and exotic with unzipped and dominating roast chile flavor, balanced heat, and a smooth, purely drinkable English-style pale ale. It

has to be brewed to believe. If you like mo hotta mo bettah, then you know how to customize this recipe to your taste. (This recipe originally appeared in *Microbrewed Adventures*.)

Ingredients for 5 gallons (19 l):

7½ lb. (3.4 kg)	pale malt
1 lb. (454 g)	crystal malt (20 L)
½ oz. (14 g)	UK Kent Goldings or Glacier hops (boiling): 3.5 HBU (98 MBU)
½ oz. (14 g)	UK Fuggles or Willamette hops (boiling): 2.5 HBU (70 MBU)
1 oz. (21 g)	UK Kent Goldings or UK Bramling Cross hops (20 minutes, flavor)
1 lb. (454 g)	fire-roasted green Anaheim, Santa Fe, Hatch, or available green chiles with roasted skins. Use freshly roasted or thawed frozen chilies
¼ tsp (1 g)	Irish moss powder

*   American-type ale yeast
¾ c. (175 ml)   corn sugar (dextrose) or 1¼ c. (300 ml) dried malt extract
                        (for bottling); or ⅓ c. (80 ml) corn sugar (dextrose) for
                        kegging

O.G.: 1.050–1.054 (12.5–13.5)
F.G.: 1.010–1.014 (2.5–3.5)
Bitterness: 35 BU; Color: 9 SRM (18 EBC); Alcohol: 5.1% by volume

A step infusion mash is employed to mash the grains. Add 8½ quarts (8.1 l) of 143-degree F (61.5 C) water to the crushed grain, stir, stabilize and hold the temperature at 132 degrees F (53 C) for 30 minutes. Add 4 quarts (3.8 l) of boiling water and add heat to bring temperature up to 155 degrees F (68 C) and hold for about 30 minutes. Then raise temperature to 167 degrees F (75 C), lauter and sparge with 3½ gallons (13.5 l) of 170-degree F (77 C) water. Collect about 5½ gallons (21 l) of runoff.

Add the boiling hops, bring to a full and vigorous boil, and boil for 60 minutes. Add the flavor hops for the last 20 minutes of the boil. Add the Irish moss for the final 10 minutes of the boil.

After a total wort boil of 60 minutes, turn off the heat and place the pot (with cover on) in a running cold-water bath for 30 minutes. Continue to chill in the immersion or use other methods to chill your wort. Then strain and sparge the wort into a sanitized fermenter. Bring the total volume to 5 gallons (19 l) with additional cold water if necessary. Aerate the wort very well.

Pitch the yeast when temperature of wort is about 70 degrees F (21 C). Ferment at about 70 degrees F (21 C) for about 1 week or until fermentation shows signs of calm and stopping. Rack from your primary to a secondary and add chopped roasted chilies. "Cellar" the beer at about 55 degrees F (12.5 C) for about 1 week.

Prime with sugar and bottle or keg when fermentation is complete.

Topple Over Anise-thetic Brown Ale (Malt Extract)

This is an extraordinarily simple English-style brown ale but with a difference. Star anise is added to the boil, imparting a licorice- or anise-like flavor. It is not for those who don't appreciate anise flavor. For those who do, this malt-emphasized beer is a real treat and ages well as the anise melds with the malt sweetness. Bitterness is kept low intentionally. A combination of bitterness and licorice may seem uninvitingly harsh. Yet the addition of wonderfully floral Mt. Hood or Santiam hops for flavor and aroma complements the spiciness and cooling sensation of star anise.

Ingredients for 5 gallons (19 l):

3.3 lb. (1.5 kg)	plain light malt extract syrup
3.3 lb. (1.5 kg)	plain dark malt extract syrup
1 oz. (28 g)	Liberty or German Hallertau hops (boiling): 4.5 HBU (126 MBU)
½ oz. (14 g)	Mt. Hood hops (2.5 HBU [70 MBU]) or 1 oz. (28 g) French Strisselspalt hops (10 minutes, flavor)
½ oz. (14 g)	Mt. Hood, American Tettnang, or Santiam hops (steeping, aroma)
2 oz. (56 g)	whole star anise
¼ tsp. (1 g)	Irish moss powder
*	ale yeast
¾ c. (175 ml)	corn sugar (dextrose) or 1¼ c. (300 ml) dried malt extract (for bottling); or ⅓ c. (80 ml) corn sugar (dextrose) for kegging

O.G.: 1.050–1.054 (12.5–13.5)
F.G.: 1.016–1.020 (4–5)
Bitterness: 20 BU; Color: 20 SRM (40 EBC); Alcohol: 4.5% by volume

Add the malt extracts and boiling hops to 2 gallons of water and bring to a vigorous boil. Boil for 60 minutes. Add the star anise for the last 20 minutes of the boil. Add the flavor hops and Irish moss for the final 10 minutes of the boil.

After a total of 60 minutes turn off heat. Add the aroma hops and let steep for 2 to 3 minutes before sparging the hot wort into a fermenter filled with 2 gallons (7.6 l) cold water.

Aerate the wort very well. Pitch the yeast when temperature of wort is about 70 degrees F (21 C). Ferment at about 70 degrees F (21 C) for about 1 week or until fermentation shows signs of calm and stopping. Rack from your primary to a secondary. "Cellar" the beer at about 55 degrees F (12.5 C) for about 1 week.

Prime with sugar and bottle or keg when fermentation is complete.

Cucurbito Pepo (Pumpkin) Ale (All Grain)

Pumpkin ale? When the homebrewing renaissance began in the last quarter of the twentieth century, this may have been considered crazy and weird, but now it is America's most popular seasonal beer. Brewed for the fall season, it far exceeds the popularity of Oktoberfest beer as a harvest seasonal favorite!

Pumpkins were used in Colonial days as an essential ingredient in many brews. Why? Because there wasn't a supply of barley or other grain from which to brew. With a bit of tradition and modern art you can brew something that is as American as apple pie. Cucurbito Pepo (Pumpkin) Ale is not too assuming. With a medium body, adequate bitterness, amber color, alcoholic warmth, and comfort spices, this beer will be an incredible contribution to your repertoire of accomplishments.

The spices that lend a typical pumpkin-pie character are not overdone, but you can opt out of the spices if you choose to brew a simpler version. This is the kind of brew for which you invite friends over to help with the ceremonies of brewing. Surely a Thanksgiving or holiday season toast with Cucurbito Pepo Ale will be one of the most memorable. England, Belgium, and Germany, eat your hearts out.

Ingredients for 5 gallons (19 l):

10 lb. (4.54 kg)	American 6-row pale lager malt or 6½ lb. (3 kg) light malt extract syrup
1 lb. (0.45 kg)	crystal or caramel malt (20–40 L)
7–10 lb. (3.2–4.5 kg)	whole pumpkin (you can substitute any tasty heirloom winter squash)
2 oz. (56 g)	Willamette or Fuggles hops (boiling): 10 HBU (280 MBU)
½ oz. (14 g)	Cascade hops (10 minutes, flavor)
1 oz. (28 g)	Mt. Hood or Santiam hops (steeping, aroma)
¾ oz. (21 g)	Czech Saaz hop pellets (dry hopping, aroma)
1 tsp. (4 g)	ground cinnamon
1	vanilla bean, chopped
½ tsp. (2 g)	freshly grated nutmeg
¼ tsp. (1 g)	ground allspice (freshly ground if possible)
½ tsp. (2 g)	ground ginger
¼ tsp. (1 g)	Irish moss powder
*	ale yeast
¾ c. (175 ml)	corn sugar (dextrose) or 1¼ c. (300 ml) dried malt extract (for bottling); or ⅓ c. (80 ml) corn sugar (dextrose) for kegging

O.G.: 1.066–1.070 (16.5–17.5)
F.G.: 1.016–1.022 (4–5.5)
Bitterness: 33 BU; Color: 12 SRM (24 EBC); Alcohol: 6.6% by volume

Chill some homebrew the day before so that it's ready to enjoy on brew day. While the beer is chilling, slice the pumpkin in half and remove seeds and stringy "veins." Roast the pumpkin in a 350-degree F (177 C) oven for about 1 hour or until soft. The roasted pulp will be used in the mash.

Use a protein-developing step mash. Add 3 gallons (11.4 l) of 130-degree F (54.4 C) water to the crushed malt. Stabilize at 122 degrees F (50 C) and hold for 30 minutes. Then add 1½ gallons (5.7 l) of boiling water and thoroughly mashed pumpkin pulp. Add heat if necessary and stabilize at 150 to 155 degrees F (65.5–68.5 C) and hold for 60 minutes. Add more heat and mash out to 165 degrees F (74 C). Sparge with about 4 gallons (15.2 l) of 170-degree F (77 C) water. Initial extract volume may be about 7 gallons (26.6 l). Anticipate a long, vigorous boil and evaporation of 2 gallons (7.6 l).

Add the boiling hops, bring to a full and vigorous boil, and boil for 1 hour 30 minutes. When the volume of boiling wort approaches 5½ gallons (21 l), add the cinnamon, nutmeg, allspice, ginger, vanilla, flavor hops, and Irish moss and continue boiling 10 more minutes.

After a total wort boil of 1 hour 30 minutes, turn off heat. Add the steeping hops and place the pot (with cover on) in a running cold-water bath for 45 minutes. Continue to chill in the immersion or use other methods to chill your wort. Then strain and sparge the wort into a sanitized fermenter. Bring the total volume to 5 gallons (19 l) with additional cold water if necessary. Aerate the wort very well.

Pitch the yeast when temperature of wort is about 70 degrees F (21 C). Ferment at about 70 degrees F (21 C) for about 1 week or until fermentation shows signs of calm and stopping. Rack from your primary to a secondary and add the aroma dry hops. "Cellar" the beer at about 55 degrees F (12.5 C) for about 1 week.

Prime with sugar and bottle or keg when fermentation is complete.

Frumentacious Framboise (Malt Extract)

In the tradition of a lightly hopped, fruit-flavored "wild" beer, Frumentacious Framboise takes the redness, fruitiness, and acidity of raspberries and blends them with a minimally hopped wort and cultured and wild yeasts to produce a pungent, extremely estery, dry and acidic raspberry lambic-type ale.

This formulation is admittedly simplified: An all-barley-malt extract base is substituted for an all-grain mash of malted barley and wheat. Even with this simplification, Frumentacious Framboise bears a strong resemblance to what one might be able to find in the small and traditional beer cafés of Brussels. The addition of *Brettanomyces lambicus* and *Brettanomyces bruxellensis* yeast cultures imparts most of the unique fermentation character. And of course, the raspberries come through exquisitely.

Ingredients for 5 gallons (19 l):

4 lb. (1.8 kg)	light dried malt extract or 4.7 lb. (2.1 kg) light malt extract syrup
1 lb. (0.45 kg)	crystal or caramel malt (20–40 L)
½ oz. (14 g)	Styrian Goldings or Fuggles hops: 2.5 HBU (70 MBU)
8 lb. (3.6 kg)	red raspberries (unsweetened)
*	American or Belgian pale ale yeast culture
*	*Brettanomyces lambicus* and *Brettanomyces bruxellensis* yeast cultures

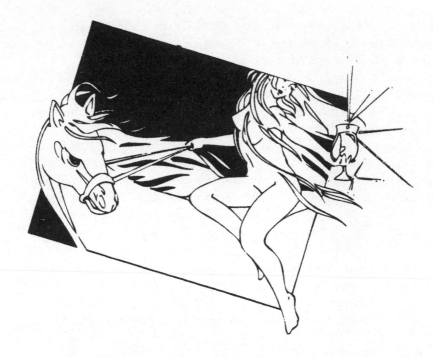

¾ c. (175 ml)   corn sugar (dextrose) or 1¼ c. (300 ml) dried malt extract
                (for bottling); or ⅓ c. (80 ml) corn sugar (dextrose)
                for kegging

O.G.: 1.046–1.050 (11.5–12.5)
F.G.: 1.004–1.008 (1–2)
Bitterness: 9 BU; Color: just plain red; Alcohol: 5.8% by volume

Add the crushed crystal malt to 2 gallons of 150-degree F (66 C) water and
hold for 30 minutes. Remove the grains with a strainer and add malt extract and
boiling hops. Boil for 60 minutes. Turn off the heat. Remove as much of the
spent hops with a strainer as possible (don't worry). Add crushed raspberries and
allow to steep at 150 to 160 degrees F (65.5–71 C) for 30 minutes to pasteurize
the fruited wort. Add this concentrated fruit-wort to cold water to make a total
volume of about 5½ gallons (21 l). If using glass fermenters, you will need to
split the batch evenly between two 5-gallon (19 l) fermenters for primary fermentation. Pitch both the ale and *Brettanomyces* yeast cultures when cool.

Allow to ferment with the fruit for 1 month. Siphon the fermentation to one
secondary fermenter, leaving behind as much fruit as possible. The specific gravity may be as low as 1.010 (2.5 degrees B) at this point. Aging for 7 to 10 more
months at about 60 degrees F (15.5 C) will allow the *Brettanomyces* to continue
breaking down carbohydrates not normally fermentable by cultured ale yeast. A

white film will cover the surface of your brew. Do not disturb this, as it helps minimize any oxidation that could occur (but don't worry). Check your fermentation lock once a month to ensure adequate water in the contraption.

Taste the brew after 4 or 5 months. If you wish the beer to be more acidic, you may add a *Lactobacillus* culture, but do so knowing that the results will be unpredictably good or perhaps not so good.

At bottling time, add priming sugar and rehydrated dried ale yeast to help ensure carbonation. Frumentacious Framboise is one beer that will stand up to years of aging. Bottling in small bottles helps preserve what will be a cherished stash. If you plan on keeping bottles for more than a year, dip the capped bottles into melted paraffin or sealing wax to create a better barrier to oxygen.

ANCIENT SPECIALTIES

Speltbrau (All Grain)

A hybrid beer combining ancient grains with modern brewing techniques and recipe formulation. Spelt, also known as dinkel, is an ancient heirloom wheat. With effort it can be found in malted form. If not, with a homebrewed determination, malted spelt and beer brewed from it can easily be made. Speltbrau may be an alternative beer for those who are allergic to barley and hybridized wheat. Spelt contains gluten. Consult your physician before consuming.

Ingredients for 2 gallons (7.6 l):

4 lb. (1.8 kg)	malted spelt
2 c. (½ l)	rice hulls (available at your homebrew supply store)
½ oz. (14 g)	Hallertau or American Tettnang hops (boiling): 2.25 HBU (63 MBU)
¼ oz. (7 g)	American Tettnang hops (dry hopping, aroma)
⅛ tsp. (1 g)	Irish moss powder
*	ale or lager yeast
⅓ c. (79 ml)	corn sugar (dextrose) (for bottling)

O.G.: 1.040–1.046 (10–11.5)
F.G.: 1.008–1.012 (2–3)
Bitterness: 22 BU; Color: 2 SRM (4 EBC); Alcohol: 4.5% by volume

Begin by malting about 6 pounds (2.73 kg) of spelt. Soak the spelt in fresh cool water for about 32 hours. Be sure to drain and change the water every 6 to 8 hours. After the soaking, drain and rinse one final time and place in a container to germinate. Meanwhile rinse the sprouting spelt with fresh water every 8 hours, or more frequently if desired. The spelt will develop rootlets and growing

acrospires. Sprouting will take place in 2 to 3 days, depending on conditions. Keep sprouting grains in a relatively cool and dark area. When the acrospires have reached a length equal to the length of the grain, it is time to dry the wet malt.

Rinse well before drying. The wet malt can be tied into a large sack and placed in a clothes dryer until dry. The malt may also be spread out on a flat surface and allowed to dry in a very warm area.

Finished malt should not be soft when chewed. It should be friable, crunchy, and have a slightly sweet flavor. The dried rootlets and shriveled acrospires will easily break off if the malt is roughly handled. They can be removed from the bulk of the malted kernel by pouring the grain from one container to another in the airstream of a fan—outdoors. Rubbing the grain over a wire screen will also serve to sieve off the dried rootlets and acrospires. But don't become worried about this.

Your spelt malt can be stored until you want to brew.

Using a protein-developing step mash, add 1 gallon (3.8 l) of 130-degree F (54.4 C) water to 4 pounds (1.8 kg) crushed malt and 2 cups (½ l) of dried rice hulls. Stabilize at 122 degrees F (50 C) and hold for 30 minutes. Then add ½ gallon (1.9 l) of boiling water. Stabilize at 152–154 degrees F (66.7–67.8 C) and hold for 60 minutes. Add heat and raise temperature to 158 degrees F (70 C) and hold for 20 minutes. Then mash out to 165 degrees F (74 C).

Slowly lauter and sparge with about 2 gallons (7.6 l) of 170-degree F (77 C) water. Because spelt does not have a husk, like barley, lautering a 100 percent spelt mash without rice hulls would be difficult. Rice hulls are added to provide a "fluff" to the mash so it will lauter more easily. If rice hulls are not available lauter, use only a 3- to 4-inch (7.6 to 10.2 cm) filter bed. This shallow bed minimizes the risk of grain bed compaction and stuck runoff. This may necessitate a series of two or three lauterings.

Initial extract volume should be about 2½ gallons (9.5 l). Anticipate evaporation of about ½ gallon (1.9 l).

Add the boiling hops, bring to a full and vigorous boil, and boil for 60 minutes. Add the Irish moss for the final 10 minutes of the boil.

After a total wort boil of 60 minutes, turn off the heat and place the pot (with cover on) in a running cold-water bath for 30 minutes. Continue to chill in the immersion or use other methods to chill your wort. Then strain and sparge the wort into a sanitized fermenter. Bring the total volume to 2 gallons (7.6 l) with additional cold water if necessary. Aerate the wort very well.

Pitch the yeast when temperature of wort is about 70 degrees F (21 C). Ferment at about 70 degrees F (21 C) for about 1 week or until fermentation shows signs of calm and stopping. Rack from your primary to a secondary and add the aroma dry hops. "Cellar" the beer at about 55 degrees F (12.5 C) for about 1 week.

Prime with sugar and bottle or keg when fermentation is complete.

Sikaru Sumerian Beer (All Grain)

Let the heart of the gakkuo [fermenting] vat be our heart!
What makes your heart feel wonderful,
Makes also our heart feel wonderful.
Our liver is happy, our heart is joyful.
You poured a libation over the brick of destiny,
You placed the foundations in peace and prosperity.
May Ninkasi live together with you!
Let her pour for you beer and wine,
Let the pouring of the sweet liquor resound pleasantly for you!
In the . . . reed buckets there is sweet beer,
I will make cupbearers, boys, and brewers stand by,
While I turn around the abundance of beer,
While I feel wonderful, I feel wonderful,
Drinking beer, in a blissful mood,
Drinking liquor, feeling exhilarated,

With joy in the heart and a happy liver—
While my heart full of joy,
And my happy liver I covered with a garment fit for a queen!
    —A 5,000-year-old toast to a woman tavern keeper in ancient Meso-
    potamia. Translated by Miguel Civil of the Oriental Institute of the
    University of Chicago, 1964

Sometime between 6,000 and 10,000 years ago the world's first grain-based beers may have been brewed. In what today is known as Iraq, Sumerians dwelled in an area referred to as Mesopotamia. Archaeologists, anthropologists, and the Anchor Brewing Company of San Francisco have done a great deal of investigative research to try to unravel the mysteries of what may have been man's first beer.

The earliest known recipe for beer is translated from Sumerian clay tablets dating back nearly 4,000 years. References to the joy of brewing and drinking were found on numerous other clay tablets inscribed in the hieroglyphic-like cuneiform written language of the Sumerians. Among these references is the

A receipt that would fill your pocket. Held in hand, perhaps once a bill of sale, this original hardened clay tablet written in cuneiform by ancient Sumerians depicts the oldest recorded recipe in the world: a 5,000-year-old recipe for beer.

"Hymn to Ninkasi." Ninkasi was the Sumerian goddess of brewing and a very revered deity.

In 1989 the Anchor Brewing Company endeavored to duplicate, as near as it could, a version of Sumerian beer. In the fall of 1989 they released the results of their first experiment. "Ninkasi" was the name they gave the beer. It was brewed from a combination of bappir, malt, dates, water, and yeast. Bappir is a type of Sumerian bread. The Anchor Brewing Company's version of bappir included water, barley, malted barley, roasted barley, and honey. It was twice baked in order that most of the moisture be removed. The resulting hard bappir bread could be stored indefinitely, as was likely the case 4,000 years ago.

Scholars surmise that bappir may have been one of the main ingredients in the brewing process, along with malted barley or spelt (ancient wheat) and dates.

One part bappir was mashed with two parts malted barley and a quantity of dates for Anchor's Ninkasi beer. This mash was lautered and then brought to a temperature just shy of boiling, to authenticate what may have been actual procedures. The wort was pitched with cultured beer yeast, fermented, and bottled without pasteurization. The result was a mild-tasting, low-alcohol, somewhat fruity wine-like beer, perhaps similar to the original 4,000-year-old version.

Following is a recipe for homemade bappir, followed by a 5-gallon (19 l) recipe for a version of sikaru that leaves much to your own imagination and creativity.

Beer author Michael Jackson (left) and professor of anthropology at the University of Pennsylvania Dr. Solomon Katz view several ancient cuneiform tablets, some depicting beer recipes 5,000 years old.

*And on the first day they made bappir. Author Charlie Papazian participates
with Anchor Brewing Company staff in preparing hundreds of loaves of bappir.
Bappir, a twice-baked hard loaf of bread made from barley, malt, and honey, was later
used as a main ingredient by the brewery in the making of an ancient
Sumerian-style beer called Ninkasi.*

Ingredients for bappir (Sumerian bread):

    2 lb. (0.9 kg)   pale malted barley, crushed
    2 lb. (0.9 kg)   barley flour
    ½ lb. (227 g)   roasted barley, crushed
    1 lb. (0.45 kg) honey
                 Adequate water

Combine the dry ingredients with honey and enough water to make a stiff dough, roughly the consistency of oatmeal cookie dough, but slightly drier. Knead and then shape into 8-inch-diameter (20.3 cm) patties about 1 inch (2.54 cm) high. Bake in a 350-degree F (176 C) oven for about 1 hour. Remove and slice into 1½-inch (3.8 cm) strips. Let cool for 1 hour and then bake again until hard and dry. Your bappir may be stored in a cool, dry place for centuries and is ready for brewing when you are.

"Bappir will get you through times with no money better than money will get you through times with no bappir." Quote from my great-great-great-great-great-great-great-great . . . great-grandmother's conversation with her husband.

Ingredients for 5 gallons (19 l) of twenty-first-century sikaru:

3 lb. (1.36 kg)	pale malted barley
2 lb. (0.91 kg)	bappir
1 lb. (0.45 kg)	chopped and pitted dates
*	ale yeast
⅔ c. (156 ml)	corn sugar (dextrose) or 1 c. (240 ml) dried malt extract (for bottling)

O.G.: 1.034–1.040 (8.5–10)
F.G.: 1.004–1.010 (1–2.5)
Bitterness: none; Color: varies; Alcohol: 3.9% by volume

Add crushed malts and bappir to 1½ gallons (5.7 l) of 168-degree F (76 C) water. The mash will stabilize at 150 to 155 degrees F (66–67 C). Hold this temperature for 60 minutes.

Sparge with 2 to 2½ gallons (7.6–9.5 l) of 170-degree F (77 C) water. Add more water to brewpot to make initial extract volume of 5½ gallons (21 l). Add chopped dates. Anticipate evaporation of ½ gallon (1.9 l). Chill the hot wort with an immersion-type system. Transfer the cooled wort with the dates to your fermenter. For brewing 5 gallons (19 l), a 6½-gallon (26.5 l) fermenter is necessary. Do not use a blow-off method of fermentation, as the dates will clog the system. Pitch chosen yeast when cool and bottle when fermentation is complete.

Variations: For perhaps more authenticity, you may use spelt rather than barley. Malt the spelt as described in the recipe for Speltbrau (page 285). Grind and use unmalted spelt in place of barley flour. Roast a portion of unmalted spelt for coloring and as a substitute for roasted barley. Keep in mind that your yields will be quite a bit less for home-malted spelt, so you may want to use 50 percent more malted ingredients in the final mash to compensate.

Want to try a yeast that may date back to Sumerian times? Write World Sourdoughs from Antiquity, P.O. Box 670, Cascade, ID 83611, U.S.A., and order their Egyptian Red Sea Culture. Surely full of wild yeast and lactobacillus, this culture may produce a beer that, if consumed fresh, may be more similar to the original sikaru. We can be quite certain that the original beers were drunk from nonpressurized containers, just as fermentation subsided.

LAGERS

LIGHT LAGERS

Come Helles or High Water (All Grain)

Here comes Helles or High Water, a Munich-style Helles lager of the type you would typically find yourself drinking liters of in a summer Bavarian beer garden. There are three essential components of the character of this style of beer. The hop bitterness is subdued and not at all aggressive. A full malt aroma and flavor should emerge with each pleasurable gulp. Relatively low in alcohol, the beer is refreshing yet full flavored. For those of us who have been lucky enough to roam the Bavarian and Franconia countryside sampling the variations among the small brewers of Germany, we often recall enjoying the unique yeast-induced "house flavors." These are not overwhelming, yet they add complexity to the character and a stamp of authenticity.

In this recipe a good dose of aromatic malt helps the biscuit-like malty character in aroma and flavor. Using Noble-type hops relatively low in alpha acid adds finesse and authenticity to the hop character emerging from this Helles. With Helles it is far better to underhop than overhop. If in doubt about alpha acid content of your hops, less is better than more. Take care to note whether you use pellets or whole hops (some varieties may only be available in one or the other form at your local shop); use 15 percent less hops when substituting pellets for whole hops.

Ingredients for 5 gallons (19 l):

8 lb. (3.6 kg)	Pilsener malt
1 lb. (454 g)	Belgian (or other) aromatic malt
¼ lb. (114 g)	CaraMunich™ malt (75 L)
¾ oz. (21 g)	any combination of German Hersbruck, Mittelfrüh, Hallertau, or Saphir hops (boiling): 6.25 HBU (175 MBU)
1 oz. (28 g)	any combination of German Hersbruck, Mittelfrueh, Hallertau, or Saphir hops (10 minutes, flavor)
½ oz. (14 g)	Crystal hops (steeping, aroma/flavor)
½ oz. (14 g)	Crystal hop pellets (dry hopping, aroma)
¼ tsp. (1 g)	Irish moss powder
*	Saflager dried lager yeast or White Labs Cry Havoc yeast
¾ c. (180 ml)	corn sugar (dextrose) or 1¼ c. (300 ml) dried malt extract (for bottling); or ⅓ c. (80 ml) corn sugar (dextrose) for kegging

O.G.: 1.048–1.052 (12–13)
F.G.: 1.014–1.016 (3.5–4 B)
Bitterness: 21 BU; Color: 10 SRM (20 EBC); Alcohol: 4.6% by volume

A step infusion mash is employed to mash the grains. Add 9 quarts (8.5 l) of 143-degree F (61.5 C) water to the crushed grain, stir, stabilize and hold the temperature at 132 degrees F (53 C) for 30 minutes. Add 4½ quarts (4.3 l) of boiling water and add heat to bring temperature up to 155 degrees F (68 C) and hold for about 30 minutes. Then raise temperature to 167 degrees F (75 C), lauter and sparge with 3½ gallons (13.5 l) of 170-degree F (77 C) water. Collect about 5½ gallons (21 l) of runoff.

Add the boiling hops, bring to a full and vigorous boil, and boil for 60 minutes. Add the flavor hops and Irish moss for the final 10 minutes of the boil.

After a total wort boil of 60 minutes, turn off the heat, add the steeping hops, and place the pot (with cover on) in a running cold-water bath for 45 minutes. Continue to chill in the immersion or use other methods to chill your wort. Then strain and sparge the wort into a sanitized fermenter. Bring the total volume to 5 gallons (19 l) with additional cold water if necessary. Aerate the wort very well.

If using the recommended Saflager dried yeast, rehydrate the yeast in 1 cup (250 ml) 90-degree F (32.5 C) clean water for 15 minutes. Pitch the yeast when temperature of wort is about 70 degrees F (21 C). Once visible signs of fermentation are evident, primary ferment at temperatures at about 55 degrees F (12.5 C) for about 1 week or until fermentation shows signs of calm and stopping. Rack from your primary to a secondary and add the hop pellets for dry hopping. "Lager" the beer at temperatures between 35 and 45 degrees F (1.5–7 C) for 3 to 6 weeks.

Prime with sugar and bottle or keg when fermentation is complete.

A Fine Time to Be Me Czech-Style Pilsener (All Grain)

The malt and body are in the style of what was the late twentieth-century character of Pilsner Urquell, before they reformulated their recipe. Use Czech or Bohemian premium 2-row Pilsener malt if available. Accept no substitute for Czech-grown Saaz hops if you want to achieve authenticity. Very soft and low mineral water is a must, but be sure your calcium ions are up to 50 ppm. A tiny amount of black roasted malt is added during the sparge to impart compounds that will help stabilize the flavor of this beer. As is the tradition in Europe, remove the trub to achieve a smoother, cleaner, crisper Pilsener. If Pils is one of your favorites, this recipe will be at the top of your list.

Ingredients for 5 gallons (19 l):

7¼ lb. (3.3 kg)	premium Pilsener 2-row lager malt
1 lb. (0.45 kg)	premium 2-row Vienna malt
½ oz. (14 g)	roasted debittered black malt
1½ oz. (42 g)	Czech Saaz hops (boiling): 6 HBU (168 MBU)
1½ oz. (42 g)	Czech Saaz hops (20 minutes, flavor)
1½ oz. (42 g)	Czech Saaz hops (10 minutes, flavor)
¾ oz. (21 g)	Czech Saaz hops (dry hopping, aroma)
¼ tsp. (1 g)	Irish moss powder
*	Czech or Bohemian lager yeast
¾ c. (175 ml)	corn sugar (dextrose) or 1¼ c. (300 ml) dried malt extract (for bottling); or ⅓ c. (80 ml) corn sugar (dextrose) for kegging

O.G.: 1.044 1.048 (11–12)
F.G.: 1.008–1.012 (2–3)
Bitterness: 36 BU; Color: 5 SRM (10 EBC); Alcohol: 5.3% by volume

A step infusion mash is employed to mash the grains. Add 8 quarts (7.6 l) of 143-degree F (61.5 C) water to the crushed grain, stir, stabilize and hold the temperature at 132 degrees F (53 C) for 30 minutes. Add 4 quarts (3.8 l) of boiling water and add heat to bring temperature up to 155 degrees F (68 C) and hold for about 30 minutes. Then raise temperature to 167 degrees F (75 C), lauter and sparge with 3½ gallons (13.5 l) of 170-degree F (77 C) water. Collect about 5½ gallons (21 l) of runoff.

Add the boiling hops, bring to a full and vigorous boil, and boil for 60 minutes. Add the 20-minute flavor hops for the last 20 minutes of the boil. Add the 10-minute flavor hops and the Irish moss for the final 10 minutes.

After a total wort boil of 60 minutes, turn off heat and place the pot (with cover on) in a running cold-water bath for 45 minutes. Continue to chill in the immersion or use other methods to chill your wort. Then strain and sparge the wort into a sanitized fermenter. If desired, use your own preferred procedures to remove hot and cold break trub. Bring the total volume to 5 gallons (19 l) with additional cold water if necessary. Aerate the wort very well.

Pitch the yeast when temperature of wort is about 70 degrees F (21 C). Once visible signs of fermentation are evident ferment at temperatures of about 55 degrees F (12.5 C) for about 1 week or until fermentation shows signs of calm and stopping. Rack from your primary to a secondary and add the hop pellets for dry hopping. "Lager" the beer at temperatures between 35 and 45 degrees F (1.5–7 C) for 3 to 6 weeks.

Prime with sugar and bottle or keg when fermentation is complete.

Creede Lily German Pilsener (All Grain)

The bitterness of a perfect northern or southern German Pils is a masterpiece of the brewer's art. German Pils such as Bitburger Pils is perfectly brewed in a way that pinpoints the sensation of hop bitterness on specific areas of the tongue and creates a special deliciousness, when done right. There are many kinds of sensations that bitterness can create; bitterness that lingers, bitterness that is assertive, overpowering, fleeting, or soft, bitterness that is sensed on the center back of the tongue, on the roof of the mouth, on the sides. All of these sensations orchestrate and punctuate the other flavors of beer. A fine German Pils has all the potential to become a dream symphony creating a infectious yearning for another and another.

Creede Lily was brewed with my German travels in mind. Its fresh taste, billowy head, and hop fragrance is something worth experiencing both in Germany and in your home.

Ingredients for 5 gallons (19 l):

8 lb. (3.6 kg)	2-row Pilsener lager malt
1¼ oz. (35 g)	German Tradition hops (boiling): 6 HBU (168 MBU)
½ oz. (14 g)	German Hallertau or Hersbruck hops (30 minutes, flavor): 2.5 HBU (70 MBU)
½ oz. (14 g)	German Hallertau or Hersbruck hops (10 minutes, flavor/aroma)
1 oz. (28 g)	German Mittelfrueh or Hersbruck hops (steeping)
¼ tsp. (1 g)	Irish moss powder
*	lager yeast, German Pilsener type
¾ c. (175 ml)	corn sugar (dextrose) or 1¼ c. (300 ml) dried malt extract (for bottling); or ⅓ c. (80 ml) corn sugar (dextrose) for kegging

O.G.: 1.045–1.049 (11–12)
F.G.: 1.008–1.012 (2–3)
Bitterness: 40 BU; Color: 4–5 SRM (8–10 EBC); Alcohol: 5.1% by volume

A step infusion mash is employed to mash the grains. Add 8 quarts (7.6 l) of 143-degree F (61.5 C) water to the crushed grain, stir, stabilize and hold the temperature at 132 degrees F (53 C) for 30 minutes. Add 4 quarts (3.8 l) of boiling water and add heat to bring temperature up to 155 degrees F (68 C) and hold for about 30 minutes. Then raise temperature to 167 degrees F (75 C), lauter and sparge with 3½ gallons (13.5 l) of 170-degree F (77 C) water. Collect about 5½ gallons (21 l) of runoff.

Add the boiling hops, bring to a full and vigorous boil, and boil for 60 minutes. Add the flavor hops for the last 30 minutes of the boil. Add the flavor hops and Irish moss for the final 10 minutes.

After a total wort boil of 60 minutes, turn off heat and place the pot (with cover on) in a running cold-water bath for 45 minutes. Continue to chill in the immersion or use other methods to chill your wort. Then strain and sparge the wort into a sanitized fermenter. If desired, use your own preferred procedures to remove hot and cold break trub. Bring the total volume to 5 gallons (19 l) with additional cold water if necessary. Aerate the wort very well.

Pitch the yeast when temperature of wort is about 70 degrees F (21 C). Once visible signs of fermentation are evident, ferment at temperatures of about 55 degrees F (12.5 C) for about 1 week or until fermentation shows signs of calm and stopping. Rack from your primary to a secondary. "Lager" the beer at temperatures between 35 and 45 degrees F (1.5–7 C) for 3 to 6 weeks.

Prime with sugar and bottle or keg when fermentation is complete.

Get Rio All-Malt Light Lager (Malt Extract)

If you have friends who have American light lager tastes and have never had homebrew, this brew is light in color and not too bitter, but with great hop flavor and the malt character that'll suit your own preferences. It's a perfect beer to wean your friends from light, light lagers to more appreciated and flavorful brews. It is in the style of a craft-brewed all-malt American light lager, but with a pleasant fullness of hop flavor not found in beers stacked a mile high and half-mile wide on the store floors and shelves.

Ingredients for 5 gallons (19 l):

6½ lb. (3 kg)	very light malt extract syrup, or 5½ lb. (2.5 kg) extra light dry malt extract
½ oz. (14 g)	German Hersbruck or Hallertau hops (boiling): 3.8 HBU (106 MBU)
¾ oz. (21 g)	Czech Saaz hops (boiling): 3 HBU (84 MBU) (flavor, 30 minutes)
½ oz. (14 g)	German Hersbruck or Tettnang hops (10 minutes, flavor/aroma)
¾ oz. (21 g)	American Tettnang hops (1 minute, aroma)
¼ tsp. (1 g)	Irish moss powder
*	lager yeast: American lager or German Pilsener type
¾ c. (175 ml)	corn sugar (dextrose) or 1¼ c. (300 ml) dried malt extract (for bottling); or ⅓ c. (80 ml) corn sugar (dextrose) for kegging

O.G.: 1.044–1.048 (11–12)
F.G.: 1.010–1.014 (2.5–3.5)
Bitterness: 20 BU; Color: 3–4 SRM (6–8 EBC); Alcohol: 4.5% by volume

Bring 2 gallons (7.6 l) of water to a boil with the malt extract and boiling hops and boil for 60 minutes. Add the 30-minute flavor hops for the last 30 minutes of the boil. Add the flavor/aroma hops and Irish moss for the last 10 minutes of the boil. Add the aroma hops for the final 1 minute.

After a total wort boil of 60 minutes, transfer the hot wort while straining out the hops into a sanitized fermenter filled with 2 gallons (7.6 l) of cold water. Top your fermenter with enough water to make 5 gallons (19 l). Aerate the wort very well.

Pitch the yeast when temperature of wort is about 70 degrees F (21 C). Once visible signs of fermentation are evident, ferment at temperatures of about 55 degrees F (12.5 C) for about 1 week or until fermentation shows signs of calm and stopping. Rack from your primary to a secondary. "Lager" the beer at temperatures between 35 and 45 degrees F (1.5–7 C) for 3 to 6 weeks.

Prime with sugar and bottle or keg when fermentation is complete.

Swingtop American Pre-Prohibition Pilsener (All Grain)

In the late part of the nineteenth century, Germans immigrated to the United States and began brewing all-malt lagers. They loved their beers. Then a new and innovative beer type called Pilsener swept the palates of Europeans, and German-American brewers sought to duplicate the crisp, light, yet full-flavored Pilseners of Europe. The problem was that the malted barley grown and malted in this country did not have the same qualities as in Europe. Ultimately their solution was to add rice or corn to duplicate the European all-malt Pilseners. This style of corn/rice Pilsener was popular up until American Prohibition shut down the brewing business for ten years, in the 1920s to the early 1930s. Pre-Prohibition-style Pilsener was gone forever—until American homebrewers discovered the recipes in old brewery archives. Here's your shot at truly satisfying "retro" brewing at its best.

Ingredients for 5 gallons (19 l):

6½ lb. (3 kg)	American pale lager malt
1½ lb. (0.68 kg)	flaked corn/maize
¾ oz. (21 g)	Northern Brewers or Perle hops (boiling): 6 HBU (168 MBU)
1 oz. (28 g)	American Tettnang or French Strisselspalt hops (30 minutes, flavor): 4 HBU (112 MBU)
½ oz. (14 g)	German Hallertau or Mt. Hood hops (10 minutes, flavor/aroma)
½ oz. (14 g)	New Zealand Mouteka or American Tettnang hops (1 minute, aroma): optional if you want to add a twenty-first-century aroma character
¼ tsp. (1 g)	Irish moss powder
*	lager yeast, Pilsener type
¾ c. (175 ml)	corn sugar (dextrose) or 1¼ c. (300 ml) dried malt extract (for bottling); or ⅓ c. (80 ml) corn sugar (dextrose) for kegging

Water used for this recipe should be very soft, low in carbonates, with about 50 ppm calcium ions.

O.G.: 1.045–1.049 (11–12)
F.G.: 1.008–1.012 (2–3)
Bitterness: 33 BU; Color: 2–3 SRM (4–6 EBC); Alcohol: 5% by volume

A step infusion mash is employed to mash the grains. Add 8 quarts (7.6 l) of 143-degree F (61.5 C) water to the crushed grain, stir, stabilize and hold the temperature at 132 degrees F (53 C) for 30 minutes. Add 4 quarts (3.8 l) of boiling water and add heat to bring temperature up to 155 degrees F (68 C) and hold for about 30 minutes. Then raise temperature to 167 degrees F (75 C), lauter and sparge with 3½ gallons (13.5 l) of 170-degree F (77 C) water. Collect about 5½ gallons (21 l) of runoff.

Add the boiling hops, bring to a full and vigorous boil, and boil for 60 minutes. Add the flavor hops for the last 30 minutes of the boil. Add the flavor/aroma hops and Irish moss for the last 10 minutes of the boil. If you like to mix twenty-first-century tastes, add the aroma hops for the final 1 minute.

After a total wort boil of 60 minutes, turn off the heat and place the pot (with cover on) in a running cold-water bath for 45 minutes. Continue to chill in the immersion or use other methods to chill your wort. Then strain and sparge the wort into a sanitized fermenter. Bring the total volume to 5 gallons (19 l) with additional cold water if necessary. Aerate the wort very well.

Pitch the yeast when temperature of wort is about 70 degrees F (21 C). Once visible signs of fermentation are evident, ferment at temperatures of about 55 degrees F (12.5 C) for about 1 week or until fermentation shows signs of calm and stopping. Rack from your primary to a secondary and add the hop pellets for dry hopping. If you have the capability, "lager" the beer at temperatures between 35 and 45 degrees F (1.5–7 C) for 3 to 6 weeks.

Prime with sugar and bottle or keg when fermentation is complete.

St. Louis Golden Lager (All Grain)

Two of America's classic light lagers are formulated from only the best malted barley, the finest rice, and the choicest hops. Different processes, yeast strains, and fermentation temperatures create the variation from one brand of American light lager to another. Here's a basic recipe that will allow you to brew an American light lager unique to your brewery and lager yeast strain. Low in bitterness, malt flavor, and body, this might be a beer you enjoy drinking because you made it. Of coors, it may make you weiser too.

Ingredients for 5 gallons (19 l):

6 lb. (2.7 kg)	2-row American pale lager malt
1½ lb. (0.71 kg)	flaked rice
¼ oz. (7 g)	Perle hops (boiling): 2 HBU (56 MBU)
⅓ oz. (8.5 g)	Hallertau hops (boiling): 1.5 HBU (42 MBU)
0.2 oz. (6 g)	American Hallertau hops (10 minutes, flavor/aroma)
¼ tsp. (1 g)	Irish moss powder

*   lager yeast, American Pilsener type
⅞ c. (207 ml)   corn sugar (dextrose) (for bottling)
Water used for this recipe should be very soft, low in carbonates,
with about 50 ppm calcium.

O.G.: 1.040–1.044 (10–11)
F.G.: 1.006–1.010 (2.5–3.5)
Bitterness: 16 BU; Color: 2–3 SRM (4–6 EBC); Alcohol: 4.5% by volume

A protein nutrient step infusion mash is employed to mash the grains. Add all except ½ lb. (227 g) of the crushed pale malt to 6 quarts (5.7 l) of 130-degree F (54.5 C) water, stir, stabilize and hold the temperature at 122 degrees F (50 C) for 30 minutes. Meanwhile add the flaked rice and ½ lb. (227 g) crushed pale malt to 5 quarts cold water and add heat to bring temperature to boiling. Stir the water, malt, and rice to prevent sticking and scorching on the bottom of your pot. As the temperature increases through the mashing temperatures it breaks down some of the rice starch and helps latter conversion and makes the cooked rice less glutinous. When this rice and malt slurry is boiling and the first step of the malt mash has reached 30 minutes, add the boiling rice slurry to the malt mash and add heat if necessary to bring temperature up to 155 degrees F (68 C). Hold this mash at temperature for about 30 minutes. Then raise temperature to 167 degrees F (75 C), lauter and sparge with 3½ gallons (13.5 l) of 170-degree F (77 C) water. Collect about 5½ gallons (21 l) of runoff.

Add the two boiling hops, bring to a full and vigorous boil, and boil for 60 minutes. Add the flavor/aroma hops and the Irish moss for the final 10 minutes of the boil.

After a total wort boil of 60 minutes, turn off the heat and place the pot (with cover on) in a running cold-water bath for 45 minutes. Continue to chill in the immersion or use other methods to chill your wort. Then strain and sparge the wort into a sanitized fermenter. Bring the total volume to 5 gallons (19 l) with additional cold water if necessary. Aerate the wort very well.

Pitch the yeast when temperature of wort is about 70 degrees F (21 C). Once visible signs of fermentation are evident, ferment at temperatures of about 55 degrees F (12.5 C) for about 1 week or until fermentation shows signs of calm and stopping. Rack from your primary to a secondary. "Lager" the beer at temperatures between 35 and 45 degrees F (1.5–7 C) for 3 to 6 weeks.

Prime with sugar and bottle or keg when fermentation is complete.

Shikata Ga Nai (Rice) Light Lager (Malt Extract)

Do you want to brew an extract-based light American lager? Well, *shikata ga nai,* meaning "I'm sorry, there's nothing anyone can do about it. I can't do anything about it. There's nothing anyone can do about it. But if there's something *you* can do about it, please let me know."

Well, it just so happens that there is something I can do about it, and so can you.

Keep in mind that there comes a time when the yard needs mowing, the sun is hot, and the air is dry. Your thirst calls out for a cold, cold thirst-quenching beer—something simple, low in alcohol, and effervescently refreshing. And just on the principle of the whole thing, you want it to be your homebrew. You know how much better your homebrew is than anything churned out of a factory.

Use quality lager yeast and you'll be able to brew an American-style light lager, superlight in color, light in body, light in bitterness, light in alcohol, but with a fresh homebrewed flavor accented with a touch of German hop flavor and aroma. This will have a bit of personality.

Ingredients for 5 gallons (19 l):

3 lb. (1.4 kg)	extra light dried malt extract or 3½ lb. (1.6 kg) extra light malt extract syrup.
2 lb. (0.9 kg)	rice extract syrup or 1.7 lb. (0.8 kg) rice extract powder
½ oz. (14 g)	German Hersbrucker or Mt. Hood hops (boiling): 2.5 HBU (70 MBU)
¾ oz. (21 g)	Santiam or French Strisselspalt hops (20 minutes, flavor): 3 HBU (84 MBU)
½ oz. (14 g)	Czech Saaz hops (10 minutes, flavor/aroma)
1 oz. (28 g)	American Tettnang hops (steeping, aroma)
¼ tsp. (1 g)	Irish moss powder
*	American lager-type yeast
¾ c. (175 ml)	corn sugar (dextrose) or 1¼ c. (300 ml) dried malt extract (for bottling); or ⅓ c. (80 ml) corn sugar (dextrose) for kegging

O.G.: 1.038–1.042 (9.5–10.5)
F.G.: 1.009–1.013 (2–3)
Bitterness: 15 BU; Color: 2–4 SRM (4–8 EBC); Alcohol: 3.8% by volume

Bring 2 gallons (7.6 l) of water to a boil with the malt, rice extract, and boiling hops. Add the flavor hops for the last 20 minutes of the boil. Add the flavor/aroma hops and Irish moss for the final 10 minutes of the boil.

After a total wort boil of 60 minutes, turn off heat and add the steeping hops. Immerse the covered pot of wort in a cold-water bath and let sit for 30 minutes or the time it takes to have a couple of homebrews.

Transfer the hot wort to a sanitized fermenter filled with 2 gallons (7.6 l) of cold water. Strain and sparge the hops. Top your fermenter with enough water to make 5 gallons (19 l).

Aerate the wort very well. Pitch the yeast when temperature of wort is about 70 degrees F (21 C). Once visible signs of fermentation are evident, ferment at temperatures of about 55 degrees F (12.5 C) for about 1 week or until fermentation shows signs of calm and stopping. Rack from your primary to a secondary. "Lager" the beer at temperatures between 35 and 45 degrees F (1.5–7 C) for 3 to 6 weeks.

Prime with sugar and bottle or keg when fermentation is complete.

Shikata ga nai. Please let me know.

Dork's Torque Mexican Crown Lager (All Grain)

If you enjoy the type of Mexican beer that is bottled in clear bottles, you can come close to duplicating it by bottling in clear glass bottles and exposing to sunlight for 30 minutes. Stuff a slice of lime into the bottle, hold your nose, smile, and serve well chilled.

Quarterbock Low Alcohol (Mash Extract)

You'll not want to pass up handing this off to your light-drinking, wide-receiving friends while you're rolling out another batch or running back to the center of town to buy ingredients for your next batch of beer. Quarterbock is one beer that won't get sacked as a tasteless second-string effort.

Now that I've fumbled that out of bounds, let's consider recovering with a winning, satisfyingly flavored, 2% low-alcohol beer.

Quarterbock is a refreshing, light-bodied (but not watery) beer, light amber in color with a bitterness that complements yet doesn't linger. It's a great beer for even overtime occasions when you're thirsty, you want a beer, and you want to

minimize the effects of alcohol on your performance. It's a great starting point for your low-alcohol beer brewing efforts. Brew it. Taste it. Enjoy it. Then darken, lighten, hop-it or add more body to it as suits your own taste with your next batch, even as a preseason draft. You can pick this one both in the first round and the last.

The secret? Well, it isn't really a secret but a trick some commercial breweries use to enhance their production. It's called high-gravity brewing, most often used to produce normal-strength beer by watering down higher-gravity beer during the packaging process. But none go the distance that you will.

The higher the beer gravity, the more esters and other flavorful fermentation by-products that are produced. These "interesting" flavors are usually not desirable in commercially available, tasteless low-alcohol beers. But for people like you and me who enjoy the flavors of beer these characters are what we want.

We want to brew a very strong doppelbock with a starting gravity of 1.096 to 1.100 (24–25). Ferment out to completion (about 1.028 to 1.032 [7–8]), then add de-aerated water at a ratio of three parts water to one part finished doppelbock. Result: a quarterbock that, after dilution, has a finished gravity of 1.008 to 1.010 (2–2.5). Brewing this as run up the middle, you'd be brewing an original gravity of 1.025 (6), but it would be more likely to ferment down to 1.003 to 1.005 (1–1.5) and would be without esters and the complexity of flavor that higher-gravity brewing creates.

You can experiment and help predict what your fermentation will taste like by diluting 2 ounces (60 ml) of your finished batch of doppelbock with 6 ounces (175 ml) of chilled seltzer water.

Because of the very high gravity of the boiled wort and the great amount of hops called for, the original gravity and bitterness units cannot be accurately calculated, partially due to the nonlinear nature of high-wort-density measurements. Hop utilization is also decreased.

Ingredients for a final net FOUR gallons (15.2 l) of mash-extract brew—but actually you will brew one gallon (3.8 l) of high-gravity beer and dilute with three gallons (11.4 l) of de-aerated water before bottling:

½ lb. (224 g)	pale malted barley
3 oz. (84 g)	Munich malt
6 oz. (170 g)	malted wheat
3 oz. (84 g)	crystal or caramel malt (40 L)
1 oz. (28 g)	roasted chocolate malt
1 lb. (0.45 kg)	light dried malt extract or 1¼ lb. (570 g) light malt extract syrup
1 oz. (28 g)	German Spalt hops (boiling): 4 HBU (112 MBU)

¼ oz. (7 g)	German Hallertau or Spalt hops (30 minutes, flavor): 1.3 HBU (36 MBU)
¼ oz. (7 g)	American Tettnang hops (10 minutes, aroma)
¼ tsp. (1 g)	Irish moss powder
*	German lager yeast or White Labs Cry Havoc yeast
⅔ c. (158 ml)	corn sugar (dextrose) or 1 c. (240 ml) dried malt extract (for bottling)

O.G. (one-gallon batch): 1.096–1.106 (24–26.5)
F.G. before dilution: 1.028–1.032 (7–8); F.G. after dilution: 1.008–1.010 (2–2.5)
Final Bitterness: 20–25 BU; Final Color: 12–16 SRM (24–32 EBC);
       Final Alcohol: 2–2.5% by volume

Using a protein-developing step mash, add 5½ cups (1.3 l) of 130-degree F (54.4 C) water to the crushed malt. Stabilize at 122 degrees F (50 C) and hold for 30 minutes. Then add 3 cups (0.71 l) of boiling water. Stabilize at 155 to 158 degrees F (68–70 C) and hold for 30 minutes. Add heat and mash out to 165 degrees F (74 C). Sparge with about 2½ quarts (2.4 l) of 170-degree F (77 C) water. Total volume should be about 1½ gallons (5.7 l).

Add the malt extract and boiling hops, bring to a full and vigorous boil, and boil for 60 minutes. Add the flavor hops for the last 30 minutes of the boil. Add the aroma hops and Irish moss for the final 10 minutes of the boil.

After a total wort boil of 60 minutes, turn off the heat, immerse the covered pot of wort in a cold-water bath and let sit for 30 minutes or the time it takes to chill down to about 70 degrees F (21 C). Have a homebrew.

Then strain out and sparge hops and direct the cooled wort into a sanitized fermenter. If necessary add additional cold water to achieve a 1-gallon (4 l) batch size. Aerate the wort very well.

Pitch the yeast when temperature of wort is about 70 degrees F (21 C). Once visible signs of fermentation are evident, ferment at temperatures of about 55 degrees F (12.5 C) for about 1 week or until fermentation shows signs of calm and stopping. Rack from your primary to a secondary. If you have the capability, "lager" the beer at temperatures between 35 and 45 degrees F (1.5–7 C) for 4 to 6 weeks.

When the beer is finished fermenting, **prepare the de-aerated dilution water**. Boil 3 gallons (11.4 l) of water and chill before adding to beer. Other options for preparing the dilution water: If you have a 3-gallon (11.4 l) or 5-gallon (19 l) soda canister for your draft system, you can add tap water to this container and bubble carbon dioxide through the "out" fixture and into and through the water, releasing the pressure through the "in" valve as you bubble the carbon dioxide. This will purge oxygen from the water and replace it with a small amount of carbon dioxide. Don't worry about the amount of carbon dioxide. The other option is to use unflavored carbonated water or seltzer water with no flavors added as your dilution water. This can be store-bought or homemade. Add vigorously to decarbonate it.

Add ⅔ c. (158 ml) corn sugar (dextrose) to finished and racked beer. Dilute 3:1 de-aerated water to beer. Mix gently and bottle. It'll be ready as soon as it carbonates. You won't want to have a Monday-morning quarterbock, but anytime after noon would be appropriate.

You could actually brew a 5-gallon (19 l) batch of 10½ percent alcohol doppelbock using the recipe called Limnian Doppelbock featured in *The Complete Joy of Homebrewing, Fourth Edition*. One gallon can go toward making 4 gallons (15.2 l) of quarterbock. The other 4 gallons (15.2 l) of doppelbock? Well, you'll know what to do, won't you?

AMBER LAGERS

Autumnal Equinox Special Reserve (Mash Extract)

Autumnal Special Reserve is our own inventive homebrewed and ramped-up Märzen-style lager, with perceived bitterness less than is typical of the normal style of Märzen. Noble varieties of Saaz, Hallertau Hersbruck, and American-grown Mt. Hood hops are sparingly used to *barely* accent the mellow, rich roundness of malt. Regal maltiness is complemented with an almost opalescent amber glow from hints of wheat and Munich-style malt.

Bavarian or Munich lager yeast should be used. They will perform best in contributing lager character even if cold lager fermentation temperatures cannot be totally achieved.

Because it matures well with the passing months, the recipe is for 10 gallons (38 l). Keg 5 gallons (19 l) and reserve for a special occasion. Celebrate the other 5 gallons at your leisure.

Ingredients for 10 gallons (38 l):

8½ lb. (3.9 kg)	amber dried malt extract or 10 lb. (4.54 kg) amber malt extract syrup
4 lb. (1.8 kg)	2-row lager barley malt
2½ lb. (1.14 kg)	Munich malt
3 lb. (1.36 kg)	wheat malt
2¼ oz. (64 g)	Czech Saaz hops (boiling): 9 HBU (252 MBU)
¼ lb. (114 g)	German Hallertau Hersbruck or Mittelfrüh hops (30 minutes, flavor): 16 HBU (448 MBU)
1 oz. (28 g)	Mt. Hood hops (1 minute, aroma)

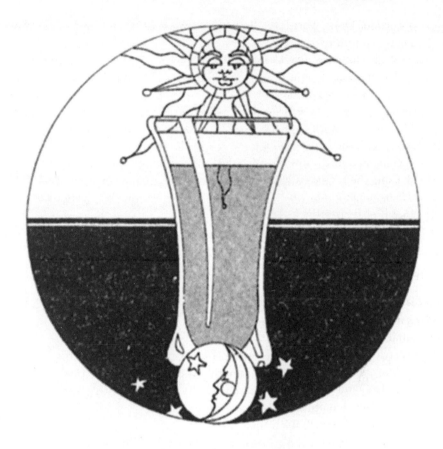

¼ tsp. (1 g)	Irish moss powder
*	Bavarian- or Munich-type lager yeast
¾ c. (175 ml)	corn sugar (dextrose) or 1¼ c. (300 ml) dried malt extract *for bottling 5 gallons (19 l)*
⅓ c. (78 ml)	corn sugar (dextrose) or ½ c. (120 ml) dried malt extract *for kegging 5 gallons (19 l)*

O.G.: 1.062–1.066 (15.5–16.5)
F.G.: 1.014–1.018 (3.5–4.5)
Bitterness: 30 BU; Color: 15 SRM (30 EBC); Alcohol: 6.5% by volume

A step infusion mash is employed to mash the grains. Add 9½ quarts (9 l) of 143-degree F (61.5 C) water to the crushed grain, stir, stabilize and hold the temperature at 132 degrees F (53 C) for 30 minutes. Add 4.75 quarts (4.5 l) of boiling water and add heat to bring temperature up to 155 degrees F (68 C) and hold for about 30 minutes. Then raise temperature to 167 degrees F (75 C), lauter and sparge with 3½ gallons (13.5 l) of 170-degree F (77 C) water. Collect about 5½ gallons (21 l) of runoff.

Add the boiling hops, bring to a full and vigorous boil, and boil for 60 minutes. Add the flavor hops for the last 30 minutes of the boil. Add the Irish moss for the last 10 minutes of the boil. Add the aroma hops for the final 1 minute.

After a total wort boil of 60 minutes, turn off the heat and place the pot (with cover on) in a running cold-water bath for 30 minutes. Sparge, strain, and add wort to your sanitized fermenter(s) partly filled with cold water. Remember, the total volume of wort will be 10 gallons. You can split the 5 gallons of boiled wort by adding 2½ gallons of hot wort to two 6½-gallon fermenters, each filled with 2 gallons of cold water. Top up to make final volume of 5 gallons in each fermenter.

Aerate the wort very well. Pitch the yeast when temperature of wort is about 70 degrees F (21 C). Once visible signs of fermentation are evident, ferment at temperatures of about 55 degrees F (12.5 C) for about 1 week or until fermentation shows signs of calm and stopping. Rack from your primary to a secondary. If you have the capability, "lager" the beer at temperatures between 35 and 45 degrees F (1.5–7 C) for 3 to 6 weeks.

Prime with sugar and bottle or keg when fermentation is complete.

If proper attention has been given to sanitation techniques, this beer will age wonderfully for eight to twelve months. When it reaches its peak flavor is a matter of personal preference. I preferred the 3- to 6-month period, but this will vary with your techniques and yeast type.

Claude of Neptune Amaizeing CopperBock (All Grain)

If I was blind, could not hear, could not taste, smell, or experience the sensation of touch, I thought to myself, what would my life be like. Would I be able to experience or interact with my surroundings? It was thought that we had only five senses. But totally independent of sound, taste, smell, sight, and touch, there is the sense called balance. It is surely our sixth sense. What is this underrecognized sense of balance all about? In everyday life it is about movement in any of several dimensions and the tendency to achieve balance and equilibrium dependent on given situations. The situation determines the state of "pleasantness" for which we strive to create balance.

That is certainly a mindful. Let's talk beer. Certainly the sensations of tasting, smelling, feeling, seeing, and even listening to beer are easily quantifiable. But whenever the subject of "balance" comes up, there seems never to be anything that can perfectly quantify a beer's balance as appropriate or not appropriate. Or so it seems.

So what is beer balance? It's a tendency for the overall impression of a beer to achieve a "center" and an equilibrium depending on a given situation. The "situation" is determined by not only the beer type but also the mood and state of mind of the beer drinker. And when you achieve balance, you achieve overall pleasantness.

(Okay—I admit I am getting a bit metaphysical, philosophizing on the meaning of beer. But the enjoyment of beer inspires, so please indulge me at least for only a few more moments before I introduce one fantastic recipe.)

Your goal as a brewer is to combine ingredients and process, striving to produce the overall sensations of pleasantness. Whether it is malt-accented bock beer, a hop-accented India pale ale, or a fruit-accented wheat beer, what you seek in a beer is determined by the moment you are in. You will seek a different balance depending on your mood and the environment with which you are enjoying beer. So naturally as a homebrewer you choose to surround yourself with beer diversity.

Beer is often defined by style guidelines. But style guidelines are only a beginning of the adventure, flavor, and diversity of beer. If you submit to beer, your quest will be the frontiers, and your desire to achieve different states of balance will be achieved, whatever the occasion. In the final experience ask yourself: Is it really through flavor, aroma, mouthfeel, listening, and appearance that I experience beer? Perhaps the only thing that matters is a sense of balance. And that's all.

Claude of Neptune is a beer that's the result of an unexpected combination of ingredients. It is a frontier beer. It is an exercise in balancing ingredients to achieve a pleasant experience. Claude of Neptune does not use any pale or Pilsener-type malts. The full flavor of Munich malt provides the foundation. The blend of aromatic, sauer, dark Munich, uniquely caramelized Belgian Special-B, and honey-accented malts adds dimension. Then with a bit of flaked corn the balance is pulled together. With so much malt emphasis care is taken not to overpower this beer with assertively oriented hops. Vanguard, Perle, and Liberty provide an earthy foundation of bitterness and flavor. At the other end of the hop spectrum, a delicate touch of Simcoe and Crystal hops offers subdued overtures that provide grace and a briefly lingering aroma and taste experience.

Claude of Neptune is different. It doesn't fit the mold of any particular style. Yet it is balanced for what it is. It achieves the experience of pleasantness.

Isn't that what beer is all about?

Ingredients for 5 gallons (19 l):

8½ lb. (3.4 kg)	Munich malt (10 L)
½ lb. (227 g)	Belgian aromatic malt
¼ lb. (114 g)	German sauer malt
¼ lb. (114 g)	German CaraMunich™ malt (75 L)
¼ lb. (114 g)	Belgian Special-B malt
¼ lb. (114 g)	Gambrinus honey malt
1 lb. (454 g)	flaked corn
¾ oz. (21 g)	Vanguard whole hops (boiling): 4.1 HBU (115 MBU)
½ oz. (14 g)	Perle whole hops (boiling): 4 HBU (112 MBU)
1¼ oz. (35 g)	Liberty whole hops (15 minutes, flavor): 5 HBU (140 MBU)
1 oz. (28 g)	Mt. Hood hops (10 minutes, flavor/aroma): 6 HBU (168 MBU)
½ oz. (14 g)	Simcoe hops (steeping, aroma)
½ oz. (14 g)	Crystal hop pellets (dry hopping, aroma)
¼ tsp. (1 g)	Irish moss powder
*	your favorite lager yeast or dried Saflager yeast
¾ c. (175 ml)	corn sugar (dextrose) or 1¼ c. (300 ml) dried malt extract (for bottling); or ⅓ c. (80 ml) corn sugar (dextrose) for kegging

O.G.: 1.060–1.064 (14.7–15.7)
F.G.: 1.016–1.020 (4–5)
Bitterness: 45 BU; Color: 21 SRM (42 EBC); Alcohol: 5.6% by volume

A step infusion mash is employed to mash the grains. Add 11 quarts (10.5 l) of 143-degree F (61.5 C) water to the crushed grains and flaked corn, stir, stabilize and hold the temperature at 132 degrees F (53 C) for 30 minutes. Add 5½ quarts (5.2 l) of boiling water and add heat to bring temperature up to 155 degrees F (68 C) and hold for about 30 minutes. Then raise temperature to 167 degrees F (75 C), lauter and sparge with 3½ gallons (13.5 l) of 170-degree F (77 C) water. Collect about 5½ gallons (21 l) of runoff. Add 60-minute hops and bring to a full and vigorous boil.

Add the two boiling hops, bring to a full and vigorous boil, and boil for 60 minutes. Add the flavor hops for the last 15 minutes of the boil. Add flavor/aroma hops and the Irish moss for the final 10 minutes of the boil.

After a total wort boil of 60 minutes, turn off the heat and add the steeping hops. Place the pot (with cover on) in a running cold-water bath for 45 minutes. Continue to chill in the immersion or use other methods to chill your wort. Then strain and sparge the wort into a sanitized fermenter. Bring the total volume to 5 gallons (19 l) with additional cold water if necessary. Aerate the wort very well.

Pitch the yeast when temperature of wort is about 70 degrees F (21 C). Once visible signs of fermentation are evident, ferment at temperatures of about 55 degrees F (12.5 C) for about 1 week or until fermentation shows signs of calm and stopping. Rack from your primary to a secondary and add the hop pellets for dry hopping. If you have the capability, "lager" the beer at temperatures between 35 and 45 degrees F (1.5–7 C) for 4 to 7 weeks.

Prime with sugar and bottle or keg when fermentation is complete.

Princess of Peace Märzen (All Grain)

This rich amber beer expresses the essence of what beer means to me. The rich, warm, and translucent color, the sweetly seductive aroma and flavor of toasted malt, and the crisp bitterness of hops—a match made in beer heaven. Full-flavored, but not heavy. Clean yet expressive.

For many, the end of August and the first few weeks of September brings a trace of autumn in the air. It is time to brew the beer that captures the final warmth of summer to feed the soul during the shorter days and cooler nights that will come soon.

Princess of Peace is an Oktoberfest Märzen that will warm your soul, compliment your friends, and inspire you to brew beer for the next fifty years. It's that good.

Ingredients for 5 gallons (19 l):

5 lb. (2.3 kg)   Pilsener/lager malt
4 lb. (1.8 kg)   Munich malt

¾ lb. (340 g)	home-toasted pale malt
1 lb. (0.45 kg)	Dextrine™ or Cara-Pils™ malt (dextrin-type malts)
3 oz. (85 g)	debittered black malt
1 oz. (28 g)	Mt. Hood or German Opal hops (boiling): 7 HBU (196 MBU)
½ oz. (14 g)	American Tettnang or Santiam (30 minutes, flavor): 2.5 HBU (70 MBU)
¾ oz. (21 g)	American Tettnang or Santiam (10 minutes, flavor/aroma)
1 oz. (28 g)	German Hallertau Hersbruck or Mittelfrueh hops (steeping, aroma)
¼ tsp. (1 g)	Irish moss powder
*	Bavarian- or Munich-type lager yeast
¾ c. (175 ml)	corn sugar (dextrose) or 1¼ c. (300 ml) dried malt extract (for bottling); or ⅓ c. (80 ml) corn sugar (dextrose) for kegging

O.G.: 1.052–1.056 (13–14)
F.G.: 1.015–1.019 (4–5)
Bitterness: 35 BU; Color: 18 SRM (36 EBC); Alcohol: 5.6% by volume

Before you begin, toast your own malt by spreading ¾ pound of whole pale malt on a cookie sheet and toasting in a 350-degree F (177 C) oven for about 10 minutes. It is done when it smells wonderful and the insides turn a slight orange color. Allow it to cool before crushing.

A step infusion mash is employed to mash the grains. Add 11 quarts (10.5 l) of 143-degree F (61.5 C) water to the crushed grain, stir, stabilize and hold the temperature at 132 degrees F (53 C) for 30 minutes. Add 5½ quarts (5.2 l) of boiling water and add heat to bring temperature up to 155 degrees F (68 C) and hold for about 30 minutes. Then raise temperature to 167 degrees F (75 C), lauter and sparge with 3½ gallons (13.5 l) of 170-degree F (77 C) water. Collect about 5½ gallons (21 l) of runoff.

Add the boiling hops, bring to a full and vigorous boil, and boil for 60 minutes. Add the flavor hops for the last 30 minutes of the boil. Add the flavor/aroma hops and the Irish moss for the final 10 minutes of the boil.

After a total wort boil of 60 minutes, turn off the heat and add the steeping hops. Immerse the covered pot of wort and place the pot (with cover on) in a running cold-water bath for 45 minutes. Continue to chill in the immersion or use other methods to chill your wort. Then strain and sparge the wort into a sanitized fermenter. Bring the total volume to 5 gallons (19 l) with additional cold water if necessary. Aerate the wort very well.

Pitch the yeast when temperature of wort is about 70 degrees F (21 C). Once visible signs of fermentation are evident, ferment at temperatures of about 55 degrees F (12.5 C) for about 1 week or until fermentation shows signs of calm and stopping. Rack from your primary to a secondary. If you have the capability "lager" the beer at temperatures between 35 and 45 degrees F (1.5–7 C) for 3 to 6 weeks.

Prime with sugar and bottle or keg when fermentation is complete.

Sweet Mischief Vienna Mild Lager (All Grain)

Every homebrewer's life needs to intersect with a bit of Sweet Mischief. This is a sessionable beer with malt and hop characters coming together to create subtle complexity and thirst-quenching satisfaction. The grains are a mashup of both Vienna-style lager and English Mild–style ale. Fermentation is pursued as a lager and the alcohol is mildly low.

The unique roasted character of brown malt and the caramel of crystal malt along with lower gravity represent mild ale-ness. The generous amount of mellow toasty Munich malt along with neutral base Pilsener malt heads in the direction of a Vienna lager. Aromatic-type malts always contribute a great goosing if a degree of rich malt aroma and flavor is asking to be present. The small amount of aromatic malt is subtle and has kind of a catalytic effect, helping emphasize the maltiness of Munich and English crystal.

Dry hopping with Crystal represents both the characters of English ales and German lagers in aroma. The overall balance of this beer emphasizes subtlety yet will satisfy your thirst on every sessionable occasion. Let's cut the shuck and jive and get on with some Sweet Mischief.

Ingredients for 5½ gallons (21 l):

4 lb. (1.82 kg)	German Munich malt (10 L)
2 oz. (56 g)	German Pils malt
1½ lb. (680 g)	English brown malt (20 L)
6 oz. (168 g)	English crystal malt (10 L)
¼ lb. (114 g)	aromatic-type malt
1¼ oz. (35 g)	German Hallertau or Saphir hops (boiling): 5.4 HBU (150 MBU)
1½ oz. (42 g)	Mt. Hood hops (45 minutes, flavor): 8 HBU (223 MBU)
½ oz. (14 g)	Crystal hop pellets (dry hopping, aroma)
¼ tsp. (1 g)	Irish moss powder
*	German- or Bavarian-type lager yeast or White Labs Cry Havoc yeast
¾ c. (175 ml)	corn sugar (dextrose) or 1¼ c. (300 ml) dried malt extract (for bottling); or ⅓ c. (80 ml) corn sugar (dextrose) for kegging

O.G.: 1.040 (10)
F.G.: 1.010 (2.5)
Bitterness: 25 BU; Color: 14 SRM (28 EBC); Alcohol: 3.9% by volume

A step infusion mash is employed to mash the grains. Add 8 quarts (7.6 l) of 143-degree F (61.5 C) water to the crushed grain, stir, stabilize and hold the temperature at 132 degrees F (53 C) for 30 minutes. Add 4 quarts (3.8 l) of boiling water and add heat to bring temperature up to 155 degrees F (68 C) and hold for about 30 minutes. Then raise temperature to 167 degrees F (75 C), lauter and sparge with 3½ gallons (13.5 l) of 170-degree F (77 C) water. Collect about 5½ gallons (21 l) of runoff.

Add the boiling hops, bring to a full and vigorous boil, and boil for 60 minutes. Add the flavor hops for the last 45 minutes of the boil. Add the Irish moss for the final 10 minutes of the boil.

After a total wort boil of 60 minutes, turn off the heat and place the pot (with cover on) in a running cold-water bath for 45 minutes. Continue to chill in the immersion or use other methods to chill your wort. Then strain and sparge the wort into a sanitized fermenter. Bring the total volume to 5½ gallons (21 l) with additional cold water if necessary. Aerate the wort very well.

Pitch the yeast when temperature of wort is about 70 degrees F (21 C). Once visible signs of fermentation are evident, ferment at temperatures of about 55 degrees F (12.5 C) for about 1 week or until fermentation shows signs of calm and stopping. Rack from your primary to a secondary and add the hop pellets for dry hopping. Lager the beer at temperatures between 35 and 45 degrees F (1.5–7 C) for 3 to 6 weeks.

Prime with sugar and bottle or keg when fermentation is complete.

DARK LAGERS

Jump Be Nimble, Jump Be Quick German Dunkel (All Grain)

The rewards are great for brewing this nimbly dark lager. Roasted chocolate malt and other aromatic and caramelized specialty malts all contribute to a spectacularly complex, nutty, velvety smooth German Dunkel. It is rich and malty yet punctuated with a balanced bitterness of roast malt and a whisper of hops. If you like dark lagers and you brew all grain, I guarantee pleasure with Jump Be Nimble, Jump Be Quick Dunkel. Your German friends will wonder where you got your brewmaster's degree.

Ingredients for 5 gallons (19 l):

5½ lb. (2.5 kg)   Pilsener or lager malt
3 lb. (1.4 kg)   Munich malt (10 L)

½ lb. (0.23 kg)   aromatic, Biscuit™ or Victory™ malt

1 lb. (0.45 g)   crystal or caramel malt (60 L)

5 oz. (140 g)   roasted chocolate malt

2 oz. (56 g)   debittered black malt

¾ oz. (21 g)   German Spalt hops (boiling): 3.8 HBU (106 MBU)

¼ oz. (7 g)   German Hallertau hops (boiling): 1 HBU (28 MBU)

1 oz. (28 g)   German Smaragd (Emerald) or French Strisselspalt hops
(30 minutes, flavor): 2.5 HBU (70 MBU)

¼ oz. (7 g)   Crystal hops (1 minute, aroma)

¼ tsp. (1 g)   Irish moss powder

*   Bavarian- or Munich-type lager yeast

¾ c. (175 ml)   corn sugar (dextrose) or 1¼ c. (300 ml) dried malt
extract (for bottling); or ⅓ c. (80 ml) corn sugar
(dextrose) for kegging

O.G.: 1.050–1.054 (12.5–13.5)
F.G.: 1.010–1.014 (2.5–3.5)
Bitterness: 26 BU; Color: 23 SRM (46 EBC); Alcohol: 5.3% by volume

A step infusion mash is employed to mash the grains. Add 10½ quarts (10 l) of 143-degree F (61.5 C) water to the crushed grain, stir, stabilize and hold the temperature at 132 degrees F (53 C) for 30 minutes. Add 5½ quarts (5.2 l) of boiling water and add heat to bring temperature up to 155 degrees F (68 C) and hold for about 30 minutes. Then raise temperature to 167 degrees F (75 C), lauter and sparge with 3½ gallons (13.5 l) of 170-degree F (77 C) water. Collect about 5½ gallons (21 l) of runoff.

Add the two boiling hops, bring to a full and vigorous boil, and boil for 60 minutes. Add the flavor hops for the last 30 minutes of the boil. Add the Irish moss for the last 10 minutes of the boil. Add the aroma hops for the final 1 minute.

After a total wort boil of 60 minutes, turn off the heat and place the pot (with cover on) in a running cold-water bath for 45 minutes. Continue to chill in the immersion or use other methods to chill your wort. Then strain and sparge the wort into a sanitized fermenter. Bring the total volume to 5 gallons (19 l) with additional cold water if necessary. Aerate the wort very well.

Pitch the yeast when temperature of wort is about 70 degrees F (21 C). Once visible signs of fermentation are evident ferment at temperatures of about 55 degrees F (12.5 C) for about 1 week or until fermentation shows signs of calm and stopping. Rack from your primary to a secondary and add the hop pellets for dry hopping. If you have the capability, "lager" the beer at temperatures between 35 and 45 degrees F (1.5–7 C) for 3 to 6 weeks.

Prime with sugar and bottle or keg when fermentation is complete.

Ivan the Wonderful's Czech Dark Lager (All Grain)

So many great beers in the world and so many great places to try them. In the city of Prague in the Czech Republic there is a brewpub that's been there since 1499. U Fleků has got to be the oldest operating brewery pub in the world. There you will find the wonderful Czech dark lager brewed by brewmaster Ivan Chramosil since 1971.

Prague is a city of beer and architecture. Though there is not a wide selection of beer types, the Czechs down on average 158 liters per person of light lager a year. They all taste similar. But Ivan's wonderful beer is something special. It's unique and for all the world it's worthy of enjoying—and if you're a homebrewer—it's worth brewing.

At the brewery Ivan tells me that U Fleků dark lager is traditionally brewed with whole hops, is cooled in a large shallow pan called a "cool ship," enjoys long ferments in wooden vessels, and is brewed at a consistent original gravity. It uses Pilsener-type malt and four other types of roasted and caramelized malts (in delicately small and balanced quantities). Ivan says he brews to a gravity of 14 degrees (1.056), with 1 to 2 weeks of primary fermentation and 3 to 4 weeks of lagering. I enjoyed many mugs of his beers without feeling the effect, so accordingly I adjusted this homebrewed recipe to a lower original gravity to feel accordingly.

If you go to U Fleků you may hear singing. If you brew this beer you'll want to sing.

Ingredients for 5 gallons (19 l):

6¼ lb.(2.8 kg)	Pilsener malt
1 lb. (454 g)	Munich malt
½ lb. (227 g)	aromatic malt
½ lb. (227 g)	dextrin-type malt
¼ lb. (114 g)	CaraMunich™ malt
¼ lb. (114 g)	debittered black malt
1 oz. (28 g)	Czech Saaz hops (boiling): 4 HBU (112 MBU)
1 oz. (28 g)	Mt. Hood hops (15 minutes, flavor): 5 HBU (140 MBU)
¼ tsp (1 g)	Irish moss powder
*	White Labs Cry Havoc yeast or Bavarian- or Munich-style lager yeast
¾ c. (175 ml)	corn sugar (dextrose) or 1¼ c. (300 ml) dried malt extract (for bottling); or ⅓ c. (80 ml) corn sugar (dextrose) for kegging

O.G.: 1.048 (12)
F.G.: 1.010–1.014 (2.5–3.5)
Bitterness: 22 BU; Color: 23 SRM (46 EBC); Alcohol: 4.7% by volume

A step infusion mash is employed to mash the grains. Add 8½ quarts (8.1 l) of 143-degree F (61.5 C) water to the crushed grain, stir, stabilize and hold the temperature at 132 degrees F (53 C) for 30 minutes. Add 4 quarts (3.8 l) of boiling water and add heat to bring temperature up to 155 degrees F (68 C) and hold for about 30 minutes. Then raise temperature to 167 degrees F (75 C), lauter and sparge with 3½ gallons (13.5 l) of 170-degree F (77 C) water. Collect about 5½ gallons (21 l) of runoff.

Add the boiling hops, bring to a full and vigorous boil, and boil for 60 minutes. Add the flavor hops for the last 15 minutes of the boil. Add the Irish moss for the final 10 minutes of the boil.

After a total wort boil of 60 minutes, turn off the heat and place the pot (with cover on) in a running cold-water bath for 45 minutes. Continue to chill in the immersion or use other methods to chill your wort. Then strain and sparge the wort into a sanitized fermenter. Bring the total volume to 5 gallons (19 l) with additional cold water if necessary. Aerate the wort very well.

Pitch the yeast when temperature of wort is about 70 degrees F (21 C). Once visible signs of fermentation are evident, ferment at temperatures of about 55 degrees F (12.5 C) for about 1 week or until fermentation shows signs of calm and stopping. Rack from your primary to a secondary. If you have the capability, "lager" the beer at temperatures between 35 and 45 degrees F (1.5–7 C) for 4 to 6 weeks.

Prime with sugar and bottle or keg when fermentation is complete.

Blinking Star Dark Lager (All Grain)

Here's a variation on Ivan the Wonderful's Czech Dark Lager. It's the same basic recipe, but with the addition of hops for flavor and aroma. The dry hopping is similar to what you might infuse into your India pale ale, but with the balance of roast and caramelized malts, the aroma hop infusions create an entirely different experience; a synergy between floral, fruity hops and sweet, cocoa, caramel malt characters creates a "whamo" experience you have to try to believe it.

¾ oz. (21 g)   French Strisselspalt hop pellets (steeping, aroma)

½ oz. (14 g)   Crystal hop pellets (dry hopping, aroma)

0.1 oz. (3 g)   Simcoe hop pellets (dry hopping, aroma)

0.1 oz. (3 g)   Citra hop pellets (dry hopping, aroma)

0.1 oz. (3 g)   New Zealand Nelson Sauvin hop pellets (dry hopping, aroma)

After the 60-minute wort boil, add the steeping hops. When racking from primary to secondary, add the dry hop pellets.

STRONG LAGERS

Shineblast Imperial Helles (All Grain)

This brew is not your typical specialty knock-your-socks-off hop and alcohol punch. It's a solemnly balanced shineblast of malt and hops with a graceful finale of alcohol. It takes you on a different path than most other American craft-made specialty beers. For one, it is a lager. With unique hop varieties used for flavor, aroma, and dry hopping, it takes you in new directions; a theme that pioneer homebrewers have been pursuing for thirty years.

When fresh and new, Shineblast Imperial Helles has a shrewdly measured hop bite. With a few short months of appropriate cellar aging at cool and stable temperatures, the intricately designed relationships between malt and hops fuse and develop—exquisitely. With a year's aging at about 50-degree F (10 C) cellar temperatures, hop, floral, and aromatic notes will begin to subside, while malt character elevates. The beer will take you on a unique and unscripted journey, surely to remain interestingly delicious, whenever you celebrate with it.

Enjoy this one with friends. Best bottle-conditioned, rather than kegged. Serve in brandy-like "globed" stemmed glassware at about 45 degrees F. Pint or 14-ounce "shaker" glasses are not a good choice of glassware for this elegant brew.

Ingredients for 5½ gallons (20 l):

13 lb. (5.9 kg)   Czech (Bohemian) floor malt, German floor malt or German Pilsener malt

½ lb. (227 g)	Belgian aromatic malt
½ lb. (227 g)	Gambrinus honey malt
¼ lb. (114 g)	Weyermann sauer malt
1 oz. (28 g)	Mt. Hood hops (boiling): 5 HBU (140 MBU)
1 oz. (28 g)	German Hallertau hops (boiling): 4.5 HBU (126 MBU)
1 oz. (28 g)	Crystal hops (1 minute, aroma)
½ oz. (14 g)	Crystal hop pellets (dry hopping)
½ oz. (14 g)	French Strisselspalt hop pellets (dry hopping)
¼ tsp. (1 g)	Irish moss powder
*	White Labs Cry Havoc yeast or Saflager dried lager yeast
¾ c. (175 ml)	corn sugar (dextrose) or 1¼ c. (300 ml) dried malt extract (for bottling); or ⅓ c. (80 ml) corn sugar (dextrose) for kegging

O.G.: 1.048 (12)
F.G.: 1.012–1.016 (3–4)
Bitterness: 32 BU; Color: 8 SRM (16 EBC); Alcohol: 7.4% by volume

A step infusion mash is employed to mash the grains. Add 14¼ quarts (13.5 l) of 143-degree F (61.5 C) water to the crushed grains, stir, stabilize and hold the temperature at 132 degrees F (53 C) for 30 minutes. Add 7 quarts (6.7 l) of boiling water and add heat to bring temperature up to 155 degrees F (68 C) and hold for about 30 minutes. Then raise temperature to 167 degrees F (75 C), lauter and sparge with 4½ gallons (17 l) of 170-degree F (77 C) water. Collect the first 6 gallons (23 l) of runoff.

Add the two boiling hops, bring to a full and vigorous boil, and boil for 60 minutes. Add the Irish moss for the last 10 minutes of the boil. Add the aroma hops for the final 1 minute.

After a total wort boil of 60 minutes, turn off the heat and place the pot (with cover on) in a running cold-water bath for 45 minutes. Continue to chill in the immersion or use other methods to chill your wort. Then strain and sparge the wort into a sanitized fermenter. Bring the total volume to 5½ gallons (21 l) with additional cold water if necessary. Aerate the wort very well.

Pitch the yeast when temperature of wort is about 70 degrees F (21 C). Once visible signs of fermentation are evident, ferment at temperatures of about 55 degrees F (12.5 C) for about 10 to 14 days or until fermentation shows signs of calm and stopping. Rack from your primary to a secondary and add the hop pellets for dry hopping. Lager the beer at temperatures between 35 and 45 degrees F (1.5–7 C) for 6 to 10 weeks.

Prime with sugar and bottle or keg when fermentation is complete.

Jah Mon Irie Doppelbock (Mash Extract)

Jah, mon, ya wanna drink this one a up side a yo fronta da face, mon.

Jah Mon Irie Doppelbock is a potent bock that welcomes you to drink it. Yes, it's strong, but ohhh, is it smooth. This is a copper-garnet-colored lager with friendly malt tones and the hop balance you come to expect from a traditional German-style doppelbock. It's mashed at lower temperatures for maximum fermentability and is lagered an extra measure. This beer keeps very well with extended lagering or bottle conditioning.

Ingredients for 5 gallons (19 l):

2 lb. (0.91 kg)	Pilsener or lager malt
1½ lb. (0.68 kg)	Munich malt (10 L)
1½ lb. (0.68 kg)	wheat malt
½ lb. (230 g)	crystal or caramel malt (10 L)
¼ lb. (114 g)	roasted chocolate malt
5 lb. (2.3 kg)	light dried malt extract
1¼ oz. (36 g)	German Hallertau or Spalt hops (boiling): 5 HBU (140 MBU)
½ oz. (14 g)	German Hallertau Hersbruck or Saphir hops (30 minutes, flavor): 2 HBU (56 MBU)
½ oz. (14 g)	German Hallertau Hersbruck or Mt. Hood hops (15 minutes, flavor)
¼ tsp. (1 g)	Irish moss powder
*	lager yeast, well-attenuating
¾ c. (175 ml)	corn sugar (dextrose) or 1¼ c. (300 ml) dried malt extract (for bottling); or ⅓ c. (80 ml) corn sugar (dextrose) for kegging

O.G.: 1.072–1.076 (18–19)
F.G.: 1.014–1.019 (3.5–5)
Bitterness: 25 BU; Color: 12–14 SRM (24–28 EBC); Alcohol: 7.6%
    by volume

Using a protein-developing step mash, add 6 quarts (5.7 l) of 130-degree F (54.4 C) water to the crushed malt. Stabilize at 122 degrees F (50 C) and hold for 30 minutes. Add 3 quarts (2.9 l) of 185-degree F (85 C) water and stabilize at 140 degrees F (60 C) for 20 minutes. Add heat to raise temperature to 152 to 154 degrees F (66.7–67.8 C) and hold for 40 minutes. Then add heat to bring temperature to 160 degrees F (71 C) and hold for 10 minutes. Mash out to 165 degrees F (74 C). Sparge with 2½ to 3 gallons (9.5–11.4 l) of 170-degree F (77 C) water. Collect 3½ to 4 gallons (13.3–15.2 l).

Add the dried malt extract and boiling hops, bring to a full and vigorous boil, and boil for 60 minutes. Add the 30-minute flavor hops for the last 30 minutes of the boil. Add the 15-minute flavor hops for the last 15 minutes of the boil. Add the Irish moss for the final 10 minutes of the boil.

After a total wort boil of 60 minutes, turn off the heat and immerse the covered pot of wort in a cold-water bath and let sit for 30 minutes or the time it takes to have a homebrew.

Then strain out and sparge hops and direct the hot wort into a sanitized fermenter to which 2 gallons (7.6 l) of cold water has been added. If necessary add more cold water to achieve a 5-gallon (19 l) batch size. Aerate the wort very well.

Sparge, strain, and add wort to your sanitized fermenter partly filled with cold water. Pitch the yeast when temperature of wort is about 70 degrees F (21 C). Once visible signs of fermentation are evident, ferment at temperatures of about 55 degrees F (12.5 C) for about 1 week or until fermentation shows signs of calm and stopping. Rack from your primary to a secondary and add the hop pellets for dry hopping. Lager the beer at temperatures between 35 and 45 degrees F (1.5–7 C) for 6 to 7 weeks.

Prime with sugar and bottle or keg when fermentation is complete. Jah Mon!

My Goodness My Bock (All Grain)

My Goodness My Bock is an immensely drinkable session bock. It's lower in alcohol than its German counterpart, but it is rich in flavor and provides a bit more kick than a lighter-styled . . . oh, shall we call it American bock? It still reflects most of the malty traditions of dark German bock beer, but with a noticeable accent of hop character and flavor, making it all the more refreshing and crisp. A terrific dark lager to introduce your friends to. This is not pint-size beer. My Goodness My Bock is good for you with its good dose of nourishment.

Ingredients for 5 gallons (19 l):

6 lb. (2.7 kg)	German Pilsener or lager malt
1½ lb. (0.68 kg)	Munich malt
1½ lb. (0.68 kg)	Vienna malt
¾ lb. (340 g)	crystal or caramel malt (10 L)
¼ lb. (112 g)	roasted chocolate malt
¼ lb. (112 g)	debittered black malt
1 oz. (28 g)	German Tradition or Spalt Select hop (boiling): 6 HBU (168 MBU)
½ oz. (14 g)	German Hallertau or Mittelfrüh hops (20 minutes, flavor)
½ oz. (14 g)	American Tettnang hops (20 minutes, flavor)
¼ tsp. (1 g)	Irish moss powder
*	Bavarian- or Munich-type lager yeast
¾ c. (175 ml)	corn sugar (dextrose) or 1¼ c. (300 ml) dried malt extract (for bottling); or ⅓ c. (80 ml) corn sugar (dextrose) for kegging

O.G.: 1.054–1.058 (13.5–14.5)
F.G.: 1.014–1.018 (4.5–5.5)
Bitterness: 29 BU; Color: 26 SRM (52 EBC); Alcohol: 5.3% by volume

A step infusion mash is employed to mash the grains. Add 10 quarts (9.5 l) of 143-degree F (61.5 C) water to the crushed grains, stir, stabilize and hold the temperature at 132 degrees F (53 C) for 30 minutes. Add 5 quarts (4.8 l) of boiling water and add heat to bring temperature up to 155 degrees F (68 C) and hold for about 30 minutes. Then raise temperature to 167 degrees F (75 C), lauter and sparge with 3½ gallons (13.5 l) of 170-degree F (77 C) water. Collect about 5½ gallons (21 l) of runoff.

Add the boiling hops, bring to a full and vigorous boil, and boil for 60 minutes. Add the two flavor hops for the last 20 minutes of the boil. Add the Irish moss for the final 10 minutes of the boil.

After a total wort boil of 60 minutes, turn off the heat and place the pot (with cover on) in a running cold-water bath for 45 minutes. Continue to chill in the immersion or use other methods to chill your wort. Then strain and sparge the wort into a sanitized fermenter. Bring the total volume to 5 gallons (19 l) with additional cold water if necessary. Aerate the wort very well.

Pitch the yeast when temperature of wort is about 70 degrees F (21 C). Once visible signs of fermentation are evident, ferment at temperatures of about 55 degrees F (12.5 C) for about 1 week or until fermentation shows signs of calm and stopping. Rack from your primary to a secondary. If you have the capability, "lager" the beer at temperatures between 35 and 45 degrees F (1.5–7 C) for 3 to 6 weeks.

Prime with sugar and bottle or keg when fermentation is complete.

SPECIALTY LAGER

Rogerfest Cherrywood Lager (All Grain)

You know you're a homebrew geek when you mentally jump up and down when you hear about a new malt or new hop variety. When I received notification from Briess Malt about their new cherrywood smoked malt, it was love at first thought.

I remember my first sip of smoked beer. It was Aecht Schlenkerla back in 1979. That was love at first sip. In those Stone Age days of homebrewing, there was no such thing as smoked malt available to homebrewers. At the time, I immediately set about to figure out how to smoke my own malt. I succeeded by wetting already malted barley and placing it on a screen in my Weber-style grill over coals and applewood. It made for some very satisfying brews.

Now there is beechwood smoked malt from German Weyermann Malt Company and cherrywood smoked malt from American Briess Malt Company. Cherrywood smoked malt will fascinate you if you're a smoked beer freak. I had a grin on my face the day a bag arrived. It is remarkably well sealed in a paper sack lined with foil. Opening the bag of malt was like being fireside. I wanted to eat the stuff.

Now here comes the interesting part. The information sheet that came with the malt suggested various amounts of smoked malt for varying degrees of intensity. I immediately was drawn to the statement at the bottom of the info sheet: "Briess Smoked Malt delivers intense smoked flavor. We recommend limiting usage up to 60% of the grist." Holy moly! Is that a dare or isn't it!? There it was confronting my homebrew sensibilities, saying to me, "I dare you to use more than 60%!" So I did.

Using smoked malt is tricky. Hop bitterness is not compatible with the phenolic character of smoke, so it's important to bitterdown (new word I just invented) the hops. I know, it's hard, but dear homebrewer, take solace in knowing there'll be other brews you make where you can throw in lots of hops. But not this one.

Dry, thin-bodied, and well-attenuated beers are not very friendly with smoke character either. With these thoughts in mind I designed a beer with sweetness, body, and sweet floral-honey-like hop aroma. Rogerfest Cherrywood Lager is like hitting a grand slam! Even friends who may not take kindly to smoked beer might be jumping up and down telling you, "Wow, this is really good beer!"

Rogerfest Cherrywood Lager is named after the late owner of Briess Malting

Company, Roger Briess. He was an original friend and fan of American home-brewers from the time of our hobby's founding. There's always a good reason to celebrate Roger's enthusiasm. For now it's with Rogerfest Cherry-wood Lager.

Ingredients for 5 gallons (19 l):

6½ lb. (3 kg)	Briess (cherrywood) smoked malt
2 lb. (908 g)	Munich-type malt (10 L)
¾ lb. (340 g)	aromatic-type malt
¼ lb. (114 g)	German sauer malt
¾ lb. (340 g)	Gambrinus honey malt
½ lb. (227 g)	German CaraMunich™ (75 L)
1¼ oz. (35 g)	Liberty or Crystal hops (boiling): 5 HBU (140 MBU)
1 oz. (28 g)	German Hallertau hops (20 minutes, flavor): 4 HBU (112 MBU)
½ oz. (14 g)	French Strisselspalt hop pellets (1 minute, aroma)
½ oz. (14 g)	Mt. Hood hop pellets (1 minute, aroma)
¼ oz. (7 g)	Crystal hop pellets (dry hopping, aroma)
¼ oz. (7 g)	French Strisselspalt hop pellets (dry hopping, aroma)
¼ tsp. (1 g)	Irish moss powder
*	White Labs Cry Havoc lager yeast or Bavarian- or Munich-type lager yeast
¾ c. (175 ml)	corn sugar (dextrose) or 1¼ c. (300 ml) dried malt extract (for bottling); or ⅓ c. (80 ml) corn sugar (dextrose) for kegging

O.G.: 1.056–1.060 (14–14.7)
F.G.: 1.016–1.020 (4–5)
Bitterness: 24 BU; Color: 16 SRM (30 EBC); Alcohol: 5.3% by volume

A step infusion mash is employed to mash the grains. Add 11 quarts (10.5 l) of 143-degree F (61.5 C) water to the crushed grains, stir, stabilize and hold the temperature at 132 degrees F (53 C) for 30 minutes. Add 5½ quarts (5.2 l) of boiling water and add heat to bring temperature up to 155 degrees F (68 C) and hold for about 30 minutes. Then raise temperature to 167 degrees F (75 C), lauter and sparge with 3½ gallons (13.5 l) of 170-degree F (77 C) water. Collect about 6 gallons (23 l) of runoff.

Add the boiling hops, bring to a full and vigorous boil, and boil for 60 minutes. Add the flavor hops for the last 20 minutes of the boil. Add the Irish moss for the last 10 minutes of the boil. Add the two aroma hops for the final 1 minute.

After a total wort boil of 60 minutes, turn off the heat and place the pot (with cover on) in a running cold-water bath for 30 minutes. Continue to chill in the immersion or use other methods to chill your wort. Then strain and sparge the wort into a sanitized fermenter. Bring the total volume to 5 gallons (19 l) with additional cold water if necessary. Aerate the wort very well.

Pitch the yeast when temperature of wort is about 70 degrees F (21 C). Once visible signs of fermentation are evident, ferment at temperatures of about 55 degrees F (12.5 C) for about 1 week or until fermentation shows signs of calm and stopping. Rack from your primary to a secondary and add the hop pellets for dry hopping. Lager the beer at temperatures between 35 and 45 degrees F (1.5–7 C) for 3 to 6 weeks.

Prime with sugar and bottle or keg when fermentation is complete.

GLUTEN-FREE/GLUTEN-REDUCED BEER

Intolerance to gluten protein is the most common genetic disorder in humans, affecting one to two percent of the American population. These estimates are even higher worldwide and many suspect American estimates are low. The disorder is called celiac (or coeliac) disease.

It's a disorder that, when certain types of gluten protein are ingested, creates an autoimmune response in the body. That response compromises the tiny absorbing and digestive villi (hairlike protrusions) within the small intestine resulting in serious digestion problems leading to several forms of ill health.

Currently those with celiac disease are advised to stop eating and drinking any food that has been made with or has content that includes the gluten protein. Therein lies the problem for beer drinkers diagnosed with celiac disease. Beer is made with barley, which along with wheat, rye, and other similar cereals contains the offending protein called prolamin/polypeptide/gluten.

One of the most common questions among homebrewers is "Can homebrewers make gluten-free beer?" The answer is yes and maybe yes. Of course if you make beer with ingredients that do not have gluten proteins and your yeast has been cultured in a gluten-free medium, you can make gluten-free beer. Currently the most common gluten-free grains used in brewing gluten-free beers are sorghum, rice, corn, and millet, which are brewed with other flavorings such as fruit, honey, flavorful sugars, and of course hops. But for the most part they are brewed to have a very light flavor profile and usually lack any beer character.

If you do decide to pursue brewing gluten-free beer with gluten-free ingredients, try toasting some of these grains in order to add caramelized flavors, roasted notes, fuller body, flavor, and complexity. Of course there's every reason to use late hopping techniques (late hop boiling and dry hopping) to help create real beer flavors and character.

Here are some fundamentals you could use in order to homebrew a beer with a sorghum syrup base:

- 7 pounds (3.2 kg) of Briess White Sorghum 45 HM Syrup in a 5-gallon (19 l) recipe will achieve about a 1.053 original gravity (13.3 P). This is about 38 points of specific gravity (9 P) per pound for each gallon.
- Lightly toast corn, rice, millet, or grain sorghum to achieve baked biscuit and caramel flavor, aroma, and character.
- Roast corn, rice, millet, or grain sorghum at higher temperatures and longer periods to develop more assertive roast flavors and aroma and achieves colors for darker beers.
- Lactose sugars can be added to create more body in the beer.
- Dry- and flavor-hop gluten-free beers just as you would traditionally brewed beer.

Can you make gluten-free beer from barley and other malts that are suitable for those with celiac disease? The answer to this is a very cautious "possibly," if certain techniques and enzymes are used. Read on.

There are many challenges in deciphering advice about whether regular beer is or can be gluten-free. There is no internationally accepted standard regarding the testing and certification of gluten-free foods and beverages, beer or otherwise. For example, European standards and measuring techniques are different from American standards. Most current standards test specifically for wheat-derived and wheat-specific gluten protein.

In the United States, the Food and Drug Administration (FDA) currently (2012) defines gluten-free food and beverages as either not made from ingredients containing the offending prolamin/polypeptide/gluten protein or the final product not containing these proteins. For the most up-to-date rulings by the FDA go to their website, www.fda.gov, and search for the current definition. At the time of this writing, here is where one really needs to consider whether this official assessment is realistic advice for beer drinkers.

The FDA rule implies that even if a beer has zero prolamin/polypeptide/gluten content, it is officially not gluten-free because it is made with gluten-containing ingredients. There are arguments emerging that lead one to consider whether offending proteins can be removed from beer. Furthermore, most standardized tests for gluten are based on measuring gluten fractions of wheat as a "marker" or indicator of gluten levels. These tests either minimize or skew the accounting for, or do not take into account, the nuances of other cereal-derived prolamin/polypeptide/gluten. There is even some inconsistency in medical opinion and research that renders inconclusive the notion that all cereal-derived prolamin/polypeptide/gluten is harmful to those with celiac disease.

All brewers are aware of a phenomenon called chill haze. Beer containing certain types of protein remains clear at room temperature, because these proteins remain dissolved. At cold temperatures this protein precipitates, appearing as a haze in the beer. It eventually settles out as sediment if kept at cold temperatures long enough. This precipitated chill-haze protein is barley malt (in the case of all barley malt beer) prolamin/polypeptide/gluten. Precipitated chill-haze protein can be cold-filtered out of beer. It's also significantly reduced or eliminated by adsorptive methods common in the beverage industry.

ANOTHER OPTION

If you doubt that the natural processing of malted barley into beer can reduce offending proteins enough, then there is another option that now promises to eliminate all offending prolamin/polypeptide/glutens from beverages. Brewers Clarex™ (aka Clarity Ferm from White Labs) is an enzyme developed by DSM Food Specialties specifically eliminating all traces of prolamin/polypeptide/gluten in beer, wine, alcohol, and fruit juices when used appropriately.

Headquartered in the Netherlands, DSM Food Specialties (www.dsm.com) has been a participant in beer industry events and trade shows for many years. They are a global supplier of advanced ingredients for the food and beverage industries, primarily manufactured with the aid of fermentation and enzyme technology.

Brewers Clarex™ (aka Clarity Ferm from White Labs) is currently marketed as a haze eliminating/reducing enzyme, specifically for "improving the colloidal stability of beer." Because of the complexity and inconsistency of international standards and "gluten-free regulations" they have not marketed this enzyme as a tool suitable for eliminating gluten in beer. They do not promote that Brewers Clarex™ (aka Clarity Ferm from White Labs) can help make beer that is suitable for those with celiac disease.

RESEARCH

Research that is relevant to Brewers Clarex™ (aka Clarity Ferm from White Labs) and its significance in addressing the health issues of those who suffer from celiac disease is ongoing. Some research indicates that a general gluten analysis is not detailed enough to determine the true benefits of Brewers Clarex™ (aka Clarity Ferm from White Labs) to persons who have celiac disease. The symptoms experienced by celiac patients are generated in particular by certain allergenic epitopes in gluten that recognize T cells and cause an immune response in the small intestine. The research DSM has conducted has shown these specific epitopes are completely degraded by Brewers Clarex™ (aka Clarity Ferm from White Labs).

There are two technical articles available on the Internet for a much more detailed explanation. They are:

- "Efficient degradation of gluten by a prolyl endoprotease in a gastrointestinal model: implications for coeliac disease," http://gut.bmj.com/cgi/content/abstract/57/1/25
- "Highly efficient gluten degradation with a newly identified prolyl endoprotease: implications for celiac disease," http://www.ncbi.nlm.nih.gov/pubmed/16690904?dopt=Citation

These were published as a result of research conducted by the University of Leiden in the Netherlands. The enzyme referred to in these articles (AN-PEP or Aspergillus niger prolyl endoprotease) is Brewers Clarex™ (aka Clarity Ferm from White Labs).

OTHER CONCERNS

Some brewers may have a concern about Brewers Clarex™ (aka Clarity Ferm from White Labs) because it is an "enzyme preparation for food use containing proline-specific endo-protease derived from a selected self-cloned strain of Aspergillus niger." For those who are opposed (for whatever reasons) to cloned or genetically modified organisms (GMO), this may be of concern. Professional brewers usually shy away from using anything that is GMO because of the associated bad publicity it often receives.

DOSAGE

The recommended dosage of Brewers Clarex™ (aka Clarity Ferm from White Labs) for use in beer is 1 to 3 grams per hectoliter (1–3 g per 0.85 barrel or 0.16–0.48 g per 5 U.S. gallons). Since Brewers Clarex™ (aka Clarity Ferm from White Labs) comes in liquid solution grams approximately converts to milliliters. For information regarding availability in the United States contact White Labs.

I've experimented with using Brewers Clarex™ (aka Clarity Ferm from White Labs) in small-batch homebrews. A pale ale I call Slithy Tove is a 5-gallon batch of homebrewed all-malt (using 10 percent wheat malt) hoppy pale ale. I added 3 milliliters of Brewers Clarex™ (aka Clarity Ferm from White Labs) to Slithy Tove at yeast pitching.

Slithy Tove Pale Ale is visually no different from a control batch of identical pale ale in which Clarex was not used. Flavor, mouthfeel, and aromatic character also remained consistent between the two batches of beer. Foam character and head retention were both superb. There was a slight haze present in the beer when refrigerated to 33 degrees F (1 C) possibly due to dry hopping.

TESTING FOR THE PRESENCE OF GLUTEN PROTEIN

I qualitatively tested Slithy Tove Pale Ale using an EZ Gluten Test Kit. This quick and easy home test is available from Elisa Technologies (www.elisa-tek.com). This test indicated a "positive" presence of gluten (note: a later batch of pale ale, with no wheat malt, tested negative). The test is a very sensitive test and guarantees a lower limit of detection of 10 ppm for barley, rye, and wheat glutens. Because this test is designed to see barley and rye glutens, the wheat fraction indicators are sometimes much more sensitive.

A more detailed quantitative analysis of gluten levels was pursued by Elisa Technologies in which they further indicated which assay should be chosen to measure the gluten in beer. There are four assay options available, but only one is suitable for measuring gluten in beer. Apparently the Gluten AOAC Assay, Prolamins Assay, and Prolamins Competitive Assay are not dependable tests for measuring gluten in food and beverage products containing alcohol. I sent my beer in to have it analyzed using their Gluten High Sensitivity Assay. This assay guarantees a lower limit of detection of 5 ppm.

SUCCESS

The Elisa Gluten High Sensitivity Assay results indicated that the gluten content in my batch of Slithy Tove Pale Ale was "less than 5 ppm." In other words less than 5 milligrams per liter of beer. That is very low.

Furthermore, the analysis report stated: "The assay utilizes ELISA techniques and is designed for the measurement of cereal gluten at low levels, nominally within the range of 5–100 ppm, e.g., in raw materials and finished food products; it detects the omega gliadin fraction of wheat as a marker of total gluten. These samples were tested using a 'high sensitivity' modification of the gluten assay procedure, which enables detection limits of levels less than 5 ppm gluten in most sample matrices. The detection limit for your samples was 5 ppm."

The laboratory director noted that my sample was tested about 10 times because it was so close to the 5 ppm threshold. The tests indicated my sample could have been about 4.6 ppm, but there was no way of knowing this degree of accuracy using this particular test. If I had used 100 percent barley malt in the recipe and had eliminated the wheat, my results would most likely indicate a much lower level of gluten.

Is Slithy Tove Pale Ale gluten-free and safe for those with celiac disease? My experimental batch of homebrew measured less than 5 ppm, but I can't say that it is safe for all or even some celiacs, because there are no dependable, consistent, and public standards offered by the U.S. government and the medical community. For liability reasons I am not giving any advice here. If you

From the Celiac Disease Glossary
http://celiacdisease.about.com/od
/celiacdiseaseglossary/g/PPM.htm

"Parts per Million" is a way to quantify very low concentrations of substances. For example, 1 ppm is equivalent to 1 milligram of something per liter of liquid (abbreviated as mg/L) or 1 milligram of something per kilogram of solid substance (abbreviated as mg/kg).

have celiac disease and wish to explore this option, you are free to do so. Please be aware that with any process, techniques and quality controls must be adhered to. I will also note that any deviation from the use of traditional ingredients and process could compromise the effectiveness of Brewers Clarex™ (aka Clarity Ferm from White Labs).

Professional brewers offering "gluten-reduced" beers for sale would be well advised to test each batch before release. At $120 an assay test this is impractical for most homebrewers. The EZ Gluten Test costs about $15 per test and can be done easily at home. As noted above, an all-barley malt recipe I brewed indicated a negative presence of gluten. If you are dealing with, or know someone who has, celiac disease and you are thirsting for a beer, it may be worthwhile to explore the Brewers Clarex™ (aka Clarity Ferm from White Labs) option. I would strongly advise medical consultation before deciding to enjoy good beer again. Five ppm is very low. I have heard that most celiacs can tolerate up to 15 milligrams of gluten a day, but these kinds of generalizing statements can be dangerous. It depends on the severity of the problem. You should consider that each celiac patient's condition is unique and different.

To find the most current regulations, go to the www.fda.gov website and search using the words "gluten-free labeling" or "fda ruling on gluten free labeling."

For some people with celiac disease, "gluten-reduced" beer in moderation may soon be a safe option. I think the future looks promising.

CROSSBREEDING BEER—THE CATYWHOMPUS SIDE OF HOMEBREWING

I regularly get requests to talk about beer styles. I can see why. Beer culture in America is vibrant. People love to talk about beer. Brewers and beer enthusiasts hang their beer hopes on every competition. Great beers are being made and better beers are being brewed with every cycle. Old and traditional styles are returning and new styles are on the cutting edge of beer talk. Flavor and diversity reign.

Since 1980 I've been involved with style development and evaluation for several competitions, including the Great American Beer Festival and the World Beer Cup, and helped establish the basis of the American Homebrewers Association and Beer Judge Certification Program style guidelines.

I admire history and tradition. My University of Virginia bachelor of science in nuclear engineering senior thesis was about the history of the Engineering School. The teacher most influential in my life and whom I most admire is Joseph Jacques, my ninth- and tenth-grade world history and modern european history teacher.

The source of creativity and new ideas is in my opinion rooted in the past. Maintaining an understanding of beer history is essential to making great beer. If you want me to talk about beer styles and relevance to beer culture, I will do it with enthusiasm and beer in hand.

But if you let me digress, I will throw my hands up in the air with a "why not?" gesture and propose going to places unzipped and unhinged. In the early 1970s my first brewed honey lager met with flabbergast and astonishment when first introduced to friends and beer lovers. Now Rocky Raccoon's Honey Lager (see *The Complete Joy of Homebrewing, Fourth Edition*) is an award winner for many brewers. Yet at the time it was first brewed, the outrageousness

of combining honey and malt to make a beer was unheard of. I recollect the sneers of professional brewers—to them it was interesting but not really beer.

My life has been all about going down a path, looking from side to side and in back of me, admiring all that surrounds and has passed. But I keep walking forward, equally admiring the prospect of a horizon that I never seem to get to.

Admire and respect tradition. Also leave yourself vulnerable to new ideas. Just for starters, consider:

- A foreign-style stout brewed with Czech Saaz hops and lager yeast?
- A robust porter brewed with Hallertau and Mt. Hood and orange peel?
- A Black Ale brewed to an IPA guideline but with roasted malts and barley, perhaps even dry hopped with Simcoe or Crystal hops. I first experimented in this direction; now it's a style brewed throughout America.
- A yarrow Pils brewed to a German-style Pilsener specification but with the addition of yarrow and fruity aromatic New Zealand hop varieties.
- An Oktoberfest lager late hopped with Fuggles and Goldings hops.
- A super-strength bock beer fermented with ale yeast.
- We know about oatmeal stout. What about rice stout, rye stout, wheat stout, corn stout? Roasted corn porter?
- An India Pale Ale dry hopped with all the "wrong" hops: Hallertau, Liberty, Hersbrucker, Mittelfrüh, Santiam, German Spalt, Saaz.
- A Czech-style Pils brewed and lagered to exception with crystal malt, British Challenger, Northdown or Progress, and perhaps a bit of American Amarillo, Cascade, and Horizon. Perhaps you've added a touch of roasted barley or Belgian Special-B malt.
- Yeast choices? Need I go there? Altbier yeast for Pilseners and stout? Pilsener yeast for an IPA? Strong Belgian beer yeast for coriandered English-style brown ale?

My quick calculation takes me to a million plus combinations when you consider all the varieties of hops, malt, yeast, fermentation temperatures, and hop schedules.

Will you win any competitions based solely on traditional style categories? Probably not, but you may pioneer a style. Will you become a better brewer? Absolutely. Will you enjoy your results? Is there really any doubt about "Yes."

ALL-GRAIN RECIPES IN *THE COMPLETE JOY OF HOMEBREWING, FOURTH EDITION*

Akka Lakka American Pale Ale

Carla's Oat Brown Ale

Dancing with Hops IPA

Dusty Mud Irish Stout

Good Life English Pale Ale

Gopher Greatness Oktoberfest

Hanging Possum (Classic American) Pilsener

Hopotheosis Rosemary Xtra Pale Ale

Humpty Dumpty English-Style Ordinary Bitter

Monkey's Paw Brown Ale

NoopleTucker Dunkel Weizen or Weizen (Dark or Pale Bavarian-Style Wheat Beer)

RU Kidding Me? Czech-Style Pils

Siam Pils

Silver Dollar Porter

Spider's Tongue German Rauchbier (Smoked Beer)

ALL-GRAIN RECIPES IN *MICROBREWED ADVENTURES*

Samuel Adams 1880 (amber lager)

Vienna-Style Ouro de Habanera (Havana Gold)

George Killians Irish Red Ale from Pellforth

1447 Belgium Zwarte Rose (black) Ale

Irish Cocoa Wood Porter

Quingdao Dark Lager

Switch and Toggles Preposterous Poorter

Zaltitis Baltic Porter

Andech's Weekday Bock

Original Dogbolter Ale—Goose & Firkin (brown ale)

Puritanical Nut Brown Ale

English-Style Bitter

Beyond the Ordinary Ordinary Bitter

"Original" Ballard Bitter

Belgian-Style Cherry–Black Currant (Kriek-Cassis) Lambic

Magic Bolo #9.1,300 (apricot ale)

New Wisconsin Apple/Raspberry/Cherry Beer

Crazy Old Man Altbier
65-65-65-65 India Pale Ale
Telluride India Pale Ale
Czech-Mex Tijuana Urquell
Klibbety Jibbit (light lager)
MickViRay Papazian Pilsener
Printz Helles German Lager
Swakapmund Cowboy (light) Lager
1982 Original Sierra Nevada Pale Ale
Piozzo Italian Pale Ale
1981 Boulder Christmas Stout
Bert Grant's Planet Imperial Stout
Brooklyn's Original Chocolate Stout
Felicitous Stout
Pumpernickel Rye Stout
Wolaver's Organic Oatmeal Stout
Jeff Bagby's Hop Whompus 2004
John 1981—a homebrewed version of Charlie 1981
Monastic Bleue Strong Belgian-Style Ale
Old Lighthouse in the Fog Barleywine Ale
Stone 03 Vertical Epic (specialty ale)
19th Century Leipziger Gose
Alaskan Winter Spruce Old Ale
Flying Fish Baby Saison Farmhouse Ale
Frog & Rosbif's Brown Wheat Coriander (mild)
Mile High Green Chile Ale
Poetic Brighella Italian-Belgian-German-English-American Ale
Vello's Gotlandsdricka (specialty ale)
Zeezuiper Spiced Nederlander Strong Ale
Zimbabwe Zephyr Sorghum Beer
Hans Weissbier
Original Pyramid Wheaten Ale

ALL-GRAIN RECIPES IN *HOME BREWER'S GOLD*

Aecht Schlenkerla Rauchbier, Brauerei Heller-Trum, Bamberg, Germany
Aventinus, Private Weissbierbrauerei G. Schneider & Son K.G., Munich, Germany
B&H Breakfast Toasted Ale, Barley & Hopp's, San Mateo, California, USA
Bow Valley Premium Lager, Bow Valley Brewing Co., Canmore, Alberta, Canada

Brick Red Baron, Brick Brewing Co. Ltd., Waterloo, Ontario, Canada
California Blonde Ale, Coast Range Brewing Co., Gilroy, California, USA
Capstone ESB, Oasis Brewery, Boulder, Colorado, USA
Cascade Pale Ale, Cascade Brewery, Hobart, Tasmania, Australia
Coriander Rye Ale, Bison Brewing Co., Berkeley, California, USA
Delaney's Ale, South China Brewing Co. Ltd., Aberdeen, Hong Kong
Derailer Doppelbock, Tabernash Brewing Co., Denver, Colorado, USA
Dos Equis Special Lager, Cerveceria Cuauhtémoc, Monterrey, Mexico
Edelweiss Dunkel, Österreichische Bräu-Aktiengesellschaft, Linz, Austria
Founders Stout, Mishawaka Brewing Co., Mishawaka, Indiana, USA
Grain D'Orge, Brasserie Jeanne D'Arc, Ronchin-Lille, France
Griffon Extra Pale Ale, McAuslan Brewing Inc., Montreal, Quebec, Canada
Hoegaarden, Brouwerij de Kluis, Hoegaarden, Belgium
Icehouse, Plank Road Brewery, Milwaukee, Wisconsin, USA
Leinenkugel's Red Lager, Jacob Leinenkugel Brewing Co., Chippewa Falls,
    Wisconsin, USA
Liefmans Frambozen, Brouwerij Liefmans, Oudenaarde, Belgium
Liefmans Goudenband, Brouwerij Liefmans, Oudenaarde, Belgium
Lindemans Cuvée René, Lindemans Farm Brew, Vlezenbeek, Belgium
Mackeson XXX Stout, Whitbread Beer Co., London, England
Miller Lite, Miller Brewing Co., Milwaukee, Wisconsin, USA
OB Lager, Oriental Brewery Co. Ltd., Seoul, South Korea
Old Rasputin Russian Imperial Stout, North Coast Brewing Co. Inc.,
    Fort Bragg, California, USA
Olde English 800 Malt Liquor, Pabst Brewing Co., Milwaukee, Wisconsin,
    USA
Ozone Ale, Hubcap Brewery/Brewing Co. of Vail, Colorado, USA
Pauwel Kwak, Brewery Bosteels, Buggenhout, Belgium
Point Amber Lager, Barton Beers Ltd., Chicago, Illinois, USA
Radegast Birell, Radegast Brewery J.S.C., Nosovice, Czech Republic
Redwood Coast Alpine Gold Pilsner, Redwood Coast Brewing Co., Alameda,
    California, USA
Redwood Coast Brown, Redwood Coast Brewing Co., Alameda, California,
    USA
Ruddles Best Bitter, Ruddles Brewery, Rutland, United Kingdom
Ruffian Mai-Bock, Mountain Valley Brew Pub, Suffern, New York, USA
Ruffian Pilsner, Mountain Valley Brew Pub, Suffern, New York, USA
Saint Brigid's Porter, Great Divide Brewing Co., Denver, Colorado, USA
San Quentin's Breakout Stout, Marin Brewing Co, Larkspur, California, USA
Scotch Ale, Samuel Adams Brewhouse, Philadelphia, Pennsylvania, USA
Seabright Session Ale, Seabright Brewery, Santa Cruz, California, USA
Slow Down Brown Ale, Il Vicino Inc., Albuquerque, New Mexico, USA

Snake River Pale Ale, Snake River Brewing Co. Inc., Jackson, Wyoming, USA

St. Charles Porter, Blackstone Restaurant & Brewery, Nashville, Tennessee, USA

Star Brew 1000 (Wheat Wine), Marin Brewing Co., Larkspur, California, USA

Stoddards ESB, Stoddards Brewhouse and Eatery, Sunnyvale, California, USA

Stoddards Kölsch, Stoddards Brewhouse and Eatery, Sunnyvale, California, USA

Stoudt's Export Gold, Stoudt Brewing Co., Adamstown, Pennsylvania, USA

Sundance Hefe-Weizen, Palmer Lake Brewing Co., Palmer Lake, Colorado, USA

Tabernash Munich Dark Lager, Tabernash Brewing Co., Denver, Colorado, USA

Thomas Kemper Hefeweizen, Thomas Kemper Lagers, Seattle, Washington, USA

Wet Mountain India Pale Ale, Il Vicino, Salida, Colorado, USA

Zoser Oatmeal Stout, Oasis Brewery, Boulder, Colorado, USA

MASH-EXTRACT RECIPES IN *MICROBREWED ADVENTURES, THE COMPLETE JOY OF HOMEBREWING, FOURTH EDITION, AND HOME BREWER'S GOLD*

MASH-EXTRACT RECIPES IN *MICROBREWED ADVENTURES*

Vienna-Style Ouro de Habanera (Havana Gold)
Quingdao Dark Lager
Switch and Toggles Preposterous Poorter
Zaltitis Baltic Porter
Masterbrewers Doppelbock
New Wisconsin Apple/Raspberry/Cherry Beer
Czech-Mex Tijuana Urquell (light lager)
Klibbety Jibbit (light lager)
Masterbrewers Celebration Light Lager
Pumpernickel Rye Stout
Wolaver's Organic Oatmeal Stout
Flying Fish Baby Saison Farmhouse Ale
Poetic Brighella Italian-Belgian-German-English-American Ale
Quito Abbey Ale-1534 (dark ale)
Vello's Gotlandsdricka (specialty ale)
Zeezuiper Spiced Nederlander Strong Ale

MASH-EXTRACT RECIPES IN *THE COMPLETE JOY OF HOMEBREWING, FOURTH EDITION*

400 Rabbits Aztec-Style Ale
Colonel Coffin Barley Wine Ale
Daisy Mae Czech Lager
Heart of the Tide Imperial Porter
Heaven's Orbit German Dunkel
Laughing Heart India Pale Ale
Limnian Wheat Doppelbock
Mayahuel—Lady of the Tortoise Throne Ale
Potlatch Doppelbock
Top Drop German Pilsener
Uckleduckfay Oatmeal Stout
What the Helles Münchner

MASH-EXTRACT RECIPES IN *HOME BREWER'S GOLD*

Aecht Schlenkerla Rauchbier, Brauerei Heller-Trum, Bamberg, Germany

B&H Breakfast Toasted Ale, Barley & Hopp's, San Mateo, California, USA

Bow Valley Premium Lager, Bow Valley Brewing Co., Canmore, Alberta, Canada

Brick Red Baron, Brick Brewing Co. Ltd., Waterloo, Ontario, Canada

California Blonde Ale, Coast Range Brewing Co., Gilroy, California, USA

Coriander Rye Ale, Bison Brewing Co., Berkeley, California, USA

Derailer Doppelbock, Tabernash Brewing Co., Denver, Colorado, USA

Grain D'Orge, Brasserie Jeanne D'Arc, Ronchin-Lille, France

Icehouse, Plank Road Brewery, Milwaukee, Wisconsin, USA

Leinenkugel's Red Lager, Jacob Leinenkugel Brewing Co., Chippewa Falls, Wisconsin, USA

Liefmans Frambozen, Brouwerij Liefmans, Oudenaarde, Belgium

Liefmans Goudenband, Brouwerij Liefmans, Oudenaarde, Belgium

Lindemans Cuvée René, Lindemans Farm Brew, Vlezenbeek, Belgium

OB Lager, Oriental Brewery Co. Ltd., Seoul, South Korea

Old Rasputin Russian Imperial Stout, North Coast Brewing Co. Inc., Fort Bragg, California, USA

Olde English 800 Malt Liquor, Pabst Brewing Co., Milwaukee, Wisconsin, USA

Radegast Birell, Radegast Brewery J.S.C., Nosovice, Czech Republic

Redwood Coast Alpine Gold Pilsner, Redwood Coast Brewing Co., Alameda, California, USA

Ruffian Mai-Bock, Mountain Valley Brew Pub, Suffern, New York, USA

Ruffian Pilsner, Mountain Valley Brew Pub, Suffern, New York, USA

Saint Brigid's Porter, Great Divide Brewing Co., Denver, Colorado, USA

San Quentin's Breakout Stout, Marin Brewing Co., Larkspur, California, USA

Scotch Ale, Samuel Adams Brewhouse, Philadelphia, Pennsylvania, USA

Seabright Session Ale, Seabright Brewery, Santa Cruz, California, USA

St. Charles Porter, Blackstone Restaurant & Brewery, Nashville, Tennessee, USA

Stoddards Kölsch, Stoddards Brewhouse and Eatery, Sunnyvale, California, USA

Stoudt's Export Gold, Stoudt Brewing Co., Adamstown, Pennsylvania, USA

Tabernash Munich Dark Lager, Tabernash Brewing Co., Denver, Colorado, USA

Thomas Kemper Hefeweizen, Thomas Kemper Lagers, Seattle, Washington, USA

Zoser Oatmeal Stout, Oasis Brewery, Boulder, Colorado, USA

OH, HONEY! LET IT BE MEAD

Yes, a friend of mead is a friend indeed.

There are many things worth remembering in life. "Firsts" are always something special. Savoring the memory is sweet. I brewed my first mead on November 25, 1974. Little did I imagine what I was unleashing that fateful evening.

I had been brewing a mere four years; many batches of beer passed between my friends and me. Honey always intrigued me—right from the start. In fact, the fifth batch of beer I brewed in Colorado (please allow me to discount the countless dump-and-stir homebrews I made in college) was my first batch of the legendary Rocky Raccoon's Crystal Honey Lager. (See *The Complete Joy of Homebrewing, Fourth Edition* for the recipe.) That was on November 26, 1973.

In those dark days of homebrew knowledge, the mere thought of using honey was like jumping off into an unknown chasm hoping for a pool of homebrew at the bottom. There was virtually no discussion with regard to using honey in beer. There were some rare English winemaking books that discussed honey and a beverage called mead, but they were written in quite a discouraging tone.

The honey lager was the first step in acquiring the confidence to concoct a honey beverage that I could call mead. And so on that memorable and exciting evening in 1974, a mead was formulated called Barkshack Gingermead, named after a river of adventure in Canada's British Columbia on Vancouver Island's wild northwest coast, a place I had a habit of visiting frequently in those days. The recipe was formulated as though it were ginger-flavored beer; except honey was used instead of malt extract. It worked. Boy, did it ever work. It was a success beyond comparison. To all of us who enjoyed its truly wondrous spirit, it was mead—sparkling, 6 to 8 percent alcohol, hopped, and ginger-flavored. It seemed that we had invented something very special. There were very few brewers who tasted this and did not go on to brew at least one special batch of sparkling Barkshack Gingermead.

It has taken many miles of traveling and much effort to uncover mead lore and factual information about the tradition of meadmaking. Over the years I have grown to respect mead as incomparable to any other beverage. It is our roots. It was the original ale, long before wine or grain beers. Its history is inspirational. To make mead is indeed a very special privilege we have as homebrewers. Mead's magical powers and closeness to all things natural are best appreciated through solemn and contemplative drinking experiences. Of course, another aspect of this special alcoholic beverage is the rousing camaraderie it inspires.

I rhapsodize. You've noticed. You will find yourself doing the same.

Since about 1974 I've been making and tasting mead. The challenge of making the simplest traditional meads of water, yeast, and honey—and nothing more—never diminishes. With the addition of fruits, spices, and sparkle, the variation and challenge become unending. Mead has its own personality. It doesn't lend itself very well to commercialization.

Reread *The Complete Joy of Homebrewing, Fourth Edition* for a thorough introduction to the many varieties and types of mead. For a more in-depth account of mead's twentieth-century roots, history, and additional recipes, see two stories in chapter 6, "Unraveling the Mysteries of Mead," in my book *Microbrewed Adventures*: (1) The Secrets of Buckfast Abbey & Brother Adam and (2) Minard Castle, Argyll, Scotland.

HONEY AND MEAD

The quality of honey is extremely important in its influence on fermentation and flavor. Equally, the influence of different yeast strains, temperatures, and creative extra ingredients is also key to mead's final character. There is very little that is consistent about mead from one batch to another, unless you are going to play doctor and aid the natural process with nutrients, acid blends, and clarifiers. These meadmaking aids are all quite permissible, though the challenge and the rewards of making a natural mead are diminished in spirit if nothing else.

Regardless, the vagaries of fermentation do always end with one consistent truth. In the end you will have a mead that befits both the most ordinary and most special occasions. It may take one month or it may take two to three years. Patience and a sense of adventure are virtues that are well rewarded.

Generally speaking, meads with original gravities of less than 1.080 (19.3

*Guidelines for Formulating Recipes for Different Types of Mead**

TYPE OF MEAD	POUNDS (KG) PER GALLON (4 LITERS)	ORIGINAL GRAVITY (° P)	FINAL GRAVITY
Sparkling	2# (0.9)	1.070–1.075 (17.1–18.2)	0.996
Dry (still)	2–2.5# (0.9–1.1)	up to 1.110 (30)	1.000–1.010 (0–2.5)
Medium (still)	2.5–3# (1.1–1.4)	1.110–1.120 (26–28)	1.010–1.015 (2.5–3.8)
Sweet (still)	3–4# (1.4–1.8)	1.120–1.135 (28–31.8)	1.020–1.050 (5–12.5)

*The addition of fruit may contribute to less predictable results.

Honey and Water: Predicting Original Gravity*

TO PREDICT THE SPECIFIC GRAVITY OF POUNDS OF HONEY PER GALLON (TOTAL VOLUME)	MIX THIS AMOUNT OF HONEY:	WITH THIS AMOUNT OF WATER:
1 lb. (0.45 kg)	¼ c. (59 ml)	21 fl. oz. (620 ml)
1½ lb. (0.68 kg)	¼ c. (59 ml)	13.2 fl. oz. (391 ml)
2 lb. (0.9 kg)	¼ c. (59 ml)	9.4 fl. oz. (279 ml)
2½ lb. (1.1 kg)	¼ c. (59 ml)	7.1 fl. oz. (211 ml)
3 lb. (1.4 kg)	¼ c. (59 ml)	5.6 fl. oz. (166 ml)
3½ lb. (1.6 kg)	¼ c. (59 ml)	4.5 fl. oz. (134 ml)

*. . . and measure the specific gravity.

Plato) are quite predictable. They will usually ferment to completion within one to two months, given the proper conditions and care. Meads 1.100 (23.7 Plato) and higher (usually up to 1.160 [about 37 Plato]) become increasingly less predictable, except that with time and patience, they will eventually finish and become clear.

The recipes included in this section offer a place to start on your meadmaking adventures. The behavior of your particular concoction is likely to vary quite significantly from these recipes and even from one identical batch to another. When in doubt, let the mead stand at 70 to 75 degrees F (21–24 C) until there are no signs of fermentation and then let it sit for a few more weeks, months—or even year or more, in the case of very high-gravity still meads. When the mead is clear and still, it is ready to bottle. If it is a traditional unflavored mead, it is also ready to drink. Fruit-flavored mead may require aging to bring the flavors into balance.

Mead is very susceptible to oxidation damage. Take extra care in minimizing the introduction of oxygen during all transfer processes and check your water-filled air lock regularly.

Sugar content of honey will vary quite a bit from one type or batch to another. Here is a simple method of predicting original gravity with a very high degree of accuracy.

One cup (240 ml) of honey weighs about 11.5 ounces (326 g). From this

TYPE OF MEAD (check one or more as appropriate):

☐ Still   ☐ Sweet   ☐ Traditional   ☐ Metheglin   ☐ Sparkling

☐ Medium   ☐ Melomel   ☐ Pyment   ☐ Dry   ☐ Cyser

BOTTLE INSPECTION Comments _____

_____

Max. Score

BOUQUET/AROMA (as appropriate for style)   10 _____

Expression of Honey, Expression of other ingredients as appropriate

Comments _____

_____

APPEARANCE (as appropriate for style)   5 _____

Clarity and Color as appropriate for style

Comments _____

_____

FLAVOR (as appropriate for style)   25 _____

Expression of Honey (5), Balance of: acidity/sweetness, alcohol strength/body, carbonation
(if appropriate), other ingredients as appropriate (15), Aftertaste(5)

Comments _____

_____

DRINKABILITY AND OVERALL IMPRESSION   10 _____

Comments _____

_____

TOTAL (50 possible points): _____

Scoring Guide		
Excellent (40-50):	Exceptionally exemplifies style, requires little or no attention
Very Good (30-39):	Exemplifies style well, requires some attention
Good (25-29):	Exemplifies style satisfactorily, but requires attention
Drinkable (20-24):	Does not exemplify style, requires attention
Problem (<20):	Problematic, requires much attention

information we know that 11.5 ounces (326 g) of honey plus 3 cups (711 ml) of water makes up one quart (950 ml). From this we can figure that 11.2 fluid ounces or 1 pound (0.45 kg) of honey plus about 117 fluid ounces (3.47 l) of water makes up one total gallon. What does all this background information mean? Well, it means that you can predict what specific gravity 1 pound (0.45 kg) of honey will contribute to a total volume of 1 gallon (3.8 l) of water and honey without actually having to mix the total volume. How? Mix and thoroughly dissolve ¼ cup (59 ml) of honey with 21 fluid ounces (620 ml) of water, and measure the gravity. Similarly, if you know what original gravity 1 pound per gallon will yield, then you know what 5 pounds per 5 gallons will yield. Refer to the chart "Honey and Water: Predicting Original Gravity."

MEADS

SPARKLING MEADS

There are several sparkling meads in the companion book *The Complete Joy of Homebrewing, Fourth Edition*, but here are two that will continue to effervesce your soul.

Waialeale Chablis Mead

Simply stated: this is a white mead champagne. The grace and delicacy of this brilliantly effervescent mead are reminiscent of the grace of the flower from which both the honey and grapes were conceived. For those who harbor an enthusiasm for fine champagnes and for the liveliness of new endeavors, making a batch of Waialeale Chablis Mead can't miss. It is incredibly simple to make, and is dry, effervescent, and refreshing. Serve chilled and when the mood suits you, because you're going to have 5 great gallons (19 l) of the stuff. Your friends will never forget you or your skills as a master meadmaker with this honey of a mead. Waialeale, Kauai, Hawaii, is the rainiest place on the planet, but with a stash of this mead, it doesn't matter.

Ingredients for 5 gallons (19 l):

5 lb. (2.3 kg)	light honey (clover, alfalfa, orange blossom, Hawaiian wildflower)
1 can	(26 fl. oz. /769 ml) Chablis grape concentrate (found at beer- and winemaking shops)
¾ c. (175 ml)	corn sugar (dextrose) or ⅞ c. (207 ml) honey for carbonation
*	champagne yeast

O.G.: 1.048–1.052 (12–13)
F.G.: 0.996–1.000 (–1–0)
Alcohol: 6.5–7% by volume

Combine honey with 1½ gallons (5.7 l) of water. Dissolve and bring to a boil and then immediately turn off heat. Skim off any coagulated white albumin protein if it forms on the surface of the boil. Add the grape concentrate. Do not boil the fruit juice. Then add this concentrated honey "wort" to a sanitized fermenter partly filled with cold water and top up with additional cold water to make 5 gallons (19 l). Aerate extremely well. Rehydrate yeast in 90-degree F (32 C) water for 15 minutes. Add rehydrated yeast when honey-juice must is cooled below 76 degrees F (24.4 C). Rack to a secondary fermenter when fermentation activity is very slow and continue fermentation or resting until mead is clear or almost clear. Bottle when fermentation is complete. Prime with corn sugar (dextrose) or honey. Waialeale Chablis Mead is ready when clear and carbonated, though it may improve with three to eight months of aging, depending on your personal preference.

A Taste of Happiness Sparkling Apple Cyser

Apple juice and honey are a natural. We probably would have realized this as children, but what we didn't know then was that there was such a thing as yeast or fermentation. The quality of your Taste of Happiness Cyser will vary tremendously with the type of apples used for the juice and, of course, the type of honey. Light honey and your favorite quality natural apple juice are recommended for starters. If buying packaged juice, be sure that there are no preservatives added. Preservatives may inhibit or prevent fermentation.

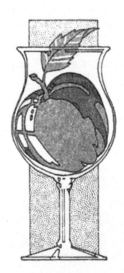

A Taste of Happiness is a dry, sparkling cider with apple tones and an alcoholic punch that should be respected and enjoyed responsibly.

If you use freshly pressed, unpasteurized apple juice, you will have to decide whether or not you want to inhibit the effect of wild yeast that naturally occurs in apple juice by using metabisulfites or by pasteurizing at 140 degrees F (60 C) for 20 to 30 minutes.

Ingredients for 5 gallons (19 l):

3 lb. (1.36 kg)	light honey (clover, alfalfa, orange blossom, or your favorite honey)
4¾ gal. (18 l)	apple juice
⅓ tsp. (2 ml)	sodium or potassium metabisulfite
¾ c. (175 ml)	corn sugar (dextrose) or ⅞ c. (207 ml) honey for carbonation
*	wine or champagne yeast

O.G.: 1.065–1.075 (16–18.2)
F.G.: 0.998–1.005 (0–1)
Alcohol: 8.8–9.2% by volume

Combine honey with apple juice. Stir and dissolve well. Add a dissolved-in-water solution of sodium or potassium metabisulfite and let the cyser-wort rest for 24 hours. The metabisulfite will react with the acidic nature of the "wort" and release sulfur dioxide gas, killing most wild yeast and other microorganisms. The gas must be allowed to vent out of the fermenter. After 24 hours aerate extremely well and add yeast culture and ferment. Rehydrate yeast in 90-degree F (32 C) water for 15 minutes. Add rehydrated yeast when honey-juice must is at or slightly below 76 degrees F (24.4 C). Rack to a secondary fermenter when fermentation activity is very slow and continue fermentation or resting until mead is clear or almost clear. Prime with corn sugar (dextrose) or honey and bottle when fermentation is complete.

A Taste of Happiness Cyser will improve with 3 to 8 months of aging.

STILL MEADS

Virgil, Plato, Plutarch, Zeus, Venus, Jupiter, Odysseus, Circe, the Argonaut, Beowulf, Aphrodite, Bacchus, Odin, Valhalla, the Sanskrit Rig-Veda, Thor, King Arthur, Queen Elizabeth, the French, Greeks, Mayans, Africans, English, Irish, Swedes, Poles, Hungarians, Germans, and even the Australian Aborigines all connected part of the enjoyment of life to mead. Man's and woman's first expression of interest in mead goes back 12,000 to 14,000 years. A cave drawing in Belgium illustrates an early man gathering honey. At the foot of a ladder leading to the tree hives, mead's aphrodisiac effects are depicted between a man and woman.

The legend of mead lives on, but often not in its traditional simple formulation of honey, water, and yeast. The variations have no boundaries. Here are a few recipes for uncarbonated still meads that offer some spectacular tasting excitement.

When bottling your still mead you may cork (or use modern substitutes for corks) in wine bottles for long-term aging. Store corked bottles on their side. If using bottlecap-able beer or champagne bottles, dip capped bottle top in melted paraffin to inhibit air ingress into bottle, minimizing oxidation.

White Angel Still Mead

This is a fully attenuated and dry mead. A batch of White Angel Mead is always handy to have around in a 5-gallon (19 l) carboy waiting to save that mysteriously stuck fermentation and very sweet mead. Usually completely fermented and clear within three to five months, White Angel can be brewed with fruits or any other flavors.

Ingredients for 5 gallons (19 l):

12½ lb. (5.7 kg)	light honey
3 lb. (1.4 kg)	ripe fruit or other flavors (optional)
¼ tsp. (1 g)	yeast extract as a nutrient
1 oz. (28 g)	dried sherry, wine, or champagne yeast; Prise de Mousse Champagne yeast works very well in combination with sherry yeast

Target O.G.: 1.100–1.110 (23.7–26)
F.G.: 0.998–1.010 (0–2.5)
Alcohol: 14–15% by volume

Combine the honey with 1 gallon (3.8 l) of water and boil for 5 minutes. Skim off the coagulated white albumin protein as it forms on the surface of the boil. Turn the heat off. Then add this concentrated honey "wort" to a sanitized fermenter and enough cold water to make 5 gallons (19 l). Aerate extremely well.

Rehydrate yeast in 90-degree F (32 C) water for 15 minutes. Add rehydrated yeast when honey-juice must is at or slightly below 76 degrees F (24.4 C). Ferment at temperatures between 70 and 77 degrees F (21—25 C). Rack to a secondary fermenter when fermentation activity is very slow or begins to clear and continue fermentation or resting until mead is clear.

If you are going to bottle this mead as is, then bottle when fermentation is complete.

If you are going to blend White Angel mead with another batch of mead, then consider these steps. Use carbon dioxide gas to purge the secondary carboy of oxygen before transferring the mead. This will minimize oxidation.

When the mead is clear and fermentation has stopped, it is ready to blend with other sweeter meads. After blending it is best to let the blended mead rest in the carboy for 3 to 4 months to ensure that fermentation doesn't begin anew. If you wish, White Angel can be stored for one to two years in a carboy and combined with sweeter meads whenever the need arises. Care should be taken to maintain the water in an air lock, or use waterless air locks that are uniquely designed and made with silicone.

Generally meads blended to a final gravity of 1.020 to 1.030 are preferred by most lovers of sweet mead, though a mead of 1.050 will mature with many years of aging. It will be your special reserve.

Love's Vision — Honey and Pepper Still Mead

Love's Vision Honey and Pepper Mead is about love. Sweet and fiery. A blend of intrigue juxtaposed with familiarity. Laughing and crying. The sweet caress of honey. The uniquely mysterious and fiery passion of exotic peppercorns. The anxious spiciness of new love. The warm intoxication of old love: trust, faith, devotion, caring, and unending endearment. Surreal, soulful, and sensual. Youthful and aged.

Love's Vision is about love.

Ingredients for 5 gallons (19 l):

15 lb. (6.8 kg)	light honey
2 Tbsp. (30 ml)	whole black peppercorns (try to find aromatic varieties when possible)
6 Tbsp. (90 ml)	whole (small black seeds and pods) Szechuan peppercorns (Note: These are not chili peppers.)
¼ tsp. (1 g)	yeast extract as a nutrient
1 oz. (28 g)	dried sherry, wine, or champagne yeast; Prise de Mousse champagne yeast works very well in combination with sherry yeast

Target O.G.: 1.120–1.130 (28–30)
F.G.: 1.020–1.035 (5–9)
Alcohol: 14–15% by volume

Combine the honey with about 1 gallon (3.8 l) of water and boil for 15 minutes. Skim off the coagulated white albumin protein as it forms on the surface of the boil. Turn the heat off. Then add this concentrated honey "wort" to a sanitized fermenter and enough cold water to make 5 gallons (19 l). Aerate the "wort" extremely well. Rehydrate yeast in 90-degree F (32 C) water for 15 minutes. Add yeast and yeast nutrient when cooled below 76 degrees F (24.4 C). Ferment at temperatures between 70 and 77 degrees F (21 and 25 C).

Rack the mead from a primary to a secondary fermenter when fermentation appears almost finished. Use carbon dioxide gas to purge the secondary carboy of oxygen before transferring the mead. This will minimize oxidation.

Grind the peppercorns to a coarse powder and add to the secondary and let age for at least three months. The pepper will eventually settle out. When the mead is clear and fermentation has stopped, it is ready to bottle. A new peppercorn can be added to each bottle at bottling time.

Love's vision? You tell me how real this mead is.

Aloi Black Raspberry Still Mead

A knockout of a mead, as fine as an exquisite red zinfandel or cabernet sauvignon— but made with rich and fruity black raspberries, honey, and water. Wine enthusiasts won't believe it when you tell them what it is. They will never be able to guess. Although this is well attenuated, the character of the black raspberries contributes a round, mellow, and delicate sweetness. Deep purple and full-flavored, Aloi Black Raspberry Mead is a superb tribute to the fascination that is mead.

Ingredients for 3 gallons (11.4 l):

10 lb. (4.5 kg)	light honey or dark honey (buckwheat, etc.)
7 lb. (3.2 kg)	ripe black raspberries
¼ tsp. (1 g)	yeast extract as a nutrient
1 oz. (28 g)	dried wine or champagne yeast; Prise de Mousse champagne yeast works very well

Target O.G.: 1.100–1.104 (23.7–24.6)
F.G.: 0.996–1.000 (0)
Alcohol: 14–15% by volume

Combine the honey with 1 gallon (3.8 l) of water and boil for 15 minutes. Skim off the coagulated white albumin protein as it forms on the surface of the boil. Turn the heat off, add crushed black raspberries, and let steep for 20 minutes at about 160 to 170 degrees F (71–76.7 C). Then add this concentrated fruit and honey "wort" to a sanitized fermenter partly filled with cold water and add more cold water to make 4 gallons (15.2 l). Aerate extremely well. Rehydrate yeast in 90-degree F (32 C) water for 15 minutes. Add yeast and yeast nutrient when cooled below 76 degrees F (24.4 C). If you allow a good 1 gallon of air space in the carboy, you may ferment the fruit in a glass primary fermenter, otherwise you'll need to do your primary fermentation in a plastic fermenter. Ferment at temperatures between 70 and 77 degrees F (21 and 25 C).

Rack the mead from a primary to a secondary fermenter after 14 days of fermentation, leaving the fruit behind in the primary. When fermentation appears almost finished, rack again and continue fermentation until clear. Use carbon dioxide gas to purge the secondary fermenters of oxygen before transferring the mead. This will minimize oxidation. By the time you've racked three times, you will have a yield of about 2½ to 3 gallons (9.5–11.4 l) of mead.

Time goes by as honey flows from a jar. Bottle when fermentation is complete and the mead is clear. This mead will mature with age.

Ruby Hooker Raspberry Still Mead
A sweet and full-flavored raspberry mead. If you love the flavor, color and aroma of red raspberries, then you'll love Ruby Hooker.

Ingredients for 5 gallons (19 l):

18½ lb. (8.4 kg)	light honey
10 lb. (4.5 kg)	ripe red raspberries

¼ tsp. (1 g)   yeast extract as a nutrient
1 oz. (28 g)   dried wine or champagne
                 yeast

Target O.G.: 1.140–1.146 (32–33.5)
F.G.: 1.020–1.030 (5–7.5)
Alcohol: 14–16% by volume

Combine the honey with 1 gallon (3.8 l) of water and boil for 15 minutes. Skim off the coagulated white albumin protein as it forms on the surface of the boil. Turn the heat off, add crushed red raspberries, and let steep for 20 minutes at about 160 to 170 degrees F (71–76.7 C). Then add this concentrated fruit and honey "wort" equally to two 5-gallon (19 l) sanitized fermenters partly filled with cold water and add more cold water to make a total of 6 gallons (22.8 l) or 3 gallons (11.4 l) in each of the two 5-gallon (19 l) glass fermenters. Allow for plenty of air space. Aerate the unfermented mead extremely well. Rehydrate yeast in 90-degree F (32 C) water for 15 minutes. Add yeast and yeast nutrient when cooled below 76 degrees F (24.4 C). Ferment the fruit in the glass primary fermenters. Ferment at temperatures between 70 and 77 degrees F (21 and 25 C).

Rack the mead from the two primary fermenters to one secondary fermenter after fourteen days of fermentation, leaving the fruit behind. When fermentation appears almost finished, rack again and continue fermentation until clear. Use carbon dioxide gas to purge the secondary fermenters of oxygen before transferring the mead. This will minimize oxidation. By the time you've racked three times, you will have a yield of about 5 gallons (19 l) of mead.

Bottle when fermentation is complete and the mead is clear. This mead will mature nicely with age.

Acermead

Although I've never tried this, the concept sounds so out of the ordinary, I'd like to inspire you. And besides, if this were ever made commercially, it would give tax collectors fits—after all, how do you tax alcohol made partially from tree sap?

Ingredients for 5 gallons (19 l):

18 lb. (8.2 kg)	light honey
4.6 gal. (17.5 l)	maple tree sap (note that no water is used in this recipe)
¼ tsp. (1 g)	yeast extract as a nutrient
1 oz. (28 g)	dried wine or champagne yeast

Target O.G.: 1.130–1.136 (32.5–34)
F.G.: 1.020–1.030 (5–7.5)
Alcohol: 14–15.5% by volume

Combine the honey with tree sap and boil for 15 minutes. Skim off the coagulated white albumin protein as it forms on the surface of the boil. Turn the heat off. Chill the hot sap-honey "wort" before adding to the fermenter. Aerate extremely well. Rehydrate yeast in 90-degree F (32 C) water for 15 minutes. Add yeast and yeast nutrient when cooled below 76 degrees F (24.4 C). Ferment at temperatures between 70 and 77 degrees F (21–25 C).

When fermentation appears almost finished, rack again and continue fermentation until clear. Use carbon dioxide gas to purge the secondary fermenters of oxygen before transferring the mead. This will minimize oxidation. Bottle when fermentation is complete and the mead is clear.

Lavender and Roses Still Mead
The aromas of lavender and roses mingle with the intoxicating character of honey to relax the mind and body. A stress-free indulgence in the spirit of wow. This mead will float you to another level of both experience and enjoyment.

Ingredients for 5 gallons (19 l):

20 lb. (9.1 kg)	light or amber honey
4–6	freshly cut or dried lavender stems with flowers
1–2 oz. (28–56 g)	dried organic rosebuds or rose petals. If fresh organic use 1–2 qt. (1–2 l)
¼ tsp. (1 g)	yeast extract as a nutrient
1 oz. (28 g)	dried sherry, wine, or champagne yeast; Prise de Mousse champagne yeast works very well in combination with sherry yeast

Target O.G.: 1.130–1.150 (30–34.3)
F.G.: 1.025–1.050 (6–12.5)
Alcohol: 14–15% by volume

Combine the honey with 1 gallon (3.8 l) of water and boil for 5 minutes. Skim off the coagulated white albumin protein as it forms on the surface of the boil. Turn the heat off. Then add this concentrated honey "wort" to a sanitized fermenter and enough cold water to make 5 gallons (19 l). Aerate extremely well. Rehydrate yeast in 90-degree F (32 C) water for 15 minutes. Add rehydrated yeast when honey-juice must is at or slightly below 76 degrees F (24.4 C). Rack to a secondary fermenter when fermentation activity is very slow or begins to clear, and continue fermentation or resting until mead is clear.

When mead is clear add the lavender and rosebuds and let mead rest in a cool place at 55–70 degrees F (13–21.5 C) for 1 to 2 months. Bottle when clear and fermentation is complete.

1944 Sack Metheglin

This recipe originally appeared in *Microbrewed Adventures* as "Castle Metheglin." It is so spectacular and loved by all who partake of its magic, it is worth reprinting here. Metheglin is a honey mead to which herbs and/or spices have been added. This recipe reflects research and discoveries made about ancient meads and what may have been a typical assortment of herbs that would have flavored the metheglins of more ancient times.

Ingredients for 5 gallons (19 l):

18½ lb. (8.2 kg)	light honey
2 oz. (56 g)	gruit (recipe follows)
¼ tsp. (1 g)	yeast extract as a nutrient
¼ tsp. (0.1 g)	zinc fortified yeast as nutrient
1 oz. (40 g)	dried champagne or mead yeast; Prise de Mousse or other champagne yeast is an excellent choice

Target O.G.: 1.130–1.138 (30.2–31.8)
Approximate F.G.: 1.028–1.038 (7–9.5)
Alcohol: 14–15% by volume

Combine honey and zinc fortified yeast with 1 gallon (3.8 l) of water and heat to 150 degrees F (65.5 C). Hold at this temperature for 20 minutes. Add this hot honey and water mixture to 2 gallons of cold water in your primary fermenter. Add more cold water as needed to achieve 5 gallons total volume. Aerate extremely well and add dissolved yeast nutrient (yeast extract).

Rehydrate yeast in 90-degree F (32 C) water for 15 minutes before pitching. When temperature is below 80 degrees F (26.5 C), add rehydrated yeast. Mead is best initially fermented between 70 and 75 degrees F (21–24 C). Ferment until fermentation activity is very low; this may take from 3 weeks to 3 months.

Rack and transfer to a secondary fermenter. Secondary can be stored at cooler temperatures. Add 2 ounces (56 g) gruit. Rack off sediment of herbs after 6 months to a year. Bottle when clear. Cork in wine bottles for long-term aging. Store corked bottles on their side. If using bottlecap-able beer or champagne bottles, dip capped bottle top in melted paraffin to inhibit air ingress into bottle.

This will be sweet still metheglin mead, whose flavors will blend and balance themselves over the years. Best after 50 years, but well worth indulging in after 1 year.

Gruit

Formulate the gruit with the following proportions of whole dried herbs (use fresh herbs when available). Note: 28 grams equals approximately 1 ounce.

Ingredients for 8½ ounces (240 g):

- 5 g   freshly grated nutmeg
- 5 g   freshly ground cloves
- 10 g ground ginger
- 10 g thyme
- 10 g peppermint leaves
- 10 g ground cinnamon
- 20 g lemon balm leaves
- 20 g rosemary
- 20 g bog myrtle (sweet gale)
- 30 g yarrow flower heads
- 50 g dried elderberry flower
- 50 g freshly crushed fennel seeds

Combine the herbs and spices and crush them all to the same consistency. Store in an airtight container in your freezer.

TASTING 60-YEAR-OLD MEADS—A JOURNEY FOR THE AGES

What do really old meads taste like?

I've been making mead since about 1975. Occasionally I discover a dusty thirty-year-old bottle of an original effervescent mead dating back to the 1970s. They are usually quite dry, retaining their effervescent champagne-like sparkle,

but a bit oxidized in a not-so-good way. I have always been intrigued with strong 14 percent to 17 percent abv still meads and how, with care, they hold up over the years.

I have always admired the passion of English mead maker and mead historian Lt. Col. Robert Gayre, who was perhaps the most knowledgeable mead historian and mead maker in modern times. In the mid- to late 1940s he commercially produced mead at the Mead House by Meadmakers Ltd., in Gulval, Cornwall, located in the southwest of England. Robert Gayre passed away shortly after my 1993 visit with him at his residence. He lived at Minard Castle on the shores of Loch Fyne, Scotland.

In early May 2008 a few close friends and I tasted seven different meads made in 1947, 1948, and 1949 by Mr. Gayre. There were four of us having the privilege of sampling and enjoying eight different bottles of sixty-year-old meads over a period of three evenings. We learned a lot about what time can do to a bottle of well-made mead. Here are my tasting notes and diary of our mead-tasting journey.

Mead, the first. May 4.   We choose a bottle of mead that has no clear indication of what it might be. It's in a Gulval Meadery bottle with a blue ribbon glued to the side. A small label singularly notes "Serve Chilled." This will be our predinner aperitif. There is no indication of when it was made, but we know that it is at least fifty-nine years old. We hold the dust-crusted bottle and with four hands very carefully lift out the crumbling cork.

We are delighted. It possesses exquisite sugarplum and sherry notes in aroma and flavor. The color is a medium amber-copper and brilliant. We speculate, perhaps a dark honey was used? Flavor impact is light despite its complexity. Its body, medium, and is perfect for chilling as the label suggests. It is very clean tasting with bright sherry-like flavor. As we slowly savor and sip, over a forty-five-minute period a coffee liqueur–like character develops. There is no sediment in the bottle, indicating that this is pure honey mead; there is no indication of fruit, herbs, or spices that would normally throw a tannic sediment.

Mead, the second. May 4.   Our second bottle transitions us to our awaiting dinner. The bottle we choose is a mystery, having no markings other than "1947" handwritten on a simple Gulval Meadery label. It is sixty-one years old. The cork is removed in its entirety without crumbling. There is no sediment. It is very clear, indicating it is a pure traditional honey mead with no fruits, spices, or herbs. It is golden and dry but not excessively so. It follows the first sweeter mead with difficulty, but on its own it evolves to become quite pleasant. At first there is a rather vegetal character, but this quickly diminishes with airing and transcends to the floral, blossom-like aroma of honey. It has a notable acidic balance. This mead inspires thoughts of food and we are beckoned to dinner.

Mead, the third. May 4.   We have chosen another adventurous-looking bottle. There is no label or markings except for a cryptic whitewashed "C" inscribed above the number "47." We assume this is a bottle of mead made in 1947 as an experimental prototype before commercial production commenced. It would be sixty-one years old. There is much sediment on the side of the rested bottle. We awaken it, carefully lifting for its uncorking and release. The cork has seeped some of its content and threatens us with crumbling. With awe, respect, and patience we masterfully remove all traces of the crumbling cork from the bottle and carefully decant it.

An aroma of apples and cider emerges with a hint of cinnamon. We now realize the whitewashed C stands for "Cyser." Cyser is a popular form of mead made from apple juice and honey.

As this mead stands and airs it improves dramatically. With time vanilla-like aromas and flavors emerge. Thirty minutes pass as we sparingly savor the nuances of this mead during dinner. Suddenly I am excited, realizing there is a faint but very distinctive aroma of *Brettanomyces* yeast. *Brettanomyces* is wild yeast that contributes a very unique character to fermented beverages. It is a signature character of Belgian-style wild yeast–fermented lambic beer and also common in Italian Chianti wine.

The *Brettanomyces* character in the sixty-one-year-old cyser mead is a wonderfully welcome revelation, which, having been brought to our attention, we all notice. It confirms our guess that this is indeed a cyser. *Brettanomyces* occurs naturally on the skin of apples. It is not an unusual character in fermented apple ciders. After sixty-one years the *Brettanomyces* emerges faintly, evident with a trained palate and after initial airing of this magnificent mead cyser. It went well with our dinner.

Mead, the fourth. May 5. We choose a fully labeled bottle of 1948 Gulval Sack Mead. The term "sack" indicates a strong, well-attenuated, dry style of mead. The cork slips out whole. There is no sediment. The label proclaims "No less than 14.5%." Our faces light up as we initiate our savoring of this evening's first mead. We take our first sip of the evening and one of us exclaims all of our feelings nicely: "This makes the whole trip worth coming for." This sixty-year-old sack mead has a clean, delicate honey character. The sherry character is deep and well integrated into the aroma, flavor, and body. Its color is a bright light amber, tending toward a polished copper color, opalescent in nature. There are no negative characters whatsoever; no vegetal, no negative oxidation character. It is super-clean in flavor and aroma.

With every sip this mead finishes with a low profile of vanilla. It's light, silky, and has a medium-bodied and velvety texture. Toffee and caramel emerge as the minutes pass, yet as suggested earlier the aftertaste is very clean.

Mead, the fifth. May 5. We choose a commercially labeled 1948 Gulval Sack Metheglin. Metheglin is an herbal infused mead. An ornamental green ribbon is taped to the side of the bottle. It is sealed with wax, which when removed reveals a crusty cork we take great care in removing. We notice and do not disturb the slight sediment.

It is drier than we had anticipated and lacks the body I would have preferred and has obviously attenuated over the years. Mint, rosemary, lavender, sage, thyme, wintergreen/sassafras-like aromatic and flavor characters are noted. These are herbs that Mr. Gayre had grown and written about during his Cornwall Meadery project. The overall blend of herbs is quite similar to the Gulval and Gayre written formulations of gruit I had discovered prior to this mead tasting.

Mead, the sixth. May 6. We begin today's mead journey as a predinner aperitif. We choose an experimental bottle of [fruit mead] Melomel. In a large, heavy, dark-green pre–World War II bottle, a typed label indicates the mead was made in 1946 and bottled in 1947. The type of fruit is not known. There is substantial sediment on the side of the bottle, an indication of fruit tannin.

The cork is sealed with a hard crusty wax that we break through. Carefully and slowly we remove the soft cork. My eyes tear up a bit at the thought of leaving a few ounces of sediment and precious nectar behind as we decant from the bottle to a carafe.

All eyes are on our glasses as we ration the pours.

The mead's color is a tawny brown with hints of red. Fruity aromas explode from our glasses. A bit of pleasant, oxidized, smoky character emerges on the

front end of our tasting. It is dry, firm, with pleasant tannin mouthfeel. The acidity is perfect and in balance for this mysteriously fruited mead. We discuss the possibilities.

One of us first suggests that we are tasting cherries. Another of us reveals a bit of English postwar history. In Sussex where this mead was probably made, there were only plums, pears, and cherries in abundance immediately after World War II. Other fruits were planted later. We guess and are quite certain that this melomel is a cherry melomel. It has held up extraordinarily. The positive oxidation has created a marvelous, complex, and well-integrated sherry character after sixty-one years.

Mead, the seventh. May 6.   We open a bottle of 1949 Gulval Bochet. It is fully labeled with a yellow ribbon affixed to the side of a musty bottle. Curiously we note there is absolutely no sediment thrown by this fifty-nine-year-old mead. We don't yet know to what the term *Bochet* refers. We conclude that due to the lack of any sediment this mead has no added fruit, herbs, or spices. It should be 100 percent honey mead.

We chip away at the hard wax seal, carefully extracting the well-preserved wet cork in its entirety. We are amazed that the cork has held up so well. We pour our glasses and continue in amazement. It is a deep copper color. How can pure honey mead have such a deep color? Bochet? The explanation was later to be revealed in the name. But at the time we remained perplexed at the dark and tawny color.

The aroma is magnificent and upon our first sip we immediately realize the magnitude of our discovery. "This exceeds all the other meads in quality. Wow." We all chuckle with boyish and girlish glee.

It has a sweet, perfumed vanilla-like aroma. One of us who has an extensive food chemistry background explains that the vanilla-like character is probably coumarin, a floral vanilla-like flavor compound that can develop during fermentation and age. He's quite certain of the character. We continue to taste, still not knowing to what *Bochet* refers.

I detect an undercurrent of yarrow (flower) and a well-integrated toffee and textured sherry-like character. I refine my visual observation—the Bochet has a dark red ruby-like color and is absolutely brilliant. There is a bit of ketone (acetone-like alcohol) that is evident, but its presence is very light, volatizing, and rapidly dissipating. The alcohol strength is not exceedingly high for mead. I am guessing it in the neighborhood of 12 percent, its body, medium dry with supple sweetness. This mead transcends to ultimate pleasure.

We later discover that *Bochet* refers to "burnt mead." There is little other information. I only assume that at the time of formulation the honey had have been scorched by heat, resulting in the caramelization of sugar. This would explain the complex toffee-like character, the deep color, and lack of tannic sediment.

Our three-day journey back in time was grueling, someone had to do it. The investigative tasting of the mysterious and the unknown revealed a promise for my aging meads at home, which will continue to "cellar" for years to come.

ROOT BEER

Roots, herbs, and spices have always been ingredients in beer. Hops are a herbaceous ingredient that is certainly regarded as essential in most beers brewed in the Western world, though they became a popular ingredient in beer only a century or two ago. Before that, all manner of herbaceous concoctions (sometimes called gruit) were added to beer to balance character. Roots, herbs, and spices—fresh or dried—have been used to make all kinds of alcoholic and non-alcoholic beverages in virtually all cultures throughout the world.

American root beer, a nonalcoholic soft drink, surely had its origins in ancient beer recipes and emerged as a nonalcoholic beer centuries ago, when beer actually did taste like a fermented blend of herbs, spices, and roots. Today root beer is an American commodity available as an alcohol-free soft drink. When mass-produced, it is artificially carbonated, with small amounts of preservative added to assure that a dangerously explosive fermentation does not occur in the package.

Most mass-produced root beer is conveniently made from extracts, artificial flavoring, water, and sugar. Some small breweries have ventured into formulating natural recipes, producing some very delicious alcohol-free root beer. Homebrewers, as well, can make this delicious soft drink in an all-natural way or with more convenient extracts if they wish.

MacJack Root Beer

An exceptionally authentic-tasting all-natural root beer, with options to vary ingredients to individual taste preferences. MacJack Root Beer is not fermented, nor are there any preservatives added to inhibit fermentation. Extreme care must be taken to avoid fermentation. Fermentation may cause dangerous explosions that can result in serious bodily harm. To help minimize this risk, artificial carbonation with a CO_2 system and keg and subsequent very cold refrigeration is recommended.

Some root beer recipes recommend adding bread or ale yeast to the sweet root beer wort in order to carbonate it. This is an extremely dangerous mix and is as good as making a bomb. The sweet wort will surely ferment in a bottle, causing foamy carbonation and exploding bottles. I know—I've been there! Sure, you could test the yeasted root beer after a few days and then refrigerate to inhibit yeast activity, but risking an eye and other vital parts of your body to such practices is simply insane and not worth it.

Ingredients for 5 gallons (19 l):

3 qt. (2.9 l)	brown molasses
2 oz. (57 g)	sassafras bark (see Note)
2 oz. (57 g)	sarsaparilla (woody), shredded
2 oz. (57 g)	wintergreen (herb)
½ oz. (14 g)	licorice bark or root (woody), shredded
1	vanilla bean, chopped
0–1 lb. (0–0.45 kg)	honey, corn or cane sugar to taste
	Other optional flavorings that could be used: teaberry, deerberry, checkerberry, boxberry, spiceberry, clove, cinnamon, star anise, ginger, ginseng, juniper berries, malt extract

O.G.: 1.035–1.045 (9–11)

Note: The U.S. government regards sassafras as having a degree of risk for being carcinogenic. Be advised and do not use if you are concerned.

Add the herbs, roots, spices, and molasses to 2 gallons of boiling water and immediately turn off heat. Let steep with lid on for 2 to 4 hours. Then strain the flavoring ingredients out of the root beer wort and add cold water to make 5 gallons (19 l). Taste and add sugar to your preference. Transfer to a keg and chill to 33 to 40 degrees F (0.5–4.5 C). Force-carbonate with CO_2 until you achieve desired carbonation.

Always maintain the keg at cold temperatures. If storing for long periods of time, check pressure weekly. If there is pressure buildup, then release pressure and consume as soon as possible.

Naturally made MacJack Root Beer is a real treat for both kids and mature adults (and immature as well, I suppose).

It is always possible to ferment root beer as you would any other beer. If you wish to experiment, add and steep 2 to 3 pounds (0.9–1.4 kg) of caramel/crystal malt in the wort in order to maintain some residual sweetness in the fully fermented beverage. Bottle with priming sugar when fermentation is complete.

NONALCOHOLIC BEERS: HOW ARE THEY MADE?

If nonalcoholic beers could actually taste like their real counterparts, they might be an achievement worthy of a Nobel Prize. Unfortunately alcohol and the process of generating alcohol both contribute very significantly to the overall character of what most of us consider real beer. Consequently the character of commercially made nonalcoholic products requires a lot of imagination if you want to call it beer. Perhaps the success of nonalcoholic beers hinges on the success of marketing beer that is so light in character that it tastes nearly like water. I suppose nonalcoholic beer can approach that.

In the United States nonalcoholic "beer" cannot legally be called nonalcoholic "beer." It is considered a "malt beverage" and cannot exceed 0.5 percent alcohol by volume. If you are looking for an alcohol-free malt beverage, seek a beverage whose label states "alcohol-free." Alcohol-free malt beverages are usually concoctions that are formulated from ingredients similar in taste to beer (at least that's the claim), carbonated, and packaged. Unlike nonalcoholic malt beverages, alcohol-free brews do not go through any fermentation process whatsoever.

Nonalcoholic brews are most commonly produced using one of a few methods:

1. Distillation
2. Reverse osmosis
3. Yeast "management"
4. Special yeasts

The goal is to have less than 0.5 percent alcohol in the final product.

Distillation is a relatively simple process whereby beer is brewed and fermented, then subjected to a distillation process. Often a vacuum is pulled on the fermented beer, lowering the boiling point of water and alcohol. The beer is heated and the alcohol is evaporated and distilled off of the beer. There are two main drawbacks of this method. Heating alters the flavor of beer, and esters and other flavor compounds contributing to the character of beer are also evaporated off.

Freeze distillation might be worth consideration on a small-scale homebrewed level. Alcohol freezes at lower temperatures than water. If fully fermented beer were to be taken down to a few degrees below freezing, a beer slush would be created. The liquid would be mostly alcohol, and the slush mostly nonalcoholic beer. You might have to go through a few stages of freezing and pouring, as alcohol will be mixed in with the beer slush. Once the process has been finished, the reduced-alcohol beer can be force-carbonated or bottle-conditioned by priming with sugar and fresh yeast. There is a major problem with this method. It is illegal in the United States to distill without proper licensing and federal and state paperwork, even if you intend to throw the alcohol away. Enough said about the freeze-distillation process.

Reverse osmosis is a method in which beer is passed by a filter membrane. Alcohol migrates through this membrane while the nonalcoholic solution flows on. The process is slow and expensive. Again, alcohol is an important part of the flavor of beer, and it is removed during the process.

Yeast "management" offers some unique methods of producing a brew that never kicks into the fermentation stage. Recall that when yeast is introduced into unfermented wort, it goes through a lag phase and respiration phase before it begins alcohol-producing fermentation. During the two initial cycles the yeast cells take up oxygen and reproduce. If conditions are controlled to force the yeast to extend its oxygen uptake and reproduction cycle (and what organism doesn't want to extend its reproduction cycle if given the opportunity?), then the carbohydrates are assimilated, and water, carbon dioxide, and other flavor compounds are produced, with very little alcohol being made. Extra oxygen can be bubbled through the wort. Temperatures can be lowered. The yeast can be overpitched. Conditions can be controlled to extend these cycles, but the cycle can't last forever and must be arrested by removing the yeast before it begins fermentation. Some of the major problems with this method can be detected in the lack of flavors that alcohols and esters contribute, but more seriously this process can contribute high levels of undesirable characters such as diacetyl.

Researchers continue to genetically engineer *special yeasts* that do not have the capability to ever kick into a fermentation cycle. So far the results have been less than desirable, but continue to improve. Problems of high diacetyl and the production of other flavor compounds make these engineered yeasts not yet usable for production of a nonalcoholic malt beverage.

What can a homebrewer do if nonalcoholic beer is desired? For the time being, that's a tough question, a very tough question. Unfortunately most commercial choices are all brewed with the American superlight lager style in mind. Perhaps if fuller-flavored styles were to be considered, success at making a "near" beer could be approachable.

Most homebrewers do not have the sophisticated equipment to distill, manage yeast, or perform reverse osmosis. But if you do, there is opportunity for experimentation. Producing a nonalcoholic beer (as homebrewers, we don't have to abide by the official government nomenclature) would be a new frontier: nonalcoholic full-flavored stout, bock, brown ale, Pilsener? You might be onto something a bit more palatable than what's available on the shelves.

CLASSIC BEER STYLES FROM AROUND THE WORLD

The beer styles that most beer drinkers regard as "classic" do not represent the complete compendium of world beer traditions. The commercially marketable beer styles of Germany, England, Belgium, Ireland, Scotland, the United States, the Czech Republic, and France may seem to take the forefront in today's world of beer. But in fairness to the rest of the world, we should appreciate that there are hundreds of millions of people who are enjoying beer styles that most Americans have absolutely no awareness of.

Traditional fermented beverages brewed from all manner of cereal grain, roots, herbs, milk, fruits, and vegetables have been made for thousands of years throughout the world. Perhaps modern production, packaging and distribution technologies, and modern marketing have not inspired their distribution. In some cases we can be reasonably assured that developing a taste for these beverages would be a significant and necessary first step. For one of my particularly adventurous beer experiences, read my firsthand account of visiting the beer gardens of Bulawayo, "The Zimbabwe Zephyr and the Beer Gardens of Bulawayo," in my book *Microbrewed Adventures*.

Over a cool glass of Pilsener, stout, bock, or pale ale we might view what's going on in the world of fermented beverages as incredible and sometimes unbelievable. Nevertheless, one should have a degree of respect for these beverages, for some of them have been enjoyed by far more people and for a much longer time than our so-called classic beers. Our beer world and perspective is but one, just as American-style light lager beer was at one time America's only perspective.

If the beer revolution in America is going to continue, homebrewers will be on the frontier. For the last 5,000 years they always have been.

INDIGENOUS BEERS AND FERMENTED BEVERAGES OF THE AMERICAS

Aca—Maize or corn beer from Peru.

Algarroba—Brewed by Central and South American Indians from ripe fruit of carob, mesquite, or other leguminous trees.

Balché (mead)—A Mayan Indian honey mead flavored with bark from the balché tree.

Camass Beer—Western North American Indians made a fermented and alcoholic brew from the bulbous root of the common camass (*Camassia quamash*), not to be confused or mistaken for the death camas, which has whitish to cream-colored flowers. (The common camass has blue flowers.) The onionlike bulbs could be boiled or roasted to develop sugars. Lewis and Clark mention this brew in their journals.

Chicha—Corn beers of the South American high country. Corn is boiled, then "mashed" by women who chew corn and spit the juice into a fermentation

pot. Enzymes in saliva are similar to the enzymes in a mash, breaking down starch to sugar.

Kentucky Sour Mash Beer—Malted wheat and/or barley beer brewed from a mash that has been soured by primarily *Lactobacillus* bacteria.

Mabi (Mavi or Mauby)—A mild alcoholic beer made in part from the root and bark of the mavi/mabi/mauby tree in Puerto Rico and other Caribbean islands.

Manioc Beer—Common throughout the world. Brewed from the starchy root of the manioc plant (also known as cassava, manioca, tapioca, *macaxeira, massato*). Manioc is often "mashed" by chewing and spitting the juice into a fermentation pot. Enzymes in saliva are similar to the enzymes in a mash and break down starch to sugar. Arawaks, the native Caribbeans, had a version of manioc beer to which they added chile pepper and fish bones.

Mescal Beer—Brewed from the juice of the mescal plant in Mexico.

Piva—Aleutian Island brew of potatoes, raisins, and sugar.

Pulque—A beer-like beverage made from the sap of several species of agave plant growing in Mexico. Sometimes called *maguey* or *pita*. Up to one ton of juice may be tapped from one plant, yielding 6 to 8 quarts (6–8 l) per day. Pulque can be naturally fermented to about 6 percent alcohol.

Tahamara Corn Beer—Corn beer brewed by Tahamara Indians of Central America.

Tesgüino—Indigenous Mexican beer made from malted corn.

Tiswin (Apache Indian "beer")—Made from malted corn, wheat, and jimsonweed (*Datura stramonium*). Jimsonweed has a drug-like effect that can be violent and can be toxic to some individuals. Experimentation is not recommended.

INDIGENOUS BEERS AND FERMENTED BEVERAGES OF ASIA

Chong/Chang/Janr—Millet, rice, maize, or barley beer of the Himalayas and surrounding area. It has the consistency of gruel. The liquid is drunk through straws.

Chiu—Wheat beer of ancient China.

Chung—Tibetan barley beer.

Kaoliang—Sorghum beer made in the ancient Szechuan province of China.

Li—Ancient Chinese rice beer.

Lida—Ossets/Iranian beer 600 BC.

Makkolli (Makgeolli)/Takju/Yakju—Homebrewed rice beer of Korea. Ale-like and unlike sake.

Ou—Beer made from glutinous/sticky rice in Nakhon Phanom, Thailand, traditionally enjoyed with straws.

Pachwaï—Type of northern Indian *Cannabis sativa* sake.

P'ei—Ancient grain-based beer of China.

Sake—Japanese rice brew. A complex process using enzymes, bacteria, and yeast.

Shoto Slake—Japanese fermented sugarcane juice.

Tongbu—Millet beer of Nepal.

Tuak/Arak—Indonesian brew made from fermented sap of a particular palm tree.

INDIGENOUS BEERS AND FERMENTED BEVERAGES OF AFRICA

Bantu/Keffir/Kaffir—Fermented mare's milk. Mare's milk will not curdle like cow's milk as the acidity of bacterial and yeast fermentation increase. Similar to Russian *Koumiss/Kumis*.

Boza/Bosa/Bouza/Booza—Made from malted millet bread, wheat, or corn. Beer of ancient Babylonia, Egypt, Turkey, and Ethiopia.

Bilbil—Once brewed in northern Egypt from malted durra, a type of sorghum/millet.

Dolo—Millet/sorghum beer of parts of Africa flavored with bitter plants, sometimes including the toxic jimsonweed (see American *Tiswin*).

Khadi—Berry honey mead of Botswana.

Korma—Egyptian barley wine beer flavored with ginger.

Mealie—South African beer made from maize and/or sorghum and flavored with plants.

Merissa—Sudanese toasted sorghum beer.

Omalofo—Kaffir, corn/millet beer of southwest Africa.

Pito—Nigerian malted sorghum beer.

Pombe ya Ndizi—Beer brewed by the Wachagga tribe on Mount Kilimanjaro, made from mashed bananas and malted millet (indigenous grain called *mbegi*).

Shimeyane—South African brown sugar, bread, and malted corn beer.

Sorghum Beer—Brewed from a grain of which millet is a variety. *Lactobacillus* bacteria souring and yeast fermentation produce a cloudy, acidic brew very popular, especially in southern Africa.

Soubya—Egyptian rice beer.

Talla—Ethiopian beer brewed from sorghum/millet, roasted barley, and sometimes corn/maize. Often flavored with herbs.

Tej—Ethiopian honey mead, often flavored with herbs.

INDIGENOUS BEERS AND FERMENTED BEVERAGES OF OCEANIA

Cassava/Manioc Beer—Brewed from the starchy root of cassava/manioc/tapioca. Cane sugar is commonly used in great quantities.

Okole—Brewed by the ancient Hawaiians from the roasted root of the ti plant. The root when roasted caramelizes to a molasses-like substance.

Topuy—Filipino rice beer.

INDIGENOUS BEERS AND FERMENTED BEVERAGES OF EUROPE

Brumalis Canna—Medieval French brew made from fruit and ginger.

Grodziskie—Also known as Grätzer, a Polish ale style brewed with smoked wheat malts.

Gotlandsdricka—Traditional beer of Swedish island Gotland, made with malted barley smoked with birchwood, juniper boughs, berries, and branches and local bread yeast.

Imiak—Malt beer homebrewed in Greenland.

Kiesel—Russian rye and oat beer.

Korma—Celtic millet beer

Kvass—A low-alcohol Russian beer brewed from dark rye bread, sometimes malted barley and/or rye, and sugar. Yeast and bacterial fermentation is encouraged. *Lablochny,* kvass with apples. *Malinovi,* kvass with raspberries.

Leipziger Gose—Spontaneously fermented German ale from Leipzig, similar to Belgian-style gueuze lambic beer. Traditionally brewed with unmalted wheat (sometimes with rye and/or oats), coriander seed, and low levels of table salt (sodium chloride). Usually served as a fresh, cloudy young beer.

Mum(m)—Sometimes called Braunschweiger Mumme or Broyhan, brewed in old Germany and currently a specialty product. Ingredients include wheat and barley malt, field beans, inner bark of blue spruce trees, buds of blue spruce trees, buds from birch trees, dried karbo-Benedictine weed, sunflower seeds, Bibernell, betonica, marjoram, Benedictine spice, bee pollen, juniper berries, thyme, cardamom, bay leaves, black burgundy, parsley, horseradish, and ten unbroken, uncracked freshly laid eggs.

Roggenbier—German beer made with malted rye.

Sahti—From Finland, a brew made from barley, rye, juniper berries, and other flavorings.

Shekar—A Hebrew beer brewed from corn, dates, honey and other flavorings.

Sicera—A strongly hopped beer brewed by the Jews when captive in Babylon.

Sikaru—Brewed 6,000 to 10,000 years ago by Sumerians of Mesopotamia. Made from ancient wheat called spelt (still available today as dinkel or spelt) or barley. Grain was malted and mashed; the wort was flavored with spices and fruits. Grains were roasted for variety and flavor.

INDIGENOUS BEERS AND FERMENTED BEVERAGES OF THE AFTERWORLD

Stelae—Although Germans sing a song with the words "In heaven there is no beer. That's why we drink it here," sources and emissaries tell us that there is beer in the afterlife called Stelae. If this is indeed true, I'll meet you at the tap—later.

Beer Evaluation: What Am I Tasting and Why Is It in Beer?

Did you like it? You've planned for, brewed, fermented, packaged, waited for your beer to be ready. A chilled bottle is uncapped and poured into your favorite glass. Of course, your favorite glass is always the one that has your beer in it—always. Isn't it? It's a matter of personal preference whether you've poured the beer down the side of the glass or straight down the middle, but practically speaking, you've probably started out by pouring it down the side and watching how lively the beer becomes as the barley and hop nectar begins to express itself. If the beer needs more head, you'll likely begin to pour it down the middle, creating the amount of foamy topping that suits your preference. So far you've given it your best shot.

You look at it, there in the glass. You smell it and then taste it. Is it any good? Well, the answer to that is quite simple. If *you* like it, then it *is* good, and nobody should ever convince you otherwise. The simple pleasures of enjoying great beer must never be forgotten.

Simple pleasure is quite enough reason to make and appreciate your own beer. However, an understanding of the basic principles of beer evaluation can offer any brewer an enhanced appreciation for beer character and can help improve or maintain quality.

BEER CHARACTER: THE DYNAMICS OF CHANGE

BEER IS A FOOD

From the moment we first brew our beer to when it is consumed, beer undergoes continual change. Flavors, aromas, sights, and sensations are layered on one another. What one perceives is the net effect. There are hundreds of different compounds that contribute to the character of beer. Some are not perceived at all, while others may be highlighted, but what is primarily perceived are characters enhanced or suppressed by the interaction of the combination of everything beer is.

As beer ages, its character will change. Certain characters will be perceived to a greater or lesser degree, or perhaps not at all. Because of the layering of so many stimulating compounds in beer, it is quite possible that the perceived development of a specific character might be something new created in the beer during the aging process or something that has been there all along, but has been suppressed by the dominance of other characters. For example, the bitterness of a beer might be perceived to increase over a period of time, not because bitter compounds are increased, but rather because malty sweetness and body are being reduced, giving a perception of increased bitterness.

Other characters that are perceived may not each exist as a single character, but may be a synergistic combination of two or more factors that creates a unique perception all its own. This synergy may also have the effect of increasing the intensity of each factor involved.

Beer changes. What we perceive in those changes is not always a clear indication of what's really happening, though often it is.

WHAT IS "FRESH" BEER?: BUNS AND ALLIGATORS

Ponce de León searched for the fountain of youth but only found himself up to his buns in alligators. Moral of the story: There is no simple answer to the question of age.

Commercially made beer is said to be *brewery fresh* just after it has been packaged and leaves the brewery. For most beer styles that's the time when beer generally will be perceived as being at its best by most beer drinkers. Some special styles of commercially made beer will be perceived as being enhanced in character with some age, but these styles are generally very strong beers with live yeast still in the bottle.

Homebrewed bottle-conditioned beer is quite another matter, but first let's examine what is happening with commercially made beer. The most significant flavor changes that will come about in sterile-filtered or pasteurized commercial beer are usually the result of time and oxidizing reactions. This is assuming that the beer is not contaminated with significant amounts of beer spoilage micro-organisms. There are countless other reactions that can also affect flavor, but the big negatives are caused by oxidation—the reaction of oxygen with flavor compounds. This reaction is accelerated by heat, light, and agitation. The character of old commercial beer is often described as tasting like wet cardboard, wet paper, vegetal, or spoiled pineapple, or as winy, sherry-like, skunky, and other not-so-wonderful adjectives.

Even if oxidation is minimal, there can be other flavor changes that are not considered true to the intent of the brewer and thus "not fresh-tasting." One significant area of change is the diminishing of hop aroma, flavor, and bitterness with time. This may be an enhancement or a disappointment, depending on the style and your own perspective.

Now then, bottle-conditioned beer is still alive in the true sense of the word. If you've brewed cleanly, then what you have is a well-brewed beer with yeast still living in the bottle. That yeast can produce both desirable and undesirable characters. Obviously desirable is the carbon dioxide that provides effervescence. The presence of yeast can reduce some of the dissolved oxygen in the beer, helping minimize future oxidizing reactions. Yeast can also reduce the diacetyl (buttery or butterscotch) character of a beer with age (though it cannot adequately reduce bacterially produced diacetyl). When yeast undergoes refermentation in the bottle, it will produce a small amount of undesirable by-products. Normally many of these by-products are released to the air in primary, secondary, and lagering fermentation, but when sealed in a bottle, these undesirables are captured and must be aged out with some time. Bottle-conditioned beer may improve with some aging. As it reaches its peak flavor, one might consider homebrew to be "fresh" and as you intended it to be.

Now then, about that harshly bitter brew that seemed to get better with age. If you hadn't put so many hops in to begin with, you wouldn't have had to age it so long to mellow it out. Yes, the perception of bitterness is often diminished with age in a very hoppy beer. The beer's bitterness may be perceived as becoming more balanced, but in the meantime, other age reactions occur, detracting from the balance. The skill to acquire is getting your bitterness proportioned correctly to begin with, so you can drink the beer sooner.

How long will homebrew maintain its fresh and intended character? It has so very much to do with how contaminant-free the beer is, at what temperature it is stored, and the type of beer it is. For beers in a range of 3 to 5½ percent alcohol, one can reasonably expect a fresh flavor to remain stable for one to three months if the beer is kept at temperatures below 60 degrees F (15.5 C). After three months, the beers will change, but if there is no bacterial or wild yeast activity, homebrew will keep for a year or two (sometimes more). However, oxidation and air ingress will eventually take their toll and the beer's character may become no better than that of an old and tired commercially brewed beer.

All of the above being said, most food and beverage labels warn with "Best Before" dates, implying that the product is not at its finest upon "expiry." Craft and homebrewers are changing the paradigm. Some beer types are best laid away to rest before enjoying. The best way to prevent excessive oxidation and to develop improved flavors in those stronger brews is to finish sealing the bottle with wax.

WHY IS A WAX SEAL IMPORTANT?

Whether a beer is corked or sealed with a bottlecap, there is oxygen "ingress" into the bottle. The seal is never perfect. Air ingress happens slowly by way of the interface between the seal material and glass. Oxygen causes an oxidizing aging process in the bottle. For stronger aged beers, this can be positive up to a point. Once that point is reached (and it varies with each beer), the beer may take on oxidized flavors that are not so pleasant. Characters in aroma and flavor discussed previously will send an otherwise classic, expensive, and highly rated beer on a downhill journey once it's "over the hill." There is always some oxygen content in bottles of the best of beers when it is packaged. Wax sealing will not prevent negative aging character a hundred percent, but it will slow it down.

I speak from experience. I dip the closures of the wines and strong beers and meads I've made in melted paraffin. Better yet, you could use sealing wax, available at most homebrew and winemaking stores. It's a simple process and will dramatically extend the age of your cherished "great" beers, provided that oxygen introduction into the bottle was minimized during the original packaging. Some of my twenty-year-old treasures have little or no oxidation character.

Sadly, I have other very old beers I had hoped would survive the years that are not drinkable. Oxidation eventually destroyed them. They were not waxed.

It's a great time to be a beer drinker. If you love to collect and sample beers later in their (and your) life, do yourself a favor—wax those closures. You'll be thankful you did.

One final thought on this subject before I open one of my seven-year-old barleywine ales: If your beer tastes good, it can never be beyond its time.

A GLOSSARY OF BEER CHARACTER DESCRIPTORS

Before we can begin to discuss beer character in any detail, a language must be learned. Over many years many of the following descriptor definitions and possible sources have been developed and utilized by both professional brewers

Desirable or undesirable? Can you recognize seventeen different flavors or aromas often present in beer?

and homebrewers; they are particularly useful in evaluating beer for competitions and educational and improvement purposes. The following terms represent the most common characters of all beers.

Acetaldehyde—Green-apple-like aroma; by-product of fermentation. Can be perceived as bread-like or solvent-like at high concentrations. Can be caused by low yeast levels and influenced by yeast strain.

Alcoholic—The general effect of ethanol and other types of alcohols. Feels warming. Tastes sweetish.

Astringent—Drying, puckering (like chewing on a grape skin); feeling often associated with sourness but is not sour. Tannin. Most often derived from boiling of grains, long mashes, oversparging or sparging with excessively hot or alkaline water. Metal ions in water or excessive trub in fermentation can contribute.

Bitter—Basic taste associated with hops; *braunhefe* or malt husks. Sensation is experienced on back of tongue.

Body—The mouthfeel sensation of beer. Full or heavy body is more cream-like in consistency, while light-bodied or dry beer is thinner.

Cheesy—Old, stale, rancid hops and sometimes (in unusual circumstances) old malt can cause this character.

Chill Haze—Haze caused by precipitation of protein-tannin compounds at cold temperatures. Does not affect flavor. Reduction of proteins or tannins in brewing or fermenting will reduce haze.

Chlorophenolic—Caused by chemical combination of chlorine and organics. Detectable at one to three parts per billion. Aroma is unique but similar to plastic-like phenolic. Avoid using chlorinated water.

Clean—Lacking off-flavors.

Cooked Vegetable/Cabbage-like—Aroma and flavor often due to long lag times and wort-spoilage bacteria that later are killed by alcohol produced in fermentation. The character persists as a by-product. Sometimes this is evident in old and oxidized beer.

Diacetyl—Described as buttery, butterscotch. Sometimes caused by abbreviated fermentation or bacteria.

DMS (dimethyl sulfide)—A sweet-corn-like aroma/flavor. Can be attributed to malt, short or nonvigorous boiling of wort, slow wort chilling, or, in extreme cases, bacterial infection.

Estery-Fruity—Similar to banana, raspberry, pear, apple, currant, cherry, or strawberry flavor; may include other fruity-estery flavors. Often accentuated with higher-temperature fermentations, stirred or agitated fermentation, high pitching rates, fermentation of higher gravity beer, excessive wort aeration, and certain yeast strains.

Fatty-Soapy—A lard-like, fatty, or soapy character contributed by the autolyzation of yeast. Dormant yeast cells explode their fatty acids and lipids into the beer.

Fusel—Refers to higher alcohols and some esters. Sometimes referred to as fusel oils because of their oily nature as a compound (see **Solvent-like**). Also can be rose-like and floral. High levels of amino acid protein in wort, high temperatures, high-gravity wort, agitated wort during fermentation, excessive yeast growth, all can contribute to higher levels of fusels.

Grainy—Raw grain flavor. Cereal-like. Some amounts are appropriate for some beer styles. Beers with high pH tend to have unpleasant grainier flavors.

Hoppy—Characteristic aroma of the essential oils of hops. Does not include hop bitterness.

Husky—see **Astringent.**

Light-Struck—Having the characteristic smell of a skunk, caused by exposure to light whose wavelength is blue-green at 520 nanometers. Some hops can contribute a similar character.

Metallic—Possibly caused by exposure to metal or by fatty acid reactions. Also described as tinny, coin, blood-like. Check your brewpot and caps. Excessive iron content in water will cause unpleasant flavors and excessive foam retention.

Moldy-Musty—Character may be contributed by water source containing algae, or by moldy hoses or plumbing. Frequent enough with corked beer to note.

Nutty—As in Brazil nut, hazelnut, or fresh walnut; sometimes sherry-like.

Oxidized-Stale—Develops in the presence of oxygen as beer ages or is exposed to high temperatures; wet cardboard, papery, rotten vegetable or pineapple, winy, sherry, uric acid. Often coupled with an increase in sour, harsh, or bitter flavors. The more aeration in bottling, filtering, and transferring or the more air in the headspace, the more quickly a beer oxidizes. Warm temperatures dramatically accelerate oxidation.

Phenolic—Can be any one or a combination of a medicinal, plastic, electrical fire, Listerine-like, Band-Aid-like, smoky, or clove-like aroma or flavor. Most often caused by wild strains of yeast or bacteria. Can be extracted from grains (see **Astringent**). Sanitizing residues left in equipment can contribute.

Salty—Flavor associated with table salt. Sensation emphasized on sides of tongue. Can be caused by presence of too much sodium chloride, calcium chloride, or magnesium sulfate (Epsom salts).

Soapy—See **Fatty-Soapy.**

Solvent-like—Flavor and aromatic character of certain alcohols, often caused by high fermentation temperatures. Like acetone, lacquer thinner.

Sour-Acidic—Pungent aroma, sharpness of taste. Basic taste is like vinegar or lemon; tart. Typically associated with lactic or acetic acid. Can be the result of bacterial infection through contamination or the use of citric acid. Sensation emphasized on sides of tongue. Acetic acid (vinegar) is usually only a problem with wooden fermenters and introduction of oxygen.

Sweet—Basic taste associated with sugar. Sensation emphasized on front tip of tongue.

Sulfur-like (H2S; Hydrogen Sulfide)—Rotten eggs, burning matches, flatulence. A by-product with certain strains of yeast. Fermentation temperature can be a big factor. Quite volatile and diminishes with age. Can be more evident with bottle-conditioned beer.

Worty—The bittersweet character of unfermented wort. Incomplete fermentation.

Yeasty—Yeast-like flavor. Often due to strains of yeast in suspension or beer sitting on sediment too long.

WHY EVALUATE BEER?

Accurately evaluating beer does not come easy. It takes dedication, training, years of practice, and a very wide variety of beer experiences. As homebrewers, you have an advantage—you know the process and understand where flavors can originate once you learn how to identify them.

If you want to learn how to evaluate beer, you have your wort cut out for you. There are more than 850 chemical compounds that occur naturally in the fermentation process. Many hundreds of these compounds remain in the beer or change to something else with time and condition. These compounds titillate the tens of thousands of taste buds in our mouths. The resulting symphony is the taste we nonchalantly identify as beer.

We find ourselves attempting to isolate and identify one or a few flavors among hundreds. How our brains manage to do this is a wonder still not fully understood. With desire we can train ourselves: first, how to recognize a type of character; and second, how to perceive various intensities or particular characters. The final test, and the most difficult, is to recognize, perceive, and isolate a number of characters among many in our glass of beloved beer.

Let's consider five reasons why brewers would want to know how to evaluate beer.

1. To Maintain Quality Control and Consistency.   Every large brewery in North America has a regular program for evaluating its beer for the sole purpose of ascertaining that its quality is consistent from batch to batch. The breweries are not necessarily trying to detect unusual flavors in order to identify their origins. Instead, beer evaluators usually are specially trained to focus on and evaluate the brewery's own brands.

2. To Be Able to Describe a Given Beer.   How does your beer taste? "This beer tastes good (or bad)." "It's a party beer." "It's less filling." "The one beer to have when you want more than one." These generic descriptions just don't cut it anymore if you want to identify for yourself or communicate to other beer enthusiasts your beer's character.

Because of the proliferation of beer styles being brewed everywhere, a language developed in the 1980s and '90s that effectively communicates the characteristics of beer. If you can evaluate your beer's strong or weak points and describe them accurately, you may be able to improve the character of your beer and make exactly what you want.

3. To Score and/or Judge in a Competition.   Beer competitions are popular. Hundreds of beer enthusiasts and brewers are spending a great deal of time learning to evaluate beer *and* determine winners in a contest. This is a specialized perspective on the art and science of evaluation, and one that has taken the direction of blending objectivity with subjectivity. The evaluators or judges use scientific and technical terms in objectively assessing beer qualities, and sometimes their subjective senses to assess the beer's drink ability and appropriateness to a style.

4. To Define Styles.   For every beer you brew, there is born a style. The skill of the brewer, combined with the tools at his or her disposal, makes for the individuality of any glass of beer. So why do definitions of styles emerge when we take pride in our own uniqueness? One reason is to appreciate traditions, inspire creativity and enthusiasm and reasons to argue about better or worse, too malty or bitter; to create identity.

5. To Detect Problems and Improve Your Own or Someone Else's Beer.
This is perhaps the most challenging of all the reasons to evaluate beer. Not only do you need to identify any one of hundreds of characters, but you also need to identify the source of the character. If you are able to evaluate a beer's flavor, aroma, appearance, mouthfeel, and aftertaste—and then identify the source of these characters—you can learn how to control, adjust, and improve the quality of your brew.

SIX SENSES FOR EVALUATION

Sophisticated equipment can be used to measure the last little molecule and the kinds and amounts of everything that could be in your beer. Technological evaluation may augment the objective and subjective findings of a trained evaluator and his palate, but it can never replace them.

The human senses of taste, smell, sight, hearing, and touch can be trained as very effective tools to evaluate beer. But it takes patience, development of confidence, time, and, above all, humility. It takes practice. I know. I have watched hundreds of beer enthusiasts and brewers improve their evaluation skills over the years, to such a degree that they enjoy beer more and brew better beer.

Sight.   You can tell a lot about a beer by just looking at it while it's in the bottle or glass. Excessive headspace in the bottle is an indication that air content may be high. This tells you that oxidized flavor and aroma characters may follow. A surface deposit ringing the inside of the bottle's neck is a clear indication of

BOTTLE INSPECTION Comments _____

_____

                                                          Max. Score

BOUQUET/AROMA (as appropriate for style)   **10** _____

Malt (3), Hops (3), Other Aromatic Characteristics (4)

Comments _____

_____

APPEARANCE (as appropriate for style)   **6** _____

Color (2), Clarity (2), Head Retention (2)

Comments _____

_____

FLAVOR (as appropriate for style)   **19** _____

Malt (3), Hops (3), Conditioning (2), Aftertaste (3), Balance (4), Other Flavor Characteristics (4)

Comments _____

_____

BODY (full or thin as appropriate for style)   **5** _____

Comments _____

_____

DRINKABILITY & OVERALL IMPRESSION   **10** _____

Comments _____

_____

                                TOTAL (50 possible points): _____

Scoring Guide		
Excellent (40-50):	Exceptionally exemplifies style, requires little or no attention
Very Good (30-39):	Exemplifies style well, requires some attention
Good (25-29):	Exemplifies style satisfactorily, but requires attention
Drinkable (20-24):	Does not exemplify style, requires attention
Problem (<20):	Problematic, requires much attention

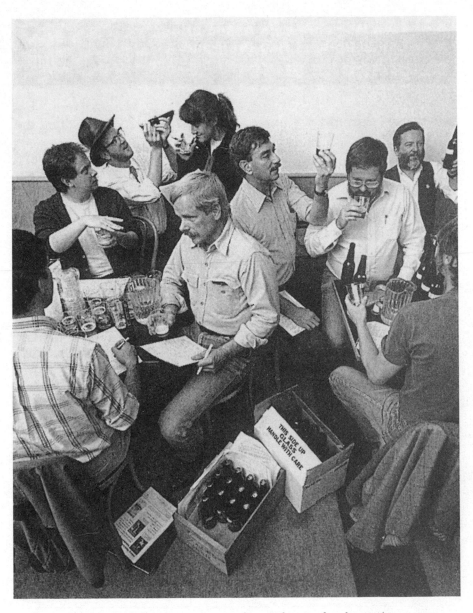

*It's a rough job, but someone's got to do it. Judging and evaluating beer is
serious business, demanding time, patience, training, practice, and humility.
But keep in mind, beer judges don't spit it out.*

bacterial or wild yeast contamination. In this case, sourness and excessive acidity may result. Gushing (another visual experience) also may be the result of bacterial or wild yeast contamination.

Sediment in a filtered, yeast-free beer may indicate an old, stale beer. Watch out for gushing. Sediment also may indicate precipitation of oxalates, a result of the brewing water lacking appropriate brewing salts—a sure cause of gushing.

Hazy beer can be the result of bacterial or yeast infection. It can be an indication of hoppy beer flavors and aromas from dry hopping. Chill haze, a precipitate of a tannin-protein compound, doesn't affect the flavor, but it can be remedied when identified.

When poured into a brandy snifter, high-alcohol beers such as doppelbocks and barleywines verify their strength by showing their legs on the sides of the glass. *Legs* refers to a coating of liquid that concentrates into streams as it runs down the side of a glass.

The complete lack of foam stability in a glass of newly poured beer (assuming the glass is beer-clean) is an indication that the beer may be stale, old, and oxidized. A very foamy, dense, and persistent head may indicate the presence of iron in the brewing water or lots of fresh hops.

Hearing.   It takes a lot of attention, but for an experienced evaluator, that sound upon opening—of gas escaping from a bottle—is music with specific tones for different volumes of carbon dioxide.

Smell.   The most acute and telling of our senses is our sense of smell. Assessing a beer's aroma should be a quick experience. Our smell detectors quickly become anesthetized to whatever we are smelling. For example, you may walk into a room and smell the strong aroma of coffee perking. Five minutes later, the smell lingers just as strongly, but you no longer notice it.

Our smell detectors reside in a side pocket of dead air along our nasal passage. In order to assess aromas, we must take air into this side pocket. The most effective way of doing this is to create a lot of turbulence in the nasal passage. Several short, strong sniffs or long, deep sniffs help get the aromatic molecules of vaporized beer smells into this pocket. Then our memory and current experience combine to identify what we smell.

Getting the aromas out of the beer doesn't happen so easily. It is best done with beers warmed to at least 45 to 50 degrees F (7–10 C) so that volatiles and aromatic compounds will evolve from liquid to gas. Swirl a half-full glass of beer to release the carbon dioxide bubbles into the air, carrying with them other aromatic gases.

Note that some constituents of beer flavor and aroma are so volatile that they virtually disappear from beer within a matter of a few minutes. This is the case with some sulfur-based compounds like DMS (a sweet-corn-like aroma), giving the beer an entirely different smell and taste after it has sat out for a period.

Taste.   The tongue is the main flavor assessor in the mouth. It can be mapped out in four distinct areas. Bitterness is emphasized at the back of the tongue, sweetness at the front tip of the tongue, and saltiness and sourness sensations on the sides of the tongue. It is interesting to note that 15 to 20 percent of Americans confuse sour with bitter and vice versa. When evaluating the perception of bitterness in one sample of beer, some will perceive no bitterness, some pleasant bitterness, and others intensely awful bitterness. Our ability to perceive intensity of flavors is genetically wired.

"Chew" the beer when evaluating. Because different areas of the tongue emphasize various flavor intensities, you must coat all of your tongue and mouth with the beer *and then swallow.* Beer evaluators—don't spit it out! It is important to assess the experience of swallowing beer for its aftertaste, exposing all parts of your mouth to beer's potential flavor. There are flavor receptors on the sides, back, and roof of the mouth independent of the tongue.

Touch and Feel.   Your mouth senses the texture of beer. Often called *body,* the texture of beer can be full-bodied or light-bodied as extremes. Astringency (also related to huskiness and graininess) can also be assessed by mouthfeel. It is not a flavor, but rather a dry, puckery feeling, exactly like chewing on grape or apple skin. This astringent sensation most often comes from tannins excessively extracted from grains as a result of oversparging, sparging with overheated water, or having a high pH. Sometimes astringency can be the result of milling your grains too finely.

Other sensations that can be felt are oily, cooling—as in menthol-like—burning, and hot or cold.

Balance.   This is a very important sixth sense. This is the close-your-eyes drinkability, the overall impression, the memorableness of the beer, the seeking of pleasure. No evaluation is complete without this final assessment. Is the beer balanced? Would you want another in the particular circumstance you find yourself in with this beer? This is the assessment and the evaluation that turned you into a homebrewer, isn't it? For a more complete perspective on beer balance, see the preface for the recipe Claude of Neptune Amaizeing Copperbock (page 314).

Our senses, like a $100,000 machine plugged into the electric socket, are sensitive to power surges, brownouts, and other ups and downs that influence the "show." Our own genetic makeup can affect our ability to detect certain chemical compounds' aromas and flavors. Also, our health is a very significant factor. Two to three days before we show the first outward symptoms of a cold or flu, our taste buds may go completely haywire. Taste panels that make million-dollar decisions consider this and do not rely on just one taster but on several in order to account for temporary inaccuracies of perception.

Finally, the environment in which beer is assessed should be comforting and not distracting. Smoke, loud music, extraneous and distracting aromas, and unusual lighting should be avoided.

In summary here's what to do:

1. Look at the beer.
2. Take a whiff. Smell the beer.
3. TASTE the beer.
4. Feel the beer.
5. Relax. Don't worry. Have a homebrew and think about balance and drinkability.

SOME FACTORS INFLUENCING THE CHARACTER OF BEER

Here is a thumbnail sketch of some of the more common factors influencing the character of beer.

INGREDIENTS

Malt and Fermentable Carbohydrates—influence color, mouthfeel, sweetness, level of astringency, alcohol strength. Brewers take a lot into consideration when evaluating and then using malt. The quality of barley is dependent on regional climate, soil, hours of sunlight, and other environmental factors. The quality of malt is influenced by both the quality of the barley and malting technique. The brewer adapts to the ingredient quality he can get and makes changes in the brewing and fermentation process to achieve the desired beer.

Hops— influence bitterness level, flavor, aroma (can be citrusy or floral). Hop variety and quality decisions, timing of their addition, amount used, and combination of hop varieties create thousands of different nuances in beer character. Interestingly, when identical hop varieties are grown in different areas of the world, the resulting hop is different in character from the originally grown hops. Certain styles of beer derive their unique qualities from hop varieties grown in specific areas of the world.

Yeast—the fungus among us. Strains and the environment they are in can affect diacetyl (buttery-butterscotch) levels; hydrogen sulfide (rotten egg smell), particularly in bottle-conditioned beer; phenolic character, including clove; plastic-like aroma and flavor; fruitiness and esters. Release of fatty acids from within cell walls can contribute to soapy, meaty, broth-like, or lard-like flavors.

Water—chlorinated water can result in harsh chlorophenolic (plastic-like) aroma and flavor. Saltiness results from an excess of certain mineral salts. High pH can result in harsh bitterness from unwanted extraction of tannin from grain and/or hops. Algae in water source can contribute moldiness or mustiness.

PROCESS

Milling—grain too finely crushed can result in husky-grainy and/or astringent character and stuck mashes. Grain too coarsely ground will yield less fermentable extract.

Mashing—temperature and type of mashing method can affect level of sweetness, alcohol level, body, mouthfeel, foam quality, head retention, perception of bitterness, aroma, astringency.

Temperature—during fermentation it can affect level of estery-fruitiness and level of fusel and higher alcohols; slow chilling of wort can increase DMS (sweetcorn-like character) levels.

Lautering—temperature, pH, mineral balance of sparge water can affect level of tannins and subsequent phenols detected in finished beer. Grain bed depth influences flavor. Speed of runoff can affect flavor, mouthfeel, head retention, and flavor stability. Agitating the grain bed can influence beer character.

Boiling—short boiling times or nonvigorous boils can result in high DMS levels; vigorous boiling precipitates proteins out of solution and helps stabilize final beer flavor. Also extracts hop bitterness, flavors, and aroma. Prolonged boiling increases caramelization of the wort.

Fermentation—at the beginning and during the height of fermentation, yeast metabolism produces a lot of heat. High temperatures can cause fusel alcohols and/or solvent-like characters; warmer temperatures can produce desirable or undesirable fruity (esters) aromas and flavors. Cooling regimes can elevate or decrease diacetyl levels in finished beer. Cold-lagering helps develop desired balance of flavors in lagered beer.

EQUIPMENT

Sanitation—lack of sanitation can result in bacterial or wild yeast contamination, causing unusual effects on flavor, aroma, appearance, texture; residues of sanitizer can contribute to medicinal-phenolic character.

Design—design of equipment—kettles, fermenters and plumbing—can grossly affect boiling regime, fermentation cycles, cleanability; the same combination of ingredients can be affected by different configurations and sizes of equipment.

Scaling batch size up or down can have significant and unforeseen effects on character of beer.

HANDLING

Temperature—warm temperatures dramatically affect the freshness of beer; warm temperatures speed up the oxidation process.

Oxygen—more than anything else, oxygen destroys the flavor of finished beer; oxygen combines with beer compounds and alcohol to produce negative flavors and aromas described as winy, stale, sherry-like, papery wet cardboard, rotten vegetables, rotten pineapple.

Light—blue-green wavelengths at 520 nanometers photochemically react with hop compounds to produce a light-struck skunky character. Green and clear glass offer no protection.

Agitation—rough handling enhances the oxidation process.

Aging/Maturation—Contradicting beer talk can get confusing to the emerging beer drinker.

So let's clarify:

- Lager is a beer that is aged *at the brewery.*
- Fresh beer is the best *and is what the brewmaster intended.*
- "Green" tasting beer is beer that isn't properly aged, *tastes like green apples and has nothing to do with St. Patrick's Day.*
- Cellaring is an English tradition of aging real ale, *but cellaring is brief and preserves complexity.*
- Belgian-style ales are aged at very warm temperatures, *in particular wild fermentations with bacteria, stronger beers, and bottle-conditioned beers (yeast in the bottle).*
- Beer needs to age in the bottle. *Some strong and hoppy ales can favorably change with time, but it is personal preference one way or the other.*
- Old beer is stale beer. *Most 4 percent to 7 percent alcohol by volume (abv) beers will lose their fresh and desired character with extended time and storage at warm or room temperatures. Stale is a polite word.*
- A barleywine before its time is like a mountain without a peak. *True. But once atop a peak, enjoy the experience. It's a journey downhill from that point on.*

TRAINING CAMP!

Becoming a knowledgeable beer drinker takes practice. It begins with tasting, observing, and bonding with your beer from its inception. Taste, smell, feel, and look at your ingredients. Watch your brewing process. Taste the liquids that are being transformed into beer as you progress. Taste the wort, taste the various rackings of fermented beer. Note appearances; note how vigorous the

(continued on page 405)

Beer Aroma/Flavor Recognition

Substances used to duplicate various beer characters (much of this information is based on Dr. Morton Meilgaard's work on the subject and my own and Greg Noonan's experience with handling samples)

MEILGAARD TERM REF. NO.	DESCRIPTOR	SUBSTANCE USED FOR RECOGNITION	CONCENTRATION IN 12 OUNCES BEER	CONCENTRATION IN 1 QUART BEER
0110	Alcoholic	Ethanol	15 ml	40 ml
0111	Clove/Spicy/DO NOT DRINK	Eugenol Allspice Cloves	100 mcg 2 g (marinate 2 or 3 cloves in beer)	265 mcg 5 g
0112	Winy/Fusely	Chablis wine	1 fl. oz.	2.7 fl. oz.
0123	Solvent-like, Acetone/DO NOT DRINK	Lacquer thinner	.03 ml	.08 ml
0133	Estery, Fruity, Solvent-like/DO NOT DRINK	Ethyl acetate	.028 ml	.076 ml
0150	Green Apples/DO NOT DRINK	Acetaldehyde	.016 ml or 16 mg	.040 ml or 40 mg
0220	Sherry	Sherry	1.25 fl. oz.	3.25 fl. oz.
0224	Almond, Nutty/DO NOT DRINK	Benzaldehyde Almond extract Almond extract	.002 ml or 2 mg 4 drops	.005 ml or 5 mg 11 drops
0503	Medicinal, Band-Aid-like, Plastic-like/DO NOT DRINK	Phenol	.003 ml or 3 mg	.010 ml or 10 mg
0620	Butter, Butterscotch/DO NOT DRINK	Diacetyl Butter-flavor extract	.00005 ml or 4 drops	.00014 ml or 11 drops

MEILGAARD TERM REF. NO.	DESCRIPTOR	SUBSTANCE USED FOR RECOGNITION	CONCENTRATION IN 12 OUNCES BEER	CONCENTRATION IN 1 QUART BEER
0710	Sulfury/Sulfitic/DO NOT DRINK Sulfur dioxide/DO NOT DRINK	Sodium or Potassium Metabisulfite	20 mg	50 mg
0721	Skunky, Light-struck	Beer exposed to sunlight for 1 hour		
0732	Sweet corn, DMS/DO NOT DRINK Cabbage/DO NOT DRINK	Dimethylsulfide/DMS (NOTE: unstable)	.00003 ml or 30 mcg	.0001 ml or 100 mcg
0800	Stale, Cardboard, Oxidation	Open bottle. Recap. Heat sample for one week at 90–100°F, or marinate cardboard in beer		
0910	Sour/Vinegar/Acetic (acid)	White vinegar	7.5 ml	25 ml
0920	Sour/Lactic (acidic) flavor only	Lactic acid	0.4 ml of 16% solution	1.1 ml of 16% solution
1000	Sweet flavor only	Sucrose sugar	5.3 g	14 g
1100	Salty flavor only	Table salt (NaCl)	1.2 g	3.2 g
1200	Bitter flavor only	Isohop extract	.0015 ml	.004 ml
—	Hop Aroma	Hop Oil	1 tiny drop	1 tiny drop

NOTE: As indicated, some of these substances are toxic and should not be tasted.

Troubleshooter's Chart

A Homebrewer's Guide to Better Beer

This chart is intended for use by brewers as a guide in helping to identify the causes of certain more commonly occurring beer flavors. It is not a complete compilation of beer flavors or their origins. Originally published by the American Homebrewers Association.

PROFILE DESCRIPTOR	INGREDIENTS	PROCESS	EQUIPMENT	HANDLING AND PROCESSING
Alcohol (ethanol)—a warming prickly sensation in the mouth and throat.	High: increase fermentable sugars through use of malt or adjuncts. NOTE: use of corn, rice, sugar, honey adds alcohol without adding body. High: healthy and attenuative yeast strains.	High: within the general 145- to 158-degree F range of mashing temperatures, the lower mash temperatures, produce more fermentables, thus more resulting alcohol. High: aeration of wort before pitching aids yeast activity. High: fusel (solvent-like) alcohols are produced at high temperatures.		Age and oxidation will convert some of the ethanol to higher solvent-like alcohols.
Astringent—(see Husky/Grainy).				
Bitter—a sensation generally perceived on the back of the tongue, and sometimes roof of the mouth, as with caffeine or hop resin.	High: black and roasted malts and grains. High: great amounts of boiling hops. High: alkaline water can draw out bitter components from grains.	High: effective boiling of hops. Low: high fermentation temperatures and quick fermentation rates will decrease hop bitterness.	Low: filtration can remove some bitterness.	

PROFILE DESCRIPTOR	INGREDIENTS	PROCESS	EQUIPMENT	HANDLING AND PROCESSING
Body—not a flavor but a sensation of viscosity in the mouth as with thick (full-bodied) beers or thin (light-bodied) beers.	Full: use of malto-dextrin, dextrinous malts, lactose, crystal malt, caramel malt, dextrine (Cara-Pils) malt. Thin: use of highly fermentable malt. Thin: use of enzymes that break down carbohydrates in mash, fermentation of storage.	Full: high-temperature mash. Low: low-temperature mash.		Low: age may reduce body. Low: wild yeast and bacteria may reduce body by breaking down carbohydrates.
Clarity—visual perception of the beer in the bottle and after it is poured.	High: use of protein-reducing enzymes (papain). Low: chill haze more likely in all-malt beers because higher protein than malt and adjunct beers. Low: wheat malt and unmalted barley cause more chill haze than malted barley and corn and rice adjuncts. Low: poor flocculant wild yeast may cause poor sedimentation. Low: bacteria cause cloudiness and haze. High: use of polyclar or activated silica gel.	Low: overmilling/grinding grain. High: long, vigorous boil and proper cooling.	Low: bacteria from dirty plastic equipment, especially siphon and blow-out hoses, scratched fermenter. High: filtration can help clear.	Low: unclean bottles can cause bacterial haze.
Color—visual perception of beer color.	Dark: dark malts (crystal, Munich, chocolate, roasted barley, black patent). Light: exclusive use of lighter malts and starch adjuncts.	Dark: scorching. Dark: caramelization with long boil.	Low: filtration can reduce color.	

(continued)

Troubleshooter's Chart (continued)

PROFILE DESCRIPTOR	INGREDIENTS	PROCESS	EQUIPMENT	HANDLING AND PROCESSING
Degree of **Carbonation**	High: bacteria and wild yeast may break down carbohydrates not normally fermentable and create overcarbonation and gushing. High: overpriming. NOTE ON GUSHING: excessive iron content causes gushing; malts containing *Fusarium* (mold) from wet harvesting of barley cause gushing; precipitates of excess salts in bottle cause gushing.	Low: cold temperatures inhibit ale yeast. Low: long-lagered beer may not have enough viable yeast for bottle conditioning (carbonating) properly.	High: unsanitary equipment can introduce bacteria which can cause overcarbonation and gushing.	High: unclean bottles can cause bacterial growth and gushing. High: overpriming kegs; prime kegs at one-third normal rate. High: agitation. Low: improper seal on bottlecap.
Diacetyl—butter or butterscotch flavor.	High: unhealthy, nonflocculating yeast. High: not enough soluble nitrogen-based yeast nutrient in wort. High: not enough oxygen in wort when pitching yeast. High: bacterial contamination. High/Low: yeast strain will influence production of diacetyl. High: excessive use of adjuncts such as corn or rice, deficient in amino acid (soluble nitrogen-based nutrients).	High: chilling fermentation too soon. High: high-temperature initial fermentation. High: premature fining takes yeast out of suspension too soon. Low: agitated extended fermentation. Low: high temperature during extended fermentation. Low: kraeusening.	High: bacteria from equipment. High/Low: configuration and size of fermenting vessel will influence production.	
Dimethyl Sulfide (DMS)—cooked cabbage or sweet-corn-like.	High: high-moisture malt, especially 6-row varieties. High: bacterial contamination of wort. Low: use of 2-row English malt. High: underpitching of yeast (lag time). High: bacterially infected yeast slurry.	Low: longer boil will diminish potential for DMS. High: oversparging at low temperatures (especially lower than 160 degrees F).	High: bacteria from equipment.	High: introduction of unfiltered CO_2 produced by fermentation. Bottle priming will produce small amounts.

PROFILE DESCRIPTOR	INGREDIENTS	PROCESS	EQUIPMENT	HANDLING AND PROCESSING
Fruity/Estery—flavors similar to fruits such as strawberry, banana, raspberry, apple, pear, currant.	Some yeast strains produce various esters. High: loaded with fruit.	High: excessive trub. High: warm fermentation. High: high pitching rates. High: high-gravity wort. High: high aeration of wort. Low: opposite of above.		Low: age will reduce esters to closely related fusel alcohols and acids (solvent-like qualities).
Head Retention—physical and visual degree of foam stability.	Good: high malt content. Poor: use of overmodified or underkilned malt. Good: mashing in of barley flakes. Good: licorice, crystal malt, dextrine (Cara-Pils) malt, wheat malt. Good: high use of hops in beer. Poor: germ oil in whole grain. Poor: elevated volumes of higher alcohols. Good: high nitrogen content.	Low: oversparging (releases fatty acids). Low: high aeration of wort before pitching. Low: extended enzymic molecular breakdown of carbohydrates in mashing. Low: fatty acid release during yeast autolysis. Low: high fermentation temperatures (production of higher alcohols). High: good rolling boil in kettle.	Poor: cleaning residues, improper rinsing of fats, oils, detergents, soaps. Poor: filtration can reduce head retention.	Low: oxidation/aging breaks down head stabilizing compounds. Low: dirty bottles, improperly rinsed. Low: improperly cleaned glasses.
Husky/Grainy (Astringent, Bitter)—raw grain-like flavor, dry, pucker-like sensation as in grape tannin.	High: alkaline or high sulfate water. High: stems and skins of fruit. High: 6-row more than 2-row malt.	High: oversparging grains. High: boiling grains. High: excess trub. High: poor hot break (improper boiling). High: overmilling/grinding. High: high temperature (above 175 degrees F) sparge water.		Low: aging reduces astringency.

(continued)

Troubleshooter's Chart (continued)

PROFILE DESCRIPTOR	INGREDIENTS	PROCESS	EQUIPMENT	HANDLING AND PROCESSING
Light-struck (skunky)—like a skunk (the British describe this character as "catty" because there are no skunks in the U.K.).	.		High: fermenting beer in glass carboy in bright light.	High: light striking beer through green or clear glass and over a prolonged time through brown glass. NOTE: effect is instantaneous with clear or green glass.
Metallic—tinny, coin-like, blood-like.	High: iron content in water.		High: mild steel, aluminum, cast iron. High: cleaning stainless steel or copper without oxidizing surfaces to form a protective layer of oxide on metal.	
Oxidation—paper- or cardboard-like, winy, sherry-like, rotten pineapple, or rotten vegetables.	Low: addition of ascorbic acid (vitamin C).	High: aeration when siphoning or pumping. High: adding tap or aerated water to finished beer.	High: malfunctioning air lock.	High: too much air space in bottle. High: warm temperatures. High: age, agitation.

PROFILE DESCRIPTOR	INGREDIENTS	PROCESS	EQUIPMENT	HANDLING AND PROCESSING
Phenolic—medicinal, Band-Aid-like, smoky, clove-like, plastic-like.	High: chlorinated (tap) water. High: wild yeast, German wheat beer yeast (clove/smoky). High: bacteria. High: roasted barley/malts (smoky).	High: oversparging of mash. High: boiling grains.	High: cleaning compound residue. High: poor quality plastic hoses and gaskets. High: bacterial and wild yeast contamination.	High: defective bottlecap linings (rare).
Salty—emphasized perception on the sides of the tongue as with table salt (sodium chloride).	High: brewing salts, particularly those containing sodium chloride (table salt) and magnesium sulfate (Epsom salts).			
Sour/Acidic—emphasized perception on the sides of the tongue as with lemon juice (citric acid).	High: introduction of lactobacillus, *Acetobacter*, and other acid-forming bacteria. High: too much refined sugar. High: addition of citric or other food-grade acid. High: excessive ascorbic acid (vitamin C).	High: mashing for long periods promotes bacterial growth and acid by-products in mash. High: bacteria in wort, fermentation. High: excessive fermentation temperatures promote bacterial growth. Low: sanitize all equipment.	High: bacteria harbored in scratched surfaces of plastic, glass, stainless, improper welds, valves, spigots, gaskets, discolored plastic. High: use of wooden spoon in cooled wort or fermentation.	High: storage at warm temperatures. High: unsanitary bottles or kegs.

(continued)

Troubleshooter's Chart (continued)

PROFILE DESCRIPTOR	INGREDIENTS	PROCESS	EQUIPMENT	HANDLING AND PROCESSING
Sulfur—sulfur dioxide, hydrogen sulfide (rotten eggs), yeast-like flavor (see DMS; Light-Struck).	High: some yeast strains will produce by-products. High: malt releases minor amounts.	High: yeast autolysis (cell breakdown): sedimented yeast in contact with beer in fermenter too long. High/Low: yeast strains will influence.		
Sweet—emphasized perception on the tip of the tongue as with sucrose (white table sugar).	High: high malt content. High: crystal malt, Munich malt, and toasted malt create sweet malt flavor. High: low hopping. High: licorice. High: low attenuation or unhealthy yeast strains.	High: within the general 145- to 150-degree F range of mashing temperatures, the higher mash temperatures produce more unfermentable carbohydrates.		Low: aging reduces sweetness.

fermentation is and how quickly it clears. Taste the beer as you bottle it, then taste it after one week, two weeks, three weeks, and a month. Talk to your beer. Accompany the beer along its way with your senses. Knowing and feeling the soul of your beer takes time and practice. Don't expect an "aha" phenomenon to occur with every batch. Your knowledge and understanding are cumulative. Use your senses more than anything else. These perceptions are your foundation for further training and development of beer awareness.

With cumulative experience and knowledge you will begin to be able to predict the outcome of your beer and how it will change before it is ready to drink. As the beer matures, you'll recognize what kind of sulfur characters come and go with age. You'll know that some phenolic characters are likely to get worse with age, and some can diminish. You'll observe the rise and fall of bitterness, diacetyl. Some esters will increase with age, and others will be perceived to diminish. You'll be able to gauge the potential of your beer. Homebrewing is different from commercial brewing. Many commercial brewing principles and theories can be appropriately applied to homebrewing, but there are exceptions. If you brew enough and use your senses, you will discover the delightful uniquenesses of homebrew.

Limber up that elbow. Taste beer. Yours, others'—commercial and home-brewed.

Serve samples at a temperature no cooler than 50 degrees F (10 C), even at 50 to 60 degrees F (10–15.6 C) for ales. Serve in an environment that is comfortable, well lit, odor-free, and quiet, for maximizing your sense of perception.
Training Aids.   On pages 396 to 397 you will find a table of substances you can add to 12 ounces (355 ml) of light-flavored beer in order to help you learn how to identify particular aroma or flavor characters.

Some of these samples are difficult to make because of the potency of the original solution, its volatility and stability. Make these doctored beer samples only 12 to 24 hours before they are actually sampled. Otherwise, many of them are so volatile and unstable that their propensities will diminish.

You may find some of the samples will be too strong, and some much too weak, as far as your senses are concerned. Remember, individual perception thresholds are different.

Some of the chemicals are intensely pungent in their concentrated form and will require a well-ventilated mixing area. A vented hood with strong fans is mandatory for chemicals such as diacetyl, ethyl acetate, and acetaldehyde. Use safety glasses to protect your eyes if handling concentrated lactic acid.

Note that lactic acid does not have an aroma in and of itself. Other by-products produced by bacteria produce aromatics in beer.

BEER AND THE ENJOYMENT OF LIFE

THE RIGHT BEER GLASS MAKES HAPPIER BEER DRINKERS

Enhance your beer-drinking experience with smart choices of glassware.

Try this at your next beer tasting. Choose a beer with a degree of obvious malt and hop character. Serve it in four or five different types of glassware. Tell your beer drinking "subjects" that you are serving them beers in five different glasses and would like for them to rate them as far as preference. You can tell them the style of beer you are serving. Then also ask them to rate the sweetness, malt character, bitterness, aroma, flavor, body, aftertaste, floral character, and so on. After this is all said and done, you'll be surprised at the discussion. Especially after you let them know that they were all the same beer!

Beer glassware design is both an art and a science. Your beer deserves to be served in the best type of glassware you have access to. The shape and design of the glassware dramatically impacts your perception of flavor, aroma, and overall impression of the beer you're drinking.

Take, for example, the same dark lager served in a narrow water glass and in a wide-rimmed glass goblet. With the wide mouth, physiologically your tongue extends forward. In the narrow glass your tongue retracts to the rear. Sweetness perception is emphasized at the tip of our tongues. You get less sweetness with the narrow glass, because the beer travels directly to the rear of our tongue, bypassing where we most perceive sweetness. The placement of our tongue on a wide-rimmed glass emphasizes the sweetness, thus beer is a sweeter beer with a wide-rimmed glass. Aromatically there are no surprises. With a larger surface area emitting the fragrance of hops and malt, the wide-rimmed glass enhances the aromatic experience.

The glass rim thickness matters too. A thick, heavy rim and a clean-cut, thin rim will evoke different psychological impressions. Thick-rimmed glassware creates a feeling that the beer is more rustic, while thin-rimmed glass promotes the sensation of an elegant beer. The same holds true with stemmed glassware: thin = elegant; thick and short = rustic. It's been shown that in blind tastings with the same beer, people react to these psychological messages in glass texture.

Where is your head at? That matters too. The physical position of your head when drinking can make you feel less or more full. Psychologically, drinkers feel fuller when tipping their head back and drinking out of a smaller glass. The length of the stem obviously influences head tilt.

Why does glassware shape matter? It influences whether people are going to drink more or less. If a certain style of glassware contributes to satiating your senses, you may drink less because of the exaggeration of beer character. Now

if you drink out of the bottle, then there's obviously less satiation, but you'll have to tilt your head back to do it. It all figures.

The absolute most important thing about using glassware is to keep it beer clean. It should be grease-, soap-, and detergent residue-free. You can use detergent for cleaning glassware, but you must thoroughly rinse all traces of detergent off the glass. If there are bubbles clinging to the inside of your glass, it is filthy and not suitable for holding the beer you made or paid good money for. If it smells like old dishwater, it hasn't been rinsed thoroughly. Make sure your beer is served cleanly.

Now, I think I'll take a break and have a stoneware mugful of my German Helles.

SAVOR THE FLAVOR—RESPONSIBLY

Drinking beer is a privilege. Drinking beer intelligently is an art.

Quality, not quantity, is what beer should be all about. Homebrewing is an endeavor that most of us pursue because we enjoy the flavor of beer and enjoy the process as a hobby and as an opportunity to improve the quality of our lives.

As homebrewers, we each must take individual responsibility for our behavior when consuming beer as an alcoholic beverage. Some may consider homebrewing a right, while others consider it a privilege. Regardless, unless we take it upon ourselves to exercise individual responsibility, then choices may be made by others on our behalf. Part of the freedom of choice and of brewing one's beer is taking on this important responsibility. Savor the flavor and do so responsibly.

Drinking any amount of alcohol can impair your ability to perform certain tasks. Driving is one of them. Chemical tests can determine your blood alcohol concentration (BAC). BAC is a helpful indication of your impairment. For example, five parts of alcohol in 10,000 parts of blood is shown as 0.05 percent BAC.

In many states, a driver of an automobile with a BAC between 0.05 and 0.09 percent is presumed to be driving while his or her ability to drive is impaired (DWAI). A driver with a BAC of 0.10 percent or more may be presumed to be driving under the influence (DUI). Laws and BAC limits can change and vary from state to state. Both DWAI and DUI convictions may mean mandatory penalties, sometimes including a jail term, a fine, public service, and possibly surrender of one's driving license.

The alcohol concentration in your body depends on several factors, some of which are:

- Your weight (see Know Your Limit on the facing page).
- The amount of food in your stomach. Food postpones alcohol absorption but will not keep you from increasing BAC, though the peak level may be less as your body begins to metabolize alcohol already in your blood. Fats and proteins delay alcohol uptake by the body more than when carbohydrates are ingested.
- The concentration of alcohol in the beverage you are consuming.
- The length of time during which you consume alcohol (see chart).
- The period of time since your last drink. It takes about one hour for your body to metabolize the alcohol in 12 ounces of $3\frac{1}{2}$ to $4\frac{1}{2}$ percent alcohol beer.
- The ability of your digestive system to produce enzymes that help break down and metabolize alcohol. The average metabolism rate for moderate drinkers produces a .017 per hour decline in their blood-alcohol content (BAC) level. For example, if your BAC is .08 percent and you have stopped drinking, it will take about 1 hour for your body to reduce BAC to .063 percent. Check out the Blood Alcohol Content Calculator at www .craftbeer.com to learn more about your limits.

Factors that determine the effects of alcohol include:

- **Gender.** Men generally have a higher alcohol tolerance because they are usually bigger and have a lower percentage of body fat than women.

Know Your Limit.

Your life and the lives of others depend on it.

Be careful driving BAC to .05% ☐   Driving impaired .05% to .09% ▨   Do not drive .10% and up ▦

1 Drink = 12 oz. beer, 4 oz. wine, or 1¼ oz. 80 proof liquor

After hours	1 Drink				2 Drinks				3 Drinks				4 Drinks			
Weight	4	3	2	1	4	3	2	1	4	3	2	1	4	3	2	1
100	–	–	–	.03	–	.02	.04	.06	.05	.07	.08	.10	.09	.10	.12	.13
120	–	–	–	.03	–	–	.03	.05	.03	.04	.06	.08	.06	.08	.09	.11
140	–	–	–	.02	–	–	.02	.05	.02	.03	.05	.07	.04	.06	.08	.09
160	–	–	–	.02	–	–	.02	.04	.01	.02	.04	.06	.03	.04	.06	.08
180	–	–	–	.01	–	–	.01	.04	–	.02	.03	.05	.02	.04	.05	.07
200	–	–	–	–	–	–	.01	.03	–	.01	.03	.05	.01	.03	.04	.06
220	–	–	–	–	–	–	–	.03	–	–	.01	.04	–	.01	.03	.06

After hours	5 Drinks				6 Drinks				7 Drinks				8 Drinks			
Weight	4	3	2	1	4	3	2	1	4	3	2	1	4	3	2	1
100	.13	.14	.16	.17	.16	.18	.19	.21	.20	.22	.23	.25	.24	.25	.27	.28
120	.09	.11	.13	.14	.13	.14	.16	.17	.15	.17	.19	.20	.19	.20	.22	.23
140	.07	.09	.10	.12	.10	.12	.13	.15	.13	.14	.16	.17	.15	.17	.18	.20
160	.06	.07	.09	.10	.08	.09	.11	.13	.10	.12	.13	.15	.13	.14	.16	.17
180	.04	.06	.07	.09	.06	.08	.09	.11	.09	.10	.12	.13	.11	.12	.14	.15
200	.03	.04	.06	.08	.05	.07	.08	.10	.07	.09	.10	.12	.09	.10	.12	.13
220	.01	.03	.05	.07	.04	.06	.07	.09	.05	.07	.08	.11	.06	.08	.10	.12

Note: This blood alcohol concentration (BAC) chart is only a guide and not sufficiently accurate to be considered legal evidence. The figures you calculate are averages. Individuals may vary somewhat in their personal alcohol tolerance. Food in the stomach slows the rate of absorption. Medication, health, and psychological conditions are also influencing factors.

- **Mental and physical health.** Illness, depression, stress, or fatigue can increase the effects of alcohol.
- **Percentage of body fat.** Alcohol will affect a physically fit individual less than someone with a higher percentage of body fat—even if both people are the same weight.
- **Medication.** Medication can increase the influence of alcohol. Follow your doctor's advice before mixing the two.

Be aware that the degree of intoxication you may develop is not a matter of how much of an alcohol-containing beverage you drink, but rather, how much alcohol you drink. One type of drink is often not equal to another kind of drink. Twelve ounces (355 ml) of a beer that's 4 percent alcohol by volume contains 0.48 fluid ounces (14.2 ml) of pure alcohol. A 6-ounce (178 ml) serving of wine that's 12 percent alcohol by volume contains 0.72 fluid ounces (21.4 ml) of pure alcohol. One ounce of 80 proof (40 percent) distilled liquor mixed with any mixer contains 0.40 fluid ounce (11.9 ml) of pure alcohol. These differences are very significant, and variation from the above can have a dramatic effect on how well you will be able to control the intoxicating effect of alcohol-containing beverages.

A beer containing 6 percent alcohol by volume will have 50 percent more alcohol than a 4 percent beer. Studies have been made implying that, for example, two beers at 6 percent will increase the potential for higher peak BAC more so than if three beers at 4 percent were drunk during the same period.*

Keep in mind that the concentration of alcohol in your drink has an influence on how quickly you will feel the effects of alcohol. A 1-ounce (30 ml) shot of 80 proof liquor will affect you more quickly than when combined with 11 ounces (327 ml) of a mixer.

There are several scales of proof for liquor. The American scale defines 100 percent alcohol as 200 proof, thus 80 proof would be 40 percent alcohol. There is a British scale that defines 100 percent alcohol as 175 proof, thus 80 proof would be 45 percent alcohol. A Canadian scale defines 100 percent alcohol as 75 overproof. And if all this were not confusing enough, there is a French scale that defines 100 percent alcohol as 100 proof.

The alcoholic content of beer is not normally indicated in terms of the proof scale, but keep these scales in mind when discussing alcohol by volume of beer and proof of distilled spirits. Pacing yourself with a 12-ounce (355 ml) bottle of beer can be done.

Savor the flavor responsibly.

---

* "How the Blood Alcohol Curve Develops After Drinking Light Beer," by Anton Piendl, *Brauwelt international*, 1993/II.

- Eat when you enjoy beer.
- Know the different ranges of alcohol content associated with the beer styles you are going to enjoy.
- Don't drive when you've had too much.
- Remember, time is the only remedy for overindulging—coffee, cold showers, or exercise will not "sober you up." Know your limits before you drink.

Beer and Nutrition

Although beer contains elements of nutrition and can promote some positive physiological and psychological effects, let's face it, we drink beer because we enjoy the flavor and we enjoy the effect that alcohol has on our bodies and minds, hopefully in moderation. In today's culture we don't drink beer because of its nutritional value, though in olden times beer was most purposefully brewed and consumed for health and nutritional value. But one must take this into perspective, since healthy food options were limited in centuries past.

Regardless of the reasons we drink beer—beer will have nutritional value when consumed in moderation. As an energy source, it is much more readily assimilated by the body than sugar, but it is a depressant, and as the intake increases, it can have a debilitating and toxic effect. Toxicity is indicated by dose and not by substance.

Beer provides varying amounts of nutrition, including calories, protein, carbohydrates, vitamins, and minerals. Fat and cholesterol are totally absent in most styles of beer. The amounts of some nutrients can vary quite drastically with the style of beer. A high-gravity beer, for example, may have an overall higher rating of the above nutrients. An unfiltered beer and especially bottle-conditioned beer will have a much greater amount of B vitamins. Let it suffice to say that nutritional value will vary with beer style and how it is processed.

Hops and other herbs can contribute added health benefits. Hops are a soporific and diuretic, helping create a relaxed mood, promoting sleep, and enhancing appetite, digestion, and water transport from the body. Alcohol is also a diuretic, and taken in excess, it can lead to dehydration.

Beer Is Not Fattening!

Please spare me. Take a look at the facts yourself. There's not a whole lot to write about in order to make my point. The data speaks for itself.

According to the U.S. government, a 12-ounce serving of "regular" beer has fewer calories than 12 ounces of apple juice, orange juice, 2 percent milk, or cola. If you are really serious about losing weight and don't want to drink beer, then drink water.

Take the time to read the nutritional values of the juices, soft drinks, and those micro-tiny package of peanuts, pretzels, and chips. A 12-ounce serving of

Nutrition in One 12-Ounce Serving of Beer

NUTRIENT	REGULAR AMERICAN LIGHT LAGER	GERMAN WHEAT BEER WITH YEAST	GERMAN DOPPELBOCK	U.S. RDA (RECOMMENDED DAILY ALLOWANCE) FOR HEALTHY MALES 25–50
Kilocalories	153	179	273	—
Protein	1.64 g	2.09	3.39	75 g
Thiamine (B_1)	0.018 mg	0.044	0.170	1.5 mg
Riboflavin (B_2)	0.089 mg	0.164	0.206	1.7 mg
Niacin	1.8 mg	3.03	6.3	20 mg
Pantothenic Acid (B_5)	0.169 mg	0.77	0.765	10 mg
Pyridoxine (B_6)	0.164 mg	0.153	429	2.0 mg
Folic Acid	20 mcg	—	—	400 mcg
Vitamin C	0	—	—	65 mg
Calcium	14 mg	5.5	6.7	1,000 mg
Copper	0.292 mg	0.047	0.008	2 mg
Iron	0.07 mg	0.043	0.11	18 mg
Magnesium	21 mg	30.8	44.2	400 mg
Phosphorus	50 mg	12.6	212	1,000 mg
Zinc	0.04 mg	.003	.039	15 mg

SOURCE: Data for American light lager taken from U.S. Department of Agriculture, National Nutrient Database for Standard Reference, Basic Report 14003, Alcoholic beverage, beer, regular. Data for RDA taken from *The Essential Guide to Vitamins and Minerals*, copyright 1992 by Health Media of America, HarperCollins Publishers, New York, NY. Data for German doppelbock and wheat beer taken from "Biere Aus Aller Welt," by Professor Anton Piendl, *Brauindustrie*, Schloss Mindelburg, Germany, 1982–1991.

beer has fewer calories than a 1-ounce serving of potato chips or peanuts. A 12-ounce serving of beer has half the calories of a just under a quarter-pound hamburger. So go ahead and eat the hamburger, but trade out the extra handful of potato chips or half handful of peanuts for two beers! I won't even get into a discussion about French fries, the cheese on the cheeseburger, or the sugar-spiked sesame seed bun!

And just in case a wine drinker ever tells you that beer is fattening, tell them 12 ounces of wine has 75 percent more calories than 12 ounces of 5 percent beer.

So please, let's cut the fat talk and get real. This data is not new. I realize I have simplified a discussion that involves many extenuating circumstances, but if the consumer is going to simplify "beer is fattening," then an equally simple response is warranted. Beer is no more fattening than so many other things we eat and drink. Enjoying beer should be about quality, not quantity. Overdoing anything is not healthy. Beer is about being an individual with individual responsibilities. Our friends need to be reminded.

There are many special interest groups that promote the healthful aspects of beer, while other special interest groups promote the unhealthful aspects of beer. Just as we must take individual responsibility to enjoy beer sensibly and with respect, we must individually take the responsibility for assessing the "facts" and "studies" for what they are. Take all that you read and learn into perspective, be wary, be smart, make your own beer, appreciate beers that others make, and think about what you are being told, who is telling you and why.

Perspective and moderation are important keys in assessing the value of the 10,000-year-old tradition of brewing and of your own enjoyment of beer. If you realize you don't have the ability to moderate your own consumption, respect yourself and consider alternatives. There is nothing wrong with appreciating and respecting beer while not being able to drink it.

ALLERGIES AND BEER

There are many reasons why people can develop allergies to beer. If allergies do develop, they are often allergies to one or a combination of the following:

- Yeast
- Gluten protein (barley, wheat, oats, rye)
- Corn
- Rice
- Hops
- Alcohol

If yeast is the cause of an allergy, then filtering beer using a filter with a porosity of less than 0.5 micron will enable the brewer to eliminate yeast from the final product, but often compounds from within the yeast cell walls will dissolve into solution if yeast cells burst or autolyze due to adverse situations. Consult your physician if you are allergic to yeast. Consider yourself fortunate if you are not allergic to yeast.

Barley, corn, wheat, and rice are the most common ingredients in commercially available beer and most homebrewed beer. If these grains or other cultivated cereal grains (rye, oats) cause allergic reactions, consult with your doctor about the possibility of tolerating ancient nonhybridized grains such as spelt (also known as Kamut or dinkel). Beers made from these home-malted grains may afford an alternative.

Not to worry is the homebrewer or the lover of beer who develops an annoying allergy to hops. Remember, beers were made with many different kinds of bitter herbs and plants before hops became popular about 100 to 200 years ago. This is an allergy that can be most easily circumvented.

If you are allergic to alcohol, well, relax, don't worry and don't have a homebrew. Find other passions in life that will allow you similar satisfaction and pleasure. They do exist.

Gone with the Wind—Flatulence and Beer

Have you ever been with a group of people touring a small brewery and sampling *Zwickelbier*, the good stuff out of the tanks before the yeast has settled or the beer's been filtered? It's funny, but not funny, if you know what I mean.

Without professing to be a doctor of flatulence, I can say with confidence that yeasted homebrew can cause flatulence. We are all sensitive to yeast to a small or large degree. When flatulence becomes a common occurrence after consumption of yeasty beer, it often, though not always, indicates an imbalance of digestive tract microflora. The wrong kind, or the lack of certain kinds, of bacteria in your gut may promote a fermentation of the undesirable sorts in your gut. Voilà!—flatulence (i.e., farting).

Sometimes imbalances are the result of having taken antibiotics. Some antibiotics can wipe out much of your digestive bacteria, creating an environment for other bacteria and even certain kinds of yeast to take hold and ferment in your gut. Consult your medical doctor or a holistic-minded physician for foods and supplements you may be able to take to get your system back in balance, thus minimizing the effect that naturally made unfiltered beer will have on your system.

One simple step is to avoid yeasty, cloudy beer and let someone else cut the cheese.

BEER, FOOD, AND UMAMI

Let's hope that the definition of an American gourmet seven-course meal never becomes a six-pack and a cheeseburger.

Meals can be an adventure. The food and beer you enjoy are a reflection of the people who made them and those who had a hand in producing, growing, or harvesting the ingredients. And as well, meals can be a reflection of your own adventurous spirit.

We are in the midst of a sustainable American adventure—appreciating our own unique heritage of fine food and beer. Years from now we will continue to recall how American homebrewers and beer enthusiasts popularized the practice of enhancing food with beer. Food cooked with beer and food accompanied by beer are an adventure worth discovering.

A FEW WORDS ABOUT COOKING WITH BEER

Essentially beer can be substituted for liquid in most recipes, in varying proportions. The finesse is using beer to enhance the flavor of the dish, not to take center stage. In this regard and considering that foods have varying degrees of flavor character and strength, it is all too obvious that the choice of beer style used in cooking is an important one. The right beer wonderfully contributes to the flavor of the food being prepared. Here are some general guidelines:

- Lighter foods—light beers
- More robust foods—dark beers and hoppy ales
- Sweet foods—maltier, stronger beers
- Fruity foods—mildly bittered fruity ales
- Sour foods and sauces—acidic beers
- Smoky foods—smoky beers

The following section on food types is excerpted from "Cooking with the Brewgal Gourmet," by Candy Schermerhorn, in the book *Brew Free or Die*. Candy is the author of *The Great American Beer Cookbook* (Brewers Publications, 1993).

Since prehistoric times, people have been enjoying beer with food in more ways than one. Preparing food with beer (while both drinking it and using it in the recipe) is one more versatile way to enjoy your homebrew.

In Breads . . . "The best reason to add beer to your bread recipe is that the yeast, malt and hops of beer impart a wonderful, full flavor and aroma. The final product is indescribable, and should be experienced at least once in a lifetime!"

In Soups . . . "Soup recipes can be modified to include beer, in several different ways. Beer can be used to make broth or stock—just add a few cups of beer to the water that bones or vegetables will be simmered in. Alternatively, beer can replace part of the stock called for in a recipe. A basic guideline of two cups of broth to one cup of beer is a good starting point."

On Meats . . . "No matter how you cook meat, you can add beer to it.

"Because beer is acidic, it works as a natural tenderizer on meat. This makes it perfect for marinades. Beer-based sauces and braising liquids can also enhance the flavor of meats."

On Poultry . . . "Because of the 'modern' methods employed in raising most commercial poultry, much of it lacks depth of flavor. By adding beer to basting sauces, marinades and stuffings, you will heighten the final flavor and expand your recipe repertoire."

On Seafood . . . "Fish and shellfish can benefit greatly from the addition of beer, but use a subtle touch; fish is easily overwhelmed by powerful flavors. Marinating, steaming, poaching and boiling are wonderful ways to incorporate beer into your seafood cooking."

On Desserts . . . "When it comes to combining beer and desserts, the sky is the limit. When substituting beer in a dessert recipe, it is important to remember that texture will play a big role in the amount of beer you can substitute. When a recipe calls for water, it is easy. You can substitute all or a part of the water with beer. When a recipe calls for fruit juice, substitute two-thirds of the amount with beer and the remaining one-third with frozen, undiluted fruit juice concentrate.

"Dairy products are used to add tenderness and flavor and often are used as a form of leavening. It is important to know the function of each dairy product in a recipe before substituting beer in its place. As an example, you may substitute one cup of milk with ¾ cup beer mixed with ½ cup powdered milk.

"Some examples of desserts made with beer: Imperial stout chocolate sour cream cake, chocolate doppelbock mousse, homemade kriek (cherry beer) and cherry ice cream, strawberries with a topping of honey mead blended with honey and sour cream."

For a more comprehensive treatment of cooking with beer, Candy Schermerhorn's *The Great American Beer Cookbook* (Brewers Publications, 1993) and Lucy Saunders's *The Best of American Beer & Food* (Brewers Publications, 2007) are indispensable adventures in cooking and beer enjoyment.

THE IMPORTANCE OF UMAMI

Most discussions regarding food and beer pairing emphasize the perfect marriages. But the really fantastic "wow" experiences of these matches is not the marriage itself but the child that emerges. It is remarkable to beginning beer enthusiasts how well beer pairs with certain foods. There are some very fundamental and easily explained reasons why beer pairs well with so many foods. Understanding these reasons forms the basis of thousands of perfect beer and food matches that result in what I call "wow" experiences. Beer pairs with food better than wine. Here's why.

We all experience a known sense of taste called umami. Umami, its origins, identity, influence, and impact in and with beer, determines much of what we experience in "great combinations of food and beer." Most individuals are aware and can identify four of the basic five taste sensations we experience in our mouth: salt, sweet, bitter, and sour. Umami is the fifth and is a dynamic taste sensation that we all experience but usually fail to acknowledge with anything other than an elevation of silent or expressed pleasure.

What is umami? It is not a single flavor; rather it is a range of flavors often insufficiently described as brothy or savory with a unique mouthfeel. There are different kinds of proteins in food. Umami is about the triggering and intensification of certain protein flavors that result in the umami "flavors and mouthfeel." Chemically the principal umami characters originate from glutamate (seaweed, certain vegetables such as tomatoes), inosinate (meat and fish), and guanylate (certain mushrooms) proteins.

Combining different elements of umami creates intensified flavor experiences. Combining acidic food and beverages with umami proteins can dramatically intensify umami flavor experiences.

Let's look at one classic beer and food combination: oysters and stout. This combination is a great example of "the child" emerging from a combination; the deliciousness of this combination is about neither the beer nor the oyster, but something else we are experiencing. The acidity from the beer fermentation and especially the acidic contribution from roasted malt and roasted barley in stout trigger the emergence of umami proteins in oysters, resulting in a "wow" experience.

Let's examine another classic Italian food presentation: carpaccio. Carpaccio is paper-thin slices of raw beef often accompanied by arugula, thinly sliced aged Parmesan cheese, olive oil, and lemon juice. Perhaps it is paired with wine, but beer is better. Here's why. Sliced raw beef by itself is rather boring, but whether the Italians know it or not, they are flirting and engaging with umami. Arugula greens have a spicy bitterness. Aged Parmesan cheese is well known to have umami proteins. Lemon juice is acidic. The combination is representative of umami "deliciousness" and can be spectacularly enhanced with a hoppy beer, Pilsener, pale or India pale ale.

Everyone would probably agree that pizza and beer is a great match. Try this experiment. Do a side-by-side beer tasting with red (tomato base) pizza and white (no tomato base) pizza. Which will you prefer? I can tell you. Most of us would prefer the combination of beer with tomato base pizza. Why? Because tomato is a great umami trigger and enhancer. There's a reason why tomatoes are great in roast beef sandwiches.

For those who enjoy the pleasure of miso soup in a Japanese restaurant or at home—it is the brothy elevation of umami that is the experience. Dried bonito flakes contain fish-derived umami protein, but boiled in water alone the bonito tastes flat and is not that interesting. Kombu seaweed contains a high level of glutamate protein and is also quite boring when boiled in water and tasted alone. When these two elements are combined along with the acidity of fermented miso, a high-profile deliciousness taste experience emerges.

What are some foods that are particularly high in umami?

- Soy sauce (a fermentation product)
- Asian fish sauce (a fermentation product)
- Parmesan cheese (the more aged, the more umami protein present)
- Slow-cured meat; prosciutto and other cured meats (the longer the age, the more umami protein present)
- Anchovies, sardines, mackerel (fresh, cured, or preserved)
- Scallops and oysters
- Ripe tomatoes, Chinese cabbage
- Shiitake and porcini mushrooms
- Seaweeds, particularly kombu
- Slow- and long-cooked chicken and meat broths developed from cooking meat and bone

When enjoying beer with meals it is worthwhile to understand:

- Umami often subdues sour/acidity, bitter, and sweet
- Umami is elevated by sour/acidity, salt, and bitterness
- Umami intensifies the taste of salt and sweet
- Umami balances bitter and acidity/sour
- Umami is present in beer
- Umami in beer comes from yeast (note: autolyzed yeast is a major flavor enhancer in many food products; listed in the ingredients)
- Umami-related compounds in beer can come from certain varieties of hops, most likely from original nonhybridized (noble and classic) varieties

Often Americans describe umami sensations as sweet. One might say scallops are sweet, but they are not actually sweet—it is the umami proteins that have been accented in skillful preparation. What you are tasting is the deliciousness and mouthfeel of umami protein. The sensation can be intensified with the enjoyment of certain wines and even more so with beer, which contributes the umami triggers of both bitterness and acidity.

Cheese is a well known and absolutely terrific pairing with beer. Cheese has umami protein (aged cheese as noted above has more than non-aged). Umami protein in cheese is accented by salt and the dramatic effect of beer's acidity and hop bitterness. The complex acidity of roasted grains in dark beers also dramatically contributes to an elevation of the pleasurable taste experience. We say beer "pairs" well with cheese. But actually what is happening is that beer is elevating the umami flavors and sensations from the combination of cheese and beer. The child emerges and is the experience.

Let's talk about some generalizations and misperceptions that have developed. People say Belgian beers go well with food. Yes they do, but are all Belgian beers suited to elevate taste experiences? If so how? It could be generalized that many Belgian beers with their fruitiness and higher alcohol concentration tend to mimic wine. Belgian beer's association with food is well established. Several types of Belgian beers with their distinctive characters are easily adapted to certain beer and food combinations. They were on the frontier of "sour" sensations and we know that acidity elevates umami. But what about the sensation of "sweet" and less bitter that can generally characterize many types of Belgian brews? This trend doesn't necessarily move toward elevating beer and food experiences. Or does it?

Perhaps there is a reason sweet beers can be good aperitifs, served before a meal. Why? Enjoying a mildly sweet beverage creates an environment in the mouth that is a precursor umami trigger. Residual sugar from sweet beverages in the mouth is acted upon by naturally occurring mouth bacteria and enzymes that produce acidity. That is why after we enjoy a sweet and fruity aperitif such as champagne or sweet-tasting beer, acidity develops in the mouth. Now then, imagine or remember sitting down to your first bite of umami-rich food such as seafood or meat and the "wow" experience you have created with your first mouthful. Very sweet beers throughout the meal, I would conclude, are not as umami-friendly, depressing sensitivity to food and their flavor potential. Personally I enjoy the bitter and natural fermented acidity of pale ales, Pilseners, and bitters as my choice of aperitif, but then taste is always a personal preference.

All beers are acidic and can react with food having umami proteins. Fermented and aged food also develops umami and umami triggers and flavor-enhancing character. Rich, robust beers and hoppy beers can have umami themselves and thus interact with food through their contribution of umami synergy. Wines contribute to umami experience but the variety and flavors of wine are limited compared with those of beer. Roasted, caramelized, torrefied, and toasted malts in beer contribute significantly in elevating umami. Yeast has umami. Try pairing foods with Hefeweizen, Kellerbier, Zwickelbier, and bottle-conditioned beer, real ale, witbier—you are flirting with umami.

Here are a few more great pairings that demonstrate umami character:

1. Present a side-by-side comparison of two different preparations of fresh high-quality raw beef as beef tartare. Add a touch of sea salt and new-pressed Italian olive oil to both. In one, blend 1 fluid ounce of

Belgian-style witbier to about 8 ounces of beef tartare. The taste of the beer should not be evident in the tartare, but you will note that the serving of tartare with added beer has an elevated taste sensation. This comes from the acidity and yeast-derived umami protein that the beer offers as a flavor enhancer. After comparing the taste of both tartares, serve a Belgian-style sour "oud" (old) brown/red ale. Discover how flavors are even more enhanced with this Belgian-style sour red Flemish-style beer.

2. Present a side-by-side comparison of two aged Parmigiano-Reggiano cheeses, one aged for 12 months, the other for 24 (you can also use young and aged Gouda, Cheddar cheese, or others). Over time, umami protein character develops and can be clearly demonstrated with this tasting. Then serve and enjoy a rich, dark porter or stout, beers rich in roasted-malt character, whose pleasant acidity greatly elevates the flavor experience of the Parmesan cheeses. The salt of the cheese becomes suppressed by the porter or stout.

3. Present a small serving of quality sardines packed in olive oil and pair it with a floral and aromatic hoppy India pale ale. First taste the beer and note flavors, then taste the sardine and note the flavors of the sardine. Take another taste of sardine and then back to beer. How are the flavors changed and enhanced. This is a really great exercise in learning how to recognize and understand the character of umami—in both the flavor and mouthfeel.

4. Present aged prosciutto with a hoppy Pilsener lager. The salt of the meat becomes suppressed by the Pilsener and a back-and-forth tasting reveals umami elevation and a separate "child" taste born of the marriage.

5. Present an 80 percent cacao chocolate paired with brown ale or rich dark/black lager; malty brews having roast and nutty characters. The process of creating quality chocolate involves fermentation of the cacao bean, slow-roasting, and managing humidity, temperature, mechanical processing, and time. I am not sure, but I strongly suspect that umami potential can be carefully developed with chocolate and that I believe is exactly what results especially with artisanal chocolate producers. That it goes so well with beer in creating its own childlike experience speaks for itself. The better the chocolate, the more "wow" the experience.

6. Food and beer is not about the marriage—it is about the child. Keep it simple—bring out umami. Elevate pleasure. Now that you've been introduced to umami, here are some simple straightforward suggestions for designing a meal.

CHOOSING BEERS TO ACCOMPANY A MEAL

The beginning of a meal sets the mood. A lively, bubbly, and unusual beer greets the palate and inspires conversation. Belgian-style fruit beers such as peach (pêche), cherry (kriek), or raspberry (framboise) beer or even a champagne-like Berliner Weisse (a sour wheat beer) are great starters.

Salads or seafood cocktails are well matched with wine-like light sour beers such as Belgian lambic gueuze or sharp porters and stouts.

If you serve steamers, mussels, or oysters, dry stout is an excellent accompaniment. Shellfish, fish, and poultry main courses go well with light yet hoppy German Pilseners or Dortmunder styles. Their pleasant bitterness and delicate hop character refresh the palate, without overpowering the flavors of seafood.

Beef and other red meat dishes go well with heartier brews such as robust Belgian Abbey ales and English pale ales.

Between the main course and dessert, a small glass of a maltier brew such as bock, Oktoberfest, or English brown ale makes you feel like you're at a carnival and the cotton candy is just around the corner.

Some beers go exceedingly well with dessert; pie, fruit, ice cream, sherbet, torte, and cakes. Some of my favorites are Belgian-style Grand Cru witbiers (a light-colored, alcoholic beer with the refreshing palate-cleansing zestiness of hops, coriander, and orange curaçao), Belgian-style tripel, caramel and toffee-like English-style barleywine ales, rich nutty brown ales, dubbels, imperial porters and stouts.

After-dinner drinks? Bring out the Cognac glasses but hold the Cognac. How about a malt "liqueur" such as sweet stout, an American-style barleywine-style ale, a Belgian-style strong Trappist-like ale, a sweet doppelbock, or a well-aged honey mead?

RESOURCES

BOOKS

American Homebrewers Association. *Victory Beers*. Boulder, Colo: Brewers Publications, 1994.

Briggs, Hough, Stevens, and Young. *Malting and Brewing Science*. Vols. 1–2. New York: Chapman and Hall, 1971.

Daniels, Steve. "Beer Filtration for Homebrewers." *Just Brew It: Beer and Brewing*. Vol. 12. Boulder, Colo.: Brewers Publications, 1992.

Eckhardt, Fred. *The Essentials of Beer Style*. Portland, Oreg.: Fred Eckhardt Associates, 1989.

———. *Sake (U.S.A.)*. Portland, Oreg.: Fred Eckhardt Communications, 1992.

Fink, Dan. "Fermentation and Beyond: Gadgets for the Homebrewer." *Brew Free or Die: Beer and Brewing*. Vol. 11. Boulder, Colo.: Brewers Publications, 1991.

Fix, Dr. George. *Principles of Brewing Science*. Boulder, Colo.: Brewers Publications, 1989.

———. *Vienna*. Boulder, Colo.: Brewers Publications, 1992.

———. "Quality Control in Small-Scale Brewing." *Beer and Brewing*. Vol. 6. Boulder, Colo.: Brewers Publications, 1986.

———. "Hop Flavor in Beer." *Beer and Brewing*. Vol. 8. Boulder, Colo.: Brewers Publications, 1988.

Forget, Carl. *Dictionary of Beer and Brewing*. Boulder, Colo.: Brewers Publications, 1988.

Foster, Dr. Terry. *Pale Ale*. Boulder, Colo.: Brewers Publications, 1990.

———. *Porter*. Boulder, Colo.: Brewers Publications, 1992.

Gayre, Lt. Col. Robert, and Charlie Papazian. *Brewing Mead*. Boulder, Colo: Brewers Publications, 1986.

———. "Hops, Beer Styles and Chemistry." *Best of Beer and Brewing*. Boulder, Colo.: Brewers Publications, 1987.

———. "Clear Beer Please." *Beer and Brewing*. Vol. 9. Boulder, Colo.: Brewers Publications, 1989.

Gordon, Dan. "Effect of Trub on Flavor and Fermentation." *Brewery Operations*. Vol. 7. Boulder, Colo.: Brewers Publications, 1991.

Gruber, Mary Anne. "Crack It Up: Understanding the Physical Properties of Malt." *Quality Brewing/Share the Experience; Brewery Operations*. Vol. 9. Boulder, Colo.: Brewers Publications, 1992.

Guinard, Jean-Xavier. *Lambic*. Boulder, Colo.: Brewers Publications, 1990.

Jackson, Michael. *The Simon and Schuster Pocket Guide to Beer*. New York: Simon and Schuster, Inc., 1991, 1994.

———. *Michael Jackson's Beer Companion*. Philadelphia: Running Press, 1993.

———. *The New World Guide to Beer*. Philadelphia: Running Press, 1989.

———. *The Great Beers of Belgium*. Cooperstown, N.Y.: Vanberg & DeWulf, 1991.

Katz, Sandor Ellix. *The Art of Fermentation*. White River Junction, Vt.: Chelsea Green Publishing, 2012.

Kieninger, Dr. Helmut. "The Influences on Beer Making." *Best of Beer and Brewing.* Vols. 1–5. Boulder, Colo.: Brewers Publications, 1987.

Klimovitz, Ray. "Is This the Malt You Ordered?" *Quality Brewing/Share the Experience; Brewery Operations.* Vol. 9. Boulder, Colo.: Brewers Publications, 1992.

Konis, Ted. "Origins of Normal and Abnormal Flavor." *Evaluating Beer.* Boulder, Colo.: Brewers Publications, 1993.

Master Brewers Association of the Americas. *The Practical Brewer,* first and second editions. Madison, Wis.: Master Brewers Association of the Americas, 1946, 1977.

Miller, Dave. *Continental Pilsener.* Boulder, Colo.: Brewers Publications, 1990.

———. *The Complete Handbook of Home Brewing.* Pownal, Vt.: Garden Way Publishing, 1988.

Morse, Roger. *Making Mead.* Ithaca, N.Y.: Wicwas Press, 1980.

Neve, R. A. *Hops.* New York: Chapman and Hall, 1991.

Narziss, Prof. Ludwig P. *Die Technologie der Würzebereitung.* Stuttgart: Ferdinand Enke Verlag, 1985.

Noonan, Greg. *Brewing Lager Beer.* Boulder, Colo.: Brewers Publications, 1986.

———. "Water: Its Effects on Hop Bitterness and Beer Flavor," *Beer and Brewing.* Vol. 6. Boulder, Colo.: Brewers Publications, 1986.

———. "Water Workshop." *Brew Free or Die: Beer and Brewing.* Vol. 8. Boulder, Colo.: Brewers Publications, 1988.

———. *Scotch Ale.* Boulder, Colo.: Brewers Publications, 1993.

Palamond, Dr. Raoul. "Training Ourselves in Flavor Perception and Tasting." *Evaluating Beer.* Boulder, Colo.: Brewers Publications, 1993.

Papazian, Charlie. *The Complete Joy of Homebrewing, Fourth Edition.* New York: Avon Books, 1991.

Rajotte, Pierre. *Belgian Ales.* Boulder, Colo.: Brewers Publications, 1992.

Remi, Bertrand. *Home Brew.* Katmandu, Nepal: Sahayogi Prakashan, 1976.

Reed, Gerald, and Tilak W. Nagodawithana. *Yeast Technology.* New York: Van Nostrand Reinhold, 1991.

Richman, Darryl. *Bock Beer.* Boulder, Colo.: Brewers Publications, 1994.

Rybacek, Vaclav, ed. *Hop Production.* New York: Elsevier, 1991.

Scheer, Fred. "Diacetyl—A Quality Control Parameter." *Quality Brewing/Share the Experience; Brewery Operations.* Vol. 9. Boulder, Colo.: Brewers Publications, 1992.

Schermerhorn, Candy. "The Brewgal Gourmet Cooks with Beer." *Brew Free or Die: Beer and Brewing.* Vol. 11. Boulder, Colo.: Brewers Publications, 1991.

———. *The Great American Beer Cookbook.* Boulder, Colo.: Brewers Publications, 1993.

Shelton, Ilse. "Flavor Profiles." *Evaluating Beer.* Boulder, Colo.: Brewers Publications, 1993.

Thomas, David. "The Magic of Malt." *Beer and Brewing.* Vol. 6. Boulder, Colo.: Brewers Publications, 1986.

Warner, Eric. *German Wheat Beer.* Boulder, Colo.: Brewers Publications, 1992.

Wood, Rebecca. *Quinoa the Supergrain.* Tokyo: Japan Publications, 1989.

PERIODICALS

Ballard, Melissa. "Tuak: Toddy of the Rice Farmers." *Zymurgy,* Fall 1986.

Brewing Techniques. Box 3222, Eugene OR 97403.

Bauer, Gary. "Raw Materials." *Zymurgy,* Fall 1990.

Clack, Johnny. "Apache Beer: Indigenous Beer of American Indians." *Zymurgy*, Winter 1984.

Cribb, Stephen. "Beer and Rocks." *Zymurgy*, Special issue, 1985.

Fix, Dr. George. "Cereal Grains." *Zymurgy*, Special issue, 1985.

———. "Yeast Cycles." *Zymurgy*, Special issue, 1985.

———. "Detriments of Hot Side Aeration." *Zymurgy*, Fall 1992.

———. "Sulfur Flavors in Beer." *Zymurgy*, Winter 1992.

———. "A Simple Technique for Evaluating Beer Color." *Zymurgy*, Fall 1988.

Great Western Malt Staff. "A Malt Primer." *Zymurgy*, Special issue, 1985.

Guinard, Jean-Xavier Mary Miranda, and Professor Michael Lewis. "Yeast Biology and Beer Fermentation." *Zymurgy*, Special issue, 1989.

Kane, Ken. "Low Alcohol Beers: Brewing Fad or Future." *Zymurgy*, Fall 1989.

Katz, Dr. Solomon. "Beer and the Origin of Cereal Grain Agriculture." *Zymurgy*, Summer 1988.

Klisch, Russel. "Proteins in Beer." *Zymurgy*, Special issue, 1985.

Kowaka, K., Kawasaki Fukuoka, and Asano Fukuoka. "The True Value of Aroma Hops in Brewing." *European Brewing Convention Congress, Lecture No. 7.* 1983.

Millspaw, Micah, and Bob Jones. "Beer Stability." *Zymurgy*, Winter 1992.

Morris, Rodney. "Beer Filtration for the Homebrewer." *Zymurgy*, Summer 1990.

Narziss, L. "Types of Beer." *Brauwelt International* II/1991.

———. "Special Malts for Greater Beer Type Variety." *Brauwelt International* IV/1991.

The New Brewer (for microbrewers and pub brewers). Institute for Brewing Studies, Box 1679, Boulder, CO 80306.

Noonan, Greg. "Decoction Mashing." *Zymurgy*, Special issue, 1985.

O'Neil, Pat. "The Mystery of Malt Extract." *Zymurgy*, Summer 1985.

Peindl, Professor Anton. From the series "Biere Aus Aller Welt." *Brauindustrie*, 1982–1991.

———. "How the Blood Alcohol Curve Develops After Drinking Light Beer." *Brauwelt International* II/1993.

Richman, Darryl. "Water Treatment: How to Calculate Salt Adjustments." *Zymurgy*, Winter 1989.

Rodin, Colin, and Glenn Colon-Bonet. "Beer From Water: Modify Minerals to Match Beer Styles." *Zymurgy*, Winter 1991.

Schisler, Ruocco, and Mabee Schisler. "Wort Trub and Its Effects on Fermentation and Beer Flavor." *American Society of Brewing Chemists.* Vol. 40 (1982).

Segal, Doralie Denenberg. "Beer and Nutrition." *Zymurgy*, Winter 1984.

Singleton, Jill. "Kvass: Back in the USSR." *Zymurgy*, Summer 1986.

Taylor, David. "The Importance of pH Control During Brewing." *Master Brewers Association of the Americas Technical Quarterly.* Vol. 27 (1990).

Taylor, Ken. "Effects of Water." *Zymurgy*, Special issue, 1985.

Tierney, Michael. "How to Keep Skunks Out of Your Homebrew." *Zymurgy*, Fall 1989.

Winship, Kihm. "Black Patent Malt and the Evolution of Porter." *Zymurgy*, Summer 1987.

Wright, Morgan. "How to Make Maple Sap Beer." *Zymurgy*, Winter 1988.

Zymurgy. American Homebrewers Association, P.O. Box 1679, Boulder, CO 80306–1679.

———. 1985 Special All-Grain Brewing Issue.

———. 1986 Special Malt Extract and Recipe Issue.

———. 1987 Special Troubleshooting Issue.

———. 1988 Special Brewers and Their Gadgets Issue.

———. 1989 Special Yeast and Beer Issue.

———. 1990 Special Hops and Beer Issue.

————. 1991 Beer Styles Issue.
————. 1992 Gadgets and Equipment.
————. 1993 World Beer Traditions: Britain, Germany, and the United States.
————. 1994 Forthcoming.

OTHER LITERATURE (PAMPHLETS, BROCHURES, ETC.)

The Great American Beer Festival Program Guide—1992. Boulder, Colo.: Association of
    Brewers.
Hops from Germany. Bonn, Germany: Centrale Marketingesellschaft der deutschen Agrar-
    wirtschaft, mbH, 1992.
Hop Variety Specifications. Yakima, Wash.: Hop Union U.S.A., Inc., 1983.

INDIVIDUALS, ASSOCIATIONS, INSTITUTES, AND BUSINESSES THAT PROVIDED TECHNICAL ASSISTANCE AND INFORMATION FOR THIS BOOK (PLACE OF RESIDENCE AT TIME OF CONSULTATION)

American Society of Brewing Chemists, 3340 Pilot Knob Road, St. Paul, MN 55121.
Bass Export Limited, Glasgow, Scotland. Arthur Seddon, Master Brewer; Jane Milroy,
    Brand Manager.
Beverage Consult International, Inc., Evergreen, Colorado. Finn Knudsen, Director.
Brewers Association, Box 1679, Boulder, CO 80306–1679
Has four divisions:

1. The American Homebrewers Association; activities include:
   - Annual National Homebrewers Conference
   - Annual National Homebrewers Competition
   - National Beer Judge Certification Program
   - Sanctioned Competition Program
   - Publisher of *Zymurgy* magazine
2. The Brewers Association Professional Division; activities include:
   - Annual National Craft Brewers Conference and BrewExpo America Trade
     Show
   - Publisher of the *New Brewer* magazine
   - Editors of *The North American Brewers Resource Directory*
   - additional services
   - Brewers Publications; publishes books on beer and brewing
3. The Great American Beer Festival[sm]; annual festival of American beers held each
   October
4. The World Beer Cup®

Brother Adam, Bee Breeder and Meadmaker, Buckfast Abbey, Buckfast Leigh, Devon, England.

Kinny Baughman, Brewer, Boone, North Carolina, for coining the phrase "Beer is my business and I'm late for work."

Briess Malting Company, Chilton, Wisconsin. Mary Anne Gruber, Director of Brewing Services; Roger Briess, President.

Cellite Corporation, Wayne, New Jersey. Ed Busch, Senior Technical Sales Representative.

Coors Company, Golden, Colorado. Willis Lyford, Corporate Communications Manager; Dave Thomas, Department Head—Malting R & D.

Crosby and Baker, Westport, Massachusetts. Seth Schneider, General Manager.

Dr. George Fix, Author, Brewing Consultant, and Brewer, Arlington, Texas.

Phil Fleming, Editor and Homebrewer, Broomfield, Colorado.

Frankenmuth Brewery, Frankenmuth, Michigan. Fred Scheer, Brewmaster.

Lt. Col. Robert Gayre, Mead Historian and Meadmaker; **Reinhold and Marion Gayre,** Minard Castle, Argyll, Scotland.

Great Western Malting Co., Vancouver, Washington. Bryan Thoet, Vice President, Sales and Services.

Guinness Ireland Limited, Guinness Brewing Worldwide Research Centre, St. James Gate, Dublin. Dr. Eddie Collins.

Hopunion U.S.A. Inc., Yakima, Washington. Dr. Gregory K. Lewis, Vice President and Technical Director; Ralph Olson, Vice President of Operations.

Michael Jackson, World Beer Journalist and Author, London, England.

Labatts Brewing Co. Ltd., London, Ontario, Canada. Dr. Inge Russel, Research Manager; Dr. Graham Stewart, Director of Technical Affairs.

Master Brewers Association of the Americas, 3340 Pilot Knob Road, St. Paul, MN 55121.

Michael Lewis, Professor, Food Science and Technology Department, University of California, Davis, California.

Liberty Malt Supply, Seattle, Washington. Charles Finkel, President.

Tracy Loysen, Editor, Homebrewer, and Creative Thinker, Alameda, California.

The Miller Brewing Co., Milwaukee, Wisconsin. Gary Luther, Senior Staff Brewer.

Rodney Morris, Homebrewer, College Station, Texas.

Munton & Fison, P.L.C., Stowmarket, England. Andy Janes, Marketing Manager.

Greg Noonan, Author, Brewmaster, and Owner of Vermont Pub and Brewery of Burlington, Vermont.

Ryouji Oda, President Japan Craft Beer Association.

Joseph L. Owades & Co., Sonoma, California. Dr. Joseph Owades, Director.

Schenk Filterbau GMBH, Waldstetten, Germany. Tom Thilert, U.S. Representative, Baltimore, Maryland; Josef Neubauer, Waldstetten.

S.S. Steiner, Inc., Yakima, Washington. Herbert Grant, Technical Consultant.

Schrier Malting Co., Sheboygan, Wisconsin. Keith Gretenhart, Vice President, Sales and Technical Services.

Siebel and Sons, Chicago, Illinois. Ron Siebel, Director.

Siebel Institute of Technology, Chicago, Illinois. Bill Siebel, Director.

Stroh Brewing Co., Detroit, Michigan. Ray Klimovitz, Director of Brewing Development.

Tabernash Brewing Company, Denver, Colorado. Eric Warner, President and Brewmaster.

Rebecca Wood, Natural Foods Authority and Great Person, Albuquerque, New Mexico.

ACKNOWLEDGMENTS

Photo on page 337 by John Abbott, Chico, California.

Scoresheets appearing on pages 348 and 389 courtesy of the American Home-brewers Association, Boulder, Colorado.

Photo on page 296 courtesy of the Anchor Brewing Company, San Francisco, California.

Tables and charts on pages 184 and 213 and excerpts from the book *Brew Free or Die* on pages 416 to 418 appear courtesy of Brewers Publications, Boulder, Colorado.

Photo on page 174 appears courtesy of Bass Export Limited, Glasgow, Scotland.

Photo on page 207 (*bottom*) appears courtesy of Cellite Corporation, Wayne, New Jersey.

Photos on pages 19, 32, and 203 courtesy of Coors Brewing Company, Golden, Colorado.

Chart on page 409 courtesy of The Great American Beer Festival, Boulder, Colorado.

Illustrations and charts by Vicki Hopewell appear on pages 132, 134, 135, 146, 147, 156, 157, 158, 175, 186, and 208.

Photos on pages 88 and 89 courtesy of Labatt's Brewing Company, London, Ontario, Canada.

Illustrations by Steve Lawing appear on pages 1, 2, 4, 11, 12, 17, 44, 48, 51, 61, 67, 69, 72, 80, 81, 85, 87, 107, 111, 124, 136, 161, 168, 217, 231, 235, 243, 251, 257, 258, 261, 264, 269, 271, 274, 282, 284, 286, 287, 290, 292, 299, 306, 307, 309, 313, 315, 321, 326, 350, 353, 356, 366, 371, 373, 374, 375, 376, and 377.

Photos by Michael Lichter appear on pages 92, 95, 106, 133, 172, 384, 390, 407, and 417.

Photos by Charles Matzen appear on page 196.

Photos by Charlie Papazian appear on pages 66, 83, 150, 294, 295, 360, and 363.

Photo on page 191 by Loran Richardson.

Photos (*top and middle*) on page 206 courtesy of Schenk Filterbau GMBH, Waldstetten, Germany.

Illustration on page 98 by Brent Warren.

Charts appearing on pages 396–404 courtesy of *Zymurgy* magazine, American Homebrewers Association, Boulder, Colorado.

INDEX

All recipe names are indexed under the Recipe listing.

Creativity in a Glass

{ Discover the person behind the pint. }

CraftBeer.com
Presented by the Brewers Association

CRAFTBEER.COM
CELEBRATING THE BEST OF AMERICAN BEER

American Homebrewers Association®

LOVE TO BReW? LEARNING TO BReW?

Join the American Homebrewers Association
BE PART OF THE HOMEBREWING COMMUNITY

AHA members enjoy these benefits:

- **AHA Member Deals**—Discounts and special offers at more than 700 breweries, bars and homebrew supply shops nationwide

- Six issues annually of *Zymurgy* **magazine**, plus Members-Only privileges for current and back issues digitally via **eZymurgy**

- Invitation to participate in the **Great American Beer Festival® Members-Only Session/General Session Ticket Pre-Sale.** Only members may purchase tickets for the special Saturday afternoon session at GABF.

- Discounts on **National Homebrew Competition** entries, and exclusive access to the **National Homebrewers Conference**

- **AHA Rallies**—Fun events at local breweries, always free to AHA members

- **Discounts on new book titles** from Brewers Publications

- **Members-Only resources** for newbies and advance homebrewers alike on HomebrewersAssociation.org

- And more!